PURO TEATRO

A LATINA ANTHOLOGY

D0062747

PURO TEATRO

A LATINA ANTHOLOGY

Edited by

Alberto Sandoval-Sánchez

Nancy Saporta Sternbach

THE UNIVERSITY OF ARIZONA PRESS
TUCSON

The University of Arizona Press
© 2000 The Arizona Board of Regents
First Printing

This book is printed on acid-free, archival-quality paper.
Manufactured in the United States of America

05 04 03 02 01 00   6 5 4 3 2 1

Library of Congress Cataloging-in-Publication Data
Puro teatro, a Latina anthology / edited by Alberto Sandoval-
Sánchez and Nancy Saporta Sternbach.
    p. cm.
    ISBN 0-8165-1826-2
    ISBN 0-8165-1827-0 (pbk.)
    1. American drama—Hispanic American authors. 2. Hispanic
American women—Drama. 3. American drama—Women authors.
4. American drama—20th century. 5. Hispanic Americans—Drama.
I. Sandoval-Sánchez, Alberto   II. Sternbach, Nancy Saporta.
    PS628.H57 P87 2000   99-6567
    812'.540809287'08968—dc21   CIP

British Library Cataloguing-in-Publication Data
A catalogue record for this book is available from the British Library.

The research for this project was partially funded by a grant from
the National Endowment for the Humanities. Publication of this
book was made possible in part by the proceeds of a separate and
permanent endowment created with the assistance of a Challenge
Grant from the National Endowment for the Humanities, a federal
agency.

For John and David, Rafael, and Tobias

Contents

Acknowledgments

THE WORK OF COMPILING AND COMPLETING this book would not have been possible without the assistance, support, and encouragement of many people. It goes without saying that the playwrights themselves have been instrumental in our acquisition of manuscripts in order to construct a history of Latina theater. *A todas y a cada una,* we want to extend our deep gratitude, with a special thanks to those who sent us photocopies of their work, even when they themselves were out of work, those who spoke to us either in person or by telephone to clarify some of the many details that arose, those who allowed themselves to be interviewed by us, even when we could not offer a possible publication of that interview or of their work. Especially important in putting together the pieces of this myriad puzzle were Dolores Prida, Migdalia Cruz, Caridad Svich, Cherríe Moraga, Edit Villarreal, Elaine Romero, Silviana Wood, Denise Chávez, Carmelita Tropicana, Marga Gomez, Monica Palacios, as well as all those playwrights whose works we, regrettably, cannot include, but who have helped us compose this book.

For theater criticism in the past and present, feminist theory, and performance theory, we acknowledge the groundbreaking work of many scholars, whose thinking in some way informed our own: Gracias a Beatriz Rizk, Diana Taylor, Tiffany López, Lillian Manzor-Coats, Yolanda Flores, Yvonne Yarbro-Bejarano, Yolanda Broyles-González, María Herrera-Sobek, Diana Rebolledo, María Teresa Marrero, and Judith Butler.

Colleagues who showed interest in our work and who supported and sustained us in our efforts are Gail Hornstein, Karen Remmler, Efraín Barradas, Silvia Spitta, Ellen McCracken, Patricia González, Reyes Lázaro, Marina Kaplan, Janie Vanpée, Rosetta Cohen, Sheila Ortiz Taylor, Lourdes Rojas, Ranu Samantrai, Jorge Román-Lagunas, Sandy Doucett, and Alan Bloomgarden. We thank them for their friendship and support. Additionally, we thank the anonymous readers for the National Endowment for the Humanities, who critiqued early versions of this project and who finally awarded us a grant to complete it.

Our two colleges generously funded these books at different stages and we thank them for assistance we received from the Faculty Grants Committee (Mount Holyoke College), and the Committee on Faculty Compensation and Development, the Stride Program, and the Office of Advancement (Smith College).

Technical assistance was forthcoming from librarians at both institutions: Robin Kinder, Sika Berger (Smith), Susan Fliss, Margaret Lavalle, Bryan Goodwin, Marilyn Dunn, Ann Drury, Kathleen Norton, and Kuang-Tien Yao (Mount Holyoke); and Jo Cannon and Anna Fessenden at the Center for Foreign Languages and Cultures at Smith. Joann Dwight's marvelous transcriptions enabled us to recall some of the many interviews we had with playwrights. Our research assistants Camile Pahwa, Laura Finney, Alexis Pott, Monica Dacumos, and Meredith Field happily scurried to libraries where we sent them on impossible missions, only to discover that they were able to unearth reviews and criticism of Latina playwrights from the depths of theater archives. Their contribution has been invaluable.

To our two families, we offer our infinite gratitude. We cannot begin to thank them enough for their patience. We thank John Schwartz for his enthusiasm in attending every opening of a play by a Latina playwright in New York City and elsewhere. The completion of this book attests to the patience and forbearance of David Le Noury for doing more than his share of parenting. We thank Rafael for his willingness to have his mom go to "one more meeting," and to Tobias, who so generously allowed his infancy to be spent being passed back and forth in front of the computer, we also offer our deepest gratitude.

Introduction

CONTEMPORARY
LATINA THEATER

FROM THE SHOESTRING BUDGETS OF THEIR collective theater collaborations in the 1970s to the high-tech, multimedia performance pieces of the 1990s, Latinas working in the theater have moved from their marginal positions backstage to become the central protagonists of an emerging, hybrid, multicultural art form. In numbers of productions growing at such a rapid and prolific rate that even scholars specialized in the field cannot keep pace with them, Latina playwrights have altered the face of ethnic theater in this country. Suddenly, hundreds of women are working in all capacities in the theater. Having literally "stolen the show" at all the recent Latino theater festivals, Latinas know the time has come for their work to reach a wider audience. In the last three decades, they have literally played every role necessary—from set designers to lighting technicians—in order to advance their theatrical projects. Of those hundreds of women, at least fifty devote themselves professionally to playwriting. What is unique and historic about this particular moment is the maturation of their once adolescent voices into a diversity of artistic manifestations that could be called a discourse that is finally their own.

This burgeoning number of productions of the plays of Latina playwrights is not an isolated cultural phenomenon. Rather, a constellation of marketplace forces, critical attention, and ethnic theatrical practices have contributed to the visibility and circulation of this emerging theater practice. The two most influential factors that brought about this reality are the commercial success of Latina novelists, and the cultural legacy of the various regional Latino teatros, especially Chicano theater, in which many contemporary playwrights participated. Yet, while Latina novelists are acknowledged as a vital component of a national conversation about race, ethnicity, class, gender, and sexuality, the same attention has not been accorded to the playwrights. With the early exception of Estela Portillo's volume, *Sor Juana and Other Plays* (1983), it was only in the nineties that Latina playwrights began to publish their own anthologies of plays, volumes which remain even today countable on the fingers of one hand (María Irene Fornes' *Fefu and Her Friends and Other Plays,* Dolores Prida's *Beautiful Señoritas and Other Plays,* and Cherríe Moraga's *Heroes and Saints and Other Plays*).

Puro Teatro places Latina playwriting and performance center stage in several ways: first of all, it acknowledges that without the pioneering efforts of Latina poets and novelists (first and second generations of a "canon" of Latina writing), Latina playwriting might never have reached the point it has today. Second, this volume acknowledges that Latina theater per se materialized as a result of socio-cultural and historical events such as feminism, the professionalization of playwriting as more Latinas choose to advance their education in theater, and moments of cultural transition such as the return home of college-educated Latinos that brought forth new hybrid identities, and new ways of doing theater.

Theater criticism, too, has responded to these factors, but not swiftly enough. *Puro Teatro* seeks to transcend the paradigmatic classification of Latinas by ethnicity and nationality that has previously defined both theoretical and archeological work on Latina literature. Our collection, in contrast, addresses the playwright specifically as a woman, to show how, once gender inflected, theatrical representations centering on women's issues began to emerge. Thus, when read together, Latina plays form a corpus of work with its own patterns and traits, common to each play but vastly different from plays written by men. While some resonance inevitably exists between Latina and Latino theater, the former contains an imprimatur all its own. One common denominator in many Latina plays, for example, is their protagonists' empowerment from having received an education, an action which often permits them to claim their agency and to question the cultural construction of gender and sexuality in their respective communities.

Our choice of the term "Latina" is both simple and complex. Simply put, it is more inclusive than terms like "Hispanic," which often offend, or terms like "Puerto Rican," which do not tell a complex enough story. However, the choice is also politically motivated: we were conscious of not limiting this book solely to Chicanas, Puerto Ricans, or Cubans, but rather, we were interested in the intersection of the interests and experiences of playwrights from these diverse places. In the selection of plays, several criteria informed our decisions. Foremost, the plays had to have both artistic and literary merit. Second, they had to represent a broad cross-section of themes, nationalities, issues, ethnicities, and concerns, without compromising dramatic excellence. Likewise, different types of contemporary theatrical projects and voices needed representation: the one-woman show, the performance piece, the dramatic monologue, the full-length play, the series of vignettes, the collaborative piece, the testimonial, the one-act play, and even the puppet show. In terms of content, we also searched broadly for the funny play, the sad or serious play, the many plays about families and home, the play about friends and community building, the play about the phases of growing up and the awareness of one's sexuality and the play that avoided this issue, the play about politics and the play devoid of them, the play about illness, and the play about death, in our attempt to recognize the multifaceted nature of Latina playwriting. For this reason, we wanted *Puro Teatro* to represent both new and established voices in Latina theater. In all cases, however, we have asked the playwrights to submit works that have never been published (or, in the case of *Botánica,* never published in English). When we intuited that women who work in the theater do not limit themselves to a single task, we realized that personal life stories and collective experiences—*testimonios*—would be a crucial component of our book. Thus, we asked playwrights, performance artists, and directors to write short statements that, in the words of Monica Palacios, "describe their work."

And yet, in spite of our attempts to be as inclusive as a single volume would permit, Latina theater is comprised of many more voices than we could include here. In some cases, we were unable to make contact with playwrights, and in others, plays were commissioned and promised elsewhere. Still, when read together, all of these voices form a choral symphony. Further, our second volume, a book of criticism tentatively entitled *Stages of Life: Cultural Performance and Identity Formation in U.S. Latina Theater,* will complement this first volume as we treat specific plays or clusters of plays.

This book places Latinas in *teatro* at the forefront of a vibrant, innovative new art form that has unfolded in the nineties in a multiplicity of places and ways of doing theater. All over the country, Latina playwriting is emerging as a new genre in all its plurality and hybridity. This book aims to recover the ephemeral nature of theatrical productions that are often works in progress. While the typical route of theatrical productions is page to stage, this book reverses that order by taking productions from the stage and rendering them onto the page. By giving these plays the visibility they so rightly deserve, we also lift the curtain for that process to reverse itself back again from the page to the stage. Accessibility to these plays and circulation of them in a variety of different venues will benefit communities, students at all levels of their education and their teachers, actors and actresses looking for material, and theaters at the community, regional, and national level. By posing the question, who is our audience?, we want to insist that in its attempt to promote multiculturalism and diversity, this book is for everyone.

PURO TEATRO

A LATINA ANTHOLOGY

Full-Length Plays

UNTIL THE MID 1980s, there appeared to be only three Latina playwrights: Dolores Prida, Maria Irene Fornes, and Estela Portillo. Lacking a history into which to insert themselves and their work, lacking an overall concept of Latina playwriting and "latinidad," and identifying themselves along ethnic and nationalist lines rather than as Latinas, their plays—when produced—were independent of one another and were perceived to be exceptional cases. With such limited representation and such a large agenda to tackle, these playwrights often faced having to try to insert their work into a largely male paradigm. Nevertheless, their participation in and commitment to theater was well established before the mid eighties. Many contemporary playwrights included in this book performed tasks that were largely invisible, yet vital to the foundation of Latino theater in general and Latina theater in particular. This long period of apprenticeship and practice in theater arts coincided with the newly emerging social movements (Chicano, women's, gay and lesbian), through which Latina playwrights gained the crucial tools necessary to develop their own dramaturgy and poetics. As feminism unfolded, Latina playwrights embraced a new politics of representation and identity, now inflected by gender. In this sense, the plays that emerged from this period not only functioned as consciousness-raisers with given political agendas, but also as artistic representations of new theatrical models.

In order to explain the consolidation of Latina theater, many factors must be taken into consideration. Among them is the recognition of the Chicano theaters, many of which operated as collectives, that sprang up throughout the country as Chicanas and Chicanos began to see themselves as the protagonists of a new social movement. Within these collectives, women's work, both as authors and as managers, was not only unrecognized but frequently invisible. Recent scholarly work examines and confirms the participation of Chicanas in this collective process.[1] The move from collective to individual endeavor signaled Chicanas taking the role of authorship into their own hands. During this time, non-Chicana Latina playwrights, too, began to make the fruit of their labors visible, stamping their signatures on their individual plays.[2]

As the eighties progressed, both in the East and the West, Latinas became more prominent in every aspect of theater production and playwriting. At the heart of their work was a model of dramatic action and theatrical representation that focused on dramatizing the identity of a woman, almost always a Latina. As Latina playwrights struggled to define themselves, their agenda privileged first and foremost their female bodies. This previously taboo subject proved to be an infinite arsenal of material as it gave rise to a cornucopia of questions and issues concerning gender relations, the articulation of subjectivities in process, and all manner of problematized constructions of race, class, gender, ethnicity, marginalization, and sexuality. Practitioners of this new art form, such as Cherríe Moraga, Denise Chávez, and Milcha Sánchez-Scott, paved the way for the explosion of Latina theater in the nineties. Those labors resulted in the first anthology of Latina plays, *Shattering the Myth*, which appeared in 1992, a banner year for Latina playwrights.

The combination of all these experiences—the collective theater followed by an increasing emphasis on individual playwrights, the social movements of the sixties and seventies, the groundwork laid by early Latina playwrights, the emergence of female protagonists, and even the so-called "Decade of the Hispanic"—facilitated the incarnation of what we may call the full-length Latina play. The Latina playwright, often equipped now with her M.F.A. in playwriting, has listened closely for decades for the myriad and diverse stories that will shape her plays. The full-length play's dominant structural paradigm—a series of interconnected vignettes—sets the parameters for the dramatic action. This action, instead of being divided into classical scenes, is often depicted as stages of a woman's life, frequently connecting the audience to the protagonist.

In this anthology, we have selected full-length plays that evidence the development of Latina theater in its many manifestations. There is no one simple prescription for a Latina play, as this section will demonstrate. What the plays all have in common is the making of a full-fledged woman protagonist by a Latina playwright. Even when these protagonists take on mythic proportions, as they do in *The Heart of the Earth*, the notion of retelling history to empower women is the driving force that unites these plays. This new perspective that informs all of these plays reveals itself in the innovative way of doing theater with new visions and dramatic situations, culminating in plays with protagonists who have hybrid identities, different from what has formerly been offered in the American theater, who demonstrate just how far Latina theater has come in such a short time.

1. In her book, *El Teatro Campesino: Theater in the Chicano Movement* (Austin: University of Texas Press, 1994), Yolanda Broyles challenges and revises what she calls the "great man conceptual framework" of viewing the early Teatro Campesino. In her extensive interviews with female members of Teatro, she documents how the collective process functioned, and then how those labors were attributed to a single person, namely Luis Valdez. See especially chapter 3, "Toward a Re-vision of Chicana/o Theater History: The Roles of Women in El Teatro Campesino" (pp. 129–163).

2. The example of the late Estela Portillo Trambley constitutes a lone departure from the paradigm of collective theater, in that she staged full-length plays and took credit as the sole author. This act of author-ity marked an attempt to carve out a space for herself in a world and on a stage dominated by men.

BOTÁNICA

Dolores Prida

CHARACTERS

DOÑA GENO (Genoveva Domínguez). Sixty-something. Born in Guayama, Puerto Rico. Has lived in New York City for the last forty years. She is the owner of Botánica La Ceiba, an herbs, candles, and religious items store in East Harlem.

ANAMÚ. Forty-something. Doña Geno's daughter. Born in Puerto Rico, raised in New York. Divorced. She is the mother of Milagros (Millie). She's indecisive, somewhat bitter, unsure of herself.

MILLIE (Milagros Castillo). Twenty-two years old. Born in New York City. She has just graduated in Business Administration from a "fancy" university.

RUBÉN. Twenty-six years old. Millie's childhood friend. Born in New York. He works in a community development organization in East Harlem.

PEPE EL INDIO. Uncertain age and nationality. He is a homeless alcoholic and philosopher who roams the neighborhood.

LUISA and CARMEN. Two clients.

SANTA BÁRBARA and SAN LÁZARO. Two saints.

SETTING

All action takes place inside the Botánica storefront. The set does not have to be realistic, but it must contain certain of the paraphernalia found at such stores: candles, religious images, herbs, beads, bottles of essence, aerosol cans, books, etc. A rather large painting of a ceiba tree dominates the scene. Under it, Doña Geno's armchair/throne. A small counter is at Stage Left, behind it a door leading to the back of the house. On Stage Right, the street door.

ACT ONE

[*As lights come up,* DOÑA GENO *is waiting on a customer.*]

LUISA: I don't believe it's another woman, Doña Geno. He doesn't have the time. The poor man is working two jobs. At first, I thought it was because of the hair, you know . . .

GENO: What hair?

LUISA: My hair. In the last few months, it's been falling out, it's become dull, flat. And I had such a beautiful head of hair! But I saw on TV, in the "Five Minutes with Mirta de Perales," that a woman wrote a letter telling Mirta how her husband had stopped even looking at her because her hair was so ugly. Mirta recommended she use Loción Mirta, and zas!, her hair became gorgeous and her husband fell in love with her all over again. I bought the same lotion, but nothing happened. Arturo doesn't even look at me. What would you recommend, Doña Geno?

GENO: Sábila. The americanos call it aloe vera. I have it in liquid, in gelatin, and in capsules.

LUISA: For the hair?

GENO: Mi'ja, it's been proven that aloe vera has medicinal properties for the treatment of arthritis, high blood pressure, asthma, vaginitis, bed wetting, warts, hemorrhoids, athlete's foot, boils, colitis, diarrhea, constipation, flu, apoplexy, dandruff, toothache, and—baldness! But that's not all. Aloe vera is also a cleansing, refreshing, moisturizing, and nutrient for the skin. It stimulates the pancreas, repels insects, and eliminates foot odor. It helps you lose weight, it's a hair conditioner and a powerful stimulant of sexual power.

LUISA: ¡Ay, Virgen! Give me six bottles of liquid, six jars of gelatin, and four bottles of capsules!

GENO: Just in case, I suggest that you burn this "Perpetual Help" incense several times a day, and put a few drops of this "Come with Me" essence in your bath water. I prepare it myself. Also, take down this spiritual prescription to bring good luck to your home. Listen carefully. Take an egg, tie a piece of white and a piece of blue ribbon around it, put a few drops of your regular lotion—

LUISA: Mirta.

GENO: —place the egg on a dish, and light up a red candle. Say three Lord's Prayers and blow the candle out. Place the egg at the foot of your bed all night. Next day, pick it up and throw it in the river.

LUISA: Which river?

GENO: Either one.

LUISA: I think I'll throw it in the Hudson. It's bigger.

GENO: The Hudson is okay, but throw it downtown. Uptown, it's kind of overloaded by the dominicanos.

LUISA: Thank you, Doña Geno, I really appreciate this. How much do I owe you?

GENO: [*Adds up bill on a piece of brown paper bag.*] $45.50.

LUISA: Ah, dear. I didn't think it was so much. I don't have all that money with me.

GENO: Don't worry, mi'jita. Give me whatever you can. I'll put it on your bill, and you pay me later.

LUISA: I'll bring it to you next week, for sure . . . when I hit the numbers. Another thing, Doña Geno. Last night, I dreamt about Elsie. Which number do you think I should play?

GENO: Who's Elsie?

LUISA: The cow on TV. Remember?

GENO: Ah, yes. Well, if you dreamt that you <u>saw</u> a cow, that means relatives will come to visit. If you dreamt that you <u>were</u> <u>milking</u> a cow, that means money is coming your way.

LUISA: I can't remember whether I was milking it or not.

GENO: Anyway, play number 744.

LUISA: 744. Hmmm, it sounds good. Listen, Doña Geno, how long do you think before I see any results?

GENO: Give it a couple of weeks. And let me know if you notice any change.

LUISA: Thank you, Doña Geno. God bless you. Good-bye.

GENO: Good-bye, mi'ja, God bless you.

[LUISA *exits.* ANAMÚ *enters from the back, wiping her hands on her apron.*]

ANAMÚ: Mamá, please, go and take a look at the plantain dough. I think it's too soft. Also, watch the amount. I don't think it'll be enough for 50. Also, taste it, it may need more salt.

GENO: Ay, mi'ja, I just sat down.

ANAMÚ: Well, Mamá, whenever you can.

GENO: You'd think it's the first time you made pasteles.

ANAMÚ: It's just that these pasteles give me bad vibes. I'm not sure it's a good idea to show up there loaded with frozen pasteles.

GENO: Why? You think those gringos in Nu Hamprish won't like them? All they eat is meat loaf and potatoes.

ANAMÚ: Mamá, they're not all from New Hampshire. There are people from all over.

GENO: Well, if the gringos don't want them, Milagritos will eat them all. She's always been very fond of pasteles. Although lately, she's taken a dislike to fried plantains. Last time she was here, she was so picky about the food, talking about becoming a vegetarian or something like that—as if plantains weren't vegetables!

ANAMÚ: Mamá, the problem is that she has never liked mashed green plantains for breakfast.

GENO: You're exaggerating. When have I served mashed plantains for breakfast?

ANAMÚ: Well, almost.

GENO: What happens is that you can't accept that Milagrito has changed a lot since she's been up there in that lily-white college.

PEPE EL INDIO: [*Off.*] Rubén, Rubén, don't let them kill your buffalo!

RUBÉN: [*Off.*] Don't worry, chief, I'm keeping an eye on them!

ANAMÚ: There goes Pepe el Indio with his cantaleta. Now he'll ask for lunch money. You spoil him.

GENO: He's a poor devil, Anamú. He doesn't even have a place to sleep.

ANAMÚ: He's a bum, Mamá. The money you give him to eat he spends on beer.

GENO: At least he doesn't spend it on drugs.

[RUBÉN *enters wearing a loud, mismatched baseball uniform. He carries a wooden baseball bat.*]

RUBÉN: Hello, what's up, ladies?

ANAMÚ: Hi, Rubén.

GENO: For God's sake, Rubén, that uniform hurts my eyes!

RUBÉN: Well, you can't look a gift horse in the mouth. José, the owner of the Bella Boricua Restaurant, donated the uniforms. I told him people would laugh at us, but he says they're to "confuse" the opponent.

GENO: He means they'll be "confused" with nausea.

RUBÉN: The bad news is that nothing confuses those Bronx Bulls. But, anyway, Doña Geno, give me some essence of "Bully Tamer."

ANAMÚ: I hope it works. Last time they gave you the nine doughnuts.

[DOÑA GENO *hands* RUBÉN *a small glass vial.*]

RUBÉN: Thank you, Doña Geno. Put it on my bill.

[*He splashes liquid on his baseball bat and rubs it on.*]

GENO: Don't worry, dear. Let me go and check that masa, and give my eyes a rest from that scandal of a uniform.

RUBÉN: Masa? She said masa? By any chance, is it plantain dough for the one and only famous pasteles by Doña Genoveva Domínguez, the Empress of the Puerto Rican Pastel?

ANAMÚ: You can stop licking your chops, Rubén. I am making them. Mamá is not feeling well. Besides, they're for Milagritos' graduation.

RUBÉN: You know the date already?

ANAMÚ: No, we're expecting her call. I think it is next weekend. We are going to freeze them. You can't make 50 pasteles in one day, you know.

RUBÉN: Mila knows you're taking these pasteles to her graduation?

ANAMÚ: No, it's a surprise.

RUBÉN: A surprise is right. Who would have thought, eh? Milagritos graduating from Business School. I say it, I hear it, and I can't believe it.

[DOÑA GENO *enters carrying a large cooking pot.*]

GENO: Anamú, this dough is bad, not even a mi—

[*Milagros enters, carrying two suitcases.*]

RUBÉN: Mila!

ANAMÚ: Milagros!

GENO: Milagritos!

ANAMÚ: Mi'ja, but—

RUBÉN: But—what are you doing here?

ANAMÚ: And the graduation?

GENO: Is something wrong? Why didn't you call?

ANAMÚ: Why didn't you let us know you were coming?

RUBÉN: What happened?

GENO: Did you graduate?

ANAMÚ: What are we going to do with all these pasteles?

MILLIE: Calm down, calm down.

ANAMÚ: Don't tell me you didn't graduate? After so much effort—

MILLIE: Mami, yes, I graduated. The graduation was yesterday. Look at the ring—and here's the diploma.

GENO: Yesterday! How can that be? Why didn't you let us know? Here your mother and I were ready to go—

ANAMÚ: With fifty frozen pasteles—well, they're not frozen yet.

RUBÉN: Milagritos—

MILLIE: Millie.

RUBÉN: Millie. I was going to drive them up there in my car. I had even bought a new jacket, and a serious tie.

MILLIE: Mami. Grandma. Rubén. I'm so sorry. It's that—er—there were prob-lems and they moved up the date. It was a private ceremony. There was hardly anyone there. There was no time to let anybody know.

GENO: There are no phones in Nu Hamprish?

MILLIE: It's that with all the rush, I got so nervous I thought I didn't want you to rush up there, all of a sudden. Besides, you didn't miss anything. It was all very boring.

ANAMÚ: Didn't miss anything! My daughter graduates from college and that is boring? I was prepared to feel so proud.

RUBÉN: [*Sensing everyone's discomfort.*] Hey, people! We can feel proud right here. Isn't that so, Mila—I mean, Millie? Let's celebrate the graduation right here. I'm not wearing my new jacket, but what the heck, this uniform is new too. Let me see that diploma, where's it? Here it is. Man, are we proud or what? Charge! To boil the pasteles!

[*Lights out. All exit.*
A few hours later. As lights come up again, MILLIE *and* RUBÉN *are talking together in the botánica.*]

RUBÉN: Just between you and me, Mila—Millie, your mother's pasteles aren't as good as your grandma's. But, you know what, today they tasted really good. Maybe it's because of the occasion. But you hardly ate.

MILLIE: I don't eat pork anymore. It poisons your system.

RUBÉN: Don't give me that. If that were true, there wouldn't be any Puerto Ricans walking around.

MILLIE: Can you imagine? Mami and Grandma showing up at my graduation with fifty frozen pasteles?

RUBÉN: Did you know they were going to do that?

MILLIE: No, but I suspected it. I know them. When I was little, we used to take the subway to Orchard Beach. All the other kids carried toys, life preserv-ers, pails, shovels, towels. Not me. I had to carry shopping bags full of pasteles and arroz con gandules. I think that's why I hate the beach.

RUBÉN: That's why you didn't want them to go to your graduation?

MILLIE: Why do you say that? Of course not. It's just that—there wasn't enough time. I couldn't work it out. I thought I'd explained all that.

RUBÉN: You've changed a lot, Milagros.

MILLIE: Millie. I don't like to be called Milagros.

RUBÉN: It's a beautiful name. What's wrong with it?

MILLIE: It's just that in college, every time I'd have to explain the meaning of my name, they'd laugh: "Miracles, what kind of a name is that?"

RUBÉN: And you listened to that crap?

MILLIE: You don't understand, Rubén. It wasn't easy, you know. To come to a place where you don't know a soul. I'd practically never left El Barrio. And end up in New Hampshire, in a school where everyone was so different from me. It wasn't easy, believe me. I had to deal with a lot of things. The name thing was one of the easiest. Milagros in El Barrio may be an everyday thing, but Miracles in New Hampshire—no way.

RUBÉN: Well, that's over and done with. You're home now. You are here and your family is very happy, even though they couldn't go to your graduation.

MILLIE: Aren't you ever going to forget that?

RUBÉN: It's just they—we—were so excited.

MILLIE: Well, that's over now. I don't want to talk about it anymore. The future is what matters.

RUBÉN: That's true. Doña Geno is getting on in years, and lately she hasn't been feeling very well.

MILLIE: How can that be? With so many remedies and miracles at her fingertips? She looks quite healthy to me. She's very strong. She says so herself. "Not even lightning can fell this ceiba tree."

RUBÉN: With your education, you'll be a great help to your mother and grandmother here in the botánica.

MILLIE: Rubén, if you think I got a degree in Business Administration to run a botánica, you're out of your mind. I have other plans.

RUBÉN: Like?

MILLIE: Like Vice President of Chase Manhattan Bank, International Department.

RUBÉN: Wow, Nena! If you are going to start at the top, why not president?

MILLIE: In a couple of years, you'll see. The fact is, I already have a job. They did recruiting on campus and I was interviewed.

RUBÉN: Does your family know that?

MILLIE: My mother knows. But we still haven't found the right moment to tell Grandma.

RUBÉN: Good luck! Doña Geno thinks you're staying. I thought so, too.

MILLIE: Nope. As soon as I start working, I'm moving downtown. I want my own place.

RUBÉN: Now I'm convinced.

MILLIE: Of what?

RUBÉN: That you lost some of your marbles up there. Even gringos are going crazy looking for apartments around here. And you can have one for free, but you're thinking of going downtown and paying a thousand dollar rent?

MILLIE: What free one?

RUBÉN: Doña Fela's, upstairs. She's retiring and moving back to Puerto Rico. Your grandmother is going to give it to you instead of renting it again. Didn't you know?

MILLIE: She hasn't said anything about it.

RUBÉN: Communication in this family is great.

MILLIE: It must be another "surprise" she's got in store for me. But I can't accept it. She needs the rent to pay the mortgage. This house is not paid for yet.

RUBÉN: No problem. You pay her the same rent as Doña Fela, and that's it. Look, the apartment is really nice. I put in new wood floors, forget la carpeta. I said to Doña Geno, "Milagros doesn't like that five-and-ten store linoleum. She likes the real thing—parquet floors." It cost a bundle. But it's outta sight. Girl, Doña Fela almost changed her mind.

MILLIE: Rubén, I don't want to live here. I won't live here. I have my own plans. I want something different. I want to leave all this behind. I want to forget the smell of fried plantains and Florida Water. I hate this business. I've always wanted to escape from the incense, the camphor, the cleansing rituals, the spirits, and the saints, from people looking for an easy way out to life's problems, from my grandmother ruling over everybody's life, like a queen in her palace of cholesterol and patchouli. I may have been born in the ghetto, but I don't have to live here.

RUBÉN: But, look, many Latino professionals are moving back here, helping to—

MILLIE: I don't care. There's a big world out there and I want to be part of it. That's why I went to college. I don't want to be like you. Dreaming about hitting home runs at Yankee Stadium, but settling for fly balls in Central Park. I'm sorry, Rubén. Forgive me, but it's just that, since I came back, I feel pressured by everyone. You all have plans for me. My life's been planned without me. It is my life, you know.

RUBÉN: I know. The thing is that I've always thought that people study and get ahead in life to—overcome—to become a better person, not to turn into a different person.

[RUBÉN *exits, as* DOÑA GENO *enters from the back.*]

MILLIE: Rubén, wait.

GENO: You're fighting already? You're always so disagreeable. I hope you didn't put him down again. That boy's been waiting for you all his life.

MILLIE: I don't know why. I've never given him a reason to wait. He's always been and always will be my childhood friend, like a brother. That's all.

GENO: To everything there's a season and a reason.

[DOÑA GENO *rummages through a shopping bag full of papers.*]

MILLIE: What are you looking for, Grandma?

GENO: Something I want to show you. A surprise.

MILLIE: I don't know if I can take another surprise.

[MILLIE *pulls out pieces of paper from Geno's shopping bag.*]

MILLIE: [*Reading.*] "Paco: apasote, marjoram, spurge. Julia: balm of Gilead, rompezaraguey. Dr. Martínez: sal'pafuera, polvos voladores, necklaces, six-inche Eleguá." What's this, Grandma?

GENO: The bills.

MILLIE: I know they're bills. The last time I was here I bought you a file cabinet and a ledger, I organized all your papers, accounts payable, accounts receivable, but I see you went back to your old system. [*Continues to fish pieces of paper out of the bag.*]

GENO: That system didn't work for me. People panicked when they saw what they owed me. This is a better system. I stick my hand in the bag, take out a little piece of paper, and I tell them an amount I know they can pay. They pay me, buy something else, and everybody's happy.

MILLIE: What would they say about this lottery system at the Harvard Business School? I think I found what you were looking for. This is a good surprise.

GENO: What is it?

MILLIE: A letter from the Ahabi Realty Company. They want to buy your building. They are offering a good price—well, compared to what you paid for it.

GENO: I'm not going to sell the house. Not at that price, which is a rip-off, nor at any price.

MILLIE: But, why, Grandma? With all that money you can pay off the mortgage and buy a house in Guayama.

GENO: What am I going to do in Guayama? I'm not ready for retirement. Besides, there's too much competition there.

MILLIE: Well, some other place. On the beach maybe.

GENO: I don't know, Milagritos, after forty years in this crazy city, I think I'd be bored to death over there with nothing to do. For the time being, this ceiba tree is rooted here. Besides, I can't leave you alone all of a sudden to run the botánica. You've got a lot to learn.

[GENO *looks behind counter.*]

MILLIE: Grandma, I want to talk to you about that.

GENO: Ah, here it is. I had to hide it from your mother.

MILLIE: What is it?

GENO: An article about your father that came out in *Réplica* magazine. Wait until you see this. Look. "Miami's Businessman of the Year—Cuban Entrepreneur Becomes a Millionaire with Line of Spiritual Products." How do you like that? A man that just a few years ago didn't even know the difference between common cress and watercress. Everything he knows, he learned from me, here at The Ceiba Tree Botánica, Lexington and 113th, El Barrio, New York. Everything. And now I'm one of his customers, paying top dollars for his stuff. Look how fat he is. And now he smokes cigars. Look at the gold pendant he's wearing, it's the size of a plantain fritter. I bet he bought it with all the money I've paid him for his Seven Powers Spray.

MILLIE: Grandma, I don't like you talking that way about Papi.

GENO: I don't know why you stand up for him all the time. Your mother doesn't know it, but I even put a spell on him so he wouldn't marry her. But it didn't work.

MILLIE: Grandma, if they hadn't gotten married, I wouldn't exist.

GENO: Of course you would! Anamú would have married the other boyfriend she had, Henry Collazo. Such a nice young man—

MILLIE and GENO: —from one of the best families in Guayama.

GENO: Ahamm! The difference would have been that you'd be 100 percent Puerto Rican. But your mother, such a romantic soul, has always believed in that poem, "Cuba and Puerto Rico are like two wings of the same bird."

MILLIE: But Grandma, there's nothing Cuban about me.

GENO: Nothing except your airs.

MILLIE: I know you couldn't stand him. But he's my father. The truth is he was very affectionate and friendly. You can't deny that he was a lot of fun. He made us happy.

GENO: Yeah, the problem was he made too many people "happy." Specially other women. Which made your mother extremely unhappy. Since the day he went crazy for that marielita and followed her to Miami, your mother walks around like a shadow. Sometimes she even forgets to comb her hair. And I have cast all kinds of spells on her. I even prepared a special spiritual cleansing bath. I even named it after her: "Anamú Despojo Bath." You wouldn't believe how many irrigations and fumigations I did in her bedroom. But she's immune to my spells.

MILLIE: She'll get over it.

GENO: It's going on eight years, mi'ja. Maybe now that you're here, you can go out with her, take her to the beauty parlor. She's still young and attractive.

She can remarry. She hasn't been past 110th Street in three years. Now that you're back—

MILLIE: Grandma, listen to me—that's what I wanted to talk to you about. [ANAMÚ *enters from the back, carrying an armload of small manila envelopes.*]

ANAMÚ: Mamá, where do I put the Mister Money Incense?

GENO: Over there, same place as usual.

ANAMÚ: Mamá, there're three full boxes back here! You told me there wasn't any left. And I ordered four boxes. We have enough incense to last till Judgment Day.

[PEPE EL INDIO *enters from the street.*]

PEPE: Doña Geno, they're killing our buffalo.

GENO: And how.

MILLIE: [*To* ANAMÚ.] Mamá, who's that man? What's he talking about?

ANAMÚ: He's a little crazy, a bum who sleeps in the vacant buildings in the neighborhood.

PEPE: Young lady, you have to protect your little buffalo. Without them, we're nothing. They've killed all of mine, and you see, I'm nothing. But don't worry. You're safe here. Yes, indeed. Because Doña Geno has her ceiba tree, and nothing can bring it down. Right, Doña Geno?

GENO: Not even lightning, chief.

PEPE: But the buffalo, that's another story.

MILLIE: What buffalo are you talking about?

PEPE: Young lady, look out there. You see all that? Well, it used to be full of buffalo. And the buffalo meant everything to us.

MILLIE: Buffalo? In El Barrio?

PEPE: Ha, you bet! There they were, over there, over here, all over. Buffalo everywhere, galloping up and down, in clouds of dust. But the white men came and pum pum pum, killed them all, and we were left with nothing. And we used to have it all, right, Doña Geno? She knows. She knows what I'm talking about, right, Doña Geno? Right?

GENO: Right.

PEPE: But Doña Geno has her ceiba tree, and nothing can knock it down, not even lightning.

GENO: [*Hands* PEPE *a dollar bill.*] Here you are, chief. Go and get yourself some hot soup.

PEPE: Thank you, Doña Geno, thanks. Young lady, don't let 'em kill your buffalo. Don't end up like me. Don't you forget it, niña, don't you forget it.

[PEPE *exits.*]

MILLIE: Who is that man?

ANAMÚ: [*Sees magazine.*] What is this doing here? I burned this magazine a month ago. I put the ashes inside a hollow coconut and threw it off the Staten Island Ferry.

GENO: Oh, dear. Why didn't you tell me? Since I couldn't find it, I went and bought another copy. I wanted to show it to Millie. I ruined your hex without meaning to. But don't worry. I'll fix it, you'll see. I'm going to concoct my "counter-burundanga hex special" right now.

MILLIE: Leave my papá alone. Remember your own words, Grandma, "Cubans have very good relations with their saints, they have influence with the spirits."

GENO: Yes, that's true. But nothing's going to bring down this ceiba tree.

[*She holds her stomach, grimacing.*]

ANAMÚ: Mamá, what's wrong?

GENO: Nothing. Something I ate.

MILLIE: It's probably the blood sausages, they're like cholesterol bombs. Take an Alka-Seltzer.

GENO: Alka-Seltzer my foot. I'll make an infusion of—

[*She exits quickly, covering her mouth with one hand, and placing the other on her behind.*]

ANAMÚ: Exactly. I'll make it for you, Mamá. Millie, watch the store for a minute.

[ANAMÚ *exits.* MILLIE *takes letter, looks up phone number, and dials.*]

MILLIE: Hello, Ahabi Realty? Yes, I'm calling for Mrs. Genoveva Domínguez. It's about Mr. Ahabi's letter . . . Yes. We're interested in his offer to buy the building . . . 113th Street, that's the one. I'd like to make an appointment with Mr. Ahabi to discuss the matter . . . Next Tuesday is fine. Thank you.

[MILLIE *hangs up the telephone. Carmen, a customer, enters from the street.*]

CARMEN: Good aftern—ay, but look who's here. What a surprise. Milagritos, how are you?

MILLIE: Fine, thank you, Carmen.

CARMEN: So, how was the graduation? Doña Geno and Anamú couldn't stop talking about it. They must have been like two proud peacocks at that graduation. Where's Doña Geno?

MILLIE: Doña Geno is resting.

CARMEN: Resting? Oh, dear, I hope she's not sick.

MILLIE: It looks like indigestion.

CARMEN: Poor thing. I'm going to light a candle and say the prayer she taught me when my mother had her gallbladder removed.

MILLIE: It isn't that bad. She ate blood sausages. But thanks anyway.

CARMEN: Don't thank me, mi'ja. Doña Geno has helped me out in very difficult times. Right now, I'm in need of her advice. But anyway, I'll come back tomorrow.

MILLIE: What is the matter?

CARMEN: I don't know. Nothing's going right. I want to change my life. My boyfriend left me—the third one this year. I need a spiritual prescription, a different irrigation, some new bath. What do you think?

MILLIE: I would advise you to go to night school, learn English, get another job. Also, buy some new clothes, and change your hairdo. That always helps.

CARMEN: Ay, but that's a lot of work. I don't have the time, nor the money.

MILLIE: It does take a lot to change your life.

CARMEN: I don't know. I need something else. I better come back tomorrow and ask Doña Geno.

MILLIE: Well, look, maybe there's something I can give you in the meantime. Here's a book. Let's see. Spiritual prescriptions for . . . good luck . . . finding work . . . getting men . . . aha, here we go. [*Reading from notebook.*] "Boil seven sprigs of fresh mint, add honey, rum, a package of 'Quick Luck' Bath, a piece of the . . . panty you're wearing that day. Let it cool and place it in front of the statue of Yemayá. Light a yellow candle. Leave it for one night. Next day, wet the bottom of your shoes with this liquid, then mop your doorstep with it, as you say these words: 'Let the man who will bring me happiness walk through this door.' Do this three Fridays in a row."

CARMEN: That will work for sure.

MILLIE: Wait, there's more. [*Pretends to read.*] "Go to the beauty parlor and change your hairdo. Say the Lord's prayer three times and buy a new dress—yellow. Improve your appearance and your life. Go to night school and learn English."

CARMEN: It says that in there? Let me see.

MILLIE: I can't show it to you. This is my grandmother's *Book of Secret and Sacred Spiritual and Herbal Prescriptions,* and she doesn't show it to anybody.

CARMEN: Well, the last part sounds kind of strange to me.

MILLIE: They are modern prescriptions.

CARMEN: No wonder. Okay. I'm going to try it. Thank you, Milagritos, and remember, I'm praying for Doña Geno.

MILLIE: Well, thank you, and good luck.

CARMEN: Good bye, mi'ja.

[CARMEN *exits.* ANAMÚ *enters from the back, feather duster in hand.*]

MILLIE: How's Grandma?

ANAMÚ: She's taking a nap.

MILLIE: That's good.

ANAMÚ: I don't see what's good about it. I don't like it. [*She dusts plaster statues nervously.*]

MILLIE: Why?

ANAMÚ: Your grandmother has never taken a nap in her life.

MILLIE: Well, then it's about time.

ANAMÚ: Nena, please put the price tags on the saints. Those over there.

MILLIE: How much are they?

ANAMÚ: $79.95.

MILLIE: Isn't that a little high?

ANAMÚ: That's almost what they cost. I'm worried about Mamá.

MILLIE: Grandma is a very strong woman, but she has to watch what she eats.

ANAMÚ: I'm not sure it's indigestion. I'm worried because, you know, her heart—it doesn't tick like before.

MILLIE: Naturally, at her age nothing works like it used to. It will happen to all of us.

ANAMÚ: Oh, if only a miracle would happen.

MILLIE: What Grandma needs to do is go to the doctor and get a thorough checkup.

ANAMÚ: No, what we need is a miracle—that you change your mind and stay here with us, instead of taking that job with the bank.

MILLIE: Mamá, I'm not going to change my plans. I've told you in any number of ways. There's nothing more to talk about. In two weeks, I start working at the bank. And that's that.

ANAMÚ: I don't know how to tell Mamá. What if she gets really sick?

MILLIE: Nothing. We sell the house. You move to Guayama. The whole family is there. There's already a buyer for the building.

ANAMÚ: But what am I going to do? A woman alone, without a husband.

MILLIE: We've always gotten along well without men here. They have come in and out of our lives. That's all. Look at Grandma. She became a widow so young, and she always managed. She raised you and she raised me, and when my father left—

ANAMÚ: That's true. We've managed on our own, and we've never lived on welfare. We've worked very hard.

MILLIE: Then you should understand what I'm saying.

ANAMÚ: I understand, dear, but I'm not like you. I'm scared. Mamá has always been like the ceiba tree she's always talking about, sheltering me in its shade, protecting me from life's thunderbolts.

MILLIE: But you were once young like me. Didn't you ever want to be your own ceiba?

ANAMÚ: Not quite. When I met your father, he was also looking for shelter and protection. And he found it here. But before that, yes. When I was in high school, I thought—I dreamed—you're going to laugh. I've never told anyone, but I wanted to be a singer.

MILLIE: Mamá, you a singer? I would have never imagined it.

ANAMÚ: I was in the school choir. Everyone told me I had such a beautiful voice.

MILLIE: But I've never heard you sing.

ANAMÚ: Yes, you have.

MILLIE: When?

ANAMÚ: When you were a little baby.

MILLIE: Ah, that doesn't count! Sing to me now.

ANAMÚ: Here? Are you crazy? What if Mamá comes and—

MILLIE: Come on, just a little bit. She's not going to hear you.

ANAMÚ: No, no.

MILLIE: Come on, Mamá.

[ANAMÚ *sings for a while, stopping abruptly when* GENO *enters.*]

ANAMÚ: Mamá, what are you doing here? I thought you were going to rest.

GENO: I'll get enough rest when I die. It was only a dizzy spell. Now I have a lot to do. I have to teach Millie about the remedies and prescriptions.

[*She picks up notebook.*]

MILLIE: Grandma, we have to talk about— [*Phone rings.* MILLIE *hesitates, then picks it up.*] Hello? Yes, it's la botánica. Millie—Milagros . . . Fine, thank you . . . No, the graduation was yesterday . . . Yes . . . No . . . Just a moment. [*Covers mouthpiece.*] Grandma, it's Gloria the hairdresser. She wants to talk to you.

GENO: Ask her what she wants.

MILLIE: Grandma is busy right now. She wants to know what's going on . . . Aha, aha. One moment. [*To* DOÑA GENO.] She says that last night she dreamt about men's underwear. And what does that mean? In my opinion, she needs a man.

GENO: Blessed Virgin! Tell her to come right over.

MILLIE: Why?

GENO: Dreaming of underwear means unhappiness in the home, and loss of money, but don't tell her that. Tell her to come over, and to bet on the number 184.

MILLIE: [*Into phone.*] Gloria, Grandma says to come by as soon as possible. And to bet on the number 184. But, look, I would recommend you read Freud. F-R-E-U-D . . . Yes, but it's pronounced Froid. *The Interpretation of Dreams* . . . No, Grandma doesn't have that book . . . No, it's not in Walter Mercado's encyclopedia. Well, what it says is that a lack of sexual relations could— [GENO *grabs phone away from* MILLIE.]

GENO: Gloria, don't pay attention to her. Come by later and I will give you an amulet . . . Yes, you can do a cleansing. Let's see, today is Saturday. Okay, take some fresh water, seven different perfumes, seven pennies, seven petals of a red flower, and a drop of Good Luck Magnet essence . . . Yes, and don't forget to bet on 184. Okay, see you later. [*Hangs up.*] What are you doing? Gloria is a saintly woman, and here you are talking about sexual relations. Are you making fun of my customers?

MILLIE: But Grandma, Gloria is a hairdresser.

GENO: So, what does that have to do with it?

MILLIE: Have you heard the conversations that take place in beauty parlors? The things you hear. I'm not making fun of her. I'm being realistic and scientific. Gloria is forty years old, she has never had a husband, and she dreams about men's underwear. What do you think that means? A horny subconscious!

What else can it be? We're almost in the 21st century and you still pretend to solve people's problems with herbs, essence, and mumbo jumbo.

ANAMÚ: Milagros, don't talk like that to your grandmother.

GENO: Thanks to that mambo-jambo, you went to college. How do you think you won that scholarship?

MILLIE: Because I studied, because I fried my brains to get good grades, because I was the token spic for that scholarship. I don't fool myself, Grandma. I deal with reality.

GENO: Endless prayers, many candles for the saints, lots of faith, <u>faith</u>, Milagros. That's why you won that scholarship. That's how we have survived. This ceiba has provided a lot of shade. And you better change your attitude, because you're going to drive away the customers. What good is all your science if you don't understand people? A botánica is not a business. It's a service.

MILLIE: I'm not going to drive away any customers, because I'm not going to work in this botánica.

GENO: What?

MILLIE: I already have a job in a bank—the temple of the only "spirit" that really counts in this world: money. [*She throws Geno's notebook on the floor.*]

ANAMÚ: That's enough, Milagros! It's sacrilegious! These are our traditions.

MILLIE: What are you talking about, sacrilegious? You have never believed in any of this. But you let yourself be trapped by traditions—you stopped singing. These are things from the past. They have nothing to do with me.

GENO: Santos y santas, spirits and powers, don't listen to her. Don't mind her. She does believe. She just forgot, but she does believe.

[GENO *falls down.*]

ANAMÚ: ¡Mamá!

MILLIE: Grandma!

GENO: The graduation . . . the graduation . . .

MILLIE: Grandma.

[DOÑA GENO *faints. Lights out.*]

ACT TWO

[*The botánica is in semi-darkness.* MILLIE *holds Doña Geno's notebook close to her chest and stares at the picture of the ceiba tree.* PEPE *enters quietly, observes* MILLIE *for a while.*]

PEPE: The ceiba tree is tottering. Right, little girl?

MILLIE: You scared me. I didn't see you come in.

PEPE: I remember the day I saw the first buffalo fall dead at my feet.

MILLIE: I have no money. We haven't sold anything today.

PEPE: I didn't come for money, little girl. I came to ask about Doña Geno.

MILLIE: There's been no change. Today they'll try a new medication. I believe she'll get better soon.

PEPE: Ah, that's very important—that you believe she's going to get better. Yes, one must believe, as hard as it may be. Look, when they started to kill my buffalo, I was left with nothing to believe in. Now it's too late for me. The first thing you have to do is not let them kill your buffalo. Remember that, niña. Remember.

[PEPE *exits.* RUBÉN *enters shortly afterwards.*]

RUBÉN: Hi.

MILLIE: Hi.

RUBÉN: I just saw Anamú in the subway. She told me the hospital had just called and that she was going to sign some papers.

MILLIE: Yeah, they're going to change her treatment and they need authorization.

RUBÉN: What do you think?

MILLIE: I don't know, Rubén, I don't know. I don't know what's going to happen. I'm very confused.

RUBÉN: There's nothing to be confused about.

MILLIE: Sometimes I feel guilty about what happened—for the way I broke the news to her all of a sudden. And because of the graduation. The last thing she said was "the graduation." It almost sounded like an accusation. If she only knew . . .

RUBÉN: You're imagining things, Millie. Doña Geno didn't—

MILLIE: Other times, I think my grandmother is trying to create her own miracle, practically dying to make me change my plans and stay here and run the botánica.

RUBÉN: Milagros, how can you even think that?

MILLIE: You don't know my grandmother like I do.

RUBÉN: But this is not the time to—

MILLIE: And when is the time?

RUBÉN: Hey, look, if you want to start another fight, I'm not in the mood, okay? Anyway, I came for another reason.

MILLIE: It's not a fight, it's a discussion. I feel like I am in the middle of a conspiracy, that I'm the victim of emotional and psychological manipulation. Even the saints look like they are blaming me. And that Indian looks like it's going to throw its tomahawk at me.

RUBÉN: Pepe?

MILLIE: No, that one. [MILLIE *points to a plaster statue of an Indian.*]

RUBÉN: Millie, I don't know what you're talking about, conspiracy. I really think you—

MILLIE: How can I make you all understand that I'm not part of any of this? These images, these beliefs, they're old baggage, from other generations, from Africa to the Caribbean, from the Caribbean to New York. But I'm from here, I was born here. These are not part of my baggage, you know what I mean? You were born here too. You understand what I'm saying?

RUBÉN: I don't know. I see things differently. Look, I don't know if I can explain it, if I have the words. I didn't go to a fancy school, like you did. I only graduated from Hostos Community College in the Bronx.

MILLIE: So, you resent my education too?

RUBÉN: No, that's not it. I don't know. What does it mean "to be from here"? Well, for me, to be from here is, well, mangoes and strawberries, alcapurrias and pretzels, Yemayá and the Yankees. What's the difference? What's the big deal? That's what we are, brunch and burundanga, quiche and rice and beans, Chase Manhattan and the numbers game. It all depends on how you pack your suitcase. But it's all part of your baggage. It's all the same. You see, I decide what it means to be from here, because out there, many people think that even if you are born here and you change your name to Joe or Millie, they think you are not from here anyway. And there on the island, they think we are not from there either. From here, from there— what do I know? There's no reason to leave it all behind, no reason to let them kill our buffalo.

MILLIE: What is it with the buffalo?

RUBÉN: Believe it or not, Pepe el Indio is a well-read man. He read that Native Americans lost not only their land, but also their culture and identity, when the white man killed their buffalo.

MILLIE: But we are not Indians.

RUBÉN: He says that when we let them kill what's important to us, we become like the tribes trapped in reservations.

MILLIE: You did not learn all that at Hostos, eh?

RUBÉN: Yes, believe it or not.

MILLIE: Rubén.

RUBÉN: Yes?

MILLIE: Thank you.

RUBÉN: What for?

MILLIE: For talking to me like this. It's a relief not having to be on the defensive.

RUBÉN: You don't have to be. [*He takes her hand in his.*]

MILLIE: [*Pulls hand away.*] Maybe.

RUBÉN: Well, why don't you come to the meeting?

MILLIE: What meeting?

RUBÉN: What a moron! I haven't told you yet. It's a neighborhood meeting we organized at work. I thought it would take your mind off things.

MILLIE: What's the meeting about?

RUBÉN: Some speculators are trying to buy buildings around here, making very low offers. What they're not talking about is their plans. As soon as they buy, they throw the tenants out. Gentrification is coming to El Barrio, Mila.

MILLIE: Rubén, I can't think about that now. The sale of the house has to be carefully thought out. It has to be a good deal. But I can't deal with it right now. I have to think.

RUBÉN: You mean they also want to buy Doña Geno's building? You are not thinking about selling!

MILLIE: Why not? I'll inherit it anyway. I talked to Ahabi, but Grandma won't even discuss it. That's something I have to deal with later. There's a lot I have to deal with.

RUBÉN: You ain't kidding.

MILLIE: I think I'm going to close the shop. There's been hardly any customers. Everybody wants Doña Geno's advice. I don't know what I'm doing here. I'm not good at this.

RUBÉN: This is not something you learn in one day. Remember what Doña Geno used—what she always says.

RUBÉN and MILLIE: "You have to learn to fry slowly."

RUBÉN: See you tomorrow, Milagros. Call me if you need me.

MILLIE: See you tomorrow.

[RUBÉN *exits.* MILLIE *locks the door behind him. She remains thoughtful for a while.*]

GENO: [*Voice-over.*] The ceiba was the only tree that survived the Flood. All the creatures and people that took shelter under it survived, and that's how the earth was replenished with life. Relics and amulets are buried at the ceiba's foot. You must never cross its shadow without asking for permission. The ceiba is our Yaya, our Great Mother, Milagritos, the mother of all spirits. In African, she's called irokó, and she's also called nkunia casa sami, and she's called mama ungundu, and she's called iggi-olorún and she's called—

MILLIE: Yaya . . . [MILLIE *looks around her. Takes a bottle of Florida Water and clumsily sprinkles some on the floor.*] Maybe I'm not doing it right, but it can't hurt.

[MILLIE *sprinkles some more Florida Water. Light change.* SANTA BÁR-BARA *and* SAN LÁZARO *enter.* MILLIE *kneels in front of* SANTA BÁRBARA.]

MILLIE: Excuse me, saint. I—I've forgotten how to do this. I don't know what to say, but, Santa Bárbara, I'll go straight to the point: please make my Grandma well.

SANTA BÁRBARA: [*With a Cuban accent.*] Oye, no falla. Nada más que se acuerdan de mí cuando truena. Y mira chiquitica, yo no spika da inglis.

MILLIE: Sorry. Didn't realize. I was praying for my grandma's life.

SANTA BÁRBARA: Ay, mi'jita, él que está a cargo de los enfermos es San Lázaro. Él sí que es bilingüe.

MILLIE: That's right. I forgot. Thanks. I forgot. But wait. Maybe I'll remember. [*Turns to* SAN LÁZARO.] Babalú-ayé, that's you, lord of the universe, healer of all suffering, patron saint of the sick, Taita cañene, I'll place stale bread behind the door. I've forgotten that I forgot about your two dogs and your crutches, your guide, and the faith of those who seek health. We are supposed to offer gold, that I remember. Yes, gold at your feet and stale bread behind the door. Let her get well, San Lázaro. And make it quick, santo, make it quick.

GENO: [*Voice-over.*] Milagritos, you are so impatient. You must learn to fry slowly, or else your life will be nothing but a plate of burnt plantains.

MILLIE: We're running out of time, Yaya, out of time, santos.

SAN LÁZARO: Child, I'm just a poor, ailing old man who makes miracles happen. Se hace lo que se puede, mi'ja. We win one, we lose one. But we keep trying.

MILLIE: Win this one, will you? Win this one, please.

SAN LÁZARO: We'll see what we can do, hija. And what will you give in return?

MILLIE: Give? I don't know what I can give. Aha, I see. You're also part of the conspiracy. If you think that I'm going to leave my job in the bank and stay here, you can forget it. I paid dearly for that diploma and I'm not letting it go to waste. Besides, I'm not asking for myself, but for her—Yaya—Grandma. She's given everything to you—her whole life.

SAN LÁZARO: You have to promise to give something. Business is business.

MILLIE: What do you mean business is business? This is not business. We're talking miracles here, okay?

SAN LÁZARO: And you think miracles don't cost?

MILLIE: I see, you want to play hardball, don't you? That's fine with me. I can play too. Look, I won't make you a promise, but I'll make you a deal—an offer you can't refuse.

SAN LÁZARO: I'm listening.

MILLIE: [*Removes graduation ring from her finger and places it at the foot of the plaster statue of San Lázaro.*] Yo, Milagros Castillo—I, Miracles Castle, have I got a deal for you!

[*Lights out. With the change of light we see a transformation take place in the botánica.* RUBÉN *comes in and hangs a new sign that reads, "Ceiba Tree Herbs and Candles Boutique."* MILLIE *places an adding machine on the counter.* ANAMÚ *switches the pedestals holding the saints for others colorfully decorated.* MILLIE *removes Doña Geno's armchair from under the painting of the ceiba tree. At the end, they all admire their work with satisfaction.*]

MILLIE: So, what do you think?

[*As lights go down on the scene, the boutique sign glows in the dark. Two months later.* DOÑA GENO *enters from the back, checks out the changes in the place. Returns her armchair to its former place under the ceiba tree. Sweeps the floor while saying some incantations.* LUISA *enters.*]

LUISA: Doña Geno, you don't know how happy I am to see you.

GENO: Luisa, muchacha, it's been so long.

LUISA: Ay, Doña Geno, you have no idea how I prayed for you. We thought we were going to lose you.

GENO: No way, mi'ja. Nothing can knock down this ceiba, not even a thunderbolt.

LUISA: You look great. How do you feel?

GENO: Like a million. You're going to have Doña Geno around for a long time.

LUISA: Look at this—this botánica looks like a boutique!

GENO: My granddaughter's idea. But tell me about you. How are things with you?

LUISA: See how great my hair looks, Doña Geno? That aloe you recommended is wonderful. I want to pick up a couple of bottles more.

GENO: And Arturo, did he mend his ways?

LUISA: The aloe had no effect whatsoever. I fed it to him by the spoonful, in capsules, I put it in his coffee, I spread it all over his face—and other parts of the body—but no dice.

GENO: I can recommend something else, or if you want to, I can make you an appointment with that witch doctor in Paterson.

LUISA: Nah, it's not worth it. I'm getting tired of it all.

GENO: Don't give up, my child. Look, why don't you try the candles? You light six candles, a white one, two blue, one red—with a few drops of Fire of Love Oil—one yellow, one purple. Then you do this. I'll write it down for you. [*She draws diagram on a piece of paper.*] You move them around in this way, for nine days and nine nights.

LUISA: Well, I've got nothing to lose by trying. Let me have the candles.

[ANAMÚ *enters.*]

LUISA: Anamú, you look beautiful! What have you done?

ANAMÚ: Nothing. Milagritos fixed my hair. That's all.

GENO: Where are you going all dressed up?

ANAMÚ: I don't know.

GENO: What do you mean?

ANAMÚ: Millie wants me to go to a natural cosmetics expo at the Convention Center to see if they have something we can sell here.

GENO: She didn't say anything about that to me.

ANAMÚ: Well, I'm on my way. [*She goes to the door, turns back.*] I don't even remember how to get there.

LUISA: I'll tell you how. I know New York from top to bottom. I'm a true New Yorker. I've been here all of three years.

ANAMÚ: Don't worry about it. Millie gave me a map.

GENO: Anyway, I'll light up a candle so you won't get lost in the subway.

ANAMÚ: Thank you, Mamá. See you later.

[ANAMÚ *exits.*]

LUISA: Anamú seems like a different person. All these changes are incredible, Doña Geno.

GENO: Yes, things are going really well since I came back from the hospital. Thanks to God, the saints, and all the spirits.

LUISA: I'm so happy for you, Doña Geno. You deserve it. And now that Milagritos moved in upstairs, you must be even happier.

GENO: She wanted to move downtown, but when she saw the rent she had to pay for a little closet of a room, she ran back here as fast as her feet could take her.

LUISA: I can imagine. Is she vice president of the bank yet?

GENO: Not yet. But she says she's happy doing what she's doing.

LUISA: I'm so glad. Well, Doña Geno, got to go. How much do I owe you?

GENO: Five dollars, hija.

LUISA: No, I mean how much do I owe you in total? You remember the number you told me to bet on before you went in the hospital? I hit it. So I'm going to pay the whole thing.

GENO: Finally! Lately I wasn't doing too good with the numbers. Here it is. Let me see. It's—give me $30 and we're even.

LUISA: No, I mean everything, really.

GENO: Everything, everything? Well, it's . . . [*Pulls out a manila folder, tries using the adding machine.*] Ay, I can't add with this machine. Four plus eight, twelve, carry the one, seven and six plus . . . Okay, it's $63.60.

LUISA: Are you sure that's all?

GENO: Yes, that's it.

LUISA: Okay. Here you are, Doña Geno. And thanks for everything. Keep the change.

GENO: But, this is a hundred-dollar bill.

LUISA: It's okay.

GENO: Boy, am I glad you won the lottery.

LUISA: Me too. Okay, Doña Geno, thanks for everything.

GENO: Here are your candles. God bless you.

[GENO *puts folder back. Arranges papers on the counter, etc. Goes to the San Lázaro statue, lights a candle, sees Millie's school ring, picks it up.*]

MILLIE: Hi, Grandma.

GENO: God bless you, mi'ja. Look what I found.

MILLIE: I hadn't lost it.

GENO: Then . . . you left it as an offering? And the bread? Did you leave some stale bread behind the door?

MILLIE: More or less. I left half a croissant.

GENO: Cruasán?

MILLIE: It's bread. French.

GENO: From France?

MILLIE: Yes. No. I bought it on 96th Street . . .

GENO: Ah, well. Then that means you made a promise.

MILLIE: [MILLIE *takes school ring away from* GENO *and puts it back at the foot of the saint.*] No such thing. I made a deal with the saints.

GENO: A deal? Child, you don't make deals with the saints. You give them and they give back to you.

MILLIE: That's a deal, isn't it, Abuela?

GENO: No, it isn't. You mean to tell me that if the saint doesn't deliver on the promise you sue him? Give him a dispossess?

MILLIE: I hadn't thought about that.

GENO: Well, and this "deal," was it about me?

MILLIE: Yes.

GENO: And for you?

MILLIE: What I need I get through my own efforts, knowledge, and discipline.

GENO: But dear, you can't live your life like a business plan.

MILLIE: Grandma, you can't live your life waiting for miracles, either. [MILLIE rubs her temples.]

GENO: What's the matter? You're not feeling well?

MILLIE: It's nothing. Just a slight headache.

GENO: I'll make you an infusion of—

MILLIE: Grandma, I don't want any infusions. I'll take a pill.

GENO: Herbs are healthier than anything that comes in a bottle. Plants are a gift from Mother Nature. Look, when the Great Flood—

MILLIE: Grandma, I'm not in the mood for stories.

GENO: That is the problem. Nowadays nobody wants to hear stories. Young people don't want to know about herbs, nor recipes. But they'll miss them one day when they're gone. Because at this rate, Mother Nature won't last much longer, with so much poison thrown into the air, and rivers and oceans—

MILLIE: Yes, yes. Mother Nature is a battered woman. Nag, nag. Cantaleta time again.

GENO: Cantaleta time, yes. Do you think that because you organized the store and hung that little sign up there and filed away the papers, you are paying back the promise you made to the saints?

MILLIE: I didn't make any promise. I made a deal. If you'd get well I was going to help make the botánica run more efficiently, and—

GENO: That's not the way it works. You can't pray to Santa Bárbara only when it thunders.

MILLIE: [Looking at the plaster statue of Santa Bárbara.] That's what she said.

GENO: What?

MILLIE: Nothing, nothing. [Pause.] If you don't think it's enough, I can do some more. We can change the shelves, paint the walls a different color. You tell me . . .

GENO: That's not what I expected.

MILLIE: And what did you expect, Grandma?

GENO: I wanted to teach you the secrets and the mysteries, the wonders of the plants, the old stories and the ceremonies, so that they won't disappear, so that your children and your grandchildren will learn it from you, just as I learned them from my mother, and she from her grandmother, and my grandmother from her mother, and her mother's mother from her grandmother and her mother . . .

MILLIE: We live in different times, Grandma. My world is not your world. This is not Guayama, nor Africa. This kind of thing has no future. Today—

GENO: Of course it has no future if young people don't learn about it, if there's no continuity, if we don't save the secrets and the mysteries, if we don't bury our valuable things at the foot of the ceiba tree.

MILLIE: Grandma, you ask too much of me. I have to live in the world out there—and I want to succeed. These things, these— They are just— sometimes you have to renounce—

GENO: And you have decided to "renounce." I don't know what they did to you in the university, Milagritos, but you've changed. Your not inviting us to the graduation—you have no idea how hurt I was. I will never understand it.

MILLIE: [*Hesitates briefly.*] The graduation. I did not invite you because I had nothing to celebrate. That was just the day they gave me a diploma. My real graduation was much earlier, Grandma, much earlier—the first year of college. That was my test of fire. I got there ready to conquer the world, to learn it all. But immediately the small cruelties began—jokes about my clothes, about my accent, about the music I liked, about my name. "Miracles, what kind of a name is that?" I did not want to be different. I wanted to be like the others. And I changed my name to Millie, and hid my salsa records. And I hid the amulets and beads you sent me—your "survival kits." One day, my roommate found the box where I had hidden it all in the back of the closet. She didn't say anything to me, but told the whole school, "Miracles Castillo from El Barrio is a witch. Guess what I found in the closet?" She asked to be transferred to another room. Earlier on, I had applied to one of the sororities. And I had been accepted. The day of the initiation, they decided to play a trick on me. They took me to the forest, and tied me to a pine tree. At my feet they put a bunch of red tissue paper. It looked like a bonfire. They lit up candles and poured a bottle of rum all over my body. One of them beat a little toy drum. The others danced around me a sort of Indian dance, and—. And—I know it was an accident, but one of them dropped her candle and that tissue paper bonfire became a real blaze. In the confusion, by the time they untied me, my rum-soaked feet—. They burned my feet, Grandma. But I didn't quit. Because that's what they want, that we give up. But I won. And I graduated. Summa cum laude.

GENO: [*Holding* MILLIE *in her arms.*] But, mi vida, what good is it to win if you are no longer who you are?

MILLIE: And who are we, Grandma? Who are we?

[*Blackout.*]

[*A few days later. As lights go up slowly, the botánica is empty.*]

PEPE: [*Offstage.*] Rubén, Rubén, hold it tight. Don't let it get away, boy.

RUBÉN: Don't worry, chief, I've got a good hold on it. Be careful not to trip there.

PEPE: This is heavier than a dead buffalo.

[RUBÉN *and* PEPE *enter carrying a huge box.*]

MILLIE: [*Entering from Backstage.*] Wait, wait. Don't drop it.

[*They take a computer, monitor, keyboard, etc. out of the box.* GENO *enters.*]

GENO: And what is that?

MILLIE: A surprise, Grandma. You'll see.

GENO: Very nice, but what is it?

MILLIE: It's a computer, Grandma.

GENO: And what am I supposed to do with it?

MILLIE: The same thing you have always done. But better and faster.

GENO: Do you think that at my age I'm going to learn to use that thing?

MILLIE: I'll teach you. Every day after work, I'll come to give you lessons. And to Mamá too.

[ANAMÚ *enters from the back.*]

ANAMÚ: What about Mamá? What are you up to?

GENO: Anamú, look at what Millie brought, a competitioner.

MILLIE: Computer, Grandma.

ANAMÚ: Where did that come from?

MILLIE: At the bank they've changed the system to a better one and sold the old ones to the employees, real cheap.

GENO: And what is it for?

MILLIE: This has a memory. It remembers everything you tell it.

GENO: I don't need a machine for that. I remember everything.

MILLIE: But with this, we all have access to the information.

GENO: And how does it work?

MILLIE: Well, first you have to feed it the information. You can copy the information on these disks, see? Here we'll list all the herbs, the remedies, the prayers, the dreams, the irrigations, fumigations, and all the weekly cleansings. In another, we'll list the inventory, that way you will always know what products and quantities are available, the cost, etc. Then you press this key and you can see the information on the screen. And if you want to print it, press the other key, and zas! It appears on paper.

ANAMÚ: And it isn't dangerous?

MILLIE: No, Mamá. It doesn't bite.

PEPE: Doña Geno, what do you think? This another white man's invention. Gotta be careful. Gotta be careful with the buffaloes, Doña Geno.

GENO: I don't know, chief. I don't know what the saints and the spirits will think about this.

MILLIE: Grandma, don't worry about that. It is okay with them, I assure you.

Here in this computer, we will bury all the secrets and mysteries, as if at the foot of the ceiba tree. How about that?

GENO: Ay, dear, I don't know. Do you think that an old woman like me can learn to use this machine?

RUBÉN: Come on, Doña Geno.

MILLIE: Yes, you can. It takes a little time, but remember, you have to learn to fry slowly.

ANAMÚ: Okay, Milagritos, show us something.

MILLIE: First we must connect everything.

ANAMÚ: And you know where all those cables go?

MILLIE: I think so.

PEPE: Not to worry, children. I know the Universal Method to Assemble and Connect Any and All Types of Apparatuses.

ANAMÚ: How's that?

PEPE: Easy. You'll see. First, you hold the thing with your left hand. With the right hand, insert the whatchamacallit into the thingamajig just below the red whositwhatsit. Then, very carefully, turn it to the right until you hear a click. Immediately, screw the long doohickey onto the yellow whatnot. Now, very important, don't, under any circumstance, let the metal gizmo make contact with the black doodad, because you can totally ruin the whatsitsname. Understand?

ALL: No.

PEPE: Don't worry. We'll do it a step at a time.

GENO: Wait, before you start— [*Sprinkles Florida Water over the computer.*]

MILLIE: Grandma, what are you doing?

GENO: Just in case.

PEPE: Good idea, Doña Geno. We have to keep evil spirits away. [*He sprinkles computer with his whiskey.*] These machines are very sensitive to bad vibes.

MILLIE. Okay, let's go, let's get this plugged—

PEPE: All right. Hold the thing with the left hand.

ANAMÚ: Which thing?

[CARMEN *enters.*]

CARMEN: Hello, everybody. Hi, Reuben, how are you? And you, Mr. Indian?

RUBÉN: Wow, you're speaking English.

CARMEN: Yes, I'm going to night school.

RUBÉN: Great.

PEPE: —just below the red whositwhatsit—

CARMEN: [*To* DOÑA GENO.] Hello, Doña Geno. How do you do? Is me, Carmen.

GENO: My, I hardly recognized you.

CARMEN: Yes, thanks to your modern spiritual prescriptions—

GENO: Modern prescriptions?

CARMEN: Yes, the ones Millie gave me when you were sick. See, I changed my hair, I got a job, I bought new clothes, I'm going to night school, and—this you won't believe—I have a boyfriend!

PEPE: Rubén, now screw the long doohickey—no, no that is the thingamajig.

RUBÉN: Sorry, chief.

ANAMÚ: [*To* CARMEN.] And who is the fortunate man?

CARMEN: I don't know if you know him. His name is Arturo. He loves my hair.

[LUISA *enters.*]

LUISA: Ay, I'm so glad you're still open. Doña Geno, I need to consult you about something.

GENO: Oh, dear, you'll have to come back tomorrow. Right now my granddaughter is doing a demonstration with this machine here. But what's the problem? Your husband?

PEPE: Careful, the metal gizmo is almost touching the doodad.

LUISA: No, that's been taken care of.

MILLIE: Rubén, be careful.

GENO: [*To* LUISA.] I knew the candles will do the trick.

LUISA: No, it wasn't the candles, Doña Geno.

GENO: What did it then?

LUISA: I gave the house a thorough cleaning, I fumigated, I irrigated, I took all the garbage out, I placed the broom behind the door, and there.

GENO: What happened?

LUISA: I threw Arturo out with the rest of the garbage.

MILLIE: Hand me the input whatchamacallit.

CARMEN: [*To* LUISA.] Arturo? Arturo is your husband?

LUISA: No more. I got rid of that monkey on my back.

ANAMÚ: Watch out, I think the whatnot is loose.

CARMEN: [*To herself.*] Blessed Virgin! [*To* DOÑA GENO.] Doña Geno, I need a little consultation—a private consultation.

MILLIE: I think it's ready.

GENO: Tomorrow, tomorrow.

PEPE: Let me check everything quickly: whatchamacallit, thingamajig, whosit-whatist, doodad, doohickey, gizmo, whatsitsname. Yes, it's ready.

LUISA: Aha, what have you here? A TV set. Now I can come to watch the soap operas.

CARMEN: Excuse me, it isn't a TV set. It's a computer.

GENO: Yes. Millie brought it. She's going to do a demonstration.

RUBÉN: Come on, turn it on.

ANAMÚ: Yes, yes, do it. I'm dying to see what good is a thing like this in a botánica.

MILLIE: You'll see. You'll see.

CARMEN: [*To herself.*] Arturo.

MILLIE: Okay. Let's start with the plants. Grandma, you tell me the name of the plant, then what it's good for, and I will type it here.

GENO: There are so many. I don't know where to begin.

RUBÉN: You can start in alphabetical order.

PEPE: That's it. In alphabetical order.

MILLIE: If you want to, but it isn't necessary. We can input them in any order, because later I press one of these keys, and the program will list them in alphabetical order all by itself.

CARMEN: You should put them in English too.

MILLIE: That's another step. First we'll input them in Spanish.

ANAMÚ: Wait, don't start yet. For my peace of my mind. [*She sprinkles Florida Water on the computer.*]

MILLIE: Mamá, that's not necessary.

ANAMÚ: Please, humor me. Just in case.

MILLIE: Okay, go ahead, Grandma.

GENO: Well, then, write in there—no, no, I can't do it.

MILLIE: Come on, Grandma.

RUBÉN: Don't give up now, Doña Geno.

ANAMÚ: I can tell you the ones I know.

MILLIE: Go ahead.

ANAMÚ: Yerba santa.

MILLIE: [*Typing.*] Yerba santa. What is it good for?

[*Blackout.*]

LUISA: ¡Ay!

GENO: I knew the saints wouldn't go for all this humbug.

[*Lights return.*]

MILLIE: I hope I didn't lose all the information.

GENO: You mean to tell me that if there's a power failure this machine won't work?

MILLIE: Of course not.

GENO: And that it can forget everything that's in there?

MILLIE: It's possible.

GENO: What kind of memory is that? I don't forget anything in the dark. I tell you, machines can't be trusted.

MILLIE: Let's see. No, everything is okay. Well, let's continue. Where were we? Ah, yes, yerba buena.

ANAMÚ: Yerba santa, dear.

CARMEN: Holy grass in English.

MILLIE: [*Typing.*] Yerba santa. What's it for?

GENO: Para la garganta.

CARMEN: For the throat.

MILLIE: [*Typing.*] For the throat. Okay, next.

ANAMÚ: Abrecamino.

GENO: Para su destino.

CARMEN: That's for your destiny.

MILLIE: [*Typing.*] Abrecamino. For your destiny.

RUBÉN: Apasote, para los frotes.

LUISA: That's for rub downs.

ANAMÚ: There's also albahaca.

CARMEN: Yes, that's for skinny people.

MILLIE: [*Typing.*] Albahaca, para la gente flaca.

PEPE: There's also vetiver, ¡para los que no ven!

MILLIE: Hey, wait a minute. This sounds familiar.

ALL: [*Singing.*] ¡Y con esa yerba se casa usted!

MILLIE: That's a song! You're making fun of me.

GENO: No, dear, no. Go on.

ANAMÚ: Type, dear, type.

[*Sings a verse of "Yerbero Moderno" song. The phone rings.* CARMEN *runs to pick it up.*]

CARMEN: Ceiba Tree Boutique. May I help you? . . . yes, one momentum please, who's calling? . . . One momentum. [*Covers mouthpiece with her hand.*] Millie, it's for you, a Mr. Ahabi. Who's this Ahabi?

GENO: The man who wants to buy the building.

MILLIE: Hello, Mr. Ahabi . . . Yes . . . No, it won't be necessary, because—because I've changed my mind. No, it's not the money. It's that—that I've decided that my buffaloes are not for sale.

GENO: A miracle. ¡Gracias, Dios mío!

ALL: Un milagro.

[*The three women embrace. Reactions of great jubilation by the rest of the company. The song "Yerbero Moderno," sung by Celia Cruz, comes on as the lights go down. The song continues as actors return for their bows. After last bow, black out. In the dark, we see a projection of a giant computer screen with a computer drawing of Santa Bárbara's face winking. Slide should remain on till the audience files out.*]

HEART OF THE EARTH

A POPOL VUH STORY

Cherríe Moraga

CHARACTERS

DAYKEEPER.

IXMUCANE. Abuela, Grandmother

IXPIYACOC. Abuelo, Grandfather

CUCUMATZ. Huracán, Kukulcan, Bahana, La Culebra Verde, Plumed Serpent

HUNAHPU. First-generation twin

VUCUB. First-generation twin

TECOLOTE. Owl

PATRIARCHAL PUS. Lord of Death

BLOOD SAUSAGE. Lord of Death

IXQUIC. Blood Woman, mother of the second-generation twins

HUNAHPU. Second-generation twin

IXBALANQUE. Second-generation twin

RAT.

WOODEN-MAN.

OLLAS. Pots

CONEJO. Rabbit

CORN PEOPLE.

SETTING

The set of the world of the Popol Vuh *features a Maya-style pyramid, where much of the action of the play takes place. The steps leading to the top of the pyramid become the highland cornfields (or milpas) where to this day Mayas cultivate maíz in tiers alongside the moun-*

tains. In the play, the Corn God appears here to offer abundance to those who pray to the spirit. Steps leading down the pyramid represent the treacherous journey to Xibalba, the underworld, where the Lords of Death reside. At the base of the pyramid is a small, hutch-like opening that serves as the site of various ritual sacrifices, a miraculous birth, and a bat house jail cell.

When in the land of the gods, Downstage Right is reserved for the activities of the women. Here Grandmother works at her metate, grinding up maíz—the substance and sustenance for humankind, and Daughter-in-law embroiders, creating designs from her dreams. Stage Left serves as the gods' "creation workshop," where together Grandfather and Feathered Serpent attempt to make "Man" out of mud and wood.

At times the entire stage becomes a ball court, where the Twins play a ball game, the style of which is drawn from the traditional pre-Columbian version, and mixed with a kind of contemporary soccer and basketball. In short, the set is versatile, and the stark contrast between the world of the gods and the underworld is achieved through dramatic shifts in lighting and music.

NOTE FROM THE PLAYWRIGHT ABOUT THE LANGUAGE:

Heart of the Earth: A Popol Vuh Story is a multi-lingual, multi-cultural adaptation of the Quiché Maya creation myth. The language employed in the play includes standard English and Spanish, Quiché, other Mayan tongues, Spanglish, Chicano speech from the Southwest, and the urban colloquialisms of U.S. city streets. I have tried to create a version of the *Popol Vuh* that honors its original language, while acknowledging that Quiché is a living language used not only among the Maya in the highlands of Guatemala, but also heard on the streets of New York City, along with Quechua, Nahuatl, Navajo, Lakota, and myriad other indigenous American tongues. As *Heart of the Earth* is being presented in the United States, the world of language I hope to evoke is one of a diverse and people-of-color América that more closely reflects its changing and beautifully darkening face as we enter the twenty-first century.

Scene One

[*The conch shell sounds.* DAYKEEPER *appears. A large cloth rests on the floor of an otherwise bare stage. A pyramid is illuminated Upstage.*]

DAYKEEPER: This is the root de la palabra anciana, in a place named Quiché. Es la raíz de un pueblo of earth and sky that we shall plant here in the hearts of its descendants. This is the story of how light was born from darkness y la luz shadowed again by the hands of the gods. We shall tell our cuento en voz alta for there is no place to read it. [*Music: "Conquistadores."*] Five hundred years ago, the bearded ones arrived in floating palacios, in search of the sun's golden secretions. They came armed with flechas of melded steel and a black book decrying their devil. [*Pause.*] Today our children know fewer and fewer Indian prayers; they put on the Ladino cloth of soldier and seller. And our book and its author keep their faces hidden.

[IXPIYACOC *enters carrying god-headdress, gives it to* DAYKEEPER, *who immediately puts it on, becoming* IXMUCANE.]

IXMUCANE: Gracias, Abuelo.

[*They pick up the cloths and begin to manipulate them in a kind of dance. The sky-earth are created.*]

IXPIYACOC: In the beginning, there was just sea and sky.

IXMUCANE: Nothing stirred.

IXPIYACOC: Uleu was a breath held back,

IXMUCANE: a speechless sea,

LOS ABUELOS: kissing the limitless sky.
[*Chanting.*] ucah tzucuxic
ucah xucutaxic
                retaxic,
ucah cheexic,
meh camaxic,
uyuc camaxic

upa cah,
upa uleu
cah tzuc
cah xucut

[*Music transition.* CUCUMATZ *emerges from inside the cloth. The green-blue Plumed Serpent dances majestically in a dramatic opening.*]

IXMUCANE: Cucumatz!

IXPIYACOC: You are named by your quetzal-feathered splendor.

IXMUCANE: Kukulcan.

IXPIYACOC: La Culebra Verde.

IXMUCANE: Nao'tsiti.

IXPIYACOC: Plumed Serpent.

IXMUCANE: Culebra Fuerte y Sabia.

IXPIYACOC: Bahana.

IXMUCANE: Corazón del Cielo.

IXPIYACOC: Huracán!

[*Los Abuelos join* CUCUMATZ *in the dance. They mark and measure the four directions, the four corners of the universe, stretching and folding the cloth, as if preparing a cornfield for planting. Counting out their footsteps in dance, they chant the following as they work, creating the site where the story of the* Popol Vuh *will unfold.*]

Chant:
The East, the place where the sun is born.
The South, el Mundo Tamanco.
The West, the place where the sun passes into darkness.
The North, el Mundo Pipil.

[*The four directions named,* CUCUMATZ *ascends the pyramid.*]

Scene Two

[*Music/lighting transition: "The World of the Gods." Los Abuelos join* CUCUMATZ *on the pyramid.*]

IXPIYACOC: This will not do at all. I am thoroughly bored. There's nothing to look at. No people, no animals, no trees, not a blade of grass. No tenemos pájaros, ni cangrejos. We have no stones, no straw, no seed, and no flowers.

IXMUCANE: What are you complaining about, viejo?

IXPIYACOC: [*Startled.*]: ¿Mande?

IXMUCANE: You're talking to yourself.

IXPIYACOC: Oh, it's just that at times, I get a little frustrated, tú sabes. There's so much in my mind and so little made manifest.

IXMUCANE: We have our sons.

IXPIYACOC: Sí, pero I have a world of ideas, corazón.

IXMUCANE: Paciencia, querido. The time draws near for all that.

CUCUMATZ: Tienes razón, comadre. It is time to proceed with the creation of the world. [*Pause.*] ¿Están listos?

IXPIYACOC: [*A bit amazed.*] Listos. Sí. Estamos muy listos.

CUCUMATZ: Bueno.

[*He gets into a meditation posture. Meditation music rises in the background.*]

CUCUMATZ: Just think about it.

[*They sit for a moment in silence.* CUCUMATZ *and* IXMUCANE *begin to chant softly.*]

IXMUCANE and CUCUMATZ: Keh, Tz'ikin, Koh, Balam, Kumatz
Pa k'im, Pa zaq'ul, Pa k'icheelah.

IXPIYACOC: [*Confused.*] Excuse me, Plumed Serpent, but—think about what?

CUCUMATZ: Piénsenlo and the creation shall begin.

[CUCUMATZ *and* IXMUCANE *begin to chant again.* IXPIYACOC *joins them. Sound and light effects, the creation of the earth is taking place.*]

Keh, Tz'ikin, Koh, Balam, Kumatz
Pa k'im, Pa zaq'ul, Pa k'icheelah.

IXMUCANE: I see it. I see the water receding, separating from the earth. [*Sound builds upon sound, beginning with a single stream of water, then the sound of animals, emerging one after the other, squawking and squeaking.*]

IXPIYACOC: Veo el llano, el cuerpo desnudo de la tierra, drying beneath the sky.

CUCUMATZ: We name her "Uleu," Madre Tierra.

IXMUCANE: I see rivers like a thousand knives sculpting cañón y arroyo.

IXPIYACOC: I see mountains emerge beneath the parting clouds.

CUCUMATZ: And el león, y el tigre, el venado, y la culebra will serve as guardians of the earth.

IXMUCANE: And the animals will multiply and make homes in branch and bush, in cave and riverbank.

CUCUMATZ: And they will praise their creators—

[*They are suddenly interrupted by a cacophony of animal sounds.*]

CUCUMATZ: What is that?

IXMUCANE: I fear it is the animals, Culebra Verde.

CUCUMATZ: [*Shouting out at the animals.*] Stop that ruckus at once! Do you hear me?

IXPIYACOC: We are your father!

IXMUCANE: And we are your mother!

CUCUMATZ: Speak now in a manner befitting of us.

IXPIYACOC: ¿Qué valen estos animales?

IXMUCANE: Son brutos.

CUCUMATZ: ¡Silencio!

[*There is sudden silence.*]

CUCUMATZ: [*To the animals.*] I hunger for echo of my name, but you creatures speak no godly language. [*Raising up his wings in a fury.*] I banish you ingrates to the caves of night and to the forests dense and dark. From this day forward, you shall be preyed upon and serve as the food for both animal and man!

IXPIYACOC: [*After a pause.*] Huracán?

CUCUMATZ: [*Annoyed.*] What is it, Grandfather!

IXPIYACOC: You mentioned food. I'm a little . . . hungry?

CUCUMATZ: [*Half-heartedly.*] Let there be maíz.

[*A sack of corn appears at the opening of the pyramid.*]

IXPIYACOC: [*Examining it.*] ¿Qué es esto? [*He passes it to* IXMUCANE.]

IXMUCANE: It's . . . corn, viejo.

IXPIYACOC: Corn?

IXMUCANE: Sí.

CUCUMATZ: [*Disinterested.*] See what you can do with it, comadre.

IXMUCANE: Sí, Bahana.

> [*She crosses with the corn to Downstage Right. She sets up the metate and begins to grind. To the music of the metate,* IXPIYACOC *and* CUCUMATZ *cross to Downstage Left.*]

IXPIYACOC: What are we going to do now, Kukulcan?

CUCUMATZ: [*Suddenly disturbed by the sound of the Twins at play.*] We need to think.

HUNAHPU: [*Sportscaster's voice.*] And Hunahpu drives the ball through the deathly ring!

CUCUMATZ: What is that racket?

VUCUB: That'll cost you your head!

IXPIYACOC: Son los chavos.

HUNAHPU: But I won!

VUCUB: The winners always get sacrificed.

IXPIYACOC: They sure love that fútbol.

VUCUB: Not by my rules!

CUCUMATZ: Well, it doesn't bode well for their longevity.

> [THE TWINS *enter, taunting each other.*]

HUNAHPU: ¡Te hice cachitos! ¡Te hice cachitos!

VUCUB: I'll get you next time!

IXMUCANE: ¡Muchachos!

HUNAHPU: We'll see!

IXMUCANE: ¡Ya, paren! ¡Ya paren! Go play en la plazuela. El Señor Culebra y su padre are planning to create the first humans.

VUCUB: Hew mans?

IXMUCANE: Váyanse. They're losing their concentration.

HUNAHPU: Can't we watch?

CUCUMATZ: No! [*To* IXPIYACOC.] Vámonos. We won't get a thing done here!

[THE GODS *exit.*]

IXMUCANE: Ya ven.

VUCUB: [*To* HUNAHPU.] C'mon. Rematch.

HUNAHPU: You're on. [*To* IXMUCANE, *as* THE TWINS *ascend the pyramid.*] Ay te watcho, jefita!

IXPIYACOC: [*Starts to respond chola-style.*] Ay— [*Stops.*] No hable así. [*To herself.*] I don't know where they pick up that barrio slang.

[IXMUCANE *exits.*]

Scene Three

[THE TWINS *are playing ball Center Stage.* TECOLOTE, *The Owl Messenger (a four-faced figure), observes the boys from a distance. "Tecolote Theme" plays in the background. It is a wordless melody, more a cry of warning than a song. A Quiché chant can also be heard from Offstage: "Ch'abi Tukur, Hu r A qan Tukur, Kaqix Tukur, Holom Tukur."* TECOLOTE *descends the pyramid.*]

TECOLOTE: [*With authority.*] I surmise you are ballplayers.

VUCUB: [*Nervously.*] Yes, ma'am.

HUNAHPU: [*Overlapping.*] That's right.

TECOLOTE: Then you are who I've come for.

HUNAHPU: You've come for us?

TECOLOTE: I have.

VUCUB: Forgive us, ma'am, but—who are you?

TECOLOTE: [*Indignant.*] I am Shooting Owl, One-legged Owl, Macaw Owl, and Skull Owl. Otherwise addressed as Tecolote. I am the messenger to the Lords of Death, from the land of Xibalba.

[*Chant in the background: "U zamahel Xibalba."*]

THE TWINS: [*In unison.*]: Xibalba!

TECOLOTE: Yes. You have the distinct honor of being summoned by the Lords to a match.

HUNAHPU: A ball game.

TECOLOTE: A ball game of significant proportion. A match with the very masters of the sport!

VUCUB: But, why us?

TECOLOTE: The Lords were duly impressed by the banter of your ball up here.

HUNAHPU: They could hear it?

TECOLOTE: It was impossible not to. All the dust you two were stirring up brought down a rain of mud and thunder in the underworld.

HUNAHPU: They were impressed, you say?

TECOLOTE: Well, let's say they were interested. And I'll say no more, except that I will be back to retrieve you at nightfall. [*He raises his stubby neck in a gesture to take flight.*]

VUCUB: You're leaving?

TECOLOTE: I'll meet you at the darkest hour of the night.

VUCUB: How will we see, traveling at that hour?

TECOLOTE: [*Bugging out his eyes.*] Four pairs of owl eyes should suffice, I think, to illuminate the dark and foreboding paths that lead to Xibalba.

[*"Tecolote Theme" rises; he takes flight.*]

VUCUB: She's awesome!

HUNAHPU: Yeah. [*Beat.*] This is gonna be great. A real game. No more of this kid's pretend-stuff.

VUCUB: I don't know, Hun, I hear those güeros are a ghostly color down there. Pale people with all the blood sucked out of 'em. That's probably why they want us—for fresh blood.

HUNAHPU: They're thirsty for blood and we're thirsty for a good challenge. Anyway, they ain't all pasties down there. Papá told me stories of how some of the women are a beautiful blood-red color.

VUCUB: Really?

HUNAHPU: Like the mountains at sunset.

VUCUB: Wow!

HUNAHPU: He said to see such beauty makes you blush red yourself, from head to toe. [*Beat.*] Mira, here comes Mamá. Let's tell her of our journey.

[IXMUCANE *enters with a stack of tortillas.*]

IXMUCANE: ¿Tienen hambre, muchachos? I've got some fresh tortillas for you both!

VUCUB: Tortillas?

HUNAHPU: What's that?

IXMUCANE: Corn cakes.

VUCUB: [*Munching on one.*] They're good.

HUNAHPU: [*Taking a bite.*] Yeah, but we'll have to take 'em to go, Abuela. We're off to Xibalba to face the Lords of Death.

VUCUB: In a ball game.

[*They start to exit.*]

IXMUCANE: My sons. Espérense. [*They stop.*] Xibalba es una jornada we all must take, but it is not as simple as you think. Los Señores del Infierno are full of trickery and deceit. Cuídense, hijos. Trust your brain, not your brawn.

VUCUB: No te preocupes, madre. We'll return.

HUNAHPU: Y como campeones.

IXMUCANE: ¡Oye! La muerte is not so easy to defeat. ¡Que los dioses los bendigan! [*She blesses them as they take their leave.*] In the name of el Tiox, los mundos, y Nantat . . .

Scene Four

[THE TWINS *exit. It is night.* THE TWINS *are met by* TECOLOTE, *who leads them through the pyramid path to the underworld of Xibalba. Underwater sound effects and lighting.*]

IXMUCANE: [*Percussion accompaniment.*]
Con Tecolote como guía, Vucub y Hunahpu navigate the watery roads of Xibalba.
The rivers run silver with spikes, but my sons are not pierced.
And though thirsty, put neither lip nor tongue to the pus-filled waters.

At the crossroads, all colors converge: el colorado, el negro, el amarillo, y el blanco.
Pero encontrará su destino on that blood-black road of Xibalba.
The land of the mirror people of pale and sickly reflection.

[HUNAHPU *and* VUCUB *complete their journey through the pyramid, arrive in Xibalba. Music/lighting to create the dark world of infierno.*]

HUNAHPU: They sure don't make it easy getting here.

VUCUB: This place gives me the creeps. Hey! Where'd Tecolote go?

HUNAHPU: He disappeared. I think we're all on our own here.

[*The Mannequins posing as the* LORDS OF DEATH *stand awkwardly in the distance.* THE TWINS *approach.*]

VUCUB: [*Whispering.*] Hun, look. I think there are the Lords.

HUNAHPU: [*Extending his hand to the Mannequin.*] Buenas noches, Señor Muerte.

VUCUB: [*Also extending his hand.*] Hello, Sir. God! They look really sick!

[*The* LORDS OF DEATH *emerge from their hiding place.*]

LORDS OF DEATH: We are sick!

[THE TWINS *grab each other. The* LORDS OF DEATH *bust up into vile and insidious laughter.*]

PATRIARCHAL PUS: Fools! We are the real Lords of Death!

LORDS OF DEATH: We are spilled blood and broken bones.
We are hemorrhage and cancer of the marrow.

We are vomited guts and infected wounds,
we drink pus and blood and like it!
Sudden deaths in subway stations,
a quick blade to the heart!
The slow dissolution of body and bone
by a hunger left in the dark.
Name the disease, we invented it!
And we daily dream up more!
Silent plagues are our favorite,
a game of cellular war.
This is the home of Cizin
who passes a gruesome gas.
No one escapes our odor
nor the call of the water-lilied path.

PATRIARCHAL PUS: You boys must be weary after your long journey. [*Indicating the "hot seat."*] Take a load off your feet.

HUNAHPU: Thanks.

VUCUB: Yeah.

[*They both sit down at once, scorching their butts.*]

THE TWINS: ¡Ay, Carajo! Ouch! My nalgas!

[*The heat of the seat tosses them onto the ground. The* LORDS OF DEATH *again are thoroughly delighted and are laughing uproariously.*]

BLOOD SAUSAGE: I hope you two haven't thoroughly ruined your backsides.

HUNAHPU: [*Holding his wounded butt, under his breath.*] We'll still kick your butts tomorrow.

BLOOD SAUSAGE: That's the spirit. Now, we must make sure that you're well rested for the Big Game.

[*The* LORDS OF DEATH *escort* THE TWINS *to a small hutch-like cell where they are to spend the night.*]

PATRIARCHAL PUS: Welcome to La Posada, our South of the Border Theme-House. You should find it [*Mispronouncing*] cómoda. Good night, gentlemen.

BLOOD SAUSAGE: And, good luck.

[*They lock the Twins in.*]

PATRIARCHAL PUS: Why wait? We should just be rid of them tonight. A human sacrifice would be equally as entertaining as any ball game.

BLOOD SAUSAGE: Yes! [*Calling out.*] Owl! The Instrument of Sacrifice! At once!

TECOLOTE: Sacrifice?

PATRIARCHAL PUS: Are you deaf, Owl? Have the gods given you those big ears for nothing?

TECOLOTE: No sir, I mean, yes sir.

[*Owl exits.*]

BLOOD SAUSAGE: These young athletic types bring such pleasure to a sacrifice.

PATRIARCHAL PUS: Yes, all those red corpuscles just pumping with life. [TECOLOTE *returns with the obsidian blade.*]

PATRIARCHAL PUS: Ah! The obsidian blade!

TECOLOTE: [*Anxiously.*] Will you be needing my services any more this morning, sirs?

BLOOD SAUSAGE: What's the rush, Owl?

TECOLOTE: No rush, your Lordship. It's merely that I'm feeling a little . . . under the weather.

BLOOD SAUSAGE: You offend me, Owl, with your complaints.

TECOLOTE: Yes, sir.

PATRIARCHAL PUS: [*Handing him the obsidian blade.*] Brother, you can do the honors.

BLOOD SAUSAGE: Most generous of you, Pat Pus.

PATRIARCHAL PUS: Owl, announce to the boys that the sun has risen.

TECOLOTE: Right away, your Lordship.

[TECOLOTE *crosses to the cell, knocks on the door.* BLOOD SAUSAGE *hovers next to him, the blade poised in the air.*]

TECOLOTE: Hunahpu! Vucub! Come, look out at the sky. The sun is rising. It is a beautiful blood-red morning.

[*As the Twins stick out their heads to look,* BLOOD SAUSAGE *decapitates them. The heads fly into the air. The* LORDS *catch them and salivate over them.*]

PATRIARCHAL PUS: Owl, here, put the elder brother's head into that old dried-up tree. No harm in giving the Xibalbans a little reminder—

BLOOD SAUSAGE: —of the price of defiance.

[TECOLOTE *places Hunahpu's head into the calabash tree which rises from the center of the pyramid.*]

Scene Five

[*Lighting/music transition: "Fertility." The once-barren tree gradually blossoms into a calabash tree, heavily laden with fruit. Hunahpu's head sits in it.*]

HUNAHPU: [*To himself, bitterly.*] All of Xibalba will be talking about how gorgeous this old tree is, now that my head's stuck into it. I wonder what they did with Vucub's head. Probably using it for a fútbol. Yep, fruit abounds now all around me. Calabash for days!

[IXQUIC *enters.*]

HUNAHPU: Who is this? ¡Qué belleza! She is exactly as Papá described her, el color de los antiplanos cuando se pone el sol. But she seems so sad. I must speak to her.

[*Starts to speak, then stops as* IXQUIC *approaches the calabash tree.*]

IXQUIC: Antes era un árbol seco
ahora estás lleno de vida.
Your branches me quieren acariciar,
and your leaves tiemblan
cuando paso por acá.

¿Por qué me atormentas así?
¿Por qué me invitas
a bailar con tus hojas en la brisa,
abrazar tus ramas fuertes,
hold your sweet fruit in my eager palm?

Te tengo que probar.
Hasta en mis sueños
te puedo saborear.

[*Spoken.*] Must I die of this relentless hunger?

HUNAHPU: No.

IXQUIC: Who speaks?

HUNAHPU: It's me. La calavera, I mean the calabash, I mean the jícara, I mean, here in the tree. See my moving mouth?

IXQUIC: Are you the devil?

HUNAHPU: No, your daddy's the devil, he's the one who got me into this gourd.

IXQUIC: I don't think you should talk about my father.

HUNAHPU: I'm sorry.

IXQUIC: [*Pause.*] What were you going to say to me?

HUNAHPU: I said, Ixquic, you shouldn't die of hunger.

IXQUIC: How do you know my name?

HUNAHPU: By your color. My father told me—. He was right. You are a beautiful earth color, Blood Woman.

IXQUIC: Too dark.

HUNAHPU: No, why do you say that?

IXQUIC: Here in Xibalba, with the blood-less Lords—they want everyone empty and bone-gray like they.

HUNAHPU: Come to my country. There the Blue-Green Kukulcan reigns. And Ixmucane and Ixpiyacoc, my parents, they love all their children.

IXQUIC: You tempt me. You do look delicious.

HUNAHPU: I am. Would you like a little sample?

IXQUIC: Yes.

HUNAHPU: Then extend your right hand.

IXQUIC: You won't harm me?

HUNAHPU: I will only give you a taste of the life you seek.

[*She extends her hand; he spits into it.*]

IXQUIC: But it's nothing but a chisguete.

HUNAHPU: That little spit will bear the sweetest fruit. It is the liquid life of our descendants that shall be born again in our children.

IXQUIC: I am to be their mother?

HUNAHPU: Yes. Through them we shall not perish. Now hurry! Súbete a la tierra. [IXQUIC *hurries away. She presses the palm of spit to her breast, and she immediately blossoms, her blood-red color deepening. Music/lighting: "Fertility." The* LORDS OF DEATH *enter.*]

PATRIARCHAL PUS: Do you smell something foul, Blood Sausage?

BLOOD SAUSAGE: Yes, there is a stench in the air.

PATRIARCHAL PUS: [*Upon the sight of* IXQUIC *pregnant.*] It is you. You have deceived me. You have dishonored our name. You are a traitoress and a slut.

IXQUIC: But, Father, I have not known a man in the biblical sense.

PATRIARCHAL PUS: This is not the bible. This is the Popol Vuh. [*Thunderous.*] Who is responsible for this crime?

IXQUIC: The crime of life?

PATRIARCHAL PUS: The crime of that swell in your belly.

BLOOD SAUSAGE: What a rotten smell.

IXQUIC: With all due respect, your honor, it's motherhood.

PATRIARCHAL PUS: It's female wantonness!

IXQUIC: It's fertility. But what would you old men know of that.

BLOOD SAUSAGE: What insolence! She must die! [*To* PATRIARCHAL PUS.] You are in accord, Brother Lord?

PATRIARCHAL PUS: [*Eyeing* IXQUIC *with utter contempt.*] So be it. [*Calling out.*] Owl!

TECOLOTE: [*Entering.*] My Lord?

PATRIARCHAL PUS: Cut her heart out and bring it to us in a jícara gourd.

IXQUIC: Father?

PATRIARCHAL PUS: I have no daughter. [*To Owl.*] Take her away at once. The sight of her pregnant with so much life revolts me.

TECOLOTE: [*Sadly.*] Come with me, Blood Woman.

[TECOLOTE *reluctantly starts to drag* IXQUIC *away, as the* LORDS OF DEATH *exit.*]

IXQUIC: No, wait. [TECOLOTE *stops.*] Betray your master, wise Owl. What I carry in my womb germinated of its own choosing as I contemplated the sudden beauty of the calabash tree. This living heart that beats next to mine is a gift from the gods. How can we refuse their generosity?

TECOLOTE: But what am I to do about your heart, Ixquic? The Lords will surely have my head were I to return without it.

IXQUIC: My heart will stay inside my breast. My breast will spill no blood, only sweet milky sap for my growing sons. Give me the filero, Teco. [TECOLOTE *does.* IXQUIC *goes to the tree.*] And a gourd. [TECOLOTE *follows with a gourd.* IXQUIC *drives the blade into the breast of the tree.*] La leche de madre—as fragrant as the sap that bleeds from this tree. [*The sap spills out.*] Now gather this copal into this jícara and present it to my cruel father and his brother of death. It will burn and curdle like my own dark blood.

[TECOLOTE *puts a gourd below the mouth of the wound to catch the bleeding sap.*]

TECOLOTE: [*Holding the gourd between them.*] Blood Woman, you must escape this hell. You have too much life for this place.

IXQUIC: Teco.

TECOLOTE: You were never meant to live beneath the Lords' ghostly shadow. [IXQUIC *wraps her hands around* TECOLOTE'S.]

IXQUIC: Querido Tecolote, I swear by my sons' divine origins, you, too, shall be freed from this place. You shall inherit the bright face of Uleu and reside upon the earth's generous countenance.

[IXQUIC *rushes off. The* LORDS OF DEATH *enter.*]

BLOOD SAUSAGE: Well, Brother, it appears by the eager look of our messenger that her task has been well executed.

PATRIARCHAL PUS: Indeed. What's that you hold trembling inside your feathered grip, Owl Messenger?

TECOLOTE: It is the heart of your deceitful daughter, your Lordship, as you requested.

BLOOD SAUSAGE: [*Rubbing his hands together, salivating.*] ¡Ah!

PATRIARCHAL PUS: Bring it here!

[TECOLOTE *presents the gourd to the* LORDS. PATRIARCHAL PUS *dips his fingers into the gourd.*]

PATRIARCHAL PUS: Oh yes, this has the look and feel of an unfaithful heart! Don't you think, Brother?

BLOOD SAUSAGE: [*Digging his fingers into the gourd.*] Delicious.

PATRIARCHAL PUS: What a marvelous fragrance!

BLOOD SAUSAGE: There is nothing sweeter.

[*The* LORDS OF DEATH *exit with the gourd, following the intoxicating scent off the stage.* TECOLOTE *remains alone on stage.*]

TECOLOTE: What have I done? I have deceived the Lords. I've saved Blood Woman's life, and my own, I think. She promises freedom, la tierra as home. Uleu, I'm trembling. Receive me, Madre.

[*Fade-out.*]

Scene Six

[IXQUIC *stands at the top of the pyramid path.*]

IXQUIC: [*Journeying, singing.*]
Without father or husband, without mother or guide,
I enter la tierra sagrada, orphaned of home and history.
The twin beating of my babies' breath is the only company I keep.
How will they receive me in this land of celestial strangers?
Will they blame me for the wickedness of my father?
. . . my delight at the taste of calabash, spilling from a once-barren tree?

[*Downstage Right,* IXMUCANE *is grinding away at her metate, periodically wiping her eyes. The tears mix with the masa as she grinds.* IXQUIC *approaches timidly.*]

IXQUIC: ¿Señora? ¿Madre?

IXMUCANE: [*Not looking up.*] Who calls me Mother?

IXQUIC: Soy tu nuera.

IXMUCANE: [*Looking up.*] I have no daughter-in-law, no children. My last born have died in Xibalba. Don't you see how my tears salt the masa of these tortillas? Why do you come here and aggravate me?

IXQUIC: No la quiero molestar. But your herencia lives inside me y cuando dé a luz you will recognize in my children's faces the features of the sons you mourn.

IXMUCANE: Impostor!

IXQUIC: And if I'm not?

[IXMUCANE *studies* IXQUIC *for a moment.*]

IXMUCANE: Bueno. [*She rises slowly, wipes her hands on her apron.*] I will have to see for myself.

IXQUIC: Test me as you must, Señora. I know who I am and I bring you no falsehoods.

IXMUCANE: Enough said. Ven conmigo. [*She gives* IXQUIC *a net for harvesting.*] If you are so sure that you are my daughter, then start behaving like one.

[*They go to the milpa. It is a barren field with one lone corn plant growing at its center.*]

IXMUCANE: Aquí está mi milpa. Tapizca this net of maíz and return it full to me.

IXQUIC: As you wish.

[*She starts to exit.*]

IXMUCANE: Full, te digo. And don't deplete my field.

IXQUIC: Sí, Señora.

[IXMUCANE *exits.*]

IXQUIC: But this is not a test. It is a trick! How am I to fill this net from such barren ground. [*Looking up to the moon.*] Querida Diosa Ixchel, Guardia del Bastimiento, te pido tu ayuda.

[*She begins to chant, praying to the four directions.*]

Chant:
ucah tzucuxic
ucah xucutaxic
 retaxic,
ucah cheexic,
umeh camaxic,
uyuc camaxic
upa cah,
upa uleu
cah tzuc
cah xucut

[*Suddenly the figure of la diosa de maíz appears at the pyramid's peak. Corn spills forth from her mouth.*]

IXQUIC: X Toh, X Q'anil, X Kakav! Las Diosas have answered my prayers!

IXMUCANE: [*Entering.*] It will soon be dawn and I have received no— [*seeing the mountain of corn.*] ¡Hija bendita! El dios de maíz te ha tocado. [*She embraces* IXQUIC.] Daughter of corn and light! ¡Basta! De verdad, ¡eres mi hija! Ayúdame, mi'ja. [*She begins stuffing the corn into the net.*] Mi viejo will be thrilled to see qué abundancia le trae su nuera a la familia. Con tanto corn, we will surely be busy con la tamalada tonight!

IXQUIC: [*Holding her womb.*] Mother, dearest, I think la tamalada will have to wait. The twins announce their entrance.

IXMUCANE: Perdón. [*Noticing that* IXQUIC *is going into labor.*] ¡Mi'jita! ¿Estás dando a luz?

IXQUIC: [*In a panic.*] Sí. ¡Ahorita!

IXMUCANE: ¡Ay, te ayudo!

[*She goes to* IXQUIC.]

IXQUIC: [*Nervously.*] ¿Eres partera?

IXMUCANE: ¿Qué crees? These hands have caught thousands of celestial beings. Now cállate y push!

[IXQUIC *goes into labor, rising before the pyramid.*]

IXMUCANE chants:
> Xa ta'jun hora o media hora
> cuya ri luz, cuya ri sak.

[IXQUIC *gives birth to* IXBALANQUE *and* HUNAHPU. *They come somersaulting out from beneath her long skirt.*]

IXMUCANE: [*Naming each twin as he emerges.*] K alaxik Hun Ah Pu X Balan ke!

[*At first, they are infants, sucking their thumbs and cuddling up to their mother and grandmother. They emit infant sounds, gurgling playfully. Then they begin to walk, trying out their first shaky steps as toddlers.* HUNAHPU, *the more aggressive one, tries first, then his brother follows suit. They fall on their butts numerous times until they get the hang of it. This may be performed as a kind of dance piece between* LOS GEMELOS *and assisted by* IXMUCANE *and* IXQUIC. *Verbal exclamations are made throughout, until finally* LOS GEMELOS *are noticeably full grown.* HUNAHPU *finds some corn and begins trying to juggle it in the air.* IXBALANQUE *joins him, tossing the corn back and forth. The women observe.*]

HUNAHPU: ¡Mira, Mamá! What do you think of this?

IXQUIC: That's nice, hijo! [*To* IXMUCANE.] I fear Hunahpu may have inherited his father's love of sports.

IXMUCANE: Es el destino, Daughter.

IXQUIC: Pero, ves al otro. [*Referring to* IXBALANQUE.] He's not quite as adept.

IXMUCANE: But a ballplayer nonetheless. I would have hoped for at least one scribe in the family!

IXQUIC: He does look intelligent.

IXMUCANE: Ni modo. Whatever they turn out to be, they must first learn the lesson of hard work.

IXQUIC: Verdad.

IXMUCANE: [*Calling out to them.*] Come here, my sweet boys, your mother has something to tell you.

[*They go to her.*]

IXBALANQUE: ¿Mande, Señora?

HUNAHPU: ¿Sí, Mamá?

IXQUIC: This field is ready for replanting. Treat the earth well and she will reward you with abundance and long life. Here are your planting sticks.

[*She hands the sticks to* LOS GEMELOS.]

HUNAHPU: Planting sticks?

IXMUCANE: Your tools. Váyanse.

[*The women exit.* LOS GEMELOS *cross to the empty field and stare at it in bewilderment.*]

HUNAHPU: And we were just getting warmed up.

IXBALANQUE: I know.

HUNAHPU: This dirt doesn't look like it can produce much of anything.

IXBALANQUE: Really.

[*Begrudingly,* IXBALANQUE *and* HUNAHPU *start digging the ground and planting seed.*]

IXBALANQUE: I don't see the reward in it. I feel like we're just wasting our time.

HUNAHPU: Well, Abuela sees it differently. [*Imitating her.*] "First they must learn the lesson of hard work."

IXBALANQUE: Truth is 'mano. I think what Abuela really sees, she ain't tellin' us.

HUNAHPU: What d'ya mean?

IXBALANQUE: I don't know. It's just a feeling.

[HUNAHPU *leans on his stick thinking on this.*]

IXBALANQUE: C'mon, Hun.

HUNAHPU: All right.

[*They return to work. Their efforts are obviously half-hearted. Suddenly they hit upon a lump in the ground.*]

RAT: Jesus H. Christ!

VUCUB: Who? Whadya say, Hun?

HUNAHPU: I didn't say anything.

[*They continue working.*]

RAT: [*Popping out of the ground.*] Hey! Watch where you're pokin' that stick.

HUNAHPU: It's a rat! Grab it!

[*Percussion/music. They grab* RAT, *tossing it back and forth. It screams out.*]

RAT: Get ya friggin' paws offa me! Put me down! Put me down, ya buncha babies. Stop! What would your ole man think of yous, pickin' on somebody ain't half your size.

[*They stop.*]

IXBALANQUE: You know our father?

RAT: You think I'd lie about a thing like that? 'Bout a person's flesh 'n' blood?

IXBALANQUE: Well, no, but—

HUNAHPU: Ah, he's bluffing. Give me him.

[HUNAHPU *grabs* RAT *out of* IXBALANQUE's *hands.*]

RAT: Put me down, punk, or I ain't tellin' you jack.

IXBALANQUE: Put him down, Hun.

HUNAHPU: [*Setting* RAT *down.*] So, tell us.

RAT: Cheezus! What your ole lady put in your corn cakes this morning?

HUNAHPU: Quit stalling.

IXBALANQUE: What do you know about our father?

RAT: I know he'd be purty broken up to find you stooped over some lump of dirt with a hoe in your hand.

[*There is a pause.*]

HUNAHPU: That's it. That's all you have to say?

RAT: You're ballplayers, dummies. Don't you get it? Jus' like your ole man and his brutha and his ole man, etcetera, etcetera, etcetera.

HUNAHPU: Abuelo, too?

RAT: Well, he don't play no more. He's old.

IXBALANQUE: Yeah, but—what's a ballplayer?

RAT: [*Somewhat exasperated.*] It's freedom! Prestige! Honor! And it sure beats bustin' your butt out here in the fields.

HUNAHPU: Sounds like our kind of game.

RAT: Yeah, but it can get a little messy at times.

IXBALANQUE: Messy?

RAT: Well, a little—bloody. But you don't have to lose your head over it. C'mon, I know where the ball equipment is stored. Yokes, handstones, hachas, the works. Every jock's dream come true.

IXBALANQUE: [*To himself.*] Jock?

HUNAHPU: [*To* IXBALANQUE.] Are you game?

IXBALANQUE: [*Hesitating for moment, then.*] Yeah, let's go. Which way, Rat?

RAT: That-a-way.

[*The Gemelos start to exit.*]

RAT: Hey! Take me with yous.

[*The Gemelos grab the* RAT *and all exit excitedly. Fade-out.*]

Scene Seven

[*Music/lighting transition.* THE GODS *reconvene.* IXPIYACOC *is molding mud into a human-like form.* CUCUMATZ *hovers over him, whispering directives.* IXMUCANE *and* IXQUIC *enter.*]

IXMUCANE: Ahora que we finally got the boys to work, we can return a nuestros quehaceres.

IXQUIC: [*Indicating her embroidery.*] Verdad. Este huipil me estaba llamando. The dream goes dim, it's time to finish it.

IXMUCANE: Pues, sí. Ya es hora. And I got a house full of men to feed. [IXMUCANE *begins turning tortillas on the comal.* IXQUIC *returns to her embroidery. They work in silence as the gods continue shaping the mud-man.*]

CUCUMATZ: [*After a pause.*] I think we're close to making something human here.

IXMUCANE: [*Overhearing.*] ¿De verdad? ¿Qué tienes?

[IXMUCANE *crosses to where* IXPIYACOC *is working.*]

IXPIYACOC: It's a mud-person.

IXMUCANE: A mud-person, but I don't think—

CUCUMATZ: [*Totally engrossed, to* IXPIYACOC.] Add a flatter forehead and a broader nose.

IXPIYACOC: How's that?

CUCUMATZ: Mejor.

IXMUCANE: Pero un cuerpo de barro no servirá ni para na . . .

IXPIYACOC: [*Ignoring her.*] ¡Eso! Terminamos. All that is required is your breath of life, Cucumatz.

[CUCUMATZ *leans over and breathes into the being.*]

IXPIYACOC: Now, speak up, little one. Sing praises to your creator.

[ALL *wait; no response.*]

IXPIYACOC: Speak up, I say!

[*Again, no response.*]

CUCUMATZ: [*Worried.*] He can't hear you.

IXPIYACOC: ¡Tal vez está sordo!

IXMUCANE: Te dije.

CUCUMATZ: Possibly I made some error in calculation, an improper balance of elements.

[IXMUCANE *picks up a small pitcher of water and pours it over the mud-man.*]

IXPIYACOC: ¿Qué 'stás haciendo, mujer?

CUCUMATZ: Have you gone mad?

IXMUCANE: With all due respect, compadres, that was your first spring rains.

IXPIYACOC: It's collapsed.

IXMUCANE: [*Nonchalant.*] Qué pena.

[IXMUCANE *returns to the comal.*]

IXMUCANE: [*To* IXQUIC *as she passes.*] Pictures speak louder than words.

[IXQUIC *smiles.*]

CUCUMATZ: [*Noticeably disturbed.*] She's right. This mud isn't strong enough to weather even one highland season.

IXPIYACOC: What shall we do now, Culebra Sabia?

CUCUMATZ: We'll have to try something else. [*Pause.*] Let's see. I know. We shall start with the finest grain of wood from the ceiba tree.

[*They are interrupted by the sound of ball-playing.*]

IXBALANQUE: Kick it, Hun!

IXMUCANE: [*Under her breath.*] Oh, no, not again.

HUNAHPU: What a shot!

CUCUMATZ: It's a miracle we get anything done around this place.

[LOS GEMELOS' *banter continues.*]

IXQUIC: I'm sorry, Don Culebra.

IXMUCANE: [*To herself.*] And I had hidden the playing equipment so well.

IXPIYACOC: [*To* IXQUIC.] Send them to la plazuela to play.

IXQUIC: Sí, señor.

[IXQUIC *exits.*]

IXMUCANE: [*To herself.*] ¡Qué arrogancia! . . . to think I could defy destiny.

CUCUMATZ: [*To* IXPIYACOC, *who holds the ceiba wood.*] Now the first penetrations into the head are very important. Follow the grain of the wood exactly.

IXPIYACOC: Yes, Cucumatz. [*He begins to carve the wood.*]

CUCUMATZ: That's right.

[LOS GEMELOS *enter with ball.*]

IXBALANQUE: Sorry about the noise, Godfathers.

HUNAHPU: [*Spying the creation.*] Hey, what are you making?

CUCUMATZ: The human race, my sons.

IXBALANQUE: What's a human race?

HUNAHPU: Can we join?

CUCUMATZ: Certainly not. You are gods.

HUNAHPU: Why can't gods be in the race?

IXPIYACOC: It's not a contest. It's a—people.

HUNAHPU: [*Not understanding.*] Oh.

IXBALANQUE: What's a people?

CUCUMATZ: Living beings who long to know the face of their creator.

IXPIYACOC: Run along now. We'll let you know when we're finished.

IXBALANQUE: Promise?

CUCUMATZ: ¡Váyanse, ya!

IXPIYACOC: Go to the plazuela to play.

HUNAHPU: Yes, sirs!

> [LOS GEMELOS *exit toward la plazuela.* CUCUMATZ *and* IXPIYACOC *return to work.* IXQUIC *goes to* IXMUCANE, *who is noticeably disturbed, grinding her distress into the corn.*]

IXQUIC: Mamá, is there something you wish to tell me?

IXMUCANE: [*Grinding.*] No.

IXQUIC: At times, my sons act as strangers. I fear they are leaving me.

IXMUCANE: It's natural.

IXQUIC: The fear? Or their leaving?

IXMUCANE: Both. Both are as common as this corn.

> [CUCUMATZ *and* IXPIYACOC *finish the final touches of a wooden sculpture of a human. It is doll-sized and Maya in features.*]

IXPIYACOC: Cucumatz, it's gorgeous. We have truly created a thing of beauty.

CUCUMATZ: [*Putting away their sculpting tools.*] Se ve bien, ¿no?

IXPIYACOC: Muy bien.

CUCUMATZ: It bears intelligence in its look.

IXPIYACOC: But can it speak?

CUCUMATZ: So be it.

WOODEN-MAN: I'm hungry.

CUCUMATZ: These are the first words of our divine creation?

[CUCUMATZ, *clearly disturbed, rethinks the problem. He reviews his steps to himself as the action continues.*]

CUCUMATZ: But the ceiba was strong and well-aged.

WOODEN-MAN: Do you hear me? I'm starving.

CUCUMATZ: We used the sharpest of obsidian edges to imbue the head with clarity and self-reflection.

WOODEN-MAN: [*Overlapping.*] ¡Tengo mucha hambre!

IXPIYACOC: [*Calling out.*] ¡Vieja!

IXMUCANE: Sí, corazón.

IXPIYACOC: Feed this stick-man something. He complains of hunger.

CUCUMATZ: What could I have forgotten? The wood was thoroughly sanded, which should have resulted in a soft-spoken being with a mild manner.

WOODEN-MAN: ¡Quiero comer!

CUCUMATZ: Feed him, please. I grow impatient to know if he can express something beyond animal needs.

IXMUCANE: Allí voy.

WOODEN-MAN: Give me something to eat!

IXMUCANE: Allí voy. Allí voy. [*She brings him two pots of food.*] He is a nice-looking fellow.

WOODEN-MAN: [*To* IXMUCANE, *copping a feel.*] ¡Tú también, te ves sabrosa!

CUCUMATZ: He's obscene.

[WOODEN-MAN *devours the food, banging the* POTS *around.*]

IXPIYACOC: Hardly godly in his manners.

WOODEN-MAN: [*Banging.*] I want more!

[*In moments, the* POTS *begin to complain.*]

OLLAS: Hey! Handle me with care.
Stop beating me, I'm fragile.
Yeah, we're just made of clay.
Watch it! You're spilling my guts.

WOODEN-MAN: Give me some more food.

[THE GODS *watch in horror as the* WOODEN-MAN *eats ravenously, without notice of his creators or the complaints of the kitchen utensils. The* POTS *rebel, begin to attack the* WOODEN-MAN.]

OLLAS: Take that, you callous thug.
Pot oppressor!
Bowl abuser!
We'll pound you down to sawdust.

[*The* POTS *beat the* WOODEN-MAN *until he falls to the ground.*]

IXPIYACOC: Well, it was just an experiment.

CUCUMATZ: A failed one.

[IXPIYACOC *picks up the broken man from the ground and* THE GODS *exit, mumbling to themselves.*]

CUCUMATZ: We didn't even get a word of thanks.

IXPIYACOC: A song of praise. A postcard.

[*Crossfade to* IXMUCANE *who is grinding corn at the metate.* IXQUIC *is embroidering.*]

IXPIYACOC: The wooden-man had no heart.

IXQUIC: Verdad. But he did look human.

IXPIYACOC: So do the monkeys.

[*The women laugh, then are suddenly interrupted by "Tecolote Theme." *TECOLOTE *appears at the top of the pyramid. They watch him as he descends. There is a sense of foreboding in the air.*]

IXMUCANE: [*To* TECOLOTE.] I imagine you will find who you are looking for, playing ball en la plazuela.

[TECOLOTE *exits without a word.*]

IXQUIC: Mother?

IXMUCANE: [*Rises, wipes her hands on her apron.*] Ya vámonos, hija. The story is already written.

[IXQUIC *accompanies* IXMUCANE *out to the patio Center Stage.* IXMU-CANE *gets down on her knees and pulls out two young corn plants from her apron pocket. She hands one to* IXQUIC.]

IXMUCANE: Toma.

IXQUIC: What is this for, Madre?

IXMUCANE: A prayer of life for your sons.

IXQUIC: I don't understand.

IXMUCANE: Siémbrala en la tierra, hija.

[*They both plant the corn stalks in the ground.*]

IXMUCANE: And each day as you enter el patio, observe the plants well. Should the plants grow dry and desert gray, Xibalba will be their resting place. But should these plants bear new leaves of green, our sons shall return to us as sun and moon and light.

[LOS GEMELOS *enter.*]

IXQUIC: ¡Hijos!

HUNAHPU: Hello, Mother.

IXBALANQUE: Beloved Grandmother.

IXMUCANE: My sons.

IXBALANQUE: Grandmother, you've already planted the corn. You've known all along, haven't you, la jornada that lies before us?

IXMUCANE: I am not ignorant of fate, as I have already suffered the loss of your father and uncle.

IXQUIC: And now I, too, understand your destiny.

[LOS GEMELOS *go to their grandmother and mother. They embrace.*]

IXMUCANE: Go now, the Lords of Death await you. [*Blessing them.*] In the name of el Tiox, Los mundos, y Nantat.

[LOS GEMELOS *take their leave and travel down the pyramid path to Xibalba.* TECOLOTE *leads the way, then vanishes. "Xibalba" theme music repeated.*]

Scene Eight

[*The Gemelos hide, just as the* LORDS OF DEATH *enter.* TECOLOTE *follows.*]

BLOOD SAUSAGE: Did you hear something, Pat Pus?

PATRIARCHAL PUS: We aren't expecting anyone at this hour.

[LOS GEMELOS *jump out of hiding.*]

HUNAHPU: Good day, Lord Blood Sausage.

BLOOD SAUSAGE: What the bloody hell?

IXBALANQUE: Señor Patriarchal Pus.

PATRIARCHAL PUS: [*Startled.*] You nearly scared us to death.

BLOOD SAUSAGE: How did you know our names?

HUNAHPU: A good guess?

BLOOD SAUSAGE: Hmph! [*Indicating the "hot seat."*] Have a seat and give us a moment to think about what to do with you.

HUNAHPU: No, sirs. It is you who have suffered the shock. Take a moment to recoup yourselves.

PATRIARCHAL PUS: He's right.

BLOOD SAUSAGE: Most thoughtful of them.

[*The* LORDS OF DEATH *unwittingly sit on the "hot seat."*]

PATRIARCHAL PUS: Ouch!

BLOOD SAUSAGE: Ooooh! My blistered buttocks!

PATRIARCHAL PUS: You busters think you're pretty smart, don't you?

IXBALANQUE: Well, sirs, we do know the difference between a comal and a couch.

BLOOD SAUSAGE: All right then, smart alecks. [*Calling out.*] Owl!

TECOLOTE: Yes, your Lordship.

BLOOD SAUSAGE: Put these hooligans in the House of Bats.

PATRIARCHAL PUS: No one survives those nocturnal navigators.

[*He escorts* LOS GEMELOS *to their cell.*]

PATRIARCHAL PUS: [*To* BLOOD SAUSAGE *as they exit.*] I don't know what it is about those boys, they feel so . . . familiar.

TECOLOTE [*Muttering.*] DNA.

[TECOLOTE *puts Los Gemelos in the hutch.*]

TECOLOTE: Keep your heads covered.

IXBALANQUE: What?

TECOLOTE: The bats. They got snouts like knives.

IXBALANQUE: Oh.

[TECOLOTE *closes the hutch door.* LOS GEMELOS *wait for the bats to arrive. Suddenly a field of moving darkness passes over the heads of* LOS GEMELOS. *A bat figure enters and dances menacingly around the hutch. The sound of beating wings and a loathsome squeaking fill the air. Then there is silence as the bat hovers above the boys' cell.*]

IXBALANQUE: [*Timidly.*] Hun?

HUNAHPU: Yeah.

IXBALANQUE: I think the bats are gone now. Can you see if it's close to dawn?

HUNAHPU: Okay, I'll go check it out.

IXBALANQUE: Be careful.

[*As* HUNAHPU *sticks out his head to look for the dawn, the bat flies by and snatches off Hunahpu's head, dancing about with it as she exits.*]

IXBALANQUE: Hun! Hun! [*He pokes his head out.*] What happened? [*Calling out.*] Tecolote! Tecolote!

TECOLOTE: What's the problem?

IXBALANQUE: It's Hunahpu. He's lost his head.

TECOLOTE: I told you to stay under cover.

[CONEJO *enters.*]

CONEJO: Oye, carnala ¿qué pasa?

TECOLOTE: Hunahpu's lost his head.

CONEJO: ¿De veras? The bats?

TECOLOTE: I tried to warn them.

CONEJO: Bloodthirsty little cabrones. I guess that was the round thing con cara de dios que was rollin' around in the ball court.

IXBALANQUE: You saw my brother's head! Can you get it back?

CONEJO: [*After a pause.*] Pues . . . I got an idea. 'Spérate aquí.

[CONEJO *disappears.*]

IXBALANQUE: What's he up to?

TECOLOTE: You'll see.

CONEJO: [*Returning with a large squash.*] ¡Toma! [*He tosses the squash to* IXBALANQUE.]

TECOLOTE: Good thinking, Rabbit.

IXBALANQUE: What's the squash for?

CONEJO: Un sub.

IXBALANQUE: A sub?

CONEJO: Un substitute.

IXBALANQUE: I still don't get it.

CONEJO: Vente.

[IXBALANQUE *and* CONEJO *huddle close together.* TECOLOTE *keeps watch.*]

CONEJO: Hunahpu's gonna hafta fake it like this squash is his cabeza-head. Otherwise, you forfeit the game.

IXBALANQUE: We can't forfeit.

CONEJO: Por eso, digo you gotta follow my game plan. They'll be using your carnal's real head as the ball today.

IXBALANQUE: Ouch!

CONEJO: No te agüites. He'll survive. [*Continuing.*] Halfway through the game, I'll whistle and that'll be la señal for you vatos to kick the ball as far out of bounds as you can. En el mismo momento, I'll bounce off like a ball p'allá in a different direction. The Lords son tan pendejos, they'll chase after anything that moves. While they're busy huffin' and puffin' after me, you make the switch.

IXBALANQUE: Oh, now I get it. And I stick Hun's real head back on.

CONEJO: ¡Eso!

IXBALANQUE: And we use the squash for the ball.

CONEJO: ¡Órale! That's the strategy.

IXBALANQUE: Will it work?

CONEJO: Este . . . [*Kisses the air.*] ¡Suavecito!

[IXBALANQUE *places the squash on Hunahpu's head.*]

IXBALANQUE: Try this on, Bro.

[HUNAHPU *emerges from hutch wearing squash-head.*]

IXBALANQUE: How you feel, melón?

HUNAHPU: [*Muffled.*] All right . . . I guess.

IXBALANQUE: [*His ear to the squash.*] Yeah, great. Okay, let's go. We got a game to win.

[*They exit.*]

Scene Nine

[*Conch shells announce the day of the ball game.* LOS GEMELOS *enter; they are in full ball-game regalia. The* LORDS OF DEATH *stand at the top of the pyramid.*]

PATRIARCHAL PUS: Xibalbans! It has been brought to our attention that Hunahpu, the son of his similarly fated father—Hunahpu the First—has generously donated his head for the purposes of today's ball game!

BLOOD SAUSAGE: A round of applause for the donor.

[*The* LORDS OF DEATH *descend with the head ceremoniously. The opponents face each other off. For a moment the* LORDS *appear a bit confused seeing* HUNAHPU *standing before them while they hold his head in their hands. But eager for a good game, they proceed. The conch shell again sounds and the ball game begins. Percussion. The ball game is a kind of death-dealing, slow-motion dance. Suddenly,* CONEJO *lets out a loud whistle and* IXBALANQUE *kicks the ball off the field.* CONEJO *runs off in a different direction, pretending to be the ball.*]

BLOOD SAUSAGE: There goes the ball.

PATRIARCHAL PUS: Let's get it.

[*The* LORDS OF DEATH *chase after* CONEJO. *In the meantime,* HUNAHPU *grabs the real ball (his own head) and replaces the squash with it. The squash now becomes the ball. They rush back into the center of the court.*]

IXBALANQUE: We've retrieved it! We've got the ball over here!

PATRIARCHAL PUS: But I don't understand. Didn't the ball roll over there?

BLOOD SAUSAGE: Who cares? Let's get back to the game.

[*The* LORDS OF DEATH *return to the ball game, a bit disoriented. The ball game ensues.* HUNAHPU *kicks the ball and hits the goal-ring at the top of the pyramid. The squash-ball splits in two.*]

HUNAHPU: Our game! We won! We won!

[LOS GEMELOS *win the game. The* LORDS OF DEATH *exit in disgust.*]

BLOOD SAUSAGE: This is an outrage!

PATRIARCHAL PUS: If word should get out that these pubescents defeated us—with a squash.

BLOOD SAUSAGE: Well, their victory will be short-lived. I assure you.

Scene Ten

[*After the ball game,* LOS GEMELOS *sit up on the pyramid.*]

HUNAHPU: We won, so why don't I feel good?

IXBALANQUE: 'Cuz that's not the point.

HUNAHPU: What? Feeling good?

IXBALANQUE: No, winning.

HUNAHPU: But winning's everything, Ix.

IXBALANQUE: Maybe when we were kids, but not now. [*Sniffing the air.*] Smell that?

HUNAHPU: What? [*Sniffing*.] It's bar-be-que.

IXBALANQUE: It's us—soon to be burned to a crisp, Big Brother. [*Pause.*] Have you forgotten? We're never getting out of here alive. This is Xibalba. We can defeat death only by surrendering to it.

HUNAHPU: The fire pit?

[TECOLOTE *enters.*]

IXBALANQUE: Right. There's Tecolote. Maybe she can help us. [*Calling.*] ¡Oye, Tecolote!

HUNAHPU: Will you help us, Teco?

TECOLOTE: I don't see that I can. Your deaths have already been divined.

IXBALANQUE: But not the matter of our bodies' disposal.

TECOLOTE: I don't understand.

IXBALANQUE: The manner in which our bones are disposed will determine if we are to see the next life.

TECOLOTE: What about the Lords?

IXBALANQUE: They will do as you suggest.

TECOLOTE: You think so?

IXBALANQUE: I know so. [IXBALANQUE *whispers in her ear.*]

TECOLOTE: Your bones! The river!

HUNAHPU: Yes!

TECOLOTE: I will try. [*With resolve.*] I will take care of your remains.

IXBALANQUE: Good. We will keep our mother's promise to you, Teco. You shall preside as guardian of the night throughout the forests of Uleu.

[*The* LORDS *can be heard entering.*]

BLOOD SAUSAGE: Boys! Oh, boys!

[TECOLOTE *puts on his owl-servant face.*]

PATRIARCHAL PUS: [*To* LOS GEMELOS.] Come, my sons. Come see what delicious meats we have cooked up for you.

BLOOD SAUSAGE: Yes, you must be famished after so much ball-playing.

[LOS GEMELOS *eye each other knowingly.*]

HUNAHPU: Ya con las mentiras, viejos. ¡No somos pendejos!

BLOOD SAUSAGE: But aren't you hungry?

IXBALANQUE: It is the mouth of that fire pit that is hungry for us.

[LOS GEMELOS *race up to the top of the pyramid, which is now the edge of the fire pit. Lighting effects. They turn to each other, wrap their arms around each other.*]

IXBALANQUE: Como cuates. . . .

HUNAHPU: Y hermanos eternos, we enter and exit this world.

[*They dive headfirst into the oven.*]

PATRIARCHAL PUS: What fools! Finally, the little bastards are out of sight.

BLOOD SAUSAGE: Let's celebrate.

[*Music. The* LORDS *begin to dance with each other.*]

TECOLOTE: [*Trying to get their attention.*] Lords! Sir Sausage, Sir Pus?

[*The music suddenly stops.*]

PATRIARCHAL PUS: What is it, Owl? Don't you know how to party?

TECOLOTE: Their death is not complete, your Lordships, until there is no trace of their remains.

BLOOD SAUSAGE: The Owl speaks truly.

TECOLOTE: I overheard the twins saying that the fate they feared most was to have their bones ground down into the finest of flour and sprinkled as ashy dust into the river. There, you see, their death will be complete and their sleep eternal.

BLOOD SAUSAGE: So be it. Keep checking the bar-be-que, Owl. When the boys are thoroughly cooked, we will follow your recommendation exactly.

[*The* LORDS *exit. Crossfade to* IXQUIC *and* IXMUCANE *entering. They sit by the two corn plants.*]

IXMUCANE: You have cried now, Daughter, for five days.

IXQUIC: And still I have rivers of tears inside me.

IXMUCANE: In the womb of that river, your sons are reborn, their ribs forming from the sculpted sands beneath the water. [*Indicating the plants.*] Mira.

IXQUIC: I see green leaves sprouting from once-withered stalks.

IXMUCANE: Your tears have watered these plants.

IXQUIC: Let us give thanks. Our sons live!

[*The plants dance. The women exit, dancing.*]

Scene Eleven

[*Music: "Carnaval."* LOS GEMELOS *enter wearing catfish faces, their clothes in tatters. They do a little dance.*]

HUNAHPU: Step right up, damas y caballeros! Come witness for yourselves the greatest, most thrilling magic show in the world.

IXBALANQUE: Or should we say the underworld.

HUNAHPU: We are magicians of the highest caliber.

IXBALANQUE: Trained by the University of Life.

HUNAHPU: And Death.

[*The* LORDS OF DEATH *enter.*]

BLOOD SAUSAGE: Enough talk and self-congratulation.

PATRIARCHAL PUS: Start the show.

[HUNAHPU *produces an obsidian blade.*]

HUNAHPU: Is this more what you had in mind, sirs?

PATRIARCHAL PUS: Ahhhh!

BLOOD SAUSAGE: Exactly!

IXBALANQUE: We now present a death-defying feat.

PATRIARCHAL PUS: But no one can defy the obsidian blade!

IXBALANQUE: We need a volunteer.

[*They come down into the audience.*]

HUNAHPU: A volunteer?

BLOOD SAUSAGE: Take that insolent owl.

TECOLOTE: Me? But what would you magicians want with me?

HUNAHPU: To remove your heart and put it back again.

IXBALANQUE: Alive!

PATRIARCHAL PUS: Impossible!

TECOLOTE: But it is a mere bird's heart.

BLOOD SAUSAGE: Oh, quit hesitating, you coward.

[*The* LORDS *push* TECOLOTE *over to the sacrificial site.*]

TECOLOTE: You will return my heart alive, you say?

IXBALANQUE: It won't miss a beat.

[LOS GEMELOS *lay* TECOLOTE *down, breast to the heavens.* HUNAHPU *raises the blade above his head. The crowd lets out a gasp. And* HUNAHPU *comes down with all his force into the feathered breast of* TECOLOTE. IXBALANQUE *digs his hands in and pulls out the beating heart.*]

BLOOD SAUSAGE: Ah yes, a marvelous excavation.

PATRIARCHAL PUS: And done with such gusto. Might we not have a taste while it still pulses?

HUNAHPU: This heart is to be restored into the breast of the bird.

PATRIARCHAL PUS: Who ever heard of such a thing?

BLOOD SAUSAGE: Brother, if these vagabond clowns can return the life to this worthless owl, I will be the next to expose my breast to the magician's blade.

PATRIARCHAL PUS: And I will follow.

BLOOD SAUSAGE: On with the show!

IXBALANQUE: And now to resurrect the life of this bird.

[LOS GEMELOS *breathe upon Tecolote's beating heart and place it reverently back into his chest. The gash in his breast they fill with feathers and wait for a sign of life. Within a moment,* TECOLOTE *sits up, a full and complete owl.*]

IXBALANQUE: How do you feel?

TECOLOTE: Well, my plumas are a little ruffled.

[*Applause.*]

PATRIARCHAL PUS: Me next! Step aside, you feathered fool.

BLOOD SAUSAGE: No, me next!

[*Pushes* PATRIARCHAL PUS *aside, approaches the sacrificial site.*]

PATRIARCHAL PUS: [*A bit insulted.*] Well.

HUNAHPU: How 'bout your head instead?

BLOOD SAUSAGE: My pleasure.

PATRIARCHAL PUS: [*Overlapping.*] Why, even better!

[BLOOD SAUSAGE *lays his head down upon the sacrificial table.* HUNAHPU *decapitates him. A sudden silence falls over the crowd as* BLOOD SAUSAGE's *head rolls onto the ground.* LOS GEMELOS *turn to* PATRIARCHAL PUS.]

PATRIARCHAL PUS: My turn! My turn! [*He rushes to the sacrificial site, starts to lay his head down for decapitation, stops.*] Now, you're sure this will work?

HUNAHPU: Absolutely!

[HUNAHPU *pushes* PATRIARCHAL PUS'S *head down onto the sacrificial table.* IXBALANQUE *chops it off. Music.* LOS GEMELOS *break out into a dance, holding the heads in the air.* TECOLOTE *joins them. There is a riff of the "Tecolote Theme," then he takes flight out of Xibalba forever.* LOS GEMELOS *watch him depart. Lighting/music transition. Moonlight.* IXQUIC *appears at the top of the pyramid as una luna creciente.*]

IXQUIC: Hijos. Do you recognize your mother?

LOS GEMELOS: We do.

[*They meet her at the top of the pyramid. She puts headdresses on them. They become the sun and the moon.*]

IXQUIC: Sons, you are transformed. No longer earthly bodies, but celestial in nature. You, Hunahpu, the one star brilliant enough to be visible at the day's zenith. And you, Ixbalanque, the guardian of the night, visible once a month en la luna's full female face. We name you Sun and Moon.

IXBALANQUE: And you, Mamá, are named by la luna's changing aspects.

HUNAHPU: Waning moon. Waxing moon. El lado oscuro de la luna.

IXQUIC: [*Pause, the music rises.*] Let us go now. Your siblings, the Four Hundred Stars, await us.

[*Lighting/music transition.* IXQUIC *and* LOS GEMELOS *descend the pyramid and exit.*]

Scene Twelve

[IXMUCANE *enters, carrying the four humans in the shape of corn dolls. She is covered with the dust of corn flour.*]

IXMUCANE: [*Calling out.*] ¡Qué maravilla! ¡Qué maravilla! Miren, I think I've done it! This morning may be the dawn of humankind. ¡Viejo! Kukulcan!

[CUCUMATZ *and* IXPIYACOC *enter excitedly.*]

IXPIYACOC: Why, they're human beings.

CUCUMATZ: ¿Cómo lo hiciste, comadre?

IXMUCANE: The water became their blood, the corn their flesh. And the oil from my hands, as I worked them, became their muscle and fat.

[*The* DANCERS *enter.* IXMUCANE *passes out the* CORN PEOPLE *to them in a ritualized fashion.* THE GODS *ascend the pyramid and chant.*]

Chant:
Ch i biih na q'ut/Ri qa bi.
K oh i q'aharizah, oh i chuch,/Oh i qahav.

[*The* CORN PEOPLE *dance and praise their creators.*]

DANCER: Corazón del Cielo.

DANCER: Heart of the Sky.

DANCER: Plumed Serpent.

DANCER: Huracán.

IXPIYACOC: They honor our names!

CUCUMATZ: At last! And so we pass onto you first humans, of the male and female kind, the project of humanity.

IXMUCANE: La raíz de la tribu maya.

IXPIYACOC: Each with his own tongue, her own land.

CUCUMATZ: Multiply and become numerous, occupy the north and the south.

IXPIYACOC: The highlands and the low.

IXMUCANE: But remember always, to lift your faces to the sky.

[*The* CORN PEOPLE *dance and call out the names of the first peoples.*]

DANCER: Balam Acab, Tigre de la Noche.

DANCER: Chomihá, Agua Hermosa y Escogida.

DANCER: Iquí Balam, Tigre de la Luna.

DANCER: Caquixahá, Agua de Guacamaya.

[THE GODS *and the* CORN PEOPLE *join together dancing and chanting.*]

ALL:

ucah tzucuxic
ucah xucutaxic
        retaxic,
ucah cheexic,

umeh camaxic,
uyuc camaxic

upa cah,
upa uleu

cah tzuc
cah xucut

[*They exit. Only* IXMUCANE *remains on stage. She removes her head-dress and once again becomes* DAYKEEPER.]

DAYKEEPER: From these men and these women we are descended—Los Qui-chés. [*Pause.*] And we turn our faces up to the sky and toward the eastern place where the sun is born, and give thanks. This is the root de la Palabra Anciana. Are, u xe 'oher tzih.

[*She bows ceremoniously. The lights fade to black.*]

THE FAT·FREE CHICANA
& THE SNOW CAP QUEEN

Elaine Romero

CHARACTERS

AMY DURÁN. A fat-free Chicana in her early twenties.

MAMI DURÁN. Amy's mother.

SILVIA DURÁN. Amy's nineteen-year-old sister.

ABUELO/MR. SUAVE. Mami's father. Mr. Suave is suave, with all his faculties.

RUMALDO SOTO. Mami's nephew. Amy and Silvia's older cousin. He should be from his late twenties to his early forties.

SNOW CAP QUEEN, also known as the Lard Lady. A Mexicana, a trickster, she claims to dwell within the blue-hued mountain of Morrell Snow Cap Lard. She has two other incarnations—the GOOD WITCH OF THE NORTH/DOÑA NORTE, a New Mexican in the tradition of *La Conquistadora* of Santa Fe, and LA CRÍTICA, a restaurant critic. She also appears as a WOMAN CUSTOMER. Her voice will be used when the script indicates WOMAN'S VOICE.

TIME

The present.

PLACE

Idaho and the desert Southwest.

SETTING

Café Lindo, a southwestern café in an old adobe building. In the interior, brightly colored Mexican blankets hang from the beam ceilings. Clear plastic tablecloths cover nicer ones. The counter opens up to a partially visible kitchen. On the exterior, stucco peels off the adobe walls. (This is where the lard pours out of the walls.)

ACT ONE

Scene One

[*On the grounds of the University of Idaho campus stands a warm-blooded person in a cold-blooded place.* AMY, *the fat-free Chicana, dressed in snow garb, clutches her arms, teeth chattering. It's snowing. The* SNOW CAP QUEEN *appears as the* GOOD WITCH OF THE NORTH. *She wears a white lace dress, carries a magic wand, clicks her heels together. She looks like La Conquistadora, the Virgin of Santa Fe, New Mexico.*]

NORTH: There's no place like home. There's no place—

AMY: [*Defensively.*] I wasn't thinking that.

NORTH: And it's nice and warm, too.

AMY: Forget your jacket?

NORTH: I'm not cold.

AMY: Girl in my dorm thought it wasn't cold. Went to class with wet hair. It broke off. [AMY *slices the air.*] It was her only good feature.

NORTH: Do the names Silvia, Mami, Abuelo, and Rumaldo mean anything to you?

AMY: Guilt-ridden daydream go away. Don't come back another day. [AMY *claps her hands together, closes her eyes tight, opens her eyes, as if relieved, and sees* NORTH *is still there.*] I'm the first grandchild to go to college in my family. I will not return home a failure. [AMY *pushes* NORTH.] These fantasies are ruining my life. Mi familia. Oh great, now you've got me speaking Spanish.

NORTH: Your familia needs you.

AMY: I'm trying to get an education here.

NORTH: There's something called summer break.

AMY: Mami and I have already discussed this.

NORTH: You lectured her.

AMY: I don't disrespect my mother.

NORTH: It's breaking her heart.

AMY: I'd love to freeze to death out here with you, but I've got a major midterm in about three minutes.

NORTH: Dietetics?

AMY: Dietetics, yes.

NORTH: That isn't what you set out to do.

AMY: Hallucinations know everything about you because they're from your own twisted, degenerate mind.

NORTH: [*Singsong.*] I know something you don't know.

AMY: Oh yeah?

NORTH: Cholesterol levels can shoot so high they'll lift tin roofs off adobe buildings.

AMY: What do you know about adobe buildings?

NORTH: There's always a way to make them fall apart.

AMY: That place has been there for—a long time.

NORTH: Longer than you think. [NORTH *claps her hands.*] Smell.

   [AMY *sniffs.*]

AMY: [*Excited.*] My mami's cooking.

NORTH: It's the smell of death.

AMY: Go away.

NORTH: She must change. Her restaurant must change. Or . . .

AMY: Or what?

[NORTH *touches* AMY'S *shoulder with the magic wand, dissipating Amy's anger and making her sleepy.*]

NORTH: Go home and make your fat-free dreams come true.

AMY: My fat-free dreams?

NORTH: Change your mami's restaurant. Create a new healthier menu.

[*It's as though* NORTH *has spoken Amy's secret desire.* AMY *hugs her.*]

AMY: Oh can I—whatever your name is?

NORTH: The Good Witch of the North, Doña Norte to you.

AMY: Oh, Doña Norte, I don't have money for the airplane.

NORTH: Pues, el hombre propone y Dios dispone.

AMY: Man proposes, God disposes?

[NORTH *exhales forcefully and disappears.* AMY *trips, reaching in the snow barehanded, discovering three one-hundred-dollar bills. She lifts them into the air.*]

AMY: Yes!

[*Crossfade.*]

Scene Two

[*A week later. Café Lindo.* SILVIA *jogs in the front door, donned in tight-fitting jogging clothes. A bilingual radio station plays Tex-Mex.* SILVIA *turns off the radio, and runs in place as she delivers her message.*]

SILVIA: Mami! Amy called. She decided to come home anyways. She's gonna be at the bus station at 2 P.M. Sharp. She needs you to pick her up.

[SILVIA *shrugs her shoulders and heads out, struggling with the screen door, still jogging in place. When she exits and slams the door, a bell clangs.* MAMI *emerges from the kitchen, dazed, wearing headphones and a flour-covered apron, oblivious, not having heard a goddamn thing. She takes the headphones off, and turns up the radio, shaking her head. Lost in the music, she dances about, busing tables. A bicycle horn sounds.* MAMI *doesn't respond. It gets louder and louder, more frantic.* MAMI *opens the door.* ABUELO, *in his late seventies, drives a power lawnmower into the café, beeping the horn.* MAMI *moves aside some chairs, pushes the lawnmower over to the corner under a picture of the Bleeding Heart of Jesus, blesses herself, and throws a Mexican blanket over the lawnmower.* ABUELO *grumbles, reaches into his shirt pocket, pulls out a traffic ticket.*]

ABUELO: [*Grumbling.*] I have to drive this piece of mierda because they say I can't see. Took away my driver's license.

MAMI: I'm sorry, Apá.

ABUELO: I was driving before they were born.

MAMI: I think that's what they're worried about.

ABUELO: Huh? Where's Silvia? She was gonna jog next to me on the way downtown.

MAMI: She's probably warming up with a twenty-mile run.

ABUELO: I wish she'd come home.

MAMI: Put some lettuce out on the front stairs again. That brought her home last time.

[ABUELO *hides his ticket, mumbling.*]

ABUELO: They want to send me to prison. I'll never see you again, mi'ja.

[ABUELO *shows her the traffic ticket.*]

MAMI: Fifteen miles on the freeway. Pa, you could have been killed.

ABUELO: It was an emergency.

MAMI: What emergency? A forty-five-dollar fine. We don't have the money for this.

[*Clanging at the door,* AMY *comes bustling in with bulging suitcases.*]

AMY: Mami, where were you? I walked all the way from the downtown bus station.

MAMI: Amy, what are you doing here?

AMY: [*Frustrated.*] Silvia!

[*A shocked* MAMI *pinches* AMY's *thin waist.*]

MAMI: No me digas. What happened, mi'ja? You got sick in Idaho.

AMY: No.

MAMI: I could have come for you. I would cook for you some pozole, some albóndigas. [*A revelation.*] Manzanilla tea!

AMY: [*Sarcastically.*] Oh, there's an original thought.

MAMI: Why don't you call me?

AMY: I wasn't sick. I just changed my diet.

MAMI: You're too young for that.

AMY: According to my height/weight chart, I was twenty pounds overweight.

MAMI: Who makes that stuff up anyways?

AMY: [*Sarcastically.*] The AMA, the American Medical Association.

MAMI: Let me cook you some lunch.

[SILVIA *enters.*]

AMY: [*Sarcastically.*] Thanks for passing on my message.

MAMI: Now, let's get you something to eat.

AMY: [*A beat.*] No.

MAMI: No. What's this no?

AMY: The Mexican diet is one of the highest-fat diets in the world. Why do you think we're all diabetics and die of heart attacks while we're still young?

MAMI: Mi'ja, you're not a diabetic.

SILVIA: We don't all die young. Look at Abuelo.

AMY: [*To* SILVIA.] Read the obituaries. [AMY *lifts a newspaper off the table, thumbs through to the obituaries, hands the paper to her mother.*] See, they're all Mexican.

MAMI: [*Sad.*] Mi'ja, stop.

AMY: No, it's all that cheese. All that greasy meat and fried food. And I'm not even talking about the lard.

MAMI: You don't like my manteca?

AMY: [*Simultaneously.*] García, Garza, González . . .

MAMI: You always loved my manteca. Just for taste.

AMY: Bad luck for the G families.

MAMI: What happened to you at college, mi'jita?

SILVIA: Not Adán Garza? He's one of our most loyal customers.

[AMY *looks at* MAMI *disapprovingly.*]

AMY: [*Looking at the paper.*] The same.

[MAMI *grabs the newspaper, crosses herself.*]

MAMI: Pobrecito. But he wasn't fat, mi'ja, honest.

AMY: It's just our diet is no way to lose weight.

SILVIA: Look at Abuelo. He's as skinny as a calavera during Lent. At least he used to be. And look at me.

AMY: All you eat is lettuce.

SILVIA: It's Mexican lettuce.

AMY: Do you think Mexican men have higher metabolisms than Mexican women?

MAMI: What words! I need a box full of dictionaries just to talk to you.

AMY: Don't you understand what I'm saying, Mami?

MAMI: Dichos no rompen panzas pero adolecen corazones.

AMY: Mami?

MAMI: Don't you understand what I'm saying, mi'ja? Words can break my heart.

AMY: Can't anybody change around here? I don't know why it's such a big deal. I haven't eaten a tortilla in a year anyways.

[MAMI *is in tears.* MAMI *makes the sign of the cross.*]

MAMI: Madre mía santísima.

AMY: They don't have good Mexican food in Idaho.

MAMI: [*With disbelief.*] We should never have sent you up there. How did you live?

AMY: I'm fine.

MAMI: I'll cook something for you. Not too much fat. Just a little fat. Just for taste.

AMY: Ma, can't you just accept it? I'm never eating at your restaurant again.

MAMI: C'mon, mi'ja, have a little something.

AMY: Never!

MAMI: What'd I do wrong, God? My daughters only eat air.

[MAMI *crosses to the kitchen shaking, puts her hand on a tub of lard for support and collapses. All freeze, except* MAMI. *The Snow Cap Queen appears as herself—an apparition—wearing pale and dark blue colors. She speaks with authority.*]

SNOW: Gloria! Gloria! Lift your head.

[MAMI *lifts her head.*]

SNOW: Don't you listen to her, mi'ja. What do they teach her at college anyways?

MAMI: María. Ave María.

SNOW: Not quite. [*Justifying.*] You have to put lard in the beans to get them to taste just right. And your tortillas would be flaky without a little manteca. Your Christmas tamales would only be good for Halloween if you used vegetable oil.

MAMI: Who are you?

SNOW: Name's Snow Cap. Snow Cap Queen to be exact. I got this modeling job when I was sixteen.

MAMI: ¿Mande?

SNOW: [*Points at the lard container.*] See that little bump right there?

[MAMI *holds the lard container close to her eyes, finally nods her head.*]

SNOW: Well, that's the top of my hair.

MAMI: [*A double take at* SNOW *and the lard container.*] A ver.

SNOW: Right there. Plain as day.

MAMI: ¡Fíjate!

SNOW: That's my hair.

MAMI: You're from manteca land.

SNOW: Actually, I'm from the Andes. South America. The lard capital of the world.

MAMI: Oh, my. You come a long way to my little restaurant.

SNOW: I know. Classy, huh?

MAMI: Such trouble for us.

SNOW: You're having a crisis—a crisis of the heart. I'm here to help, if you'll let me. [SNOW *reaches out her hand.* MAMI *reluctantly shakes it. Beat.*] That daughter of yours gives you some trouble, no?

MAMI: That's just Amy. She's always like that. Always has something going.

SNOW: We can fix that.

MAMI: She's okay. She'll get over it.

SNOW: She doesn't like your food. She said she's never going to eat in your restaurant again.

MAMI: She's just talking. The second she smells the first tortilla, she'll rip it out of my hands.

SNOW: She could be bad for business. It's slow this time of year, no?

MAMI: We do all right with the RVs.

SNOW: You should see the kinds of crowds the lady across the street at El Saguaro de Suárez is getting. The bean committee from the newspaper has been there twice already tasting their beans.

MAMI: What do you know about the bean committee?

SNOW: I know they've been having second thoughts.

MAMI: Don't be silly. We have a reputation for having the best beans in town. The newspaper has voted us number one five years in a row.

SNOW: Well, she's trying to change all that.

MAMI: She wouldn't know a good bean if she soaked it overnight.

SNOW: Con lo que sana Susana cae enferma Juana.

MAMI: I know one girl's food is the other girl's poison. But I know the secret.

SNOW: About adding the birria juice to make it taste just right?

MAMI: [*Alarmed.*] Who told you about the birria juice? [*Summoning her.*] Amy!

SNOW: It's only a matter of time before she steals not only your business, but your title.

[MAMI *bites her fingernails.*]

MAMI: What should we do?

SNOW: [*A loud whisper.*] Buy more lard.

MAMI: Are you sure this isn't one of your commercials? [*Singing a jingle: "For you and your familia there's nothing more."*]

SNOW: Than Snow Cap Lard. It's me. It's the truth. Listen to that song or close your doors forever.

[*Lights flicker.* SNOW *disappears in a white cloud of dust.* MAMI *reaches out to her, collapses on the ground.*]

AMY: Call 9-1-1.

SILVIA: Mami, wake up.

AMY: What happened, Mami?

[*As if on auto-pilot,* MAMI *takes her money out of her bra, handing the cash to* SILVIA.]

MAMI: Silvia, go to the store. Buy three cases of lard.

AMY: Are you trying to kill us all?

[SILVIA *takes the money.*]

SILVIA: Sure, Ma, anything you want.

AMY: Kiss up.

SILVIA: You shouldn't be so disrespectful.

[SILVIA *runs out the door.*]

MAMI: [*Firmly.*] Mi'ja, this is my restaurant.

AMY: Did you know that one chimichanga has the same amount of fat as one dozen glazed donuts?

MAMI: ¿Mi'ja, porqué te importa? We never ever served chimichangas.

AMY: Mami, you just don't want to face the facts—Mexican food can kill you.

[AMY *starts to leave.*]

MAMI: Where are you going, young lady?

AMY: To look for a summer job.

MAMI: You're not working here? Mi'ja, I rely on you for the summer visitors in their RVs.

AMY: [*Simultaneously.*] RVs. You don't want me to anyways.

MAMI: I never said that.

[RUMALDO, *a Chicano with a red bandanna wrapped around his head, bursts in with an oversized graffiti art sign that reads "Café Lindo." Below that, it reads "Voted the Best Beans in Town Eight Years in a Row." It's so large it could take up half the outside wall of the restaurant.*]

MAMI: Rumaldo!

RUMALDO: Tía, I've got your new sign. I was worried if it was big enough or not.

[*All look at him questioningly.*]

RUMALDO: Amy, you're home. Come here and hug your favorite cousin.

[RUMALDO *reaches out to hug* AMY. *She doesn't respond.* RUMALDO *looks devastated.*]

AMY: [*Pointing to* RUMALDO*'s sign.*] What's that?

RUMALDO: It's the latest. It's called graffiti art.

AMY: [*Looking at sign.*] While you're at it, you might as well change that sign. Call the place something new. Call it "The Heart Attack Café."

[AMY *slams the door.* RUMALDO *still has his arms outstretched for her to hug him.*]

MAMI: Aren't you gonna embrace your favorite cousin?

RUMALDO: What's into her?

[*Crossfade.*]

Scene Three

[*The next morning.* AMY, *dressed in a white apron, begrudgingly cleans tables.* MAMI, *dressed up and ready to go, kisses her on the cheek. The sign hangs on the outside wall.* MAMI *sprays herself with perfume, and then sprays some in* AMY's *face.*]

MAMI: Smell that.

AMY: [*Waving her hand under her nose.*] Bug spray.

MAMI: French perfume. It should take until this afternoon. Then, I'll help you cook.

AMY: Don't count on it. You know how much time bureaucrats like to waste.

MAMI: Well, they said it would be 20 minutes. I added the three hours.

AMY: You're learning.

MAMI: Rumaldo makes all the messes, and I have to clean them up.

AMY: Nobody's gonna accept that as art.

MAMI: I thought you'd be out there doing just what he does like you always do.

AMY: I don't always do that.

MAMI: However you want to remember it, mi'ja. [*Beat.*] The sign code. Have you heard of such a thing?

AMY: They're just trying to beautify the neighborhood.

MAMI: Our little sign beautifies the neighborhood. What do they mean?

AMY: I think they mean something smaller. Something that doesn't take up the front wall of the restaurant and encourage gang activity.

MAMI: It makes a nice statement—that's what Rumaldo said.

AMY: Did he?

MAMI: They'd rather we all starve to death and put in a Denny's across the street, than to let my nephew Rumaldo, with all his artistic talent, express himself in our own little neighborhood.

AMY: He should have just called it a mural.

MAMI: He doesn't paint murals.

AMY: Graffiti art. That's dumb.

MAMI: Oh God, I'm late. You okay for the cooking?

AMY: Ready to kill people with a smile.

MAMI: Okay, bribona, I'm going. By the way, Silvia couldn't make it. She was—

AMY: Jogging.

MAMI: You know. Some contest or something. [MAMI *slams the door and looks up at the new sign across the street.*] No me digas.

AMY: What?

MAMI: El Saguaro de Suárez has a new name. [*Quickly.*] "El Burrito Preparado Más Pronto Con Los Frijoles Mejores En Todo El Pueblo, En Todo El Mundo. Chinga el Periódico."

[*Inadvertently having cursed,* MAMI *makes a quick sign of the cross.*]

AMY: The quickest burrito with the best beans in the whole town, in the whole world. Fuck the newspaper. That's not a name. It's two sentences.

MAMI: They can't put that word on a sign.

AMY: It's in Spanish. Nobody'll know the difference.

MAMI: I guess I can't blame her. She got that place in the divorce. It was named after her ex-husband's family.

AMY: El Saguaro de Suárez?

MAMI: [*Bends her finger.*] But the little cactus died.

AMY: She's pathetic.

MAMI: Why doesn't the sign code go after her? Ay, I'd better go before the Just Say No to Graffiti people paint over Rumaldo's sign with white paint. Dios mío, you should have seen what they did to Maria's fifteen-year-old son's Aztec mural.

[AMY *kisses her mother on the cheek.* MAMI *exits. The sound of* ABUELO'S *horn.* AMY *opens the door, lets him in.* ABUELO *holds a paper bag full of groceries in one arm, honks with the other.*]

AMY: Were there any problems with the order?

ABUELO: Huh?

AMY: [*Louder.*] The order. Was it okay?

ABUELO: Huh?

[AMY *nods her head at* ABUELO. *He catches on, starts nodding back.*]

ABUELO: They laughed at me when I showed them the new grocery list.

AMY: Oh, Abuelo. I'm sorry.

[AMY *takes the groceries out.*]

ABUELO: Huh?

AMY: Egg beaters, fat-free cheese, fat-free sour cream. For the tourists and their enchiladas. Good job, Abuelo.

ABUELO: Huh?

AMY: I said, good job!

ABUELO: I need to go to the park. I told Silvia I'd follow her in my car.

[AMY *looks at the lawnmower.*]

AMY: Don't embarrass her.

ABUELO: I won't. No one will even know I'm there.

AMY: Why not?

ABUELO: I cut the grass.

AMY: Don't you want to stay and help me in the kitchen?

[ABUELO *grumbles, rolls away on his lawnmower, honking the horn.*]

AMY: I'm teasing. Let's see.

[AMY *starts grating the cheese. She hums to herself, stops, turns on the radio, flips through some sappy pop music, and switches to the bilingual Tex-Mex station. As the DJ speaks,* AMY *drops her head sadly. Vicente Fernández's song "Por Tu Maldito Amor" plays.* AMY *sings along, dancing with the cheese up against her chest. At the end of the song, she kisses the package of cheese and sets it down. Light show. Like magic,* SNOW *appears.*]

SNOW: Ah, mi'ja, you don't think your mother can tell the difference?

AMY: [*Taken aback.*] Hallucination, hallucination go away. Don't come back another day.

SNOW: Don't pretend you don't know me.

AMY: Don't come back.

SNOW: I'm your madrina.

AMY: My godmother died right after my baptism.

SNOW: Ugly baby.

AMY: Indigestion.

SNOW: I took one look and my little heart couldn't take it.

AMY: No, I remember my madrina. Big bulging eyes springing out of her eye sockets before she collapsed. On the parish priest. The priest was so stunned, he didn't give her the last rites. So now she wanders in Purgatory like La Llorona because of him, but we pray for her on Holy Days of Obligation, like on Los Días de los Muertos and Mother's Day.

[SNOW *starts to check out the non-fat foods.*]

SNOW: You know this food is gonna taste like it was made by termites.

[AMY *grabs the non-fat cheese out of* SNOW's *hand.*]

SNOW: I'm sorry. He's your novio, I forgot.

[AMY *starts pushing* SNOW *out the door.*]

AMY: We're not open till 2:00.

SNOW: What about the lunch crowd?

AMY: We're on MPT, Mexican people's time.

SNOW: You'll never get away with this. You'll ruin your mother's business. Everybody who eats here will know you're not giving them the real Martinez.

AMY: Oh yeah?

SNOW: Your mother will go bankrupt and wander the streets looking for little children to eat because of you.

AMY: Is this a curse?

SNOW: Yes.

AMY: [*Sarcastically.*] I'm threatened.

SNOW: I curse every meal you make with your little college girl hands. May your customers gag and have strong cravings for a little gristle for their meat, good wholesome saturated fat in their cheese, and most of all, manteca—All-American, South American lard dripping through their veins.

AMY: You don't scare me, you evil little witch of the south. Bruja del sur.

SNOW: And may this curse, which I have drummed up in defense of la cultura, la raza, remain in full effect until you have a change of heart, mi'jita of the big ideas and grand schemes.

AMY: I'll never have a change of heart, and I'm not your daughter. Get out of my restaurant before I call a priest to exorcise you to purgatorio, where you will spend eternity being tortured by my real-life madrina with her bulging eyes.

SNOW: [*Smiling.*] I've already disappeared.

[SNOW *vanishes.* AMY *looks around, worried. She shakes her head, disgruntled.*]

AMY: Maldita.

[SILVIA *enters, jogging.* AMY *doesn't see her.*]

SILVIA: You look like you just saw the Virgin Mary having sex.

AMY: I'm just behind on the cooking.

SILVIA: You can't be behind. Mami made a whole bunch of food yesterday so she could go to her meeting.

AMY: Well, it got freezer burned.

SILVIA: Overnight?

[AMY *shrugs.* SILVIA *jogs over to her, grabs a piece of shredded lettuce. Her delight immediately turns to distaste as she spits the lettuce out.*]

SILVIA: Ay Chihuahua, what'd you do to the lettuce?

AMY: [*Defensively.*] Nothing.

SILVIA: It tastes like it's been marinated in pesticides. César Chávez is going to come back from the dead just to boycott.

AMY: It's organic.

SILVIA: You bought two-dollar lettuce?

AMY: Of course. Mami may think it's okay to poison the customers, but I don't. I thought you were running for Christ, or something.

SILVIA: Heart disease.

[AMY *looks up at the picture of the Bleeding Heart of Jesus.*]

AMY: Oh, that's why Jesus looks like that.

[AMY *laughs, thinks better of it, and makes the sign of the cross.*]

SILVIA: You're lucky it's his policy to forgive you.

AMY: You're all so superstitious.

SILVIA: I'm three miles ahead. In the race. Ah, I get lazy always being in the lead.

AMY: That's not possible.

SILVIA: With practice, hermanita, todo es posible.

AMY: Silvia, they'd have to be crawling on their butts with both cheeks stuck together with Super Glue.

SILVIA: No montaña is too high. No ocean is too deep and yadda, yadda, yadda. All you need is a little feo.

AMY: Fe. It's fe.

SILVIA: You got so silly in college, hermanita.

AMY: Hey, stop it with that little sister stuff.

SILVIA: I'm taller.

AMY: Oh yeah. You're just towering over me.

SILVIA: I've got to get back out there so we can get this Ukrainian guy a heart transplant. Although I feel a little bad about the chimpanzee.

AMY: You're running so some Ukrainian guy can get a heart transplant from a chimpanzee?

SILVIA: Gotta run, hermanita.

[AMY *chases* SILVIA. SILVIA *slams the door in* AMY's *face. Crossfade to two hours later.*]

Scene Four

[*Two hours later.* MR. SUAVE *and* LA CRÍTICA *sit at a table in the middle of the restaurant.* MR. SUAVE, *played by the same actor who plays Abuelo, is all over* LA CRÍTICA, *who is* SNOW *in disguise.* MR. SUAVE *and* LA CRÍTICA *seem to like to mix sex and food.*]

MR. SUAVE: [*To* LA CRÍTICA.] So, you say the food here is good.

LA CRÍTICA: You never look at me when I'm talking. It was the one across the street I ate at the last time I was in town. La Saguaro de Suárez or whatever they're calling it nowadays.

MR. SUAVE: Oh, well.

LA CRÍTICA: Let's try this place. How bad could it be?

[MR. SUAVE *pulls out* LA CRÍTICA's *chair.* AMY *hands them menus.*]

MR. SUAVE: For you, my dear.

LA CRÍTICA: Thank you, sweets.

[AMY *hands them chips and salsa.*]

AMY: Chips and salsa.

[AMY *steps away.* MR. SUAVE *dips* LA CRÍTICA's *fingers in the salsa and sucks on them.* AMY *returns, winces, clears her throat, breaking them apart.*]

AMY: May I take your order?

LA CRÍTICA: Enchiladas with rice and beans. And a little chorizo on the side.

MR. SUAVE: The same.

AMY: Oh, that's great. We've got the best enchiladas in town. And the best beans. Sorry, no chorizo.

[LA CRÍTICA *looks at* AMY *knowingly.*]

AMY: Do I know you?

LA CRÍTICA: We're just passing through town. And you?

AMY: I live here. Actually, I'm in Idaho going to school. It just looks like I live here.

[MR. SUAVE *gives* AMY *a dismissive look. She steps away. He chews* LA CRÍTICA's *ear.* AMY *crosses to behind the counter.*]

AMY: You two are so lucky. I just made these a couple of minutes ago.

[AMY *re-enters with the food.*]

LA CRÍTICA: Bon appétit.

MR. SUAVE: [*Simultaneously.*] Bon appétit, ma cherie.

[*They click water glasses. They dig into their enchiladas—immediately gagging.*]

MR. SUAVE: Oh my—

LA CRÍTICA: —God.

MR. SUAVE: Poison.

LA CRÍTICA: Water.

[MR. SUAVE *spits out his food.* LA CRÍTICA *holds her throat like she's choking.*]

MR. SUAVE: It's disgusting.

LA CRÍTICA: Hurry.

[AMY *rushes to the table with extra water.* LA CRÍTICA *drinks from the pitcher, knocks it over. She scoops the water off the table, drinking from her hands.*]

MR. SUAVE: I'll call the Health Department on you.

LA CRÍTICA: Thank God.

MR. SUAVE: I'll sue you. I'll take it all the way to La Corte Suprema.

[LA CRÍTICA *and* MR. SUAVE *get up, start for the door.* AMY *holds their check meekly.*]

AMY: Your check.

MR. SUAVE: What check?

AMY: I'm sorry, sir. But it costs us money to cook that food.

MR. SUAVE: I'm not paying.

AMY: I could make you something else.

MR. SUAVE: I don't want something else.

AMY: I could bring you dessert. Some fresh fruit.

MR. SUAVE: I don't want fresh fruit.

AMY: Sir, you must pay. That will be $9.50.

MR. SUAVE: You don't seem to understand.

AMY: I understand that you . . . lost your appetite.

MR. SUAVE: Lost my appetite? This food is abhorrent.

AMY: You don't need to make a big deal out of it. Fine. Don't pay.

MR. SUAVE: You're missing the point.

AMY: What point?

[MR. SUAVE *grabs* AMY, *starts pushing her face toward the enchiladas.*]

MR. SUAVE: Have you tasted this food? Taste this.

[MAMI *enters, sees* MR. SUAVE *holding* AMY'S *face in the food.*]

MAMI: Madre mía. Leave her alone.

[MAMI *wrestles* MR. SUAVE *off* AMY. *He grabs* AMY *again. She is dazed and weak.*]

MR. SUAVE: She tried to poison us.

MAMI: ¡Mentiroso!

MR. SUAVE: Have you tried these enchiladas?

MAMI: Sir, I made them last night.

MR. SUAVE: She said she made them.

MAMI: You didn't hear her right.

MR. SUAVE: Expect a visit from your local health department.

[AMY *rests her head on the table, losing consciousness.* MR. SUAVE *escorts* LA CRÍTICA *out of the door.* AMY *is sick, coughing, semi-conscious.* MAMI *panics.*]

MAMI: Oh, mi'ja. I should never have left you alone like that. I should have told Silvia. You've got to stop your jogging, girl.

[MAMI *splashes water on* AMY's *face.* AMY *awakens suddenly.*]

AMY: Mi madrina.

MAMI: ¡Qué milagro! You saw your madrina at the end of the tunnel. She and Jesus were coming to get you. I made it in the nick of time. [MAMI *holds* AMY. *Sitting on the floor, stroking* AMY's *arms,* MAMI *looks heavenward.*] You can't have her, Jesus. No, no, no. She's mine. You get her when she's eighty. No, ninety. You're gonna be luckier than God if I ever let you have her at all.

AMY: Mami?

MAMI: Amy, mi'ja, are you okay?

AMY: Everything is so fuzzy.

MAMI: It's just God. He got confused, but it was a mistake! [*Quick beat.*] How's your godmother?

AMY: [*Dazed.*] Madrina is fine. She don't like my cooking, but—

MAMI: All you had to do was put it in the microwave.

AMY: She says everything tastes like a little termite made it.

MAMI: Nonsense. You're the second-best cook in town.

[MAMI *lifts* AMY, *sits her up.* AMY's *head plunges to the table.* MAMI *goes to the kitchen, immediately notices the fat-free cheese packages, looks horrified.*]

AMY: [*Simultaneously.*] Ah, Mami, thanks so much. It's so good to have a mother like you.

MAMI: Bribona!

[*Abuelo's horn goes off outside.* ABUELO *rolls in on his lawnmower. He is on the verge of speaking.*]

MAMI: A terrorista—that's what we've got on our hands. A little girl who thinks she can do what she pleases. In my restaurant. [MAMI *puts the "Closed" sign in the window.*] We're closing because of you.

[ABUELO *beeps his horn.*]

MAMI: I will not feed this health food to my customers. They come here to get real Mexican food like their abuelas used to make.

ABUELO: Silvia. She collapsed. In the race.

MAMI: Two daughters collapsed. God, why didn't you give me sons?

[AMY *lifts up her head to put in her two cents.*]

AMY: Oh, Silvia, mi hermanita. Don't let them give your heart to that Ukrainian guy. Greedy organ harvesters. My sister's life is worth more than that chimpanzee's.

[AMY *drops her head again.*]

MAMI: You've done enough damage for one afternoon. A whole day lost because of you and your crazy dieta. Why can't you be overweight and be happy like everybody else in America?

[MAMI *storms out of the restaurant.* ABUELO *beeps the horn behind her. They exit.* AMY *groggily lifts her head. Magical music. She looks up to see that* SNOW *has returned.*]

AMY: Doña Norte, is that you? You've got to help me.

SNOW: See, now. You're in trouble with your mamá 'cause of your inflexible ways.

AMY: Oh, it's the bad witch again. Where's the good witch?

SNOW: You had no right to change her recipes.

AMY: Fat-free tastes just as good as normal food when it's not cursed by some maldita with a fat-tooth.

SNOW: Always excuses, you college kids.

AMY: Leave my education out of this.

SNOW: What're you studying?

AMY: [*Under her breath.*] Dietetics.

SNOW: I thought you were studying Chicano history.

AMY: I don't want to talk about it—La Llorona who drowned her children in the Río Grande, and then afterwards lied to her mother and went out dancing with the devil.

SNOW: I thought your cousin Rumaldo taught you to love Chicano history.

AMY: Well, they didn't know about it.

SNOW: About what?

AMY: [*Under her breath.*] California, Texas, New Mexico, Arizona, Colorado.

SNOW: Yes.

AMY: They didn't know about them being part of Mexico.

SNOW: What?

AMY: The school was in Idaho, you know.

SNOW: That's no excuse. ¡Qué estúpido! ¡Qué terrible! ¡Qué barbaridad!

AMY: Besides, there are more important things to study.

SNOW: Like majoring in weight loss for one?

AMY: You make me so mad. Right when I'm on the verge of proving to my mom how tasty healthy food is, you come in and curse it.

SNOW: Well, have you thought any more about our little deal—about the change of heart?

AMY: I'm not going to accept this nonsense. My mom may not want to join the rest of society, but I'm not ignoring medical science. I'm not going to sit by and watch my mother kill her customers with her little smiles and her little coma, coma. No more coma, coma—my mother's a murderer. She's as bad as a sexually compulsive serial killer—and I'm not changing my heart.

[*Blackout.*]

Scene Five

[*Lights up. The sound of Abuelo's horn blasts.* MAMI *can be heard swearing.* MAMI *opens the door.* SILVIA's *limp body is sprawled across the back of Abuelo's lawnmower.* MAMI *rushes to the kitchen, gets water.*]

AMY: Why'd you bring her here? Mami, are you trying to kill her?

MAMI: Cállate.

AMY: Call 9-1-1. Come on, Mami.

MAMI: She said you fed her poisoned lettuce.

AMY: She spoke?

MAMI: The lettuce?

AMY: Normal lettuce. I washed it in the sink.

MAMI: You know we can't drink the water out of the sink. Híjole.

AMY: Ma, we've been drinking the water our whole lives.

MAMI: It has some kind of poison in it, mi'ja. It's been giving people cancer and making them sick all over our barrio.

AMY: Cancer?

MAMI: Sometimes I think you were raised in a shoe box. Pa, wake Silvia up.

[*No response.* MAMI *signals to* ABUELO *to beep his horn. He does.* SILVIA *comes to consciousness.*]

SILVIA: [*Dreamily.*] I saw her. She spoke to me. She came to me like a vision—

blue and blue, standing on a tub of lard. And you were all there. Amy and Mami. Sorry, Abuelo, you weren't there, but the rest of you were. She came to me and she said, "I am from the Andes. I am your Indian mother— no, I am your mestiza mother. I know the ways of our people, and we have always swum in rivers of fat and felt those little fat cells pulsating through our veins, so we could feel alive again. That is our history. That is our destino, she says. That is the real dieta de la raza, mi'ja." [*Beat.*] And she said no more lettuce for a while. Yuck. [SILVIA *spits.*] No more of that vile green leafy stuff until I bleed.

AMY: No lettuce until your period?

MAMI: [*Reprimanding* AMY.] ¡Hija! Not in front of your grandfather.

AMY: Abuelo knows what a period is.

SILVIA: "For six moons you haven't bled," she said, "and you must eat other foods until you bleed."

AMY: You haven't had your period in six months. This is what you're saying? [SILVIA *drops her head, embarrassed.*]

SILVIA: From running.

AMY: Silvia, you can get osteoporosis from that. Don't you know anything?

SILVIA: [*Starting to cry.*] I was just trying to be healthy.

AMY: Mami, take her to the doctor.

MAMI: Running off to the doctor for every little thing. If you ran this household, we'd all be on welfare with the doctor bills.

[ABUELO *has finally heard something—welfare!*]

ABUELO: Welfare! There's never been nobody on welfare in this family.

AMY: No one, Abuelo. We're all workaholics. Except Silvia, she's a jogaholic or whatever you call it.

ABUELO: We're a proud family. We're descendants of Hernando De Soto de España's [*Pronounced as "Ethpaña."*] brother-in-law.

SILVIA: Who was an Indian.

AMY: [*Loudly.*] Don't worry. We all work. It's just some work goes unappreciated even though we spend all day doing it.

MAMI: A cada uno su gusto lo engorde. Just let people eat their dinners, you know.

AMY: Taste it. You can't even tell the difference.

MAMI: I'd eat across the street first.

AMY: You're not being supportive.

MAMI: It's dangerous to change my recipes, mi'ja.

[MAMI *makes the sign of the cross.*]

AMY: Mami, things have to change or something terrible is going to happen. [*The phone rings.* MAMI *answers.*]

MAMI: The local health department. Amy, I'm gonna slice you and dice you, and send La Llorona to eat you and your little evil packages of fat-free cheese.

AMY: Mami. Just a taste. Try my enchiladas. They don't know what they're talking about. You'll see.

[SNOW, *dressed as a health official, stands at the door.*]

MAMI: They said they'd send you right over. They meant it.

SNOW: [*Addressing* MAMI.] You—Mami Durán?

MAMI: Sí, Señora. Will you be dining alone or with a friend?

SNOW: You're under arrest.

MAMI: Oh, God, the sign—I forgot. We'll take it down right away. But my nephew made a mistake. He didn't mean graffiti art—he meant mural art.

[SNOW *scribbles on her note pad.*]

SNOW: We'll have to send the sign code people back later. No, Señora Durán, you are under arrest for serving los amantes, two beautiful young lovers, the worst lunch of their lives. [*Beat.*] Alberto Higuera is an attorney and his lover, Marita Sena, is a restaurant critic for *The New York Times.* It seems, Mrs. Durán, that your ticket is up, your número is looking you in the face, not even members of your own familia will be dining at this establishment until we get to the bottom of this—this outrage.

MAMI: But I've been in business for fifteen years.

SNOW: I'm taking you to jail.

[SNOW *handcuffs* MAMI. MAMI *is crying.* SILVIA *is groaning.* AMY *is looking guilty.* SNOW *leads* MAMI *out of the restaurant.* ABUELO *follows them, beeping his horn.*]

ABUELO: Bring my hija back, you Jezebel!

[SILVIA *yells, but she is still reclined on the table. She stays weak, but feisty, throughout the scene.*]

SILVIA: [*Weakly.*] You go get her, Abuelo. You get her.

AMY: [*To* SILVIA.] Are you going to be all right? I feel I should follow them. Considering the circumstances.

SILVIA: It's your fault, right?

AMY: What?

SILVIA: It's always your fault when this family gets into trouble. Like when you tricked Abuelo into taking you to the clinic to get birth control. Donating blood, my ass.

[AMY *tries to interrupt.* SILVIA *won't let her.*]

SILVIA: Now, make me the greasiest taco you can, and do it quick.

AMY: Silvia, your appetite.

SILVIA: Now. I said now.

[AMY *starts preparing the food. A loud alarm sounds. Red lights flash. A* WOMAN'S VOICE *comes over the loudspeaker. It's* SNOW *in disguise.*]

WOMAN'S VOICE: Red alert. Red alert. Do not touch, I say, do not touch that ground beef.

[AMY *puts her hand on the ground beef.*]

WOMAN'S VOICE: That ground beef.

[AMY *pulls her hand back.*]

WOMAN'S VOICE: This restaurant is closed, condemned, out of order until further notice. Anyone who trespasses and eats here will die.

[AMY *looks at* SILVIA, *shocked.* SILVIA *shakes her head, disgusted.* AMY *bites her hand.*]

WOMAN'S VOICE: That hand included.

[AMY *takes her hand out of her mouth, shakes it, looking helpless. Blackout.*]

ACT TWO

Scene One

[*Outside of Café Lindo.*
Late night. AMY *stands in a white nightgown.*]

AMY: Doña Norte, where are you? You've got to help me. [*Beat.*] I did what you said. I started the fat-free restaurant, only it didn't work out like I'd planned. The Snow Cap Queen came, and . . . Now, Mami's in jail, and Silvia's eating everything except people and small animals. And, and . . . I just want everything to be back to normal. [*Beat.*] I've been sitting in this building every day since I've been back. It's been such a long time since I've been here. I wonder about this building. Where did it come from? I don't know anything about it. I don't know how long it's been here, and I don't know the name of the person who made it. Something tells me when I come here that it's special. It isn't like the outside world. At least it wasn't until she came along. If only I could trick her, everything would work out fine. Thanks, Doña Norte. Wherever you are. Thanks for your advice.

[*Blackout.*]

Scene Two

[*Lights up. Later that morning.* SILVIA *and* AMY *sneak in the front door of the restaurant.* SILVIA *has a bag full of greasy tacos in a commercial fast-food paper bag.* AMY *has a salad.*]

SILVIA: [*Really loud.*] We're gonna get caught.

[SILVIA *moves quietly, looking around, worried.*]

AMY: No, we're not. Escúchame. Silvia, listen. We can fix all this. We can get Mami out of jail.

SILVIA: How?

AMY: [*Pointing to the taco bag.*] I need those.

SILVIA: [*Holding the taco bag against her chest.*] But these are my lettuce-free tacos.

AMY: We'll buy more. A bargain at 59 cents.

[SILVIA *reluctantly gives* AMY *one taco.* AMY *gags, swabbing her hands, wiping the grease on her pants.*]

AMY: All of them, Sylvia.

[SILVIA *hands them over.*]

SILVIA: This better be good. This is my breakfast.

AMY: No self-respecting Mexican would eat this crap.

[*Back to her mission,* AMY *hums as she works. She spreads the tacos out on the counter, taking the ground beef out and separating it carefully like a casserole.*]

SILVIA: What're you doing? You're crazy. You're going to get Mami in worse trouble with the Health Department.

AMY: Silvia, are we eating it?

[SILVIA *reluctantly shakes her head no.* AMY *begins an incantation, swinging her arms in a dance-like prayer.*]

AMY: Oh, mestiza mother. [AMY *looks at the Snow Cap Lard container.*] Blue mother of the Andes. Speak to us.

SILVIA: Who are you talking to?

AMY: Look who's talking. "She came to me like a vision."

SILVIA: At least I'm her real friend.

AMY: Do you want to get Mami back or not?

[SILVIA *nods.*]

AMY: Oh, blue mother.

[SILVIA *mimics the motion, screws it up, stops.*]

SILVIA: I don't get what we're doing.

[AMY *lifts her finger to her mouth to silence* SILVIA. *She grabs* SILVIA *by the hand and hides with her underneath a table.* SILVIA *pulls the table-cloth down around her head like she's the Virgin Mary.*]

AMY: You know how you used to like lettuce?

[SILVIA *nods.* AMY *points to the counter top. A blue mist appears.* SNOW *emerges. She rubs her hand along the ground beef, sniffing, animal-like.*]

AMY: [*Calling.*] Oh, mestiza mother!

[SNOW *jumps back, surprised.*]

AMY: You like my little tacos, Mamá? There's more where that came from.

SNOW: [*Quickly regaining her composure.*] Oh, I don't need them. I'm not hungry.

AMY: Your fat-tooth's raging out of control.

SNOW: Don't be silly. Where's your mamá?

AMY: Arrested.

SNOW: [*Laughs.*] The public officials always mistake that graffiti art for gang signs.

AMY: It was the Health Department. Actually, my cooking. [AMY *starts to cry. Beat.*] I've had the change, mestiza mother. It came to me. Silvia and I had five tacos apiece this morning. They were so good. I'm stuffed. [*Beat.*] I've had it—like you asked. I've had my change of heart.

[SNOW *plays with the taco meat, delighting in the grease between her fingers.*]

AMY: You can eat that. It's an offering, Mother. It's my change of heart. On a plate. For you.

SNOW: [*Having a difficult time resisting the food.*] No, thanks. I'm not hungry. [*Beat.*] You say you've changed. Then, eat this.

[AMY *gulps.* SILVIA, *who has been staring at* SNOW *in amazement, steps out from under the table and crosses to* SNOW. *She embraces her emotionally, crying.*]

SILVIA: Mamá.

SNOW: Mi'ja.

[SNOW *inadvertently drops the taco meat on the floor.* AMY *sighs, relieved.*]

SILVIA: I feel so much better now that you're here.

SNOW: Oh good.

SILVIA: Except.

SNOW: What's wrong?

SILVIA: [*Putting a hand on her abdomen.*] It's like there are 2,000 angry men—

SNOW: Let's not be sexist.

SILVIA: Angry women then, knocking on the insides of my abdomen, screaming to get out of my uterus.

SNOW: You haven't bled yet?

[SILVIA *shakes her head.*]

SNOW: That's what I thought. It's stuck blood.

[SNOW *lifts a teapot, runs water into it.*]

AMY: Don't. The alarm.

[*No alarm goes off.*]

SNOW: A problem?

AMY: I guess not.

[SNOW *reaches into her multi-colored pouch. She takes out some leaves and pours them into the water, stirs.*]

SNOW: Drink this. It will make you bleed.

[SILVIA *drinks it, cramps up. She lets out a loud cry and runs to the restroom.*]

AMY: Since I've changed my heart, we need to reopen this restaurant.

SNOW: Yes, mi'ja.

AMY: Aren't you gonna do anything?

[SNOW *scrapes the taco meat off the floor, hands it to* AMY.]

SNOW: Lose your appetite?

AMY: That's not fair. That's gross. I changed.

SNOW: You flunked the test.

AMY: But I ate all those tacos.

SNOW: [*Lifting up the salad.*] You picked at this, salad muncher.

AMY: I'm not like her. It's not what you think. [*Beat.*] It's not my mother's fault that I can't stomach it. Please, get her out of jail.

SNOW: Not till you change your real heart.

[SNOW *snaps her finger, blue smoke. She disappears.* SILVIA *rushes out of the bathroom, a new woman.*]

SILVIA: Mamá, it's a miracle. It is. It's gushing. I'm well. All the women—they came out of me, and they're not angry anymore. They're peaceful, sweet. They want to spend all day in the kitchen making flour tortillas by hand.

AMY: What are you rambling about?

SILVIA: The little women who were pumping through my veins, pounding on the walls of my abdomen, making me miserable.

AMY: Enough of this silliness. We have to free Mami.

SILVIA: Where's that healer anyways? The one from the Andes. The Snow Cap lady. I want to thank her.

AMY: She's not a healer.

SILVIA: Yes, she is.

AMY: I've made her so angry. She won't free Mami from jail. What am I gonna do?

SILVIA: I bled, Amy, I bled.

AMY: And I'm very proud of you for that. I am.

[*There is a ruckus outside.* RUMALDO *pounds nails into the side of his graffiti sign. He makes slits of rope for his hands and installs metal supports for his feet, so he can hang there crucifixion-style.*]

RUMALDO: I will not take down this sign! It's art. For my tía, who's being held against her will in the county jail. I will not budge from this sign, or I will die defending my right to this unique form of Chicano artistic expression in our community.

[RUMALDO *steps up into his crucifixion pose.*]

AMY: Rumaldo, what are you doing up there?

RUMALDO: It's a protest to free your mami from jail.

AMY: Protesting doesn't work.

RUMALDO: Come up here and join me. It'll be like old times. I can make the little slits for your feet.

AMY: No, it's okay. I've gotta work while she's gone.

RUMALDO: Mi prima favorita, tell me about college. [*Wide-eyed.*] Tell me about M.E.Ch.A.

AMY: I don't know.

RUMALDO: What do you mean you don't know?

AMY: They didn't have M.E.Ch.A in Idaho.

RUMALDO: M.E.Ch.A—Movimiento Estudiantil Chicano de Aztlán. It's a national organization. Of course they have it. Didn't you look for them—your Chicano brothers and sisters on your local college campus?

AMY: I have other interests than being a professional Mexican.

RUMALDO: Put a stake through my heart, prima.

AMY: You look silly up there.

[MAMI *enters.*]

MAMI: ¡Qué milagro! What're you doing, Rumaldito?

RUMALDO: Tía, don't call me that.

AMY: It's a protest. To free you from jail.

MAMI: But I'm not in the jail anymore.

RUMALDO: I didn't know that when I got up here.

MAMI: They let me out for poisoning the people.

AMY: I'm sorry.

RUMALDO: How'd you get off?

[RUMALDO *tries to come down; he catches his leg.*]

MAMI: Technicality.

[SILVIA *comes running out.*]

SILVIA: Mami!

[RUMALDO *looks at his hands and feet, feeling a little stupid.*]

RUMALDO: I guess everybody's happy. [*To* MAMI.] Tía, I was willing to crucify myself for you.

MAMI: I know, Rumaldo, I know.

RUMALDO: Anything for you. Sister of mi padre. Daughter of mi abuela. Patron saint of la raza.

AMY: See, Mami. There is justice.

MAMI: They forgot to read me my rights.

RUMALDO: They're always trying to forget our rights. Remember that sixteen-year-old Mexican kid who got shot by that off-duty police officer who was drunk?

AMY: That kid had a knife.

MAMI: Mi'ja, you don't believe what the papers tell you?

RUMALDO: That's why this graffiti art is so importante. Kids like that shouldn't just disappear.

AMY: If they had a case, somebody would have said something.

SILVIA: People protested. You just weren't there.

AMY: But it wasn't on the news.

SILVIA: Why do you think it would be on the news?

RUMALDO: [*Shouts.*] What do we want?

SILVIA: Justice!

RUMALDO: When do we want it?

SILVIA: Now!

RUMALDO: What do we want?

SILVIA: Justice!

RUMALDO: When do we want it?

SILVIA: Now!

[RUMALDO *continues the chant.* AMY *tries to drown him out.*]

AMY: Now he's got you doing that old stuff. But his ideas don't work. We can't live in America and be hung up on those things.

RUMALDO: [*Correcting her.*] The United States. [*Shouting.*] What do we want?

SILVIA: Justice!

RUMALDO: When do we want it?

[RUMALDO *takes one hand out, fist raised. "Snow music" comes up.* RUMALDO *freezes.* AMY *tries to help* RUMALDO *down.* SNOW *appears.*]

SNOW: He can't be moved.

AMY: What's that?

SNOW: Your heart holds a grudge, like a thousand angry butterflies pounding on the chamber of that little muscle inside your chest.

AMY: You're talking about my heart?

SILVIA: [*Nodding.*] Why do I get women and she only gets butterflies?

SNOW: Unspoken apologies freeze the tongue. In this case, they freeze tu primo.

[SNOW *points up at* RUMALDO, *who looks uncomfortable frozen.* AMY *tries unsuccessfully to move* RUMALDO. *She gives up.*]

AMY: [*Bluffing.*] I think he makes a nice statement. We'll just leave him up there. Thanks, Snow. [*Beat.*] It would mean a lot to him to say something. With his entire body like that.

SILVIA: But he's the perfect bull's-eye for a drive-by shooting.

AMY: Silvia, would they shoot Jesus?

[SILVIA *shakes her head no.* MAMI *goes into the restaurant, gets a Mexican blanket and covers* RUMALDO. SILVIA *runs into the restaurant and gets a beef taco. She moves the blanket and lifts the taco to his lips, bringing him to consciousness. He continues his speech.*]

RUMALDO: I was willing to be crucified for you, Tía.

[SNOW *snaps her fingers with disappointment.* MAMI *unhooks* RUMALDO *with ease. He leaps to the ground, shakes out his arms.*]

MAMI: You're free.

RUMALDO: I had a revelation. While I was on the sign.

AMY: Do share.

RUMALDO: The public outcry against graffiti art is not about the fact that our buildings are our canvas.

[SNOW *sneaks off unnoticed.*]

AMY: You mean, other people's buildings.

RUMALDO: The Just Say No to Graffiti Committee is about suppressing our self-expression. It's about people not wanting our youth to have any visibility or a voice that says, "Hey, this is who I am." If you don't see the art, maybe you don't see the kid who made it either.

SILVIA: We could hang some up in the bathrooms.

RUMALDO: Graffiti art belongs on the street. Con la gente. [*To* AMY.] With the people.

AMY: I know what la gente means.

SILVIA: We could do up the whole inside of the restaurant.

MAMI: I'm not sure. We already got good decorations.

AMY: The Bleeding Heart of Jesus, for one.

MAMI: You don't like my Jesus?

RUMALDO: I could do all the outside walls of the restaurant.

MAMI: I don't think I want any changes with the restaurant for a while.

AMY: I'm not touching the menu. Hey, what a disaster with that witch messing everything up.

SILVIA: She's a curandera.

MAMI: Who?

AMY: The lady in blue.

RUMALDO: We'll catch her. She can't fool us.

[SNOW *enters, a bureaucrat with a clipboard.*]

SNOW: [*To* MAMI.] Is this your establishment?

AMY: That's her.

SILVIA: No, it's not. [*To* MAMI.] She carries a pouch with magical leaves in it that can make you well.

MAMI: Yes, ma'am. We got rid of that food that was—disappointing. We're getting back to our normal business operation this afternoon. One for lunch?

[SNOW *walks up to* RUMALDO's *sign, reads his signature.*]

SNOW: You Rumaldo Soto?

AMY: Mami, it's her.

SILVIA: Leave it alone.

RUMALDO: Maybe.

SNOW: Is this your artistic work?

RUMALDO: Actually, yes.

AMY: Mami.

SNOW: You've been giving this woman grief.

RUMALDO: No.

SNOW: You will. [*To* MAMI.] You have been found in violation of Code 12345 of Section 54321. [SNOW *scribbles something and hands* MAMI *a ticket.*] In other words, take down this sign within the next 24 hours, or you'll have to pay a $500 fine.

AMY: Just rip it up. It's not a real ticket.

SILVIA: Shhh.

MAMI: Okay, ma'am.

[SNOW *leaves.* MAMI *starts taking the sign down.*]

MAMI: I'm sorry, Rumaldo. No sign.

RUMALDO: But it's the principle of the thing.

MAMI: No, it's $500.

RUMALDO: But . . .

MAMI: The sign's coming down.

RUMALDO: Tía.

MAMI: We don't have that kind of money.

RUMALDO: This is really important. We've got to take a stand. You know there are some ignorant people out there who think that three or more jóvenes make up a gang. I know some young people who will only walk in twos for fear of there being any confusion. They don't want to get shot by the cops and watch them get off. That's got to stop.

[MAMI *hands him the sign.*]

MAMI: You can keep it out as long as it doesn't touch the building.

RUMALDO: Gracias.

MAMI: See, this little strip of land here. I give it to you. It's yours. For your graffiti art. You can make billboards.

[RUMALDO *kisses* MAMI.]

RUMALDO: You won't regret it.

MAMI: [*To herself.*] I already do. But you seem so . . .

RUMALDO: Committed and ready to take a stand for my political beliefs in spite of harassment by government organizations and the local police department?

MAMI: Yes.

RUMALDO: I am.

MAMI: Good.

[RUMALDO *exits.*]

AMY: I can't believe you even believe she's real.

SILVIA: Amy, if they don't pay that fine, you know they'll just layer more fines on top of that one. One girl I know, they emptied her whole savings account for a parking ticket. And she was rich. She had three hundred dollars.

MAMI: The whole thing makes me tired. Amy, come help me with the cooking.

AMY: Okay.

MAMI: No cheating.

AMY: Never.

SILVIA: Mami, don't you want my help?

MAMI: All three. It will be like old days.

[MAMI, SILVIA, and AMY enter the restaurant. SILVIA dives for the chips. She takes a bite. "North music" as NORTH appears. All freeze, except AMY.]

NORTH: You came with a goal, and you backed down.

AMY: My goal was unrealistic.

[NORTH crosses to MAMI, places the magic wand on her shoulder.]

AMY: Get away from her. [Beat.] Who are you anyways—but some overdressed princess with an attitude?

NORTH: I'm the Good Witch of the North. Not too long ago you were calling my name. [Imitating her.] Doña Norte.

AMY: Yeah, the good witch from the Dietetics Department at the University of Idaho.

NORTH: Not that north—the other north.

AMY: Well, those ideas don't work down here. They don't work in action.

NORTH: I'm a descendent of los Conquistadores de España. [Pronounced "Ethpaña."]

AMY: You look like a regular Mexican to me.

NORTH: Your mother is dying and you know how to save her.

AMY: [Alarmed.] What?

NORTH: [Pointing at SILVIA.] When I lift my wand, your mother's heart will stop. But you can change all that . . . if you'll only try.

AMY: Stop!

NORTH: I almost forgot. [NORTH *points her wand at* SILVIA.] You'll have to save her, too.

AMY: You're going to give them both heart attacks?

NORTH: No.

AMY: What am I supposed to save her from?

NORTH: [*Beat.*] From sadness.

AMY: What sadness?

NORTH: Why do you think she eats so much?

AMY: She's hungry. She only ate lettuce for six years.

NORTH: Tell me why she's sad.

AMY: You tell me. You seem to have some idea about our—

NORTH: Hearts.

AMY: Our lives. Different than the other witch.

NORTH: [*Bluffing.*] Who?

AMY: Your mischievous sister.

NORTH: What do you mean witch?

AMY: She's just a figment of my family's collective imagination. We're so tight we can't even hallucinate alone.

NORTH: [*Lifting her wand.*] Tell me why she's sad.

AMY: Don't!

[NORTH *waves the wand.* NORTH *exits.*]

AMY: What about my mother?

[MAMI *collapses.* AMY *rushes to her.* SILVIA *drops the tortilla chip on the table.*]

AMY: Silvia, call 9-1-1.

SILVIA: You know how Mami feels about going to the doctor.

[AMY *calls.*
Blackout.]

Scene Three

[*A week later.* AMY *pushes* MAMI *in a wheelchair into the restaurant.*
ABUELO *follows closely behind. White paint covers Rumaldo's graffiti art*
sign.]

MAMI: A heart attack only felt like the flu.

AMY: A cholesterol level of 325. Mami, don't you watch your diet at all?

MAMI: Well, I tried to after the doctor told me to watch what I ate.

AMY: So, you watched it go in and out, or what?

MAMI: It's hard, mi'ja. Cooking all day for the restaurant, testing the food to make sure it's just right.

AMY: [*Grabs the lard.*] We'll give this to the Goodwill. God have mercy on the poor.

MAMI: But what am I supposed to do? You want me to quit cooking? You want me to give up the one thing I do good?

AMY: No. I just want you to do it a new way. You know, grill the meat instead of frying it. Soften the corn tortillas in the microwave instead of dipping them in lard.

MAMI: Tortillas in the microwave. ¡Ay!

AMY: Just little changes. That's all.

MAMI: In the meantime, that pest across the street is stealing all our business. Nobody from the bean committee has even been in here to taste our beans.

AMY: [*Consoling her.*] They'll come.

[SILVIA *enters, visibly heavier. She stuffs her face with chips.* AMY *glares*
at her.]

MAMI: Silvia, help your sister with the restaurant.

AMY: Abuelo, take Mami home to rest.

ABUELO: What?

AMY: [*Loudly.*] Home.

ABUELO: [*Misunderstanding.*] I'll watch the restaurant. You can go home. I'll be fine.

AMY: [*Louder.*] Take Mami home.

[AMY *kisses* MAMI. ABUELO *escorts* MAMI *off.* SILVIA *sits at the table, stuffs her face.*]

AMY: The first thing we're doing is canola chips.

SILVIA: [*Excited.*] Chips?

AMY: What's into you?

SILVIA: Nothing.

AMY: C'mon, you can tell me.

SILVIA: [*With her mouth full.*] Can you make me another tostada?

AMY: I'm not going to participate in this . . . behavior.

[SILVIA's *look says, what behavior?*]

AMY: You've already eaten four combination plates.

SILVIA: C'mon, Sis. I'm hungry.

AMY: Why?

SILVIA: I don't know. I just am.

AMY: You can't be. It's not physically possible. [*Beat.*] They have groups for this. You can get help.

SILVIA: I don't want help. I want a tostada, and I want it now.

[AMY *crosses to the kitchen.* SILVIA *puts cash on the table.*]

SILVIA: Extra guacamole.

AMY: Do you know how much fat there is in one avocado? I wouldn't be doing this if you weren't the only paying customer we had today.

SILVIA: I'm not the one who got our mother in trouble with the Health Department.

AMY: I'm making up for what I did.

SILVIA: You can't never make up for that.

AMY: [*Singing.*] Canola. Canola is the answer. [*Excited.*] We'll put it in the beans.

SILVIA: I will not let you touch my mami's beans.

AMY: They're brimming with grease.

SILVIA: People love them.

AMY: Right.

SILVIA: You're just going to make things worse with this canola bird.

AMY: Oil. It's oil. Not a bird.

SILVIA: Where does it come from?

AMY: [*Beat.*] The store.

SILVIA: It comes from bird droppings. I saw it on public television.

AMY: That's gross.

SILVIA: I'm gonna run home and tell mom.

AMY: I doubt it.

SILVIA: As she's sitting there helpless in that wheelchair, I'm gonna tell her about this canola conspiracy.

AMY: I'm trying to save Mom.

SILVIA: My mami's not going back to jail because you have a hang-up about food.

AMY: I have a hang-up about food?

SILVIA: That's why you care what everybody's eating. Let people eat. Let them enjoy themselves. Life is too short.

AMY: Exactly my point.

SILVIA: My mami will never stare at the world through the bars of a jail cell again.

AMY: Mami won't go to jail. It was that healer of yours that did that, but this time, I'm wise to her ways.

SILVIA: Just get me that tostada.

AMY: Cook it yourself. You'll burn a few calories making your way to the kitchen.

SILVIA: [*Lays her money on the table.*] But I'm paying.

AMY: [*As in, with her life.*] I know you are.

[*A moment.* AMY *reluctantly gets* SILVIA *a large tostada.*]

SILVIA: [*Beat; suddenly sad.*] You know. I feel really sad.

AMY: About what?

SILVIA: Mami. She could have died from that heart attack, you know. I could see her spirit trying to lift up into the blue sky of heaven, but it got blocked by a cloud. We were lucky.

AMY: I know.

SILVIA: Amy, it's like I thought it would be. Now that I've started eating again, I can't stop. [*Beat.*] I think it's because of you.

AMY: Me?

SILVIA: You weren't supposed to come back. You went away to college. You were supposed to stay there. Forever. I was supposed to stay here and help Mami with the restaurant. I was supposed to be the second-best cook in town.

AMY: I won't be here forever.

SILVIA: But you belong here. Better than I do. Can't you see it?

AMY: I don't belong here.

SILVIA: You're not going to leave.

AMY: I'm not staying.

SILVIA: You are. You just don't know it yet. It's like this building.

AMY: What about the building?

SILVIA: It's very special. [SILVIA *pushes a basket toward* AMY.] Could you get me more chips?

AMY: Silvia, you're overeating.

[AMY *reluctantly takes the basket and crosses to the kitchen.*]

SILVIA: It's a losing battle, but somebody's got to fight it.

AMY: What's special about the building?

SILVIA: Something Rumaldo told me.

AMY: You can't believe everything our political activist cousin says, Silvia. He's got an agenda.

SILVIA: I believe this.

AMY: Yeah.

SILVIA: He said our restaurant pre-dates the occupation of northern Mexico.

AMY: What does he mean occupation of northern Mexico?

SILVIA: You know exactly what he means. Sometimes, sister, I think you're forgetting who we are.

AMY: I haven't forgotten.

SILVIA: But I know you. You'll remember. Inside you there is somebody who will remember. Everything. And it's stronger than that other part of you that went up north to get an education and, instead, she was erased.

AMY: I'm somebody new. It's called maturing.

SILVIA: How can people who don't know who you really are help you to grow into somebody new? You have to take your old self with you when you grow—build on who you are—not toss it in a gutter and piss on it.

AMY: You're full of ideas.

SILVIA: Yes, when I stopped running, I started thinking. Now, I think all the time. It comes from sitting here. In this old building that pre-dates the occupation of northern Mexico.

[RUMALDO *enters, sees his whitewashed sign.*]

RUMALDO: I'll kill them. I'll teach them not to whitewash my work.

[RUMALDO *exits.* AMY *looks out the door.*]

SILVIA: What's cousin Rumaldo doing?

AMY: The Just Say No to Graffiti Committee blotted out his sign. The city's paying for all their white paint, but there's no grant money left in the arts for his.

[*Crossfade.*]

[*Early evening. The restaurant is dark. The "Closed" sign hangs in the window.* RUMALDO *has camped out on his land, snoring. A sign that reads "Graffiti Art Speaks to the Chicano Heart" stands next to him.* SNOW *tiptoes in, pulling a red wheelbarrow filled with a mountain of lard.* SNOW *plasters the building and Rumaldo's new sign with the lard. She puts a drop on* RUMALDO's *nose. He smears it.* SNOW *accidentally drops the shovel onto the wheelbarrow.* RUMALDO *gets up, touches his sign.* SNOW *exits.*]

RUMALDO: Oh my God. What is it? [RUMALDO *starts removing the lard with his hands, wiping it on his clothes. He is buried in the stuff.*] Terrorists.

[AMY *and* SILVIA *enter.* SILVIA *sucks on a peppermint candy cane. She runs up to the building, excited. She starts licking the lard off Rumaldo's sign.* RUMALDO *looks at her disgusted, then starts licking, too.* AMY *tries to pull* SILVIA *away, but* SILVIA *has her tongue thoroughly engaged, and she's fighting to stay there. "North music" comes up.* NORTH *gestures with her wand. Sparks fly.* SILVIA *is frozen with her tongue attached to the sign.*]

AMY: Oh, I hate when you do that.

NORTH: Tell her that it's okay to stop.

AMY: She knows that. That isn't going to help.

NORTH: Tell her. And him. Tell him to get a life.

AMY: Hey, I didn't invite you here to come and insult mi familia. In fact, I didn't invite you at all.

[AMY *pushes* NORTH.]

NORTH: If you kick me out of here, I'll leave those two just as they are.

AMY: I dare you.

[NORTH *disappears.* SILVIA *and* RUMALDO *remain frozen.*]

AMY: Me and my big mouth. Now I went and froze up my sister. And the artist. Oh, shit.

[AMY *rushes into the restaurant, grabs two Mexican blankets, throws* one over SILVIA *and the other over* RUMALDO. *She hangs a sign that reads* "Open" *around* RUMALDO's *neck. Crossfade.*]

Scene Five

[SILVIA *now wears a sign that reads "Fat-Free/Cholesterol-Free Food Served at this Location." * AMY *is humming, setting up the restaurant.* ABUELO *rolls in on his lawnmower. An American flag on a stick stands on the back of it. He honks.*]

ABUELO: [*Singing.*] From the halls of Montezuma. To the shores of Tripoli.

[ABUELO *drives up to the frozen* SILVIA, *reads the sign, but misses that it's her.*]

ABUELO: We got a couple of new signs out there.

AMY: Yeah.

ABUELO: Where's Silvia?

AMY: She went to some jogging camp.

ABUELO: What?

AMY: Jogging.

ABUELO: Smoking? She knows better than to start smoking.

AMY: [*Loudly.*] Can you buy me the food for next week?

ABUELO: Your mami doesn't like it when I buy the bad food.

AMY: But it's Mami's list. Please, Abuelito.

ABUELO: Normal food?

[AMY *nods her head until* ABUELO *nods.*]

AMY: Mami's list.

ABUELO: Okay.

[ABUELO *kisses* AMY *and starts to exit.*]

AMY: Your lawnmower.

ABUELO: I'm going to walk. It's good for mi corazón.

[ABUELO *exits to outside the restaurant. He sniffs something, checks out the frozen* RUMALDO. *He finds the lard residue, lifts it up to his nose, licks it.*]

ABUELO: The building's sweating manteca.

[AMY *crosses to the door.*]

AMY: That's silly. Take your walk.

[ABUELO *exits.* AMY *rushes outside and pushes* RUMALDO. *He doesn't move. She's hums to herself, touches the building.*]

AMY: ¡No me digas¡

[AMY *cleans the building furiously. "North music" comes up.* NORTH *enters.*]

AMY: Unfreeze them. I can't lie about Silvia being at jogging camp forever, and someone's going to eventually notice that Rumaldo isn't camping out.

NORTH: That stuff won't come off.

AMY: It's got to.

NORTH: Sorry.

AMY: Why not?

NORTH: Because it's breathing lard.

AMY: It can't be breathing lard, except by your dark magic. You bruja.

NORTH: How dare you insult me? I'm a proud descendant of los Conquistadores de España. [*Pronounced "Ethpaña."*]

AMY: Whatever.

NORTH: Your restaurant is alive, Amy, and it wants to convince your family to keep up the status quo. Only you can stop them.

AMY: How?

NORTH: You can reverse the heart attack.

AMY: I can't. Nobody can.

NORTH: You can get Silvia to stop stuffing her face, too.

AMY: Yeah, right.

NORTH: Here, let me take you to the kitchen.

[*They cross to the restaurant and walk into the kitchen.*]

NORTH: Here's your low-fat food. Now, feed it to your mother.

AMY: That's all? That's easy.

NORTH: She has to like them. She has to decide they're what she wants. And when she does that, we'll see what we can do about reversing it.

AMY: Is it going to save her or not? Don't play games.

NORTH: We know nothing really before it happens, although we hope we might.

AMY: You'll try to save my mother.

NORTH: And your sister. And there's the thing about the fat leaking out of the building.

AMY: You did all that.

NORTH: No, afraid not. It seems you cursed someone. The woman in blue— you have to forgive her for all the trouble she's caused.

AMY: And?

NORTH: Just remember one thing, you can't tell anyone what you're doing or it will break the spell.

AMY: You're leaving things worse than when you came.

NORTH: You're breaking your mother's heart.

AMY: Yeah. How?

NORTH: You're not trying hard enough.

AMY: But—

[NORTH *removes the blankets from* SILVIA *and* RUMALDO. *They move.*]

NORTH: You'll have to do the rest yourself.

AMY: How? You didn't tell me how. North. North!

SILVIA: [*Becoming unsteady, a little physically strained.*] Who you yelling at, girl?

[RUMALDO *stops himself mid-lick.*]

RUMALDO: Yuck. This building tastes like—yuck.

[RUMALDO *crosses to* SILVIA. *They seem to have some sort of unspeakable connection.* SILVIA *yawns.*]

AMY: Hey, you guys. You guys.

SILVIA: What? What?

AMY: We've got a problem.

[AMY *points to the front of the restaurant; lard seeps out of the cracks in the adobe walls.*]

SILVIA: Hey, that's manteca pouring out of the walls.

AMY: That's the problem.

[*The faint sound of horse hooves beating.*]

AMY: What's that sound? Is it my mother's shattering heart?

NORTH [*V.O.*]: It's death coming to get her. Feed your mother something she likes. Now!

[ABUELO *wheels* MAMI *in on the wheelchair.* AMY *goes to the kitchen, quickly throws together some tacos, brings one out, puts it by* MAMI's *discriminating nose.* MAMI *smacks the taco on the ground. Hoof beats beating.* AMY *desperately pushes* MAMI *through the restaurant door.*]

AMY: Enchiladas?

[MAMI *shakes her head no.*]

AMY: Chile colorado? [MAMI *shakes her head no again.*]

AMY: Albóndigas soup? [*Beat.*] Tamales?

[MAMI *starts nodding her head.*]

AMY: She would have to choose tamales.

[*As* AMY *cooks, the hoof beats get louder and louder.* AMY *starts the tamales.*]

SILVIA: What are you doing? She's hungry.

AMY: Do you know how to make vegetable tamales? Make a tamale, stuff it with these vegetables. Leave out the cheese, the lard—and the meat.

SILVIA: Are you sure you can even call it a tamale?

AMY: [*Forcefully.*] It's a tamale and you're making it.

SILVIA: [*As* AMY *leaves.*] Where are you going?

AMY: To consult with Quetzalcoatl. Las brujas can't run everything without a god's permission.

SILVIA: You're leaving?

AMY: Hurry, we don't have a lot of time.

[AMY *walks off.* SILVIA *continues preparing tamales.* SNOW *enters.*]

SNOW: You should put a little manteca in that.

SILVIA: Polluter.

[SNOW *starts shaking.*]

SILVIA: Oh, what's wrong? Can I get you something?

SNOW: I'm more worried about her. [SNOW *points to* MAMI, *who is sleeping.*] She needs something . . . familiar to eat.

SILVIA: No. Amy said just this.

[SNOW *slips* SILVIA *a tamale that she grabs from her sack.*]

SNOW: Look, it's already made. You don't want to make those. They take so much time.

SILVIA: I don't want to hurt my mami.

SNOW: Give it to her with a little manzanilla tea. She'll be fine.

[SNOW *peels the corn husk off the tamale. She puts the tamale under* SILVIA'S *nose.* SILVIA *is having a hard time controlling her impulses.* SNOW *leaves the tamale on the counter.* SNOW *begins to exit.* AMY *walks right past her.* AMY *doesn't see* SNOW. SILVIA *puts the tamale on a plate, dresses it up. She sticks a little Mexican flag in the beans.*]

AMY: You finished already?

SILVIA: The fastest tamales in the West.

AMY: Wow, I'm impressed.

SILVIA: They're not so hard. I got a lot of practice when you went to college.

AMY: You just made them?

SILVIA: No. Yes.

AMY: You made it exactly the way I told you?

SILVIA: Perfectly.

[NORTH *appears, shaking her finger no.* AMY *doesn't automatically see her at first. Then she does.* AMY *reluctantly walks over to* MAMI's *plate, snatches it away.*]

AMY: We're not giving her this.

SILVIA: Why not? I—

AMY: Cheated.

SILVIA: It takes too long to make those damn things.

AMY: Where'd you get it? From across the street? They're running us out of business.

[SILVIA *shakes her head no.*]

AMY: Where'd you get it then?

SILVIA: I don't know. I saw her and she gave me this.

AMY: [*Cuts the tamale open with a knife.*] Her, who? See, it's cheese and lard.

[SILVIA *nods.* AMY *plays with the masa.* MAMI *bangs the table now.*]

MAMI: ¡Tamales! ¡Tamales! ¡Tamales!

SILVIA: We gotta give her something.

[SILVIA *reaches for the plate.* AMY *knocks it on the ground.*]

AMY: Are you trying to kill her?

SILVIA: No, Jesus. It won't hurt just one more time.

MAMI: ¡Tamales! ¡Tamales!

AMY: Why are you all so obsessed with food?

SILVIA: She's eaten this way her whole life.

[*A loud bugle sounds.* RUMALDO *stands in the doorway.*]

AMY: Rumaldo, get me the lard. The Snow Cap lard.

[RUMALDO *takes out a bunch of lard.*]

AMY: Set them up.

[*As Native American flute music plays,* RUMALDO *builds a pyramid out of the lard cans. In the manner of an Aztec sacrifice, he acknowledges the four directions with the top can.*]

AMY: There's a folk tale from the Andes about a woman who's as evil as La Llorona on a bad day and as nice as the Virgin Mary on a worse one. It just depends on the way you point the weather vane at any moment. Sometimes you look down and she's got goat's feet or chicken's feet, and other times, she's got a halo around her head.

[SNOW *appears, approaches* RUMALDO, *misses hitting him when he steps away. She falls and bangs her head against the wall.*]

AMY: She cursed this place, but some curses can be lifted without that La Lloronita's presence. She can be locked up if you say the right words, in the right sequence. Rumaldo, you know the poem. It's written in your Chicano heart.

RUMALDO: Lady, lady, dressed in blue/May God call you something other than you./May the devil know you hoard/his little evil devil claws./May God shine on you and bring to be/the Virgin Mary inside of me. [RUMALDO *blushes.*] It rhymed.

[SILVIA *looks at* AMY *confused.* SNOW *writhes, falls to the ground, lifts herself up.*]

RUMALDO: [*To* SNOW.] Boo.

[SNOW *crawls away, defeated.* MAMI *stands. She is well. Christmas lights light up the inside of Café Lindo. Mexican music blasts.*]

SILVIA: Thank you, Rumaldo. You freed us.

AMY: You're better than a priest and not half as demanding. Three thousand Hail Marys for this. Three thousand Hail Marys for that.

MAMI: C'mon Amy. I've been thinking. About this fat thing.

AMY: You have?

MAMI: I think we can come up with an agreement.

AMY: You do?

MAMI: There will be no more dying people in my restaurant. No more original-style taquitos. No more deep-fat frying. From here on out, it's clean living.

[*Music starts,* NORTH *enters, puts her wand on* AMY'S *shoulder. All freeze, except* AMY.]

NORTH: She'll live a long time now because of you.

AMY: Oh, will she?

NORTH: Take the next step and you'll see.

[NORTH *blows* AMY *a kiss.* NORTH *exits. Magical music plays. Blackout.*]

Scene Six

[*A week later.* SILVIA *eats a salad. New semi-graffiti art signs hang inside the restaurant indicating the restaurant has changed.* RUMALDO *puts the finishing touches on two signs. One reads: "Order From Our Original-Style or Third-Generation Menu." Another reads: "Low-Fat Food Available Here."* MAMI *stands behind the counter. There is a small tap at the door.* AMY *opens the door. A weary* SNOW *crawls inside.*]

SNOW: [*Looking at* MAMI.] Your cousin was right. Half the time I'm La Llorona and the other half of the time I'm the Virgin Mary.

AMY: Get out. You're not allowed in our restaurant anymore.

[*The sound of Abuelo's horn almost knocks* SNOW *over.* ABUELO *drives his lawnmower into the restaurant.*]

SNOW: That's what I thought. That's what's happening to everybody.

SILVIA: I suggest you get another job.

SNOW: Another modeling contract. At my age? [*To* AMY.] Hear me out. [*Beat.*] It's just my heart is weak from all these attacks. Little attacks of the heart. [*She stops.*] I have eaten this food since I was a little girl. Our tears fell in our pozole when we were sad. We chopped lettuce and onions in the kitchen together, smiling through our tears. [SNOW *looks at* MAMI *as if to say, remember? For a moment, it seems the two women might be sisters.*] It seems to me that we cannot see inside our arteries, but we can see inside our hearts, that this is the one thing—the only thing—that links generation one and generation three or four. I'm not from the Andes as I have claimed, as you now all must know. I've come from México. I've come to watch you cook and laugh together in your kitchen, as you make your scrumptious home-cooked Mexican food, the way my abuela used to make it.

[SNOW *is crying.* MAMI *is crying.* AMY *is crying.* SILVIA *is crying.* ABUELO *is crying, although he doesn't know why.* RUMALDO *is still painting, but he wipes a tear away after making sure nobody is looking.*]

SNOW: [*Beat.*] I lift my curse off this restaurant. May all who enter here feel joy and relish the food. And may you all love one another.

[AMY *crosses to* RUMALDO, *taps him on the shoulder. He turns.* AMY *offers him the hug she refused him earlier.*]

AMY: I'm sorry.

[*A moment. Paintbrush and all,* RUMALDO *hugs* AMY *exuberantly, lifting her up.*]

MAMI: C'mon. This calls for a feast. A Mexican feast. [*To* SNOW.] Come here, we'll show you what you can do for us.

SNOW: Really?

AMY: I'll plan dinner. I'm the third-best cook in town.

[AMY *looks at* SILVIA, *who relishes the acknowledgment.* SILVIA *embraces* AMY.]

SILVIA: See, I told you you'd stay.

AMY: [*Knuckles* SILVIA.] Who said anything about staying?

SILVIA: We have a university here, you know.

AMY: I think I'm going to change my major though.

RUMALDO: [*With hope.*] And join M.E.Ch.A?

AMY: Definitely.

SNOW: I'm starving. I would love a chimichanga.

AMY: We don't have chimichangas. We haven't never had chimichangas.

MAMI: [*Simultaneously.*] We haven't never had—

[SNOW *drops her head.*]

AMY: I'll make one just for you. Baked or fried?

SNOW: I ought to try the baked. Oh, why not?

MAMI: I'm glad to have you home, mi'ja.

AMY: I'm glad to be here.

MAMI: I wonder if the lady at Los Frijoles Menor ever got that bean recipe.

[SNOW *takes the recipe out of her bra.*]

SNOW: Your recipe never left my breast. She thinks you add beer, not birria. They taste horrible.

[RUMALDO *begins to leave.*]

MAMI: Rumaldito, where are you going?

RUMALDO: Off to buy spray paint.

AMY: Hey, Rumaldo. I want you to come with me. College isn't just for kids, you know. We can take classes together. In Chicano studies.

[RUMALDO *looks at* AMY, *touched. This time, he can't hide his tears. He gently strikes his heart.*]

RUMALDO: My favorite cousin. You're home.

[*Blackout.*]

One - Act Plays

MANY ARE THE REASONS WOMEN playwrights have chosen to write the one-act play. First of all, in terms of practicality, the one-act play offers many theatrical and economic advantages to the playwright. If, for example, she needs a "real" job to support her playwriting, the shorter one-act play form is less demanding on her time. If she wants her work to be performed by local or regional theater groups, Latino or otherwise, the one-act play often requires fewer cast members, less rehearsal and production time, and less financial commitment to a group that may be monetarily strapped. Furthermore, a shorter play's message—sometimes urgent—can be succinct and direct and therefore reach the community faster and more effectively.

Certainly this was the case with the celebrated Actos of El Teatro Campesino, whose influence affects even those playwrights too young today to have participated in the fervor of the sixties and seventies. It should not be surprising, then, that the one-act Chicana plays included here also share the Teatro's legacy and theatrical platform, with the stated goal: "Inspire the audience to social action. Illuminate specific points about social problems. Satirize the opposition. Show or hint at a solution. Express what people are feeling."[1] The oral tradition and socio-political circumstances of El Teatro's actos interfaced with other forms of political theater of the times, such as agit-prop theater, teatro de protesta, street theater, and the many Brechtian ways of doing theater.

Nor can we underestimate the Latin American connections to Latino/a theater. While contemporary Latino theater was in its embryonic stages during the late sixties and early seventies, Latin Americans, among them visual artists, playwrights, writers, and all manner of intellectuals, were confronted with the most severe and repressive military regimes of the century. Consequently, the mass exodus that occurred while these countries were ravaged by military coups resulted in large emigrations from Argentina, Chile, Uruguay, and other Latin American nations to the United States. It was precisely this exile to the United States, which coincided with the civil rights movements, social activism, and the rise of Latino theater in the United States, that is itself paradigmatic of the rise in consciousness that permeated Latino communities. This coalescence of Latin Americans and United States Latinos in urban spaces set in motion a symbiosis whereby each could gain from the other's experiences. The Latin Americans, who knew repression and dictatorship firsthand, and who had emigrated from Latin America's "lettered cities,"[2] were accustomed to a professional urban theater that played to an educated, theater-going audience. Latinos in the United States, on the other hand, were often the first generation in their families to receive a formal education. Their political activism, which emanated from their Latino communities, showed the Latin Americans how to define their Latino and/or Latin American identity as such. Once these Latin Americans resided in the United States, they found themselves classified as "minorities," which precipitated their need to define and negotiate their identities vis-à-vis the dominant Anglo culture. One transitional tool for this enterprise was Osvaldo Dragún's one-act play, *El hombre que se convirtió en perro,* which toured widely and played to Chicano communities and students. At the same time that it dramatized the inhuman working conditions of capitalism, it served theater practitioners of the Americas as an example of the way in which a playwright can use the techniques of the one-act play to communicate about oppression which, when applied to Chicano theater, included issues of race consciousness.

If in the Southwest and California a theatrical legacy of church, conquest, and colonialism played a significant role in the conversion of indigenous peoples to Catholicism,[3] in the East, Protestant and Puritan ideologies found other methods for their hegemonic project. Due to these circumstances, Latino/a theater on the East Coast is not nearly as rooted in a hybrid past, whose heritage includes Spain, indigenous myth and ritual, and cultural and allegorical models of theater (i.e., the auto-sacramental, *La Pastorela,* and passion plays) as Chicano theater. Nevertheless, by adopting and adapting these cultural and dramatic models, Teatro Campesino reactivated and rescued a theatrical tradition that had never been completely lost, and therefore, was familiar to their audiences.

In contrast to Teatro Campesino's group efforts, theater in the East germinated, emerged, and flourished in an urban environment where religion per se was displaced and the individual was exalted. Secular plays were sanitized from any visual and iconic representation favoring the psychological development of the character. Consequently, the theater that cities such as New York have sustained faces a set of omnipresent factors and values that propagate a bourgeois modus vivendi, regulated by secularization, commercialization, and the Protestant ethic of individualism. Because Broadway foments, promotes, and finances plays of two acts as a dominant model, the one-act play is virtually non-existent. It is only when we move off-Broadway that one-act plays and performance pieces become visible again. It is within this latter paradigm that we place one-act plays by Latinas, particularly those by Maria Irene Fornes (*Fefu and Her Friends* and *The Conduct of Life*), who has received seven Obies for her off-Broadway productions. Given that she has become the mentor of a new generation of Latina playwrights, her effectiveness in writing one-act plays and the avant-garde has become pivotal since the eighties, when she began her playwriting-in-progress workshops. Her signature on Latina playwriting can also be detected in full-length plays by Latinas, wherein the dramatic action is developed in a series of vignettes that constitute a hybrid form of a full-length play structured as a series of one-acts. Works by Caridad Svich, Josefina López, Edit Villarreal, Maria Irene Fornes, and Midgalia Cruz in *Anywhere but Here, Simply Maria or the American Dream, My Visits with MGM, Sarita,* and *Miriam's Flowers* exemplify this pattern.

The plays we introduce in this section showcase the spectrum of Latina playwriting we describe above. The work of the two Chicanas and one Puerto Rican playwright included here evidences a variety of topics, themes, generations, messages, dramatic situations, and techniques. Underlying all of them, though, regardless of their provenance, is a politics of articulating a new identity and the representation of new ethnicities that function bilingually and biculturally.

1. Valdez, Luis. *Early Works.* Houston: Arte Público Press, 1990, p. 12.
2. Rama, Angel. *La ciudad letrada.* Hanover, N.H.: Ediciones del Norte, 1984.
3. Versenyi, Adam. *El teatro en América Latina.* Cambridge: Cambridge University Press, 1996.

LAS NUEVAS TAMALERAS

Alicia Mena

CHARACTERS

DOÑA MERCEDES. A woman in her sixties, very severe, old-guard type. She is dressed in dark Victorian clothes.

DOÑA JUANITA. A woman in her fifties, very tenderhearted, likes to gossip. Wears 1950s-style clothes.

SILVIA. A very bossy and methodical woman in her twenties or thirties.

JOSIE. A very malleable, mediating woman in her twenties or thirties.

PATSY. A slightly younger woman, very anglocized, tends to whine. Is dressed totally inappropriately for making tamales, such as high heels, etc.

SETTING

Scene One: Heaven
Scenes Two–Seven: Silvia's Kitchen
A day and evening in December, in the present.
The set should consist of two areas, one that represents heaven and the other a modern kitchen.

Scene One

[*After the lights come up on an empty stage,* DOÑA MERCEDES *enters, followed by* DOÑA JUANITA. *They are engaged in an ongoing conversation.*]

DOÑA MERCEDES: No, para el cólico yo siempre usé el anís, un buen té de anís.

DOÑA JUANITA: Pos, I always used la yerba buena, yerba buena con canela and a little honey, el anís, that's for the stomach.

DOÑA MERCEDES: Bueno, pos; ¿y qué diablos es el cólico si no un dolor de panza, dígame?

DOÑA JUANITA: It's a little bit different, Doña Mercedes; babies get the colic.

DOÑA MERCEDES: ¡Ah, es la misma cosa!

[DOÑA JUANITA *suddenly turns, thinking she sees something off in the distance.* DOÑA MERCEDES, *noticing, gets a bit excited.*]

DOÑA MERCEDES: ¿Qué es, Doña Juanita? ¿Pasa algo por allá?

DOÑA JUANITA: No, parecía, pero no. [*Disappointed.*] Nothing ever happens around here.

DOÑA MERCEDES: [*To Stage Left.*] Uuuuh, ¡sería un milagro que algo pasara por aquí!

DOÑA JUANITA: ¡Ay, don't be like that! We have peace and quiet here.

DOÑA MERCEDES: Sí, yo sé que tenemos paz y tranquilidad aquí—pero, dígame, ¿que no se aburre un poco usted?

DOÑA JUANITA: Ay, no, Doña Mercedes. No, I do not get bored.

DOÑA MERCEDES: Pos, ¡yo sí! Yo, sí me aburro y hasta de vez en cuando extraño "ciertas" cosas de la vida.

DOÑA JUANITA: Ay, Doña Mercedes, you shouldn't be saying those things. ¡Persígnese!

DOÑA MERCEDES: N'ombre, no sea mal pensada, Doña Juanita, lo que más extraño y ¡lo que me gustaría organizar aquí es una buena tamalada!

DOÑA JUANITA: [*At first excited by the idea.*] Oh! [*Then thinks again.*] Oh, no, Doña Mercedes, they won't let us make tamales here in heaven.

DOÑA MERCEDES: A'Dio, y ¿po'qué no?

DOÑA JUANITA: Pos porque when you make tamales siempre hay chisme—y St. Peter, he don't like the gossip.

DOÑA MERCEDES: Pos, ¡qué lástima porque a mí cómo me gustaría meter las manos en una buena masa! Ah, cómo me gustaba hacer tamales.

DOÑA JUANITA: Oooh, me too! I liked it cuando all the women got together— mis cuñadas, mi suegra—all of us. It was a lot of hard work, that's for sure, but we had a lot of fun talking. It brought us closer together, no sé cómo, but it did. ¿Será que hay algún chemical en la masa?

DOÑA MERCEDES: Pos quien sabe, ¡yo no sé nada de la "ciencia" si yo apenas alcancé a aprender a leer y a escribir! Pero sí le digo que hacer tamales era algo que a mí me gustaba mucho. Todas las mujeres de los ranchos cercanos nos juntábamos. [*Now excited, obviously enjoying telling it.*] Mire, primero juntábamos bastante maíz, lo desgranábamos y lo molíamos en el metate para hacer el nixtamal para luego hacer la masa. Ah, y qué buena masa hacíamos. ¡Nosotros no andábamos con medias tazas! Después los hombres mataban a un marrano gordotote y le sacábamos el cebo para la manteca—ah y pos también había que juntar la leña para cocer los tamales, ¿no? ¡Si era un trabajal! ¡Y todavía faltaba hacer los tamales! Pero así éramos las mujeres en mi día, ¡la mujer de la época porfiriana era muy trabajadora! Y fíjese, con todo y el trabajo que nos costaba hacer tamales, como quiera lo extraño, de veras que sí.

DOÑA JUANITA: I know, I miss it too. Bueno, my cuñadas y mi suegra y yo, well, we didn't have to work as hard as you did. We didn't have to grind the corn to make the masa. In my day you could already go to the molino to buy it. Y para la manteca, pos al HEB.

DOÑA MERCEDES: ¿Comprar la masa? ¡Ni lo mande Dios! Bueno, ¿de veras no cree que nos dejen hacer tamales aquí?

DOÑA JUANITA: No, I don't think they would let us.

DOÑA MERCEDES: Pos, qué lástima.

[*Blackout.*]

Scene Two

[*Music comes up full volume at blackout and continues as lights come up on Scene Two. If production is at Christmas, the music can be a conjunto version of "Silent Night" or any Christmas song. If it is at another time of year, any polka or any type of music can be used, as long as it is representative of contemporary Chicanos/Latinos.*

As the lights come up on a modern kitchen with every new appliance known to man in it, SILVIA *enters followed by* JOSIE *and* PATSY. *The feeling is upbeat; they dance to the rhythm of the music coming from the radio on the counter. They have great expectations.* SILVIA, *always ready to tackle any project, goes directly to the masa bowl on the counter and carries it to the table.* JOSIE *and* PATSY *are a little less eager and dance a bit more. Finally,* JOSIE *picks up a bowl with the peppers and spices in it and carries it to the table where a molcajete, a box of lard, and a package of hojas sit.*]

SILVIA: [*Slapping the masa.*] Okay, the masa, [*Picks up the hojas.*] the hojas—

JOSIE: The chiles. [*Picks up a chile, the spices.*] The spices. [*She is about to pick up the box of lard when she sees that* PATSY, *who is bending over straightening the front of her high heels, is giving her a perfect target. She slaps* PATSY's *behind.*] ¡La manteca!

PATSY: [*Whining.*] Stop it, Josie.

[*A friendly push-and-shove scuffle begins.*]

SILVIA: [*All business, crosses to counter and abruptly turns off the radio, which stops the scuffle instantly.*] Miren, no empiecen. We don't have time for that. We really have to concentrate on what we're doing.

PATSY: We don't even know what we're doing.

SILVIA: Yes we do. I do anyway.

PATSY: You've only done it once.

JOSIE: So? That doesn't matter, it's in our blood, no seas tan negative, Patsy. [*To* SILVIA.] Where do we start?

PATSY: [*Sitting.*] By praying.

SILVIA: Be quiet. I have to concentrate. Okay, first we have to organize ourselves, that way we don't make a big mess in my kitchen.

[SILVIA *puts on a very practical chef's apron.*]

JOSIE: Right. We organize ourselves, ¿y luego?

PATSY: [*Still sitting.*] We pray.

JOSIE: Mira, tú tan religious all of a sudden.

PATSY: Well, why not? We need all the help we can get. Hey! I have an idea. Why don't we light a candle? [*Now really getting into the joke of it.*] Yeah, that's it, let's light a candle. Maybe if we light a candle, some spirit or something will come and help us. Oh, God, can you just see it?

[*During this speech,* SILVIA *strikes the masa against the counter (Stage Right) and takes hojas and manteca to counter (Stage Left).*]

SILVIA: [*Has been fussing with things and organizing, trying to ignore* PATSY, *interrupts.*] Patsy, you need to take things more seriously.

PATSY: [*Stage Left.*] Well, Silvia, I was just kidding.

SILVIA: [*Stage Right.*] Besides, we can do this by ourselves.

JOSIE: [*Center Stage.*] Yeah, we can do this by ourselves. [SILVIA, *satisfied that she has an ally, turns her attention to the stove. As soon as she does,* JOSIE *continues, to* PATSY.] Pero como quiera, why don't you go light a candle, nomás, you know, por si acaso.

[*They laugh and run off to light the candle Downstage Left.*]

SILVIA: Look, you two—come back in here, Patsy.

PATSY: [*Off.*] Okay, okay, in a minute. I'm lighting a candle.

SILVIA: Patsy!

[*Silvia exits Downstage Left.*]

PATSY: [*Off.*] There. It's lit.

[*Suddenly the lights flicker on and off. An eerie, magical sound cue is heard. A wind blows the curtains, and* DOÑA MERCEDES *and* DOÑA JUANITA *appear on stage in a puff of smoke.*]

DOÑA MERCEDES: [*Stunned.*] ¡Ave María Purísima! ¿Dónde estamos, Doña Juanita?

DOÑA JUANITA: [*Very confused.*] I don't know where we are, Doña Mercedes.

[*They start to investigate their new whereabouts when they see* JOSIE, PATSY, *and* SILVIA *returning to the kitchen. They quickly hide behind the refrigerator. As soon as* JOSIE *and* PATSY *enter the kitchen they sense that something strange has happened.* PATSY *is holding a Virgen de Guadalupe candle. They are looking around, somewhat confused.* SILVIA *brings up the rear. She is in too much of a huff to notice anything strange.* JOSIE *crosses to Downstage of table to Stage Right.*]

SILVIA: [*Crosses to Upstage Center.*] Put that candle down. Okay, now, we've all been to college, right?

PATSY and JOSIE: Right.

SILVIA: Well then, I think we can handle making a few dozen tamales, don't you?

[*At hearing this,* DOÑA JUANITA, *who is very metiche and has been leaning as far as she can from behind the refrigerator, nearly falls. She quickly tries to hide again so the girls don't see her, but when they don't react, she begins to suspect that they can't see her. She decides to test them.*]

SILVIA: Besides that, we committed ourselves, didn't we?

[*The other two nod their heads in response.*]

SILVIA: I distinctly remember that it was you, Josie, who suggested it in the first place.

[DOÑA JUANITA *sneaks behind* SILVIA *and waves her hand in front of her when she is talking to* JOSIE. *Then she does the same when* SILVIA *is addressing* PATSY. *When she gets no reaction, she quickly brings* DOÑA MERCEDES *into it, and* DOÑA MERCEDES *tries it too. They now become bolder.*]

SILVIA: And you, Patsy, you thought it was a "fun" idea. Didn't we agree to do this by ourselves? ¿Entonces? Well, then, does anybody want to bail out?

JOSIE: No!

[PATSY *doesn't respond right away and the others stare at her.*]

PATSY: Not me, hey!

SILVIA: Entonces let's get to work! [*Crosses to stove.*] There's much work to be done. Let's see, first we cook the meat. No, wait. I've already done that. [*Crosses to table.*] First we boil the chiles, well, not really boil them, we have to blanch them.

[JOSIE *follows* SILVIA *readily;* PATSY *hangs back.*]

DOÑA MERCEDES: ¿Qué dicen, Doña Juanita?

DOÑA JUANITA: Pos, qué van a planchar los chiles, o algo así.

DOÑA MERCEDES: ¿Que van a planchar los chiles? ¿Cómo qué van a planchar los chiles, están locas o qué? ¡Necesitan echarle agua bien hervida a esos chiles!

DOÑA JUANITA: [*To Stage Left of* PATSY.] I think these girls really need our help.

[*At this point, the old women decide to become involved in the task at* hand. DOÑA JUANITA *is everywhere.* DOÑA MERCEDES *is somewhat distracted by the modern surroundings and appliances.*]

JOSIE: Blanch them. What's that?

SILVIA: Just go boil some water. [*Crosses back to table.*] Now, Patsy, you grind the spices.

PATSY: [*Crosses to Center Stage.*] Me? In what?

SILVIA: In the molcajete, of course.

DOÑA JUANITA: Ay, at least they have a molcajete. That's a good sign.

PATSY: So how much of this stuff do I use?

SILVIA: Uh—a lot.

JOSIE: [*At stove.*] The water's boiling. Now what?

SILVIA: [*From table.*] Pour it on the chiles and wait a while. [*Crosses to stove.*] Well, now, let's see, I already put the pork roast in the pressure cooker.

[*At this point,* DOÑA MERCEDES *realizes there is a very important item missing in the kitchen and starts looking around for it.*]

JOSIE: [*From sink.*] The pork roast?

SILVIA: [*From stove.*] Yes, the pork roast. You didn't really expect us to chop up a cabeza, did you?

DOÑA MERCEDES: [*Stage Left of table.*] ¿Y dónde está la cabeza?

SILVIA: [*At the stove.*] I wasn't about to chop up a pig's nose or its ears.

[DOÑA JUANITA *checks the pressure cooker to convince herself that they actually are not using a cabeza.*]

PATSY: Ugh! Or its eyes. Gross!

JOSIE: [*At sink.*] Yuck, me either, ¡olvídalo!

DOÑA JUANITA: [*Rushing over to give* DOÑA MERCEDES *the bad news.*] Pos que they aren't going to use a cabeza.

DOÑA MERCEDES: [*Unconvinced.*] ¿No? ¿Cómo que no? ¡Es el único modo! ¿Cómo van hacer tamales sin la cabeza? [*Now goes to* PATSY, *who is busy grinding the spices with the wrong end of the molcajete stone.*] ¡Y mira tienen que rebanar todo, todo finito, bien finito, las orejas, la trompa, los ojos, pa'que no queden trocetes grandotes, no sea que luego a alguien le vaya a tocar medio ojo en un tamal!

PATSY: Is this ground up enough, Silvia?

SILVIA: [*Takes molcajete stone out of* PATSY's *hand and rights it.*] No.

DOÑA JUANITA: No, they aren't ready yet, y besides, you're going to need more ajo in there, mi'ja.

DOÑA MERCEDES: No, no, no, ¿cómo qué ajo? Necesita más comino. Es el comino lo que le da el buen sabor al guisado.

SILVIA: I think you're gonna need some comino in there.

[DOÑA MERCEDES *is very pleased.* DOÑA JUANITA *is not.*]

SILVIA: And I think you're gonna need some more ajo, también.

[*Now the old ladies have the reverse reactions.*]

JOSIE: [*From sink.*] The chiles are blanched, now what?

[PATSY *sits.*]

SILVIA: [*Crosses to Stage Right of* JOSIE.] Now we take the skins off and the seeds out.

JOSIE: [*At sink.*] Oh, just like that, huh? We take the skins off and the seeds out. How?

SILVIA: How? Well, now let's see. How?

DOÑA JUANITA: [*Whispers to* JOSIE.] Mi'ja, try the cold water.

JOSIE: Maybe I should put them in cold water.

PATSY: Silvia—

DOÑA MERCEDES: [*Pushes* DOÑA JUANITA *out of the way.*] ¡Qué agua fría ni que nada!

PATSY: Silvia!

JOSIE: And then again, maybe I shouldn't.

[JOSIE *shoves chiles in* SILVIA's *face.*]

PATSY: [*Bringing up the molcajete, also shoves it in* SILVIA'S *face.*] Hey, Silvia, is this ground up enough yet?

SILVIA: [*Pressured.*] Uh, yes.

PATSY: Thank God!

[*Blackout.*]

Scene Three

[*All the women are gathered around the blender with* SILVIA *in the middle with the attitude of a surgeon performing major surgery. The old women are jockeying for positions so as not to miss anything.*]

SILVIA: [*With back to the audience.*] All right, Josie. Hand me the chiles.

JOSIE: [*Handing* SILVIA *the chiles.*] Chiles.

SILVIA: Patsy, hand me the spices.

PATSY: [*Handing them over.*] Spices.

SILVIA: Now, we put them all together in the blender.

DOÑA MERCEDES: [*Stage Left of* DOÑA JUANITA.] ¿En el qué?

DOÑA JUANITA: [*Behind* JOSIE.] En el blender.

DOÑA MERCEDES: ¿Y eso qué es?

DOÑA JUANITA: Pos, es como un molcajete, muele todo, pero it's electric. You died antes de que it was invented.

DOÑA MERCEDES: Pero eso no parece un molcajete.

DOÑA JUANITA: [*Not wanting to deal with her anymore for fear of missing something.*] Pos, don't worry about it.

[SILVIA *finishes putting the spices and chiles in the blender and turns it on. The loud noise alarms* DOÑA MERCEDES *very much.*]

DOÑA MERCEDES: [*Running for cover.*] Oye, ¡qué ruidoso es ese! ¿Por qué hace tanto ruido ese aparato?

DOÑA JUANITA: Pos, así es, hombre. Don't worry about it.

[DOÑA MERCEDES *slowly, carefully, peeks from behind the stove.*]

SILVIA: [*Turning off the blender.*] I think it's ready.

PATSY: Oooooh, let me taste it.

JOSIE: I'll taste it.

SILVIA: [*Quickly holding the other two back.*] I'll taste it. [*Crosses to stove.*] It's perfect!

PATSY: [*Taking over the blender.*] Let me see.

JOSIE: Me too.

SILVIA: [*Excitedly, already at the stove.*] Okay, the pork roast is ready, so all we have to do now is add that to it and cook it for a while.

DOÑA MERCEDES: Pos, ¿qué están haciendo estas muchachas? ¿Y cuándo van a rebanar la cabeza?

DOÑA JUANITA: [*Crosses Stage Left of* JOSIE.] Mi'jas, you have to chop up the meat first.

JOSIE: [*Crosses Downstage a few steps.*] Don't we have to shred the meat or chop it up or something?

SILVIA: Chop it up? Oh, yeah, of course. That's what I said. First, we chop up the meat, and then we add the chiles and the spices to it. So, what are we waiting for, huh? Let's start chopping!

[*Blackout.*]

Scene Four

[*The pork roast has been chopped.* JOSIE *and* PATSY *are at the stove tasting the guisado.* DOÑA JUANITA *and* DOÑA MERCEDES *are also at the stove, waiting their turn to taste.* SILVIA *is wiping the table.*]

JOSIE: [*Crosses Stage Right behind the stove.*] It tastes pretty good to me.

[*She crosses to Stage Left chair and sits.*]

PATSY: [*Really selling it since she doesn't want to be stuck grinding spices again.*] Hmmmm, I like it. [*Crosses to Center Stage.*] What do you think, Silvia?

SILVIA: I think it needs something.

[PATSY *holds her breath, hoping* SILVIA *doesn't think it needs more spices.*]

SILVIA: But I'm not sure what.

DOÑA MERCEDES: [*In front of stove.*] Le falta comino.

DOÑA JUANITA: [*Behind stove.*] No, le falta nada. It's ready, mi'jas.

DOÑA MERCEDES: [*To* SILVIA.] A ver, ¿dónde está el comino?

[*Annoyed when she gets no response,* DOÑA MERCEDES *decides to find the comino on her own.* DOÑA JUANITA, *getting wind of that, decides to guard the guisado with her life, if necessary. They tussle for a moment, but* DOÑA MERCEDES *wins. All this action is going on while the girls continue their dialogue.*]

PATSY: [*Standing Center Stage.*] Well, I think it tastes real good. It doesn't need any more spices, that's for sure.

JOSIE: [*Sitting Stage Left.*] Oh, sí, you just don't want to grind any more. I think it could use a little more spices.

PATSY: Then you grind them.

SILVIA: All right, you two. Let's just leave it like it is. We need to start working on the masa.

DOÑA MERCEDES: [*Hearing this,* DOÑA MERCEDES *loses interest in the guisado and rushes to the table, and so does* DOÑA JUANITA, *of course.*] ¡¿La masa?!

PATSY: [*Following* SILVIA *as she prepares ingredients.*] Are we all going to work on the masa?

SILVIA: Nope. I'll do it.

PATSY: Why? Can't we all take turns?

SILVIA: We can't do that. Only one person can work the masa.

PATSY: [*Insistent.*] Why?

SILVIA: Because it's a messy job, that's why. [*Crosses to dish drainer and back to table with big spoon.*] I'll need you to hand me things. I won't be able to stop once I start. You aren't supposed to stop kneading the masa once you start.

PATSY: [*Not at all convinced.*] Right.

JOSIE: Yeah, you aren't supposed to stop.

PATSY: Well, any one of us could do it and not stop.

SILVIA: You have to have strong arms to do this.

PATSY: No, you don't. My mother-in-law told me you could put it in the mixer first.

[SILVIA *and* JOSIE *scoff at the idea and proceed to be really buddy-buddy about preparing the masa, measuring out the manteca, etc., ignoring* PATSY *completely.*]

DOÑA MERCEDES: ¿En el qué?

DOÑA JUANITA: En el mixer, es una batidora eléctrica.

DOÑA MERCEDES: [*Crosses to Stage Right to* DOÑA JUANITA.] Pos, ¿cómo diablos trabaja eso?

DOÑA JUANITA: Well, que la suegra le dijo que it was easier like that, que el mixer batiera la masa y así no tienen que usar los brazos para amasar.

DOÑA MERCEDES: [*Completely outraged.*] ¡Cómo! ¡No! ¡Eso nunca! ¡Estas muchachitas van por muy mal camino! Pos ¿cómo que no van a usar los brazos para amasar? ¡Pero mira nomás qué ocurrencias! [*Now goes directly to the girls—to all.*] No, muchachitas, tienen que usar los brazos y las manos para amasar. [*To* PATSY.] Se tiene que trabajar [*To* SILVIA.] para que salgan buenos los tamales se tiene que sudar. [*No response.*] ¡Esto es el colmo!

[*She is so upset she swoons and has to support herself on the counter.* PATSY, *in the meantime, has been pouting and watching the other two prepare the masa. She decides to make her move and lunges for the masa bowl.* SILVIA *blocks her with her body.*]

SILVIA: [*Crosses Stage Right of table.*] Olvídalo, Patsy! I want to feel the masa in my hands.

PATSY: [*Whining, Center Stage.*] Well, so do I.

SILVIA: [*Crosses Stage Right.*] I told you before, Patsy. We can't all work the masa.

[PATSY *flops onto a chair, pouting.*]

JOSIE: [*Crosses Stage Left.*] Y besides, you wanted to do it con el mixer.

DOÑA JUANITA: [*Crosses Stage Left.*] Ya, give her a break. [*Crosses Upstage, behind* JOSIE.] Era la idea de la mother-in-law, not hers. No te dejes, mi'ja.

[DOÑA JUANITA *crosses to between* PATSY *and* JOSIE.]

DOÑA MERCEDES: [*Recovered and unable to stay away any longer, crosses Stage Right of* SILVIA.] Bueno, pos ¿qué esperan? ¿Cuándo van a empezar a amasar?

SILVIA: [*Giving in, crosses Stage Right.*] Okay, okay, you want to do the masa? Fine then, do it.

[SILVIA *leaves table, crosses Upstage to stove and counter.*]

JOSIE: [*Crosses Upstage.*] You're gonna let her do it?

[PATSY, *happy to be getting her way, enthusiastically prepares to get her hands in the masa, painted press-on nails and all.* DOÑA MERCEDES *rolls up her sleeves and delves right in behind* SILVIA *to Stage Right of* PATSY.]

Scene Five

[*As the lights come up,* PATSY *is still kneading the masa, but not enthusiastically anymore. She has masa on her hair, face, and arms.* DOÑA MERCEDES *is kneading away.*]

PATSY: [*Center Stage, wiping her brow with the back of her arm and whining.*] Wow, this is a real workout.

SILVIA: [*Wiping her stove with a spray bottle of all-purpose cleaner in her hand.*] Uh-huh, and you have a long way to go todavía.

JOSIE: [*Sitting in one of the kitchen chairs Stage Left, looking very relaxed.*] And you have to knead it harder than that.

[PATSY *stops kneading to give her a dirty look.*]

DOÑA MERCEDES: [*Stage Right of* PATSY.] Ándale, muchachita, amásale, amásale con ganas. Mira, así.

SILVIA: [*Crossing to table Stage Right, checking the masa at table.*] I think we're going to have to put some more manteca in there.

JOSIE: [*Crosses Stage Left.*] More? We already put three pounds of it in there. What if we use too much?

DOÑA JUANITA: [*Crosses Stage Left of* JOSIE.] No, mi'jita. I got news for you. You can never put too much manteca in a tamal.

SILVIA: [*Crosses Stage Right of table.*] You better go put some more on the stove to soften it up, pero put it on "low," okay? And watch it.

[JOSIE *takes the manteca to the stove.* DOÑA JUANITA *follows her.* DOÑA JUANITA *stands behind stove Stage Right.*]

DOÑA MERCEDES: [*Crosses Stage Right of* PATSY.] Ah, pero qué arrastradas son, hasta tienen que suavizar la manteca.

SILVIA: [*Getting comfortable in a chair Stage Right, to* PATSY.] Now, what were you saying about Rosalinda and Frank?

PATSY: [*Kneading half-heartedly.*] Well, she asked him for a divorce.

JOSIE: [*Rushing over and leaving the manteca unattended.*] She what?

DOÑA JUANITA: [*From stove.*] Mi'ja, don't forget the manteca.

SILVIA: [*To* JOSIE.] Rosalinda asked Frank for a divorce.

JOSIE: Well, it was about time, after all the shit he's done to her.

DOÑA JUANITA: [*Now getting interested in the gossip, leaves the manteca, too.*] Pos, just what has he done to her?

DOÑA MERCEDES: ¿Usted también? ¡Cuidado con la manteca!

[*She leaves the masa and, wiping her hands, crosses over to the stove.*]

PATSY: [*Standing Center Stage.*] It's the kids I feel sorry for.

[DOÑA JUANITA *sympathizes, crosses Stage Left of* PATSY.]

SILVIA: [*Sitting Stage Right.*] She never should have had that last one. They were already having so many problems.

DOÑA MERCEDES: [*Behind the girls.*] ¡La manteca!

JOSIE: I don't know how she stood it as long as she did.

DOÑA MERCEDES: [*Getting frantic, to* PATSY.] ¡La manteca se va a quemar!

PATSY: Low self-esteem, probably.

DOÑA MERCEDES: [*Even more frantic, trying to work the stove.*] Ay, ¿cómo trabaja este aparato? ¿En dónde ponen la leña?

DOÑA JUANITA: [*Between* PATSY *and* JOSIE.] Y andaba messing around?

JOSIE: Has he moved out?

SILVIA: Well, what do you think? [*To* PATSY.] Has he?

PATSY: Well, I heard—

SILVIA: Wait a minute. [*Sniffing the air.*] What's that smell?

DOÑA MERCEDES: [*Crosses to behind stove.*] ¡La manteca, pendejas!

JOSIE: The manteca!

SILVIA: You idiot! I told you to watch it!

[SILVIA *rushes to the stove.* DOÑA JUANITA *crosses to stove Stage Left of* SILVIA.]

JOSIE: [*Sits, defensively.*] Well, I can't do everything.

PATSY: [*Kicks off her heels.*] Oh, I'm exhausted and my back hurts. I don't know how women used to do this all the time.

DOÑA JUANITA: [*Crosses Stage Right of* PATSY.] A puro huevo, mi'ja.

JOSIE: [*Sitting Stage Left.*] You wanted to do it, ahora ya te pesa, ¿verdad?

PATSY: [*Faking it, makes it sound real peppy.*] No, it's kind of fun.

[PATSY *turns so* JOSIE *can't see her face and grimaces.*]

JOSIE: Oh, sure, it's kind of fun.

SILVIA: [*Returning with hot lard to table, Stage Right,* DOÑA JUANITA *following her.*] Now we have to wait until this stuff cools off and all because of your carelessness.

JOSIE: Te digo que I can't do everything.

DOÑA MERCEDES: [*Crosses Stage Right.*] Ya dejen de pelearse.

DOÑA JUANITA: [*Stage Right of* SILVIA, *Stage Left of* DOÑA MERCEDES.] You got a lot of work to do.

DOÑA MERCEDES: [*Stage Right of* DOÑA JUANITA.] Sí, están perdiendo el tiempo.

PATSY: Can't we just put it in like that?

SILVIA: I think it's too hot.

DOÑA MERCEDES: Esa manteca está muy caliente. [*Crosses Stage Right to* SILVIA.] No se le vayan a echar a la masa todavía.

JOSIE: Oh, let's just do it.

DOÑA MERCEDES: [*Crosses Stage Left of* JOSIE.] Tú, ¡cállate! [*Crosses Stage Left of* SILVIA, *to* SILVIA.] ¡No se le vayas a echar!

SILVIA: Well okay. [*Pours the manteca into the masa.*]

DOÑA MERCEDES: [*Crosses Stage Right to stove.*] Ay, ¡qué cabezudas!

SILVIA: Now, you have to work it in real good.

PATSY: I am.

SILVIA: You have to work it in better than that!

PATSY: I'm trying!

JOSIE: [*Crosses Upstage Left.*] Yeah, you have to work it in better than that.

PATSY: It's ho-o-o-o-t-t!

JOSIE: [*At table.*] You wanted to do it.

SILVIA: [*Pushes* PATSY *out of the way.*] Here, let me finish that. I should have known better than to let you do it in the first place.

[PATSY *crosses Upstage to counter.*]

DOÑA JUANITA: [*Crosses to* PATSY, *then back to Stage Right of* SILVIA.] Ay, give her a break. At least así it will blend in better, mi'ja. Ahora, you have to put in some spices so the masa can have a good flavor.

DOÑA MERCEDES: [*Crosses Stage Right of* DOÑA JUANITA.]: Y ¿para qué van a hacer eso? ¡No, señora! ¡La masa no necesita todo ese mugrero! Las especias nomás se le echan al guisado.

DOÑA JUANITA: El ajo y el comino give better flavor to the masa. I should know, mis tamales were famous. Go ahead, girls, put them in!

DOÑA MERCEDES: Mis tamales eran los mejores de toda la región, todo el mundo me lo decía, y nunca, nunca le eché especias a la masa. [*Pushes out* · *of the way.*] ¡No le pongan ese mugrero!

[DOÑA MERCEDES *crosses Stage Right of* SILVIA.]

SILVIA: Patsy, hand me the spices for the masa.

[PATSY, *who is pouting by the counter, ignores* SILVIA.]

DOÑA MERCEDES: No, ¡no hagan eso! Ahora verán, ¡condenadas!

[DOÑA MERCEDES *crosses to counter, picks molcajete up from counter with back to audience.*]

JOSIE: [*Stage Left, chair.*] Do you think you should do that? I don't remember my mother ever putting spices in the masa.

DOÑA MERCEDES: [*Turns to audience.*] No, ¡claro que no!

[DOÑA JUANITA *sees the molcajete in her hand and starts after her.* DOÑA MERCEDES *takes off with* DOÑA JUANITA *close behind her. They exit.*]

JOSIE: What do you think, Patsy?

PATSY: [*Full of attitude; at Stage Right counter.*] I don't know. My mother never made tamales. We had a lady who made them for us.

SILVIA: [*Center Stage.*] Well, my mother made tamales every Christmas. But I can't remember if she put the spices in or not. Oh, well, we have the spices. We might as well go ahead and put them in. It can't hurt. Bring them over here, Patsy.

[DOÑA JUANITA *comes in running. She has the molcajete in her hands this time and* DOÑA MERCEDES *is in hot pursuit.* DOÑA JUANITA *wants to put the spices back where* PATSY *left them and she almost does.* DOÑA MERCEDES *manages to get them away from her and she runs off, with* DOÑA JUANITA *chasing her again. They exit.*]

PATSY: [*Looks around for molcajete.*] Hey, they aren't here.

SILVIA: [*Still at Center Stage table.*] What do you mean, "they aren't here"? Patsy, you would lose your head if it wasn't attached to your body. Mira, if I have to go over there—

PATSY: [*At counter.*] I left them right here. I know I did.

[*In her frantic attempt to find the molcajete,* PATSY *picks up the package of hojas that was on the counter and spills them all over, making a huge mess.*]

SILVIA: [*Still Center Stage facing Downstage.*] You always make such a mess, it's no wonder you can't ever find anything. Josie, go help her look. [*Now she turns and sees counter as* JOSIE *crosses Stage Right of* PATSY.] Oh my God! ¡Mira, cómo me tienes el counter! What bad work habits you have.

PATSY: [*Crosses Stage Right to stove.*] Maybe I put them over here.

JOSIE: ¡Tonta!

[DOÑA JUANITA *runs in and this time manages to put the spices back— just in time for* SILVIA *to find them.*]

SILVIA: If I find them— [*Crosses to counter, looking.*] ¡Mira! And what's this? Chingao, Patsy, no te digo. C'mon, get your hands back in that masa. You thought you were gonna get out of it, huh?

[*They all go back to the masa and end up putting the spices in.*]

DOÑA JUANITA: Ahora sí, mi'jas, put those spices in. Now, work them in real good.

DOÑA MERCEDES: ¡Cabezudas!

[*Blackout.*]

Scene Six

[*As the scene opens,* SILVIA *is at the counter cleaning up. The rest of the women are around the table watching* PATSY *as she works the spices into the masa.*]

PATSY: [*After a beat, stops kneading.*] What do you think, Silvia?

[SILVIA *crosses Stage Right of* PATSY.]

PATSY: Do you think it's ready?

SILVIA: Let's see. [*Tests the masa with her fingers.*] Yes, I think it's ready.

[SILVIA *crosses back to sink and washes her hands.*]

PATSY: [*Practically collapsing.*] Thank God! I couldn't have held out much longer.

[PATSY *sits Center Stage.*]

JOSIE: [*Sitting Stage Right.*] Hey, you're a woman now, Patsy. ¡Te hiciste mujer!

DOÑA JUANITA: [*Stage Left of* PATSY, *checking the masa.*] Yes, ya está ready!

DOÑA MERCEDES: [*Pushing* DOÑA JUANITA *out of the way.*] A ver, a ver, sí, ya está lista.

SILVIA: [*Crosses back to Center Stage table.*] Let's get this show on the road—bring the guisado over here. Get the hojas.

JOSIE: [*Excited, goes right to it;* DOÑA JUANITA *follows her to help.*] You got it. The guisado, the hojas— [*Stops and takes a few steps toward the stove and then some toward the counter where the hojas are;* DOÑA JUANITA *is doing the exact same thing.*] Wait a minute, the guisado or the hojas? I tell you, I can't do everything.

SILVIA: Just bring the guisado. Patsy, you bring me the hojas. Okay, now, we have to be very organized.

DOÑA MERCEDES: [*Anxiously.*] Pero qué tanto se tardan, ¿cuándo van a empezar a embarrar?

SILVIA: I think we need to do this assembly line. It will be neater that way. I'll put the masa on the hojas and the two of you put in the meat.

PATSY: I thought I could put the masa on the hojas.

SILVIA: Have you ever done it before?

PATSY: No, but—

SILVIA: I have. I know how to do it. It'll save us time if I do it, ¿entiendes?

JOSIE: [*Taunting.*] Y besides, you already did the masa. Qué selfish eres.

DOÑA MERCEDES: Bueno ya, ¡por fin empiezan!

SILVIA: Let's just get started.

PATSY: [*Pouting again.*] Fine.

SILVIA: [*Very know-it-all-ish.*] A ver, if I remember correctly, you spread it like this. [SILVIA *is having much difficulty. The other two laugh at her.*] No. Well, maybe it was like this.

[*She tries again; it still doesn't work. She's getting frustrated.*]

DOÑA MERCEDES: ¡No! ¡Así no, muchacha!

DOÑA JUANITA: Ay, mi'ja, not like that.

PATSY: [*Anxious to do it, tries to grab the hoja from* SILVIA.] Let me try it.

SILVIA: No! I can do it.

JOSIE: [*Also tries to take the hoja.*] Maybe you should try doing—

SILVIA: I can do it.

[*Now getting very manic, Sylvia tries over and over to spread the masa on the hojas. The harder she tries, the worse it gets.*]

DOÑA MERCEDES: Pero qué tanto misterio, pos nomás toma la hoja en la mano y embárrale la masa, muchacha.

DOÑA JUANITA: Ay, it's not that easy for them, pobrecitas. Mira, mi'ja, you are getting too excited. Calm down. Take your time. Con más calma . . . I always took my time y mis tamales were famous.

DOÑA MERCEDES: Si yo estuviera viva, mira ya hubiera acabado—así [*Snapping her fingers.*] en un dos por tres. Y mis tamales eran los mejores de toda la región.

SILVIA: [*Has worked herself into a frenzy.*] Dammit! Stay on there.

PATSY: I think you're trying too hard.

JOSIE: [*Talking to her soothingly, as if to someone on the verge of a breakdown.*] Yeah, you need to relax. I'll get you a nice cold beer.

DOÑA JUANITA: ¡Ándale! That's it, give her a beer.

[*She follows JOSIE to the refrigerator to help.*]

DOÑA MERCEDES: ¡Qué cerveza ni qué nada!, ¡pónganse a embarrar!

PATSY: Get me one too, Josie.

SILVIA: [*Feeling that she is losing control.*] We just need to get organized. I need to concentrate harder.

DOÑA JUANITA: You just need to relax, mi'ja. Drink your beer.

DOÑA MERCEDES: Les está dando muy malos consejos, Doña Juanita.

JOSIE: [*Returning with beers, hands one to Patsy and then to SILVIA, again speaking to her firmly, but soothingly.*] Let's just drink our beer and relax for a while, okay?

PATSY: Yeah, I'm tired, kneading that masa was hard work. It felt like my arms were gonna fall off.

[*They all sit down to relax and* DOÑA JUANITA, *approving, goes to find herself a good spot to relax also.* DOÑA MERCEDES, *incredulous, takes it all in for a moment.*]

DOÑA MERCEDES: ¿Y ahora? ¡Qué bonito!, ¿no? ¡Aquí nomás sentadotas! Estas van a estar aquí todo el año nomás para hacer unas cuantas docenas de tamales. No, en mi día, allá en aquellos tiempos, la mujer era de veras mujer. Yo te podía hacer cincuenta docenas de tamales así, mira [*Snapping her fingers in* DOÑA JUANITA's *face.*] en un dos por tres. Estas te aseguro que no te saben lavar ni un calzón. No te digo, ¡estas muchachitas van por muy mal camino!

DOÑA JUANITA: Pos, they might not make you fifty dozen tamales just like that. [*Snaps her fingers back in* DOÑA MERCEDES' *face.*] Pero at least they are trying. There's a lot of them out there that don't even care about learning.

SILVIA: ¿Saben qué? That beer did relax me.

PATSY: Me too.

JOSIE: A mí también. You want another one?

[PATSY *agrees and* JOSIE *is up and ready to get some more beer.* DOÑA JUANITA, *ready to help, rushes over to the refrigerator, but* DOÑA MER-CEDES *quickly stands in front of the refrigerator door, blocking the way.*]

SILVIA: [*Stops* JOSIE.] No. It's getting late. It's almost four. What time did we start?

PATSY: A year ago, it seems.

JOSIE: Ay, at noon.

SILVIA: ¿Ya ven? It's getting late and we still have a long way to go. Let me try this again. [*Preparing herself, takes a deep breath, really concentrating.*] Okay, you take the hoja like this, and you put the masa on it like this . . . [*In spite of all her care and concentration, the masa rolls right off the hoja.*] Dammit!

[*In a rage,* SILVIA *flings the hoja and the spoon into the masa bowl and marches over to the counter to calm down.*]

JOSIE: [*Taking the hoja.*] Maybe you should try doing it . . . así.

[JOSIE *does it perfectly. The women around the table react.*]

DOÑA JUANITA: [*Joyfully.*] Oh yes, mi'ja, you got it. She's a natural.

DOÑA MERCEDES: [*Proudly.*] Sí, así se hace.

PATSY: [*Gasping.*] You lied, Josie, you have done it before.

SILVIA: [*Jealous.*] When did you learn that?

JOSIE: No, no, I didn't lie. I never have done it before. But when I was a little girl, I remember watching my mother and my tías, and this is how they did it.

SILVIA: Okay, fine. Josie, you spread and Patsy and I will fill.

JOSIE: Me?

SILVIA: Yes, you. Now do it, it's getting late!

[JOSIE *starts spreading the masa on the hojas.*]

DOÑA JUANITA: Sí, mi'jas, and you still have to cook them.

PATSY: [*Sitting down.*] It is getting late, and the back of my neck really hurts. I didn't think it was going to take us this long. Maybe we should finish this tomorrow.

DOÑA MERCEDES: ¡No! ¡Ésta no es de rancho!

SILVIA: [*Tired, losing her patience.*] Mira, Patsy, we are going to finish today. Now, I'm just as tired as you are, pero we committed ourselves. Ever since you were in elementary school, Patsy, you could never finish any project you started. Well, you're gonna finish this one if it kills you.

DOÑA MERCEDES: ¡Sí, sí! ¡Muy bien dicho, muy bien dicho!

JOSIE: [*Noticing that* PATSY's *feelings are really hurt, tries to mediate.*] Look, I have a lot of hojas ready. C'mon.

[SILVIA *comes to fill the hojas, but* PATSY *remains sitting. Everyone stares at her. After a tense beat,* PATSY *gets up and heads for the door.*]

JOSIE: C'mon, Patsy, the sooner we start the sooner we finish.

[PATSY *stops at the door.* SILVIA *leaves the table and goes to the sink busying herself.*]

DOÑA JUANITA: What are you waiting for? Ándale, mi'jita.

DOÑA MERCEDES: ¿Pos, qué esperas, muchacha?

JOSIE: [*Coaxing.*] C'mon, Patsy, please.

[PATSY *finally turns around, returns to the table, and starts to fill an hoja.*]

PATSY: [*Her voice shaking.*] Fine!

[*Blackout.*]

Scene Seven

[*As the scene opens, all the women are waiting for the tamales to cook.* SILVIA *is wiping the table (or counter),* JOSIE *and* PATSY *are sitting at the kitchen table drinking a beer, and* DOÑA JUANITA *and* DOÑA MERCEDES *are watching the pot impatiently while listening to the girls' conversation.*]

SILVIA: So, you don't think men have an ego problem, huh, Patsy?

JOSIE: Ay, Patsy, of course they do.

PATSY: They don't have any bigger problem with it than women do.

SILVIA: [*Sitting.*] That's not true.

JOSIE: No way! Just look at it from a historical point of view—

SILVIA: [*Interrupting, corrects her.*] An historical.

JOSIE: Yeah, yeah, an historical—anyway, what do you think made Diego Rivera be such an asshole to Frida Kahlo? Ego, that's what.

SILVIA: That's right. And what did she do? Huh? Nothing but be completely devoted to him.

PATSY: Oh, pu-lease. She messed around too.

JOSIE: She had to.

SILVIA: That's right. She had to. Because his ego was larger than his murals.

PATSY: Oh, please.

SILVIA: And that's the same kind of ego that makes your husband, Pete, go to happy hour every Friday after work with the rest of the guys from his law office, and not get home till ten, ya todo drunk.

[PATSY *gets up, taking her beer, and leaves the room.* SILVIA, *raising her voice so* PATSY *can still hear her.*]

SILVIA: Even though he knows you don't like it.

JOSIE: [*Getting up and following* PATSY.] Yeah, because se tienen que maderiar, that's men.

SILVIA: [*Also getting up and following the others, exits.*] That's ego.

DOÑA MERCEDES: Oiga, Doña Juanita, pos ¿qué tanto hablan estas muchachas de higos? ¿A poco les gustan mucho?

DOÑA JUANITA: Pos, dicen que it's what makes los hombres act muy macho, fíjese.

DOÑA MERCEDES: ¿Cómo cuando agarran una parranda?

DOÑA JUANITA: Pos, sí, I think so.

DOÑA MERCEDES: No, ¿cómo que los higos? Pero, ¡mira nomás que tonterías! [*Shouting to the girls offstage.*] Es el licor, el tequila. Eso es lo que los hace que hagan tarugada y media. [*Now back in conversation with* DOÑA JUANITA.] Pero así son los hombres. Siempre lo han sido y siempre lo serán. Mire, mi esposo, había veces que agarraba unas parrandas y no regresaba al rancho por muchos días. Y luego, otras veces me venía la gente con chismes . . . ¿y yo? Pos ¿qué podía hacer? De primero sí era bien duro, pos, yo estaba bien jovencita. Me quedaba allí solita en el rancho. . . . Ya después se acostumbra uno, pos ¿qué le va hacer? Ya con una bola de chiquillos. No, la mujer no puede hacer lo mismo que el hombre. Se tiene que aguantar. Se tiene que dar su lugar . . . ¡se tiene que dar a respetar!

DOÑA JUANITA: Pos, mi Ángel, and that's just what he was, an angel. He always treated me con respeto from the very beginning. I can see him right now. Era mi fifteenth birthday y mi 'apá had given me a great big baile. All of a sudden, there was this very handsome man asking me to dance, pero con tanto respeto, you know? Y así fué toda su vida. Oh, sí, se tomaba sus cervecitas, no digo que no, pero allí, at home. He didn't go to las cantinas, no señor. Y siempre, muy trabajador. He wanted more for his kids than we had. He wanted them to have an education, por eso fué que he worked so hard all his life. Pa' que fueran al college. I tell you, Doña Mercedes, they aren't all bad.

DOÑA MERCEDES: Pos no sabría decirle, Doña Juanita, porque yo nomás conocí a un hombre en toda mi vida, y ese—¡era un desgraciado!

PATSY: [*Returning from the living room, followed by* JOSIE *and then* SILVIA.] You guys sound like man-haters. So, Silvia, if you hate men so much, why did you marry Victor? And you, Josie, I suppose you can't stand the sight of Carlos.

JOSIE: Sometimes.

SILVIA: We aren't man-haters. We just said they have an ego problem.

JOSIE: Yeah, that's all we said.

SILVIA: And that's why they act like jerks. Like Frank with Rosalinda, for example. He's always at all the parties, dancing with all the women, and Rosalinda? At home with the kids.

JOSIE: Yeah, I'm glad she's divorcing him.

SILVIA: Mira, even the better ones act like jerks sometimes. When I first met Victor in college, he came on to me con que "I am el Nuevo Hombre, compañera." The New Man! Hah! Después, I had my work cut out trying to make him live up to it.

PATSY: Oh, you're just a perfectionist, Silvia. You have to admit that some women act like jerks too. Look, all I'm saying is that ego is not exclusively a man's problem.

SILVIA: Well, maybe you're right. No, you are right. Ego is not exclusively a man's problem. It's just that more men are afflicted with the problem.

[DOÑA JUANITA *comes up behind* JOSIE *and whispers for her to come check the tamales.*]

JOSIE: Hey, why don't we go check the tamales?

SILVIA: Okay.

JOSIE: Do you think they're done?

SILVIA: I don't know. It takes a long time.

[SILVIA, *followed by* JOSIE, *goes to the stove to check the tamales.* DOÑA MERCEDES *and* DOÑA JUANITA *are already there.* PATSY *hangs back at the table.*]

PATSY: It's been two hours—two long hours. They have to be done.

DOÑA MERCEDES: Esos tamales ya se cocieron, apágales la lumbre y destápalos.

[SILVIA *follows these directions.*]

DOÑA JUANITA: Oh, sí, they're done.

JOSIE: [*Excited.*] Take one out and let's taste it. Oooh, I'll get the salsita I brought.

[JOSIE *goes off to get salsa.*]

SILVIA: I want mine without the salsa. I want to taste every bit of the flavor.

PATSY: What if they aren't any good?

[*Everyone stops in mid-action and stares at her, horrified.*]

PATSY: Well, what if they aren't?

SILVIA: [*Trying to sound very confident.*] Of course they're going to be good. [*Now weaker.*] Why wouldn't they be any good?

PATSY: They could be too hard, or too mushy.

JOSIE: [*Rushing over to* SILVIA, *anxiously.*] Take one out and let's see.

SILVIA: [*Frantically takes a tamal out of the pot and takes it to the table to taste it. Everyone has followed her and all hold their breath as they wait for the verdict, finally.*] It's—. It's—. Perfect!

JOSIE: We did it!

PATSY: [*Snatching the tamal from* SILVIA.] Let me taste it. Hmmmmm!

DOÑA JUANITA: [*Crosses to where the Virgen de Guadalupe candle is and makes the sign of the cross.*] Thank you, Virgencita.

DOÑA MERCEDES: Mira nomás, ¡qué guapas mis muchachitas! ¡Yo sabía que con mis buenos consejos podían hacer unos buenos tamales! Bueno, no tan sabrosos como los míos, pero ya aprenderán. Con más práctica, con más práctica.

JOSIE: Let me have some of that tamal.

PATSY: [*Eating the last bite.*] It's all gone.

JOSIE: You ate it all? Qué selfish eres!

SILVIA: [*Bringing some more tamales to the table.*] Ya, here's some more.

JOSIE: Hmmmmm, I want some salsa.

SILVIA: [*Bringing some plates and forks, sits down.*] Well, now, I think a toast is in order here, ¿qué no?

JOSIE: Yeah!

PATSY: For sure!

SILVIA: [*Raising her beer.*] Here's to us! ¡Las nuevas tamaleras!

PATSY: Here! Here!

JOSIE: ¡Órale!

SILVIA: ¿Sabes qué, Patsy?

PATSY: [*Expecting another attack.*] What?

SILVIA: You did the right thing when you lit that candle. I think we should drink a toast to our mothers.

JOSIE: And our tías.

PATSY: And our abuelitas también.

SILVIA: And to all the women who ever made tamales . . . We couldn't have done it without them.

[*They raise their beers and toast.*]

DOÑA JUANITA: [*Dabbing her eyes with her apron.*] Ay, mi'jas, you did all the work.

DOÑA MERCEDES: [*Now a little misty-eyed, too.*] Sí, muchachitas, trabajaron muy duro y estamos muy orgullosas de ustedes . . . y qué Dios las bendiga.

PATSY: These tamales are all different sizes.

JOSIE: Who cares, they taste great.

SILVIA: [*Determined.*] Next time—. Next time, they'll all be the same size.

[PATSY *and* JOSIE *exchange a worried look. The lights begin to dim on the girls.*]

DOÑA MERCEDES: [*Suddenly very friendly.*] Oiga, Doña Juanita, ¿no le gustaría hacer esto más seguido?

DOÑA JUANITA: You mean como un partnership?

DOÑA MERCEDES: Sí, algo así.

DOÑA JUANITA: Pos, we did help, didn't we? La idea tiene sus possibilities. Let's talk.

[*Blackout.*]

AND WHERE WAS PANCHO VILLA
WHEN YOU REALLY NEEDED HIM?

Silviana Wood

CHARACTERS*

APPLICANT/NARRATOR. May be male or female. Dressed in some kind of working-class uniform, such as a fast-food server, janitor, or sanitation worker.

TRAINEE/PEANUT BUTTER. Female, dressed flashily, heavy makeup, but not "hooker-looking." Tries to act seductively but vulnerability comes through.

JANITOR/MAROMAS. Male, the class clown. Dressed in gray work uniform.

TRAINEE/PENGUIN. Male, ex-con. Heavily tattooed, longish hair, white T-shirt, khakis, tough exterior.

RECEPTIONIST/FIDELIA. Female, the class snob. Dresses in department-store "career" outfits.

*At the beginning of the acto, all of the actors are the same age, which could be late teens, early twenties, etc. However, the older the age, the greater the irony. They become sixth-graders immediately after the first freeze, and return to their "real" age at the end of the acto. Since the acto is composed of many demanding freezes, it is suggested that rehearsal warm-ups, stretches, and body/face "statue" exercises be scheduled as early as possible to allow actors to find dramatic, but comfortable, poses and facial expressions. Also, the director will find a sound cue that is not too intrusive or eerie before each freeze.

Program note: Contains adult language.

An employment training and education center for adults. The walls are drab and covered with various signs regarding health, safety, and griev- ance procedures. There is a water cooler, school desks, and book- shelves. Training manuals, writing supplies, and books are casually strewn around the room. Stage Right, there is a green easel chalkboard with chalk and erasers, and Stage Left, there is an easel with newsprint or "butcher" paper and a thick black marking pen. The receptionist's desktop is messy with papers, books, pens and pencils, calendar, and telephone. A single, dusty, red plastic rose in a vase sits on a corner of the desk.

[*Music: something by Frank Sinatra.*
ALL ACTORS *enter and freeze in position.* FIDELIA, *the receptionist, is at her desk handing an application form to* APPLICANT, *the narrator, who is reaching for the form.* MAROMAS, *the janitor, is "nodding off," leaning on a push broom.* PENGUIN, *a trainee, is sitting at a desk, bored, playing cards.* PEANUT BUTTER, *another trainee, is sitting at a desk behind* MARO- MAS, *applying makeup diligently.*]

APPLICANT: [*Breaks freeze and walks towards a desk, reading application form.*] "Circle last grade completed." [*Beat, direct address to audience.*] Why do they always want to know that? [*Looks around the office.*] What difference does it make anyway? I don't even remember what grade I "completed." It's like I have this big, dark hole in my memory when it comes to school. I remember the sixth grade really good, but I know I went to school after that. Maybe even up to the tenth grade. [*Sits down.*] Did I complete the tenth grade? I can't remember. What I do remember is almost every single day of the sixth grade up to the last day when every- thing in our room got destroyed. Well, it really got destroyed the night before, but Pirulli, the janitor, found it destroyed the morning of the last day of school. I remember how the room looked . . . and nothing after that. I remember the very first day when I started the sixth grade at Davis Elementary School. The new teacher was late.

[*Sound cue: first bell rings.*
ALL *break freeze and move quickly and noisily as they become sixth- graders once again.* FIDELIA *walks to a desk, sits down, and primly stuffs her green crocodile notebook with writing paper, pens, pencils, and sharpeners.* PEANUT BUTTER *takes one of* PENGUIN'S *cards and stuffs it*

down the front of her blouse, then runs to APPLICANT. APPLICANT *stands up and* PEANUT BUTTER *hides behind* APPLICANT. MAROMAS *sneaks up behind* PEANUT BUTTER *and tries to pull up her skirt with the push-broom handle.* APPLICANT *leaps to desk chair and tries to pull the push broom away from* MAROMAS. FIDELIA *runs around, excited but involved at a distance.*
Sound cue: Second bell rings. ALL *freeze.*]

APPLICANT: [*Breaks freeze and sits down, to audience.*] Our new teacher walked in.

PENGUIN: [*Breaks freeze and sits down, to audience.*] We all shut up when we saw her.

MAROMAS: [*Breaks freeze and sits down, to audience.*] We didn't breathe.

PEANUT BUTTER: [*Breaks freeze and sits down, to audience.*] She was so beautiful—like a movie star.

FIDELIA: [*Breaks freeze and sits down, to audience.*] She smiled sweetly. [FIDELIA *smiles sweetly.*] And then she walked to her desk [*Walks to the receptionist's desk.*] and put away her things: a bottle of lotion, a sewing kit, a box of tissues, a desk calendar, a clay kangaroo with pencils and pens in its stomach, and a white vase with red plastic roses. [*Picks up the vase and sets it down again.*]

PEANUT BUTTER: She went to the chalkboard and wrote her name. [PEANUT BUTTER *goes to the chalkboard and writes.*] Miss Folsom. Her fingernails were long and polished, the same color like her lipstick. Then she went to her desk, got a Kleenex, and wiped the chalk from her hands.

[PEANUT BUTTER *does these actions and stands next to* FIDELIA.]

FIDELIA: [*Moves quickly away from* PEANUT BUTTER, *and goes to the chalkboard.*] Again the teacher smiled to us. [*Smiles, as Miss Folsom.*] My name is Miss Folsom. Can everyone say, "Miss Folsom"?

ALL: [*Loudly.*] Miss Folsom.

APPLICANT: [*Walks to the desk and picks up a class list, as Miss Folsom.*] Fine. And now I have to learn your names. [*Reads list.*] Uh-oh, I can see problems already. [*Reads list.*] My four years of torturous high school Spanish won't help me here. Well, I'll just have to seat you in alphabetical order until I've learned your names. When I call your name, step up to the desk I'm pointing to. Please be patient and we can change around later, after I've learned your names. She began to read our names.

MAROMAS: [*Goes to desk and peers over* APPLICANT's *shoulder, as Miss Folsom.*] Goo-ee-ler-mo? Goo-ee-ler-mo Al-may-zan?

PENGUIN: [*After a beat, pointing to a desk.*] Yemo. Eres tú, baboso. La mensa teacher no sabe decir "Guillermo."

ALL: [*Running towards the desk and teasing the invisible Yemo.*] Gooey! Gooey! La teacher dice que te llamas "Gooey."

APPLICANT: [*As Miss Folsom.*] And just what does Goo-ee-ler-mo mean?

FIDELIA: Guillermo means William.

APPLICANT: [*Still as Miss Folsom.*] Ah, William. A noble name. [*Points.*] Take the first desk, Willie.

[MAROMAS *takes out a whistle from his pants pocket and becomes a traffic cop at a parade, blowing the whistle and waving his arms to stop and move the pedestrians.* PENGUIN *and* PEANUT BUTTER *pantomime, turning a jump rope as* APPLICANT *jumps "rope."* ALL *quickly change positions. The chanting and jumping becomes more frenetic as the actors quickly run to different desks as though playing "musical chairs" as their Spanish names get Americanized.*]

ALL: [*In unison.*] "Ice-cream soda, Delaware-y Punch, tell me the initial of your own honey bunch." Francisco became Frankie, Fernando became Fernie, and Alejandro became Alex. "Charlie Chaplin went to France to teach the ladies the hula-hula dance." And then the girls were next—Maria Elena became Mary Helen, Margarita became Margaret, and Julieta became Julie. "Salute to the Captain; bow to the Queen; make a funny face at the old fat King."

[ALL *make a funny face and freeze.*]

MAROMAS: [*Breaks freeze, walks to a front desk, to audience.*] My name is Antonio, but everyone calls me "Maromas." Maromas means somersaults, and my jefita says it's 'cause when I was in her stomach, that's all I did. Maromas.

[MAROMAS *sits down.*]

PENGUIN: [*Breaks freeze, walks to a front desk, to audience.*] My name is Juan

Cardenas, but everyone calls me "Penguin." It's a long story, but I better say it 'cause it's probably the only chance I'll get to say it. See, last year, I got sent to Fort Grant, the reform school way out in the desert. The judge, who was a Mexican but didn't <u>act</u> like one, sent all of us "truants, shoplifters, vagrants, and incorrigibles" to Fort Grant 'cause it was the <u>best thing for us</u>. My only crime was playing hooky. That and having a borracha for a mother. A drunkard. At Fort Grant, they used to lock up our boots so we couldn't escape barefooted through the desert. But that didn't stop me. I ran away without my boots, and when I finally got to Tucson, my feet were all cut up and swollen, so I walked like a penguin in a zoo. Well, they captured me right away and sent me back to Fort Grant. That's when I decided I liked penguins and had one tattooed right here on my arm. See?

[PENGUIN *sits down.*]

PEANUT BUTTER: [*Breaks freeze, walks to a front desk, to audience.*] My real name is Virginia Jaramillo, but the teacher changed it to Virgie. She never learned to say my last name right. It's easy: Jaramillo. But anyway everybody calls me PEANUT BUTTER. And that's because the guys in junior high say that I'm just like the commercial on TV for peanut butter. "Smooth, creamy, and easy to spread." [*Beat.*] I don't get it.

[PEANUT BUTTER *sits down.*]

FIDELIA: [*Breaks freeze, walks to a front desk, to audience.*] My name is Fidelia—that means "faithful"—but everyone calls me Della.

MAROMAS: Lambiona, lengona.

ALL: [*Chanting.*] Liar, liar, pants on fire, hanging on the telephone wire, ¡con las putas de la Calle Meyer!

FIDELIA: [*Ignores them and continues.*] I'm the teacher's pet, and nobody can beat me up 'cause I have a father who can speak real good English, and he'll come to school and make the principal paddle their ass. Oops, I mean paddle their behinds. I speak real good English, too, and I don't belong with these burros.

[FIDELIA *sits down.*]

APPLICANT: [*Breaks freeze, walks to a front desk, to audience.*] The teacher changed my name to—. Miss Folsom finished off the names quick. Chop, chop, and she was done. By the end of the first week, we were all using the new names she gave us. Some of us even forgot our old names.

ALL: [*After a beat.*] But, really, Miss Folsom was the <u>best</u> teacher we ever had in our entire lives.

[ALL *freeze, smiling.*]

FIDELIA: [*Breaks freeze and claps her hands as Miss Folsom.*] Class, class. Attention, please. During the month of October, we will be working on some very special projects. Today, I am going to teach you how to make some wonderful masks.

[ALL *break freeze and take out masks from desks.*]

FIDELIA: [*As Miss Folsom.*] Here are some wonderful materials that I brought from home for you: plaster of Paris, paints, brushes, and artificial hair for mustaches and beards. Let's get to work quickly. [*Claps hands again and* ALL *work on masks, beat.*] Are we done? Let's see your artistic endeavors.

[ALL *stand up holding masks at waist level.*]

FIDELIA: [*As Miss Folsom.*] Wonderful! Now guess what wonderful holiday these masks are for?

ALL: Pa 'l Día de los Muertos.

[ALL *put the calavera masks to their faces.*]

FIDELIA: [*As Miss Folsom.*] No, no, no. Not [*Mispronounces.*] Día de los Muertos. They're for Halloween.

ALL: Halloween? [*Beat.*] Oh.

[ALL *put masks away.*]

FIDELIA: [*As Miss Folsom.*] For the month of November, we will be celebrating the very wonderful Thanksgiving holiday. First, we will create a cornucopia—

ALL: A corna—what?

FIDELIA: Cornucopia. [*Forgets herself.*] Burros, babosos. Oops. [*As Miss Folsom.*] Cornucopia means a horn of plenty overflowing with nature's bounty: fruits, vegetables, grains—forget it. We'll just bake pumpkin pies, and we'll draw a big turkey for the hall bulletin, and I want everyone to bring feathers.

ALL: Feathers?

PENGUIN: Yo sé quien tiene feathers. Las chickens de Doña Nicha!

[ALL *pantomime, silently stalking and pouncing on unsuspecting "chickens."*]

ALL: Teacher! Teacher! Here's the feathers for the turkey.

[ALL *leap forward, proudly holding chicken feathers.* ALL *freeze.*]

MAROMAS: [*Breaks freeze, to audience.*] So for that winter, Doña Nicha's chickens went around without any feathers on their culos and I ate so much pumpkin pie, I got diarrhea all night—for not waiting for it to cool and eating it hot.

APPLICANT: [*Breaks freeze, to audience.*] The Christmas project was the best. Miss Folsom wrote a Christmas play, and everybody in the whole school got to be in it.

FIDELIA: [*Breaks freeze, to audience.*] Right away, I got to be the Virgin Mary.

[FIDELIA *moves to front of stage, kneels, and looks holy.*]

PENGUIN: [*Breaks freeze, to audience.*] Me, Maromas, and Pelón got to be the shepherds "watching o'er the sheep at night."

[PENGUIN *stands behind* FIDELIA.]

PEANUT BUTTER: [*Breaks freeze, to audience.*] I got to be the Virgin Mary's friend, or cousin, who gets pregnant first by the angels—or somebody. [*Beat.*] I forget.

[PEANUT BUTTER *stands next to* FIDELIA, *who quickly moves away from her.* MAROMAS *gets either the push broom or a chalkboard pointer and tiptoes to* PEANUT BUTTER *to lift her skirt.*]

FIDELIA: [*As Miss Folsom, sees* MAROMAS, *stands up.*] Tony! Stop that this instant. Okay, you're no longer a shepherd; you're now one of the Three Wise Men, so you, Johnny, and you [*Points to* APPLICANT.] come and stand here, right next to me where I can keep an eye on you. Places. Places, everyone. Pay attention. I'll be standing at the piano, and when I turn and nod my head, like this, that's your cue for you to sing your song.

[FIDELIA *nods her head.*]

MAROMAS, PENGUIN, and APPLICANT [*Singing.*]: We three kings of Orient are/ bearing gifts we travel afar—

FIDELIA: [*Walking to her former place as Virgin Mary, kneels, to audience.*] It was the best Christmas show ever seen in the history of Davis Elementary School. The best.

ALL: [*Singing.*] Moor and mountain/field and fountain/following yonder star. [ALL *freeze.*]

APPLICANT: [*Breaks freeze, to audience.*] After Christmas vacation, we had to learn everything all over again. We had talked in Spanish for two whole weeks, and now nothing sounded right to Miss Folsom. We were the worst when the words had the "ch" sound in them.

PEANUT BUTTER: [*Breaks freeze, to audience.*] Miss Folsom would stick out her lips like a monkey on "Tarzan" and say a hundred times: "ch, ch, ch, ch."

MAROMAS: [*Breaks freeze, to audience.*] She would write long lists and make us say a sentence with the word.

[MAROMAS *goes to chalkboard or easel and writes words: check, church, chicken, chairs, and change.*]

PENGUIN: [*Breaks freeze.*] My mother gets a welfare sheck.

MAROMAS: [*Breaks freeze.*] We go to shursh every Sunday.

FIDELIA: [*Breaks freeze.*] Liar! [*Beat, showing off.*] When my father gets his <u>check</u> from working in the mines, we go to <u>church</u>, and then we eat <u>chicken</u> in the basket at Kippy's, sitting on the <u>chairs</u> outside, waiting for the <u>change</u>.

PEANUT BUTTER: [*As Miss Folsom.*] Very good, Della. But let's keep working on that "ch" sound. [*Goes to write.*] Let's review our "sh" words so that we can hear the difference between the "ch" sound and the "sh" sound. [*Writes.*] Please notice these words with the "ch" sound: chip, cheap, and chip. And now [*Writes the "sh" list.*] notice these words with the "sh" sound: ship, sheep, and sheet.

ALL: [*Reciting.*] Chip, cheap, chip, ship, shee—shit!

[ALL *freeze.*]

APPLICANT: [*Breaks freeze, to audience.*] I guess something was wrong with our tongues or ears 'cause it always sounded right to us, and I couldn't see any difference between how Miss Folsom said the words and how we said them. Anyway, just when I thought I was getting the "ch" sound and the "sh" sound, Miss Folsom gets me for adding an extra "g" to the words ending with "g" plus the "ing" You know, like in ring, sing, and bring. She said I said: ring-ging, sing-ging, and bring-ging, but I never heard that extra "g." And how about when all those words sound the same but are spelled different? Like so, sew, and sow? Or if the words are spelled exactly the same but sound way different? Like sow, [APPLICANT *goes to chalkboard or easel and writes word.*] like the farmer and his land, and sow, the mama pig? It seemed like everything I said was wrong. But my very worst mistake was not knowing the difference between "anywhere" and "nowhere." [APPLICANT *writes these two words.*] It got so I didn't want to talk in English. Or Spanish. Talking was giving me a headache, and sometimes I even felt like crying. [APPLICANT *goes to a desk.*] I sat in the last chair, and I never put up my hand to ask Miss Folsom anything or to give an answer. [APPLICANT *sits down.*] If she asked me a question, I wouldn't answer, and someone else would eventually answer for me. Finally, she stopped asking me anything, and I felt like the Invisible Man. [APPLICANT *puts head down.*]

FIDELIA: [*Breaks freeze, as Miss Folsom.*] It's raining, and I realize it's not fun having to stay inside all day, but we must review our fractions.

[*She turns to write.*]

MAROMAS: [*Breaks freeze, to* PEANUT BUTTER.] Hey, Peanut Butter. Look into your blouse and spell "attic."

[APPLICANT *looks up.*]

PEANUT BUTTER: [*Breaks freeze, looks into her blouse.*] Spell qué?

PENGUIN: [*Breaks freeze, to* PEANUT BUTTER.] Attic, babosa. Look. [PENGUIN *writes on piece of paper.*] Attic.

FIDELIA: [*As Miss Folsom, having drawn a circle.*] This circle represents a pie—

MAROMAS: What kind of pie? Apple, peaches, pumpkin pie?

FIDELIA: [*As Miss Folsom.*] Tony, if you divide the pie into eighths, and you ate three-quarters of the pie, how many eighths would you have left?

APPLICANT: Penguin knew right away that Miss Folsom was trying to trick Maromas, so he tried to show Maromas two fingers for the answer. But Maromas didn't see the two fingers, so he pretended to think real hard. He wrinkled his face, squinted his eyes, and put one finger to his brain.

[MAROMAS *does these things.*]

APPLICANT: Then he said, real happy—

MAROMAS: No eighths, no eighths left at all. If I had a pie, I would eat it all.

[ALL *laugh as if it's the funniest thing they've ever heard.* ALL *freeze.*]

APPLICANT: [*Breaks freeze, to audience.*] When it finally stopped raining, it got hot again. And then, the very worst thing that could ever happen to a kid in school—

ALL: [*After a beat, break freeze, to audience.*] ¡Piojos!

[*Music: "Blue Danube" waltz.*
ALL, *with identical, synchronized movements, begin to scratch the napes of their heads slowly, with tentative movements, with one hand. Their hands move up slowly to the back of their heads. Then the other hand comes up to scratch the nape of their heads, then both hands slowly move upward. The movements speed up until all are scratching their heads furiously with both hands.* ALL *freeze.*]

APPLICANT: [*Breaks freeze, to audience.*] Miss Folsom finally figured out what was wrong, and she called the Health Department to send a visiting nurse to check our heads for piojos. This visiting nurse sure didn't like to visit us, especially if it was to check for cooties. We could tell because she wouldn't even touch us.

[FIDELIA *pantomimes or uses real props as* APPLICANT *describes.*]

APPLICANT: She wore rubber gloves and separated our hair with two throat sticks.

FIDELIA: [*As Visiting Nurse, checks* PEANUT BUTTER's *hair.*] My, my.

APPLICANT: That's all she ever said: my, my. And that meant cooties for sure.

FIDELIA: [*As Visiting Nurse, goes to* PENGUIN *and checks his head.*] My, my. [*Goes to* MAROMAS *and checks his head.*] My, my. [*Goes to* APPLICANT *and checks his head.*] My, my.

[*The Visiting Nurse checks her own head.*]

ALL: My, my.

[ALL *freeze.*]

APPLICANT: [*Breaks freeze, to audience.*] Piojos weren't so bad really. They just needed a head to live in. When I didn't want to read, I would watch the cooties in the head in front of me, crossing from one side of the braids to the other, like in a busy street corner. Or sometimes, the piojos would visit in the middle of the braids like two families visiting over a fence yard. Or it would turn into a war with marching soldiers and sneaky spies. What was really bad about the piojos was the stinky green medicine the visiting nurse made us take home, or the girls having to get their braids cut off. Which is what happened to Fidelia—Della—one time. Her father even came to school walking and talking like a tough Texan, wanting to know who gave his daughter the cooties: "¿Cuál de ustedes cabrones le dio sus piojos a mi hija?" But nobody knew. [*Beat.*] Since we couldn't hear the difference on how to talk good English, Miss Folsom brought her tape recorder to class. We had to stand in front of everybody and give our names into it with a story about our family. When it was my turn, I wouldn't go to the front, so Miss Folsom came to my desk and put the microphone in my face.

FIDELIA: [*Breaks freeze, goes to* APPLICANT *as Miss Folsom, with tape recorder and microphone.*] Describe your family, starting with your parents. What is your father's name? What does he do for a living?

[FIDELIA *freezes.*]

APPLICANT: [*To audience.*] What father? I didn't have a father. [*Beat.*] My throat was drying up, and I didn't have saliva to swallow. I felt like a tunnel was between my ears and my brains. I felt like I was choking and exploding at the same time. I felt—

MAROMAS: [*Breaks freeze and jumps up, goes to* FIDELIA *and grabs the microphone, and pretends to be a television show host.*] Which door do you choose? Number one? A Westinghouse freezer, refrigerator, and range. Number two? An unforgettable vacation for two in Barcelona, Spain.

[*Music cue: "El relicario."*]

PEANUT BUTTER: [*Breaks freeze, runs to desk, grabs a plastic red rose, sticks it into her mouth, and pulls up her skirt.*] Pick door number two and dance the flamingo in Barcelona, Spain.

[PEANUT BUTTER *dances what she thinks are flamenco steps.*]

PENGUIN: [*Breaks freeze, becomes a suave matador, to* MAROMAS.] ¡Olé! ¡Olé! [PENGUIN *swings a cape and* MAROMAS, *as bull, charges the cape.*]

ALL: ¡Olé!

[ALL *freeze.*]

FIDELIA: [*Breaks freeze, as Miss Folsom.*] Class, class. Since you obviously cannot cooperate with my efforts, you will now have to stay after school and write your life stories.

MAROMAS: [*Breaks freeze.*] Miss! Miss! Can I have a shit of paper?

FIDELIA: [*As Miss Folsom.*] A what?

ALL: [*Break freeze.*] A shit of paper.

MAROMAS: A shit of paper. For my story.

FIDELIA: [*As Miss Folsom, gives writing assignment.*] I want each one of you to write what you want to be when you grow up. Use your imagination and let nothing stop your thoughts. Be as original and creative as you can possibly—

PENGUIN: Miss. Miss. The principal wants to see you. Right now.

PEANUT BUTTER: [*Writing.*] I want to be a nurse, or a secretary, or a waitress at Kippy's Hamburgers.

MAROMAS: [*Writing.*] I want to be a television movie star, or a dentist, or a fireman.

PENGUIN: [*Writing.*] I want to be a public defender, or a judge, or a prison guard.

FIDELIA: [*Writing.*] I want to be an astro-physicist, or a corporate lawyer, or a crooked politician. Just kidding.

APPLICANT: [*Writing.*] I want to be—. I want to be a—

PENGUIN: [*Gets tape recorder and recites his favorite poem.*] "¡Pancho Villa mató a su tía, con un cuchillo que no servía!" [*Sings.*] "Guadalajara, Guadalajara, 'garra un palito y come cagada."

PEANUT BUTTER: [*Goes to* PENGUIN *and sings romantically, like Rocío Durcal.*] Yo a ti un beso te pedí, y tú me lo negaste, ¡un chingazo te metí!

MAROMAS: [*To* APPLICANT.] Eh, pues, you never said what you want to be someday.

APPLICANT: I want—. I want to be a—something!

PENGUIN: A something? You're already a something, ¿qué no?

APPLICANT: No, I'm not. [*Insists.*] I want to be a something.

MAROMAS: A something what? You gotta be a something something.

APPLICANT: I don't know. Whatever. Lo que sea.

PEANUT BUTTER: [*Goes to* APPLICANT.] ¿Lo que sea? [*Beat.*] Qué será, será, ¿qué no?

[ALL *group themselves around* APPLICANT *and sing chorus of "Qué Será, Será" like Doris Day. Then* ALL *freeze.*]

APPLICANT: [*Breaks freeze, to audience.*] By the time school was almost over—the very last week—people were saying that it was going to be the hottest summer in the history of Arizona. It was so hot, even with all the windows opened. Miss Folsom wouldn't let us wet our faces and hair, or put wet paper towels on our foreheads or our necks because she said it would just make us hotter. I don't know how, but that's what she said.

FIDELIA: [*Breaks freeze, as Miss Folsom, to the class.*] The best thing to do is to think of cool places, like Alaska, or cool things, like snow.

APPLICANT: And she never sweated, so it worked for her. [*Beat.*] So maybe, just maybe, it was the heat that destroyed the room. Like I said, it was the last week of school—hey, why don't <u>you</u> figure out what happened?

[APPLICANT *moves to observe. The following is fast paced, kaleidoscope-like, Downstage, with defined lights.*]

PENGUIN: [*Breaks freeze, to audience.*] I hadn't been to school for almost six days 'cause my jefita was "sick."

PEANUT BUTTER: [*Breaks freeze, goes to* PENGUIN, *as la drunken jefita.*] No chingues conmigo, Penguin. And don't get so high and mighty 'cause I'll kick your ass. Pues, quién eres tú, to tell me what I can or can't do?

PENGUIN: 'amá, I'm not telling you anything. But I didn't go to school all last week, and I had to miss today 'cause you're sick and throwing up. This is the last week of school, and I don't want to flunk again. Or get sent to Fort Grant for truancy. La teacher dijo que—

PEANUT BUTTER: Que coma mierda la teacher. [*Setting table.*] What does she know anyway? All she does is stand there, looking pretty. She should try working on the assembly line for just one day. Like I do. Roasting to death right along with the potato chips. And all that salt flying around in the air, in your mouth, in your lungs. Then see if she wouldn't die for a nice cold beer after work. [*Beat, changes tone.*] Mira, mi'jo, I made your favorite: chile con carne. Refried beans and tortillas, too. Siéntate, hijo. Where did I leave my beer? Ah, here it is. [*Pointedly.*] La comida mexicana no es comida sin una cervecita, ¿verdad?

ALL: [*Break freeze.*] We'll drink to that!

[ALL *freeze.*]

PENGUIN: [*To audience.*] So la jefita's getting drunk, someone's knocking at the door, and it's Miss Folsom. La jefita thinks it's the television reporter from Channel 9, then she thinks Miss Folsom's from the "Juvie," so she starts to cry.

FIDELIA: [*Breaks freeze, as Miss Folsom.*] You do realize, don't you, that I have no choice but to report this to the proper authorities?

[LA JEFITA *wails drunkenly.* FIDELIA, PENGUIN, *and* PEANUT BUTTER *react and freeze.*]

APPLICANT: [*To audience.*] That happened on Monday. On Tuesday, Miss Folsom decided to check our lunches to see if they were healthy, you know, with food from the basic food groups she always wanted us to be eating. Like a quart of milk a day. Fresh vegetables and fruits. Meat and fish. She went up to Maromas.

MAROMAS: [*Breaks freeze, to audience.*] I'm ready to eat my lunch when she comes right up behind me.

FIDELIA: [*Breaks freeze, as Miss Folsom.*] Tony, let me see your lunch. [*Beat.*] Tony, if you don't let me see your lunch, you will not be permitted to attend the picnic and swimming party Friday. Let me see your lunch.

MAROMAS: She had one hand on my shoulder and was gonna reach down to grab my lunch. But I jerked away, and then she got a hold of my shirt real tight. I stood up and the shirt got torned. I pushed her hard and told her to stick the picnic up her ass. You know why I wouldn't let her see my lunch? Because it was just burritos de frijoles, and nothing from the fucking basic groups she had on the walls. I didn't learn much in school, but one thing I did learn was you have the right to be left alone. And that includes your lunch, ¿qué no?

ALL: [*Break freeze, to audience.*] Damn right. Your burritos de frijoles are protected by the Constitution and the Bill of Rights.

[ALL *freeze.*]

APPLICANT: [*To audience.*] On Wednesday, Miss Folsom brought a box of her used winter clothes and gave them to Peanut Butter right in front of everybody.

PEANUT BUTTER: I was so embarrassed. All my clothes were from the second-hand. And sometimes they didn't even fit me right.

[PEANUT BUTTER *hunches her shoulders.*]

FIDELIA: [*Breaks freeze, as Miss Folsom, showing* PEANUT BUTTER *the clothes.*] Virginia, these are for you. They're almost brand new and will fit you much better than what you're wearing now. Of course, you'll have to wait until it's wintertime. [*Reverts to* FIDELIA *and taunts* PEANUT BUTTER.] A ver si te dio un bra, chichona. [FIDELIA *laughs.*]

PEANUT BUTTER: Well, you know that after school I beat the shit out of her. And she never even told her father 'cause she knew she was guilty. For laughing. [*Beat.*] But the one I really wanted to beat was Miss Folsom, for being so—

ALL: [*Break freeze.*] ¡Pendeja!

[ALL *freeze.*]

APPLICANT: Nothing exciting happened on Thursday. We were all excited because of the picnic and swimming party next day. And because school was finally ending. Since we were behind in our reading in the history book, Miss Folsom wanted us to catch up. So we had to read all day because we were barely in World War II, and Miss Folsom wanted us to reach the Korean War before lunch. Maromas kept asking questions to stall around.

MAROMAS: [*Breaks freeze.*] Miss! Miss! How come we had to bomb Japan and kill so many people?

FIDELIA: [*Breaks freeze, as Miss Folsom, sternly and out of patience.*] Because sometimes you have to destroy in order to end destruction.

[ALL *freeze.*]

APPLICANT: [*To audience.*] She sounded just like my hero—Superman. [*Beat.*]

After lunch, Miss Folsom introduced a lady who was going to teach fifth grade the next year, and Miss Folsom made us keep reading to ourselves while she showed the new teacher what we did for projects. Miss Folsom showed her the giant teeth that she used to teach us how to brush our teeth, the charts and stars, the medicine and the special combs for the piojos, and the tape recorder she was using every single day now. [*Beat.*] I was bored with the reading, so I pretended to read, but I was really listening to the two teachers. They were talking in real big words about low motivation, low achievement, inflated grades, unrealistic goals, and where to keep the yogurt, when the bell rang.

[*Sound cue: Bell rings.* ALL *break freeze and get in line.*]

APPLICANT [*Breaks freeze.*] Miss Folsom was passing out the permission slips we needed for the picnic and swimming next day. Peanut Butter was going to show the boys a new underwater game, and everybody right away wanted to be the octopus. About half of us were still in line when the new teacher went to the tape recorder on top of Miss Folsom's desk and started to play it. Me, Penguin, Maromas, and Peanut Butter were the closest to her when my voice came out of the tape recorder. The new teacher heard my voice and started to laugh. At first it was a soft laugh, and then it got bigger and bigger. Like when you break a window and the breaking glass spreads out and then falls to the ground.

FIDELIA: [*After a beat, breaks freeze, as the new teacher, laughing.*] My God, Charlene, do they all speak like that?

[FIDELIA *freezes.*]

APPLICANT: Miss Folsom looked at us. It seemed like we were all frozen. My ears had that tunnel feeling, but I could hear the wind moving the venetian blinds on the windows, making them rattle. Miss Folsom still just looked at us, and then finally at the new teacher. A funny look went between them, but I don't know what it meant. [*Beat.*] And that's the last thing I remember about the last week of school and the day before school ended. I remember the new teacher's laugh, and Miss Folsom's look to us. But what I remember the most was the look Miss Folsom gave the new teacher. [*Beat.*] And I remembered what she had told Maromas about the bombing in Japan: "sometimes you have to destroy in order to end destruction." So I waited for Pancho Villa to come charging into the room. [*Beat.*] But I waited for nothing.

[Sound cue: trumpet or bugle.
Music cue: "La marcha de Zacatecas."
As music plays, all actors pantomime their destruction of the room
in stylized movement and end with synchronized movements in the
drum or trumpet section of the song, and freeze.]

APPLICANT: [*Breaks freeze, to audience.*] The next morning, we lined up outside to say the "Pledge of Allegiance" and sing, "Oh, say can you see," and we marched up the stairs with Miss Folsom. When she opened the door for us, she looked inside the room. Her face was white, then green-like. She looked like she was going to throw up, so Fidelia ran for the principal. The rest of us went past Miss Folsom and looked at the room. It was like an explosion had broken everything in the room. The "Five Basic Food Groups" pictures on the wall were cut up into confetti. Miss Folsom's tape recorder was smashed, and pieces of the black plastic were all over the room. And the tapes were like tangled spaghetti. Paint of all colors was on everything. The stinky cootie medicine was green and sticky on all the books. Miss Folsom's desk looked like someone had hit it with an ax. On the back table sat the giant teeth, only now some of the teeth were missing or just hanging. It looked like they had been glued together shut, with something like denture adhesive. The principal came up and made us sit in the library while Pirulli, the janitor, cleaned it all up while we waited.

PENGUIN: [*Breaks freeze, as Pirulli, the school janitor, with push broom.*] Bunch of goddamn animals.

[PENGUIN *cleans quietly.*]

FIDELIA: [*Breaks freeze, to audience.*] The principal put his arm on Miss Folsom's shoulder and told her to go home, but she wouldn't. She just sat there blowing her nose while the principal talked to each one of the burros to find out who did it. But nobody knew. I sure didn't know.

MAROMAS: [*Breaks freeze, to audience.*] Through the window, we could see the other kids going to the park for the picnic and swimming. They were going to eat hot dogs, potato chips, and sodas.

PEANUT BUTTER: [*Breaks freeze, to audience.*] When Pirulli was finally done cleaning, he came and told Miss Folsom he was done. Miss Folsom thanked him and told us to go home. Everyone grabbed their towels and shorts and ran down the stairs to catch up with the principal to ask him if we could still go to the picnic. He said okay.

APPLICANT: I got my towel and shorts, too, and started to go. But halfway there I changed my mind. [APPLICANT *walks to the board or easel that has the words "anywhere" and "nowhere" written on it. Beat. Points to "anywhere."*] I didn't go anywhere. [*Erases or rips the paper off, and looks around at the others.*] <u>We</u> didn't go anywhere.

[*After a beat, music: Same Frank Sinatra tune.*
ALL *move slowly to music until they end up in exact freeze position at start of acto.*]

APPLICANT: [*Breaks freeze and takes the application form from the* RECEPTIONIST, *walks to a desk but does not sit down, reads.*] "Circle last grade completed."

[APPLICANT *starts to sit down angrily and freezes before reaching bottom of chair.*]

F U C H S I A

Janis Astor del Valle

CHARACTERS

NINA. A Puerto Rican lesbian, hopeful romantic whose hopes often get punctured by circumstance. Her friends equal her family—they are everything to her—but she sometimes lets herself get sidetracked by unworthy people. Twenty-thirty–something.

RED. Nina's best friend, an African American gay male diva. Very dependable, inclined to demand honesty. Twenty-thirty–something.

MANNY. Nina's other best friend, a gay papi chulo (an irresistibly cute and charming man, the kind you love to hate). Puerto Rican, loving, but has a tendency to be unreliable, twenty-something.

ALONSO. Another of Nina's best friends, a gay Cuban man. Bittersweet realist, with a tendency toward elitism, twenty-thirty–something.

CHICKY. Nina's estranged longtime friend, an African American–Puerto Rican lesbian. Tough but sweet and passionate, owns a bodega, thirty-something.

SANTOS. Nina's 38-year-old uncle, a gay Puerto Rican. Lovable, battles tragedy with humor.

SETTING

The action takes place late Tuesday evening into early Wednesday morning, late February 1995.

Set Notes: The set should be divided into four sections: a) a studio apartment (Scene One); b) a van (Scenes Two, Four, Five); c) a bodega (Scene Three); and d) a hospital room (Scenes One, Four, Five).

(a) The studio apartment is a railroad-type structure, consisting of a small kitchen area with full-size sink, stove/oven, and refrigerator, as well as ample counter space to double as an eating area (two stools can fit under the counter). The one and only entrance to the apartment is through the kitchen; a coat tree stands near the front door.

(b) The van in Scene Three is almost constantly moving, except for a short stop at Sucelt, the Latina comida–coffee shop. This effect can be achieved by setting up four chairs (with or without) cushions and arranging creative lighting and sound to give the illusion of a motor vehicle in motion. In Scene Four, the van is moving until a flat tire renders it stationary on the Manhattan Bridge, midway between the two boroughs. As the lights go out in the middle of the scene, the chairs can be slightly altered—even pushed partially offstage—to indicate the van's been pulled over, and a spare tire can be rolled out to imply the changing of the tire.

(c) Chicky's bodega in Scene Three should have a very compact but tidy atmosphere—there may be barely enough room for everything, but everything's in its place, very clean, very neat. Many Spanish products should be displayed (i.e., Goya beans, Cafe Bustelo), as well as a candy rack featuring plain and peanut M&M's. The bodega is in East New York.

d] The hospital room is a single one (Santos may be in isolation), complete with bed, two visitors' chairs, small refrigerator, night table, and rolling tray. SANTOS has an IV attached to his arm; the bag for this IV hangs upon a six-foot-long metal rod with hooks at the top and wheels on the bottom.

This play is inspired by, and dedicated to, Raymond del Valle, Titi Esther, Carmen, Eric, Victor, Roylan, Stacy, and Judith.

Scene One

[At rise: "Lluvia Gris" ("Stormy Weather"), by Olga Guillot, plays. Lights up slowly on Santos' hospital room; SANTOS sits in his wheelchair. Lights up slowly on Nina's studio apartment, East Village, New York City, 9:45 P.M., Tuesday, late February 1995. In the kitchen area, NINA hovers at the oven, basting and tending to a pernil; RED sits on a stool near the counter.]

SANTOS: Nina? Is that you? What month is it?

[Lights down on hospital.]

RED: How is he?

NINA: I didn't see him today; I had to make the pernil. Where's papi chulo?

RED: I don't even wanna know.

NINA: I'm not re-heating this for him.

RED: You better not. We're not waiting—when it's ready, it's ready.

NINA: It's been ready.

RED: Let's eat.

NINA: Sure you don't want some wine?

RED: Nina, we don't need it; the juice is fine.

NINA: [*Serving pernil and arroz con pollo to* RED.] Mira, I fucked up the rice—I don't think I put enough water; some of it may be a little hard. Pues, it was my first time, so you're my guinea pig.

RED: You never made arroz con pollo before?

NINA: No. [*Serves herself.*] This is it.

RED: [*Tasting.*] Damn, it's good.

NINA: Ay, stop. You don't have to pretend.

RED: No, I'm serious. I like your fuck-ups.

NINA: 'Pérate. [NINA *takes* RED's *hand.*] Gracias a Dios for these gifts we receive, we take these blessings to nourish our bodies in Christ's name, y por favor watch over Santos y toda la familia. Amen. [*Silence.*] He's not coming.

RED: He's coming.

NINA: Alonso will be here right after work.

RED: He'll probably show up before the papi.

NINA: Bueno, if Manny's gonna be that late he shouldn't bother to come at all. I've had it with him.

RED: You and me both. [*Pause.*] So, you didn't talk to Santos today?

NINA: [*Defensive.*] No. I told you I was cooking. How's the pernil?

RED: ¡Perfecto! Como siempre. [*Silence.*] Hey, where's Vanessa?

[NINA *shoots* RED *a look.*]

RED: Oh, shit. ¿Qué pasó?

NINA: Yo no sé. [*Pause.*] I told her to get the fuck out. [*Eyeing his plate.*] You don't like olives?

RED: No. What did she do?

NINA: She got the fuck out.

RED: I mean, what did she do to make you say that?

NINA: It's what she didn't do.

[*The intercom buzzer sounds.* RED *and* NINA *exchange a look; neither one moves for a beat.* NINA *rises to speak into the intercom.*]

NINA: [*Pressing the "talk" and "listen" buttons alternately.*] ¿Quién es?

MANNY: [*Offstage, through the intercom.*] Manny.

[NINA *buzzes him in, then sits.*]

NINA: I'm not serving him.

RED: You shouldn't even open the door.

NINA: More juice?

RED: [*Rising.*] I got it.

[*Doorbell rings;* NINA *starts to rise.*]

RED: Siéntate and enjoy your meal.

[RED *opens the door.* MANNY *stands, carrying a dozen long-stemmed red roses.*]

MANNY: Hola.

[MANNY *tries to plant a kiss on* RED's *lips, but* RED *turns his face so the kiss lands on his cheek.* MANNY *enters, crossing to* NINA.]

MANNY: Ay, you wouldn't believe what I've been through.

RED: [*Sitting.*] We've already started.

MANNY: [*Handing* NINA *flowers.*] Mira, for you.

NINA: Gracias.

[NINA *embraces* MANNY.]

MANNY: Pues, you look good.

[NINA *smiles sadly and begins looking for a vase.*]

MANNY: [*Taking flowers from* NINA.] Dame, I'll do it. I left work early so I could get to Century 21's one-day sale, and ended up spending two and a half hours in line.

NINA: [*Sitting.*] Everything's on the stove; there's some pernil already sliced, but I don't know if it's still warm.

RED: He knows how to use the microwave.

MANNY: Claro. [*To* NINA.] Don't worry, I'll do it—you just relax. [MANNY *starts fixing a plate.*] Ay, y la gente, pushing and shoving and grabbing—mira, I almost had it out with this queen—

RED: [*Cutting* MANNY *off.*] I bet you did.

MANNY: —over the last pair of Calvin black bikinis—extra large.

RED: [*Cutting.*] You mean extra small.

MANNY: I had picked up the box first and before I knew what hit me, with one swoosh, she snatched them up, out of my hands—I said, "Oh, no, Mary, don't even think about it," and snatched them right back. Where's the garlic bread?

NINA: Ay, Dios mío! I forgot the garlic bread.

RED: We can do without.

MANNY: I'll go get some.

NINA: No, I bought a whole loaf this morning.

MANNY: Italian or French?

NINA: French.

MANNY: You got fresh garlic?

NINA: Sí.

MANNY: Entonces, I'll make it. [*Opening the fridge.*] ¿Dónde?

NINA: [*Gets up to show him.*] Aquí.

[NINA *sits back down.*]

MANNY: ¿Y Nessa?

[RED *tries to signal* MANNY, *who doesn't get it at first.*]

NINA: She may drop by later.

MANNY: [*Realizing.*] Ay, no. Who left who?

RED: Manny.

NINA: [*To* RED.] It's okay. [*To* MANNY.] She left.

RED: After you threw her out.

NINA: Red.

RED: C'mon, Nina, if you're gonna tell it, tell it right.

NINA: [*To* MANNY.] Put a little oregano.

MANNY: [*Searching the cabinets.*] No lo veo.

[NINA *rises to get oregano.*]

MANNY: Oh, pero, the best buy—and I have to say, this was really smart shopping on my part—was the Donna Karan silk ties. They were $25.99 each, pero I found a tiny section of the table that no one else seemed to notice, it had seven for $149, that's like a $5.00 savings on each tie—so, I got one for every color of the rainbow.

NINA: [*To* MANNY.] Entonces, where you been?

MANNY: Shopping.

NINA: I mean after that.

MANNY: I told you how long I stood in line.

NINA: Yeah, but c'mon, you left work early, that means 1:00 for you.

MANNY: I didn't leave that early. I had lunch first.

NINA: Todavía, that was hours ago. What else have you been doing?

MANNY: Oye, what's with you, givin' me the third degree? You sound like my fuckin' mother.

[NINA *stares at* MANNY *in hurt anger for a beat, then goes to the living room, puts on a CD—Ella Fitzgerald, "Blues in the Night."*]

RED: [*To* MANNY.] Dinner was supposed to be at eight.

MANNY: I told her I would be a little late.

RED: Oh, like you just had to have a new pair of Calvins tonight. Please.

MANNY: I had to take care of some—

RED: C–A–R–L–O–S.

MANNY: It ain't even about that.

RED: Oh, please. You gonna tell me you didn't see him?

MANNY: Only for a minute. But it wasn't—

RED: You couldn't go one day without a little piece?

MANNY: Fuck you!

RED: You already tried, and it didn't work—remember?

MANNY: You're really a shit, ¿tú sabes?

RED: At least I show up.

MANNY: I really didn't think it was gonna be such a big deal. She got you.

RED: But she needs everybody. Manny, I don't think you realize—

MANNY: I know this thing with her uncle is breakin' her—

RED: This "thing"? This "thing" is fuckin' killin' him, day by fuckin' day. This "thing" has a name. Why can't we just say it? Santos has AIDS.

MANNY: Red. Not so loud.

RED: No, I'm tired of tiptoein' around. Santos was never quiet, so why should we be?

NINA: [*Calling from the living room.*] Stop fighting and watch the garlic bread. If you burn it this time, you're never setting foot in my cocina again.

[MANNY *and* RED *exchange a look.* NINA *returns to the kitchen.*]

NINA: Oye, I can't leave you two alone for one minute without you goin' at it.

MANNY: We weren't fighting, we were debating—

RED: Debunking.

MANNY: Discoursing.

RED: DISS-ing.

NINA: Ay, coño, ¡basta!

[*The doorbell sounds.* NINA *immediately rises.*]

MANNY: [*Rising.*] I'll get it.

NINA: [*Crossing to the door.*] No, no—please, allow me.

RED: You're upsetting her.

MANNY: Me?

RED: Is the sky blue? Are the beans black?

MANNY: That's right, I'm always the villain.

[NINA *opens the door,* ALONSO *enters with a bouquet of eucalyptus. They kiss hello.*]

ALONSO: [*Waving to* RED *and* MANNY.] Hi, guys.

NINA: [*Taking the eucalyptus.*] My favorite. Oye, how did you get in?

[*Throughout the following,* NINA *gets a vase, fills with water, arranges the eucalyptus.*]

ALONSO: A cute blonde.

NINA: Did you get his number?

ALONSO: No, I wanted to check him out with you first. 6' 1", green eyes, Hugh Grant's hair, Denzel's body, Antonio Banderas' lower lip.

MANNY: What was he wearing?

ALONSO: Versace, cómo no.

NINA: Midwestern accent?

ALONSO: Yeah.

NINA: Bubble butt?

ALONSO: That's the one.

NINA: 3A, track lights, Puccini, Art Deco, mucho spinach pasta, romano cheese.

ALONSO: Romano cheese? Ay, no! Grated parmesan reggiano or nothing at all.

MANNY: Tú sabes, I almost bought a Versace suit today, but I chose an [*Mispronouncing.*] Armani instead.

ALONSO: Oh, please.

MANNY: Say what you want, but I know how to shop. I never pay full price for anything. Why should I, when I know I can hit the clearance racks? It all comes down to patience and timing. Mira, I got a dozen Perry Ellis oxfords—salmon pink, sky blue, sea green, and sunny yellow—

RED: To go with the ties. Rainbows and pastels—how colorful.

ALONSO: Sounds like you raided the Crayola crayon factory.

MANNY: Ha, ha, very funny. I was at the Century 21 one-day sale.

ALONSO: You are so Puerto Rican.

MANNY: You should go there sometime—

ALONSO: ¡Ave María! No self-respecting Cuban would be caught dead in there.

NINA: ¡'Pérate! I only counted four colors. You said you bought twelve.

MANNY: Three of each. I never buy one of anything. That's the secret to keeping clothes fresh. Speaking of fresh, wait 'til you see the pinstriped Armani suit I got. That thing is fierce. It's gonna look so crisp when it's pressed.

ALONSO: Speaking of pressed, where is Miss Thing?

NINA: Which one? I got two of 'em right here.

ALONSO: Your Miss Thing—Nessa.

NINA: She's probably on her way to L.A. by now.

ALONSO: She got a gig?

NINA: Yeah.

ALONSO: How long?

NINA: No lo sé. [*Crossing to the stove.*] Hungry?

ALONSO: I can get it.

MANNY: Here, lemme serve him.

[MANNY *begins fixing a plate for Alonso.*]

ALONSO: Be still, mi corazón. [*To* MANNY.] I didn't know you liked to serve.

MANNY: There's a lotta things you don't know about me.

NINA: And don't wanna know.

MANNY: [*To* NINA.] You don't got anymore knives.

ALONSO: [*To* NINA.] Entonces, you still breakin' up?

NINA: [*At the sink, cleaning a knife.*] We broke.

[NINA *hands the knife to* MANNY.]

ALONSO: Ay, you'll fly to L.A. and she'll be fuckin' your brains out by tomorrow night.

NINA: I don't think so. I told her to get the fuck out.

ALONSO: Ay, Dios mío, you're right—you're not gonna get laid for at least another month.

NINA: She took Gato.

ALONSO: The CD or the cat?

NINA: The cat.

ALONSO: Ay, pobrecita, it's serious.

NINA: He was a vicious little shit anyway. [*To* ALONSO.] Thirsty?

MANNY: I'll get it, I'll get it. [*To* ALONSO.] What would you like to drink?

ALONSO: Bourbon, straight up—no pun intended.

RED: No alcohol. We havin' a drug-free evenin'.

ALONSO: Not even cognac?

RED: Nada.

MANNY: Banana Passion or Caribbean Delight?

ALONSO: What's with these third world juices? Pellegrino will suffice.

MANNY: No hay Pellegrino; it's Canada Dry Seltzer or East Village tap.

ALONSO: ¡Ave María! Guess I'll go for the Banana Passion. [*To* NINA.] Girl, what's happenin' to you? Don't you watch Martha Stewart?

MANNY: [*As he serves* ALONSO *food and drink.*] ¿Quién es Martha Stewart?

ALONSO: Whitest woman in America.

NINA: Pues, I was ready to pop open a bottle of Cordón Negro, but somebody wouldn't let me. [NINA *and* RED *exchange a look.*] Tú sabes, I was dyin' to use the new corkscrew Santos gave me for Christmas, the one with the tetas.

ALONSO: Honey, you don't need a corkscrew for Cordón Negro. All you need is blind faith and a lack of taste. How is he, anyway—Santos?

NINA: He was doin' a little better yesterday, but I haven't seen him since—[*To* RED.] Mira, can't we at least smoke a blunt?

RED: No.

[NINA *turns to* MANNY *for support.*]

MANNY: [*To* NINA.] Don't look at me, you know I don't smoke that shit. The last time I got high, I slept with you.

ALONSO: And liked it.

RED: [*Shocked.*] What?

[*The following lines are overlapping.*]

ALONSO: Por favor, don't play dumb. Everybody knows.

MANNY: What do you mean, everybody? Nina, you swore you would never tell.

RED: The two of you? And you never told me? But you told him? [*To* ALONSO.] And why didn't you ever say anything?

ALONSO: I really thought you knew.

MANNY: It happened so long ago, I almost forgot.

RED: Almost, but not quite.

NINA: He was a virgin. He practically begged me.

RED: I don't wanna hear it.

NINA: I was just tryin' to help him out.

RED: I said I don't wanna hear it.

NINA: Anybody want dessert?

ALONSO: I'd say somebody already had theirs.

NINA: Ya! We were in college for Chrissakes. [*Pause.*] Okay, mira, a pinroll between the four of us.

RED: No!

NINA: Why the fuck not?

RED: I don't want you to stop feeling.

NINA: Well, fuck you! What the fuck do you know about feelings?

RED: I know that I lost a lover, a sister, and five friends, and when the last one was gone, I tried to lose my mind in a bottle.

NINA: I'm not you.

RED: No, but you were stoned all day yesterday.

NINA: Off one joint. One lousy joint all day.

ALONSO: How can you be stoned all day off one joint?

MANNY: Must've been Californian, tú sabes.

NINA: If I roll it with herbs it cuts down—

RED: Fine. You do what you want. It's your life, your death.

[RED *exits to the bathroom, slamming the door. Silence.*]

MANNY: Mira, why don't we go for a ride? I got the agency van.

ALONSO: The one you use to drive los viejitos around?

MANNY: Yeah.

ALONSO: Ay, no, that van always smells like Ben Gay.

MANNY: ¡Vámonos!

ALONSO: Where the hell are we gonna go on a Tuesday night?

MANNY: We don't have to go anywhere. We could just drive around.

ALONSO: You're so high school, Manny.

MANNY: ¡Ay, cállate! Nina?

NINA: Yeah, let's get the fuck outta here.

[NINA *grabs her black leather jacket off the coat tree and exits.*]

ALONSO: I haven't finished eating.

MANNY: Bring it with you. [*Crossing to the bathroom, knocks on the door.*] Hey, Red, open up. Red.

[ALONSO *wraps his dish in aluminum foil, grabs the container of Banana Passion and his jacket, then exits.* RED *opens the bathroom door, steps out.*]

MANNY: C'mon, we're goin' for a ride.

RED: Where?

MANNY: Wherever you wanna go.

RED: Hmph! Baby, there's not a man on earth right now who could take me where I wanna go.

MANNY: ¡Ay, Dios! [*Grabbing his jacket off the coat tree.*] Are you comin' or not?

RED: [*Swiftly lifting his jacket from the coat tree.*] I'm comin'.

[ALL *exit. A beat as lights begin to fade.* NINA *re-enters, covers the pan of pernil with aluminum foil, then takes it with her and exits. Lights down on apartment. Lights up on hospital.*]

SANTOS: Nina? What day is it? Dime, did you eat? Tell the truth. You gotta make the time, otherwise you'll end up bulimic like Jane . . . Fonda. That's right, girlfriend, how else you think she look so good in the videos? After every sit-up, she do a throw-up. Ay, please, if you lose any more off your culo, you ain't gonna have anything left—and you didn't have much to begin with, mi'ja.

[*Lights down.*]

Scene Two

[*At rise: Melissa Etheridge's "Like The Way I Do" plays on the radio. When it ends,* MANNY *and* RED *take turns, constantly changing station— we never hear one song play very long throughout the following. Interior of Manny's company van, lower Manhattan, 10:30 P.M., Tuesday.* MANNY *is driving.* RED *sits in the front passenger seat. In the back seat,* ALONSO *sits directly behind* RED. NINA *is behind* MANNY *with the pan of pernil on her lap.*]

ALONSO: Where the fuck are we going?

MANNY: How 'bout Christopher Street?

NINA: [*Sarcastic.*] Oh, yeah, just pull up by the PATH station, we could watch 'em comin' in and out.

MANNY: Ay, Nina, por favor, like you never look.

NINA: Not at the guys.

ALONSO: Manny, your problem is you look at everything.

NINA: Remember last Halloween, when we went to Dolores' party and Manny got so drunk he danced with Chi Chi's mannequin and thought it was a real man?

RED: That's 'cause he's never had a real man. Didn't you hear—he's got a date with a blow-up doll tomorrow.

MANNY: Oye, stop talkin' about me like I'm not here. I seem to remember we all got ripped at that party and did some pretty wild shit. Red, the flaquito gorilla—that costume was so big on you, the crotch was down to your knees. Y Alonso, didn't you go as Martha Stewart?

ALONSO: Margaret Thatcher.

NINA: Same difference.

MANNY: All I know is your pumps matched your nails—I was impressed.

ALONSO: [*To* NINA.] Y, how about you, Paul Bunyon, grinding an axe all night cause Nessa wouldn't dance with you.

NINA: Nobody would dance with me—I scared all the girls away.

RED: Big bad butch.

MANNY: Them overalls Santos made you were fierce—with the little opening for your culo. I thought you were kinda sexy.

RED: You would.

MANNY: In a friendly kind of way.

NINA: Remember, Santos dressed up like Madonna with that breastplate and teddy and thong?

ALONSO: Don't forget the garters.

NINA: And nothing on underneath—

ALONSO: Except his hairy legs and pits.

MANNY: That's right, he didn't shave a thing.

NINA: Not even his mustache.

MANNY: Wasn't he singing on the way home?

ALONSO: He wasn't singing. Girlfriend performed.

ALONSO, RED, MANNY, and NINA: [*SONG*] Put your love to the test, you know you got to, got to express yourself, express yourself.

NINA: Wavin' his platinum blonde wig like a baton from the first to the last car of the number five, all the way from Dyre Avenue to Union Square. Ay, he's too much. Tú sabes, Santos is the only person I know who can sing all the words to "Stormy Weather" in Spanish.

ALONSO: I know it too. Everybody in Cuba knows it.

MANNY: Oye, Nina, didn't you tell me Dolores is havin' another costume party soon?

NINA: Valentine's Day.

MANNY: We should all go.

RED: Yeah, maybe this time you'll dance with a mannequin and think it's a real woman.

ALONSO: [*To* NINA.] Where do you suggest we go now?

NINA: Henrietta's. Or Nanny's.

MANNY: And do what?

NINA: They got pool tables.

ALONSO: [*Sarcastic.*] Oh, how urbane.

NINA: [*To* ALONSO.] ¡Pal carajo!

MANNY: Red, any ideas?

RED: No. But you better unlock the windows and the vents or find some other way to air this shit out. Between the Ben Gay, your Rasta man oils, and the pernil number five, I'm gonna die of asphyxiation.

MANNY: Pues, I could use some café con leche. Anybody else?

ALONSO: You're not gonna get café con leche around here.

NINA: Sucelt on 14th and 7th.

MANNY: Oh, you just wanna go there to see la cubana.

NINA: She's not Cuban, she's Dominican. Besides, she works days. [*Sings along with the radio.*] Manny, can you turn it up? I love this part.

MANNY: [*Turns up the music.*] I'm starving. Mami, make me a little sandwich, por favor.

NINA: I only brought the pernil.

MANNY: ¡Coño!

ALONSO: Can we hear some real music now?

[*As "Like The Way I Do" ends,* RED *changes the station. We hear a variety of music—everything from Toni Braxton to Neil Diamond to merengue to reggae to rap.* RED *finally settles on WBGO, Jazz 88 FM, which plays Billie Holliday's "My Man."*]

ALONSO: ¡Ay, no!

MANNY: [*Starting to change the station.*] What is this slit-your-wrist shit?

RED: [*Intense.*] Don't you touch that dial.

NINA: [*Closing her eyes, leaning back in the seat.*] This is classic jazz.

[MANNY *pulls in front of Sucelt, the comida Latina–coffee shop.*]

MANNY: Ay, you two, Mr. and Mrs. Prozac. Mira, we're here. Who wants what?

ALONSO: [*Getting out of the car.*] I'm comin' with you.

NINA: Café con leche con un Sweet and Low.

MANNY: Red?

RED: Nothing.

> [MANNY *gets out of the car; he and* ALONSO *exit to Sucelt.* RED *turns up the radio.* NINA *picks at the pernil.*]

NINA: Are you off tomorrow? [*Not getting a response, she gets louder.*] Are you off tomorrow?

RED: What?

NINA: Can you lower that a bit?

> [RED *complies.*]

NINA: I said, are you off tomorrow?

RED: Yes.

> [RED *turns the radio back up.*]

NINA: [*Pause.*] Red? Red? [*Louder.*] Red!

RED: [*Turning the radio down, snapping.*] What the fuck do you want?

NINA: [*Glaring at him.*] Nothing.

> [RED *turns the radio back up.* ALONSO *returns, gets in the car.*]

ALONSO: Ay, Red, can you turn that down?

> [RED *complies.*]

ALONSO: The cook's tryin' to pick up Manny.

RED: So what else is new?

ALONSO: It's a woman.

RED: Like I said, what else is new?

NINA: Not the one with really long, black, wavy hair?

ALONSO: No, this one's got very short hair, very macha.

> [MANNY *returns, gets in the car, gives* NINA *her café and a bag of garlic bread.*]

NINA: The one with long hair—se llama Ana—she makes the best sopita. [*Referring to the bag.*] ¿Qué es esto?

MANNY: I got some garlic bread. Will you make me a sandwich, por favor?

NINA: Ay, tú eres jodón.

[NINA *makes* MANNY *a sandwich.*]

MANNY: [*To* RED.] I got your favorite. (hands a bag to RED) Maduros.

RED: [*To* MANNY.] Take me home.

MANNY: I thought you were sleepin' over tonight.

RED: I am sleepin' in my own queen-size bed tonight—alone. Take me home.

MANNY: Fine. Oye, this may be classic jazz, but I can't take it anymore. How 'bout a compromise?

RED: Play what you want. I heard all I needed to hear.

[MANNY *finds a soft rock station.*]

ALONSO: Anybody want M&M's?

NINA: You got the new ones?

ALONSO: What new ones?

NINA: There's new colors. I heard from somebody—Manny, was it you?

MANNY: No, no tengo ni idea.

NINA: Fuchsia. Fuchsia's one of the new colors.

ALONSO: Fuchsia? Who told you that, your mother?

NINA: No. [*Pause.*] Santos.

[RED *and* MANNY *exchange a look. Silence, save for the music.*]

ALONSO: Mi'ja, there's no new colors.

NINA: [*On the verge of hysteria.*] It's dark in here, maybe you just can't see— dame the pack and I'll check. Manny, por favor, turn on the light.

[MANNY *turns on the car light.*]

ALONSO: Nina—

NINA: Dame the pack.

ALONSO: Nina, por—

NINA: [*Losin' it.*] Dame the fuckin' M&M's.

> [ALONSO *hands* NINA *the pack of M&M's.* NINA *empties the pack into her hand, feverishly checking each M&M. Upon realizing there are no fuchsia ones, she starts to cry.* ALONSO *puts his arm around her.* NINA *leans on him, letting him hold her.*]

RED: [*Softly, to* MANNY.] Turn off the light.

> [MANNY *turns off the car light. Billy Joel's "Innocent Man" plays.*]

NINA: [*Barely audible.*] I love this song. [*Sings "Innocent Man" chorus softly.*]

MANNY: I'm ready for some house music.

> [MANNY *changes the station to HOT 97.*]

NINA: [*Sitting up.*] What the fuck are you doing?

ALONSO: She was singing.

MANNY: I'm sorry, Mami, I didn't hear.

> [MANNY *returns to the station playing Billy Joel.*]

NINA: Vámonos a Chicky's.

ALONSO: Chicky's? In fuckin' Brownsville?

NINA: It's not Brownsville. It's East New York.

ALONSO: Same difference.

MANNY: I could drop you and Red off. It's on the way.

ALONSO: No, that's okay .

MANNY: Red?

RED: I don't wanna go home—yet.

MANNY: Okay, vámonos a Chicky's.

ALONSO: ¡Ay, coño! Lock the doors.

> [NINA *again sings softly from "Innocent Man."*
> *Music and lights fade.*]

Scene Three

[*"No Vale la Pena" plays as lights come up slowly on Chicky's bodega, East New York, 11:30 P.M., Tuesday.* CHICKY *is at the register, behind the counter.* NINA *enters hurriedly.*]

NINA: Chicky.

CHICKY: [*With biting sarcasm.*] Do I know you?

NINA: Chicky, mira, I need to find—

CHICKY: Yeah, that's the only time you come around here—when you need somethin'.

NINA: Ay, Chicky, por favor, I gotta—

CHICKY: [*She crosses in front of the counter to face* NINA.] Two and a half months, Nina, two and a half fuckin' months I sat up here waitin' on you, and not so much as a Kwaanza card passed through my door. Tú sabes, the first hour, I said, "Oh, she's just runnin' late," and so I turned off the paella, but left it on the stove. The second hour, I started to get a little worried, thinkin' all kinds of things coulda happened to you: you got jumped, the train crashed, the bridge collapsed, the World Trade Center blew up again and this time maybe you were in it—or maybe, maybe you just blew me off again for Nessa or somebody else. I shoved the paella in the fridge, between your guava and your mangoes. The third hour, I called, and you had the cojones to pick up the phone. As soon as I heard that breathy little "Hola," I hung up. I put the paella in a Tupperware and stuck it in the freezer. And there it stayed. And every day, I forgot about that paella a little bit more. Then, on January 15, I was listenin' to BLS, and they had one of King's speeches on, somethin' about freedom. And, suddenly, I remembered the paella. I grabbed it from the freezer, ran straight to the incinerator and set it free, Tupperware and all. Pues, guess what, girlfriend, I ain't waitin' on you no more.

[CHICKY *turns away from* NINA.]

NINA: Chicky, I am sorry about that night. I really am. But I wasn't ready.

CHICKY: For what? I wasn't proposin' no goddamn marriage. Fuckin' dinner. You weren't ready for a fuckin' dinner?

NINA: C'mon, Chicky, you know it was more than that.

CHICKY: How would I know? You never gave it a chance.

NINA: I was with Vanessa five years. We lived together. I even had her under my insurance. I couldn't just end it like that.

CHICKY: Shit, Nina, not even a fuckin' phone call?

NINA: I figured if I couldn't come to you the way you wanted me to, I shouldn't come at all.

CHICKY: So why in the hell are you here now?

[*Silence.*]

NINA: [*Tearful.*] I needed—I needed to know if you had the M&M's with—

CHICKY: [*Incredulously, with hurt anger.*] M&M's? You want M&M's? [*Losing it.*] I'll give you M&M's. [CHICKY *takes a carton of M&M's from the candy shelf and dumps it upon* NINA.] ¡Toma! Toma los M&M's. [CHICKY *begins crying and picking up individual packs of M&M's, throwing them at* NINA *and beating on* NINA *with her fists.*] Fuck your M&M's.

NINA: [*Crying and grabbing* CHICKY's *arms.*] Chicky, ¡por favor! Stop! Chicky! Por favor, Chicky—

[CHICKY *stops fighting* NINA, *breaks down in her arms;* NINA *holds* CHICKY.]

NINA: I'm sorry, Dios sabe I'm sorry. [*Pause.*] Santos—Santos been askin' about you. He's in the hospital again. Been there almost two weeks. The other day, he told me they had these new M&M's—two new colors—one was fuchsia. He couldn't remember the other. He doesn't remember some things so good anymore, like what day it is or who came to visit, but he remembers you, and the shininess of that midnight-blue sequined dress you wore to his Christmas party four years ago. He wanted to know if you still had that dress, and would you wear it for him so he could take a picture because he says he never got to take your picture. But I know he got the picture—it's on his mirror at home. See, I don't know if it's the medication or—tú sabes. It could be anything. I forget what day it is sometimes. He's only 38. He still watches "Jeopardy," and he still wins most of the time. So when he asked me to bring him the new M&M's, I didn't think twice. But I couldn't find them anywhere, and everyone I asked looked at me kinda funny, like I was losin' it—even the guys didn't know what I was talkin' about. Tonight, Alonso gave me one of those looks, and I started to think I was losin' it. Dime, Chicky, am I losin' it? Am I?

[NINA *cries.*]

CHICKY: [*Holding* NINA.] No, baby, you're not losin' it. There's three new colors to pick from—one of them is fuchsia—but they haven't made them yet—you gotta call in and vote. They got a toll-free number and everything. I saw it on channel 11 the other day. Yeah, they doin' it for Easter, tú sabes, a big promotion, pastel colors, almonds an' shit—they got it goin' on.

NINA: [*Half laughing.*] Serious?

CHICKY: I don't lie to you.

NINA: Yo sé. That's why I love you so—

CHICKY: Don't start that shit.

NINA: It's true.

CHICKY: You're makin' me mad again.

NINA: Things are different now that—

CHICKY: Y Nessa? Does she know they're "different"?

NINA: Se fue.

CHICKY: She'll be back.

NINA: I told her to leave.

CHICKY: And I told you I stopped waitin' a long time ago. Nina, you got what you came for, ¿verdad? So, vete.

NINA: [*Searching* CHICKY's *eyes.*] Let me at least help you clean—

CHICKY: No.

[*Silence.* NINA *starts to leave.*]

CHICKY: I'd like to see him.

NINA: He'd like that too.

CHICKY: St. Vincent's?

NINA: 826. [*Pause.*] I try to go every day. Si tú quieres, one time, we could go together.

CHICKY: Are you askin' me out?

NINA: Pues, yeah.

CHICKY: What kind of a fuckin' date is that, to a hospital? Now you are losin' it. Girl, you better throw dinner in there somewhere.

NINA: Casilda's?

CHICKY: No, you gonna cook for me, honey.

NINA: ¡Con gusto! Mañana, ¿a las cinco?

CHICKY: Yo no sé. You sure she's gone?

NINA: Segura.

CHICKY: [*Pause.*] Te llamo.

NINA: I'll wait.

[NINA *kisses* CHICKY *goodbye, then turns, starting to exit.*]

NINA: [*Turning around to* CHICKY.] Chicky, when is Easter?

CHICKY: April.

NINA: [*Sadly.*] April.

[NINA *turns to exit.* CHICKY *picks up a pack of plain M&M's.*]

CHICKY: ¡Mira!

[NINA *turns to face* CHICKY, *who then tosses the pack of M&M's to her.* NINA *catches them, smiles, and exits.* CHICKY *watches her go as lights fade.*]

Scene Four

[*Lights up on hospital room.*]

SANTOS: Nina? What month is it? Oh. Was that crazy-ass Tom Hayden messed up her life. Gracias a Dios, she got Ted Turner now. That's what I say, honey, don't marry for love, marry for money—pero, in your case, mi'ja, you can have both with Chicky. She got her own bodega y el corazón tuyo también. She got it goin' on! Oh. I thought you were Nina. I'm full. Leave it—that's for my niece. Please, just put it in the fridge. She'll be here. She'll be here.

[*Lights down on hospital room. Lights up on interior of Manny's company van, downtown Brooklyn, 1:00 A.M., Wednesday.* MANNY *is driving. Everyone is seated as he or she was in Scene Two.* NINA *hands a pack of M&M's to* ALONSO.]

RED: Chicky looked good.

NINA: Yeah.

ALONSO: [*To* NINA.] So?

NINA: So what?

MANNY: Mira, she's gettin' all coy and shit.

NINA: What?

ALONSO: You left out the part about what happened after the M&M's.

NINA: Nothing. She confirmed that there will be new colors and that was it.

RED: Oh, please. Who you think you talkin' to?

NINA: Arright. She may come over for dinner tomorrow.

MANNY: What are you makin'?

NINA: Yo no sé—it's not definite. She said she'll call.

ALONSO, MANNY, and RED: She'll call.

NINA: Ay, Manny, don't go over the Manhattan bridge.

MANNY: Too late.

NINA: [*Closes her eyes.*] ¡Ay, no!

ALONSO: [*To* NINA.] ¿Por qué no?

NINA: This thing is a piece of shit. Remember how they had to close it down 'cause it was crumblin'? Whole chunks were fallin' out. And these grates, ¡coño!

MANNY: Ay, coño, it's startin' to rain.

RED: What, you never drove in a little rain before?

MANNY: Not with one windshield wiper.

NINA: [*Shouting.*] ¡Coño!

MANNY: Would you listen to the drama queen back there?

RED: Takes one to know one.

MANNY: Oh, shit—the steering.

RED: Stop trying to scare her.

MANNY: I'm not—there's something really wrong, I can't control the steering. [*A loud thud is heard, followed by a tin rattling and a series of thumping noises.*]

MANNY, RED, ALONSO and NINA: [*Screaming together.*] ¡Ayyy, coño!

[*Lights out. A beat. Lights up to reveal* RED *and* NINA *standing, shivering, outside the van, which is parked, Manhattan-bound, on the right side of the Manhattan bridge, midway between the two boroughs.* MANNY *kneels by the flat tire on the rear right side of the van; he's unsuccessfully trying to remove the last lug nut with a crowbar.* ALONSO *rolls a tire toward* MANNY.]

ALONSO: Are you sure this spare is good?

MANNY: It has to be.

NINA: It's fuckin' cold out here. [NINA *looks down.*] ¡Ay, carajo!

RED: [*Putting his arm around* NINA.] It's okay. It's okay. Just don't look down.

NINA: [*Looking down.*] Mira, you guys, in case we all fall off this bridge, I just wanna say, I really love you. Although, Manny, when this is over, te mato.

MANNY: Yeah, I love you, too, Mami. Shit!

RED: What's wrong?

ALONSO: The last lug is stuck. Here, lemme try. [*He tries to remove the lug nut.*] Fuck.

NINA: Red, all those things I said before, when we were at my house—I'm sorry. I acted like a shit and I'm really sorry. You were just tryin' to help and I didn't wanna see it. I mean, you, more than anybody else, know what it's like.

RED: Yeah, I do. That's why you're forgiven.

[RED *hugs* NINA.]

NINA: And that thing with Manny—I was just doin' him a favor.

RED: But why didn't you just tell me?

NINA: Ay, it wasn't even that good. You know, he was the last man I ever slept with. I'm sorry, Red. From now on, no more secrets, okay?

RED: Okay.

NINA: Ay, I been feelin' worse than usual. I mean, it seems like it's getting harder to be with Santos. My visits are getting shorter, and today, tú sabes, I didn't even go, [*Tearful.*] and I feel really bad about that, 'cause he's alone all day. Our family mostly comes on the weekend, and I don't want him to be alone during the week, but sometimes, I just can't . . . yo no sé.

RED: Nina, you gotta give yourself a break. It's okay. He knows how much you love him.

NINA: Think so?

RED: I know so.

ALONSO: [*To* MANNY.] No, you push, I pull.

MANNY: I was.

ALONSO: Push!

RED: What the fuck are they doin'?

NINA: The two of them on a crowbar? It can't be pretty.

RED: C'mon.

[RED *and* NINA *join* MANNY *and* ALONSO.]

RED: Lemme have a whirl. [*Taking the crowbar, unsuccessfully trying to remove the lug nut.*] Damn! Papi, why you got this so tight?

NINA: May I?

ALONSO: Oh, please.

NINA: I'll have you know I took shop for four years.

[NINA *takes the crowbar and successfully removes the lug nut.*]

MANNY: ¡Coño!

ALONSO: Holy shit!

NINA: Lesbian hands to the rescue again.

RED: Chicky's in trouble.

NINA: Oye, I only got you started. Y'all can finish the job.

ALONSO: [*To* NINA.] And just where did you learn to un-screw like that? I'm sure they didn't teach you it in shop.

RED: You really don't wanna know.

NINA: Ay, Manny, they're picking on me again. Hurry up.

MANNY: Okay, okay, we're almost there. [*Taking over, he removes the flat, puts on new tire, etc.*] Entonces, I told you I'd get you all home safe and I meant it—I'm a man of my word. Mira, since we're stopped here, I might as well show yous my new clothes.

[MANNY *searches the trunk.*]

ALONSO, RED, and NINA: ¡Ay, no!

RED: Let's just get the fuck outta here.

ALONSO: Don't show us anything until you learn how to pronounce the names.

MANNY: ¡'Pérate! Alonso, what did you do with my shopping bags? Did you hide them somewhere?

NINA: Mira, there's one.

MANNY: Ay, no, it's empty. Where are my clothes? Alonso, this isn't funny— where'd you put them?

ALONSO: Manny, I didn't touch your clothes, believe me.

NINA: Mira, the lock's been jimmied.

MANNY: Ay, no, someone stole my clothes. We have to go to the police.

ALONSO, RED and NINA: Ay, no.

RED: Manny, chill out and come back—

MANNY: [*Hysterical.*] No, no, no! We have to go to the police. I have nothing to wear.

ALONSO, RED, and NINA: Ay, coño.

[*Lights fade.*]

Scene Five

[*Outside St. Vincent's Hospital, New York City, 2:00 A.M., Wednesday. Interior of Manny's car, seating arrangements as in Scenes Two and Four.*]

NINA: Mira, Papi, you don't gotta take me home. Just drop me off at St. Vincent's.

[MANNY, RED, *and* ALONSO *exchange looks.*]

RED: Sure you don't want some company?

NINA: I'm sure. Okay, guys, I'll see you.

[NINA *kisses* ALONSO, RED, *and* MANNY.]

ALONSO: Llámame to let me know what happens with Chicky.

RED: Me too.

MANNY: Me three.

NINA: I'll send you the video, how 'bout that? Y'all need to get some real men in your lives, that's your problem. [NINA *gets out of the van.*] Take it easy.

[*As* NINA *starts to walk into the hospital,* MANNY *jumps out of the van.*]

MANNY: ¡'Pérate, Nina! [*He runs up to* NINA *and embraces her.*] Mami, I love you.

NINA: I love you, too, Papi.

MANNY: I'm really sorry for bein' so late tonight. I promise I'll never be late for dinner—or anything else—again.

NINA: Uh-huh.

MANNY: I'm serious. You'll see.

NINA: Okay. [*She kisses him.*] Now vete, before those boys freeze their huevos off.

[NINA *exits to the hospital.* MANNY *returns to the car.*]

ALONSO: They're not gonna let her in there at this time—it's two o'clock in the fuckin' mornin'.

RED: She'll get in.

MANNY: How?

RED: You know Miss Thing can flirt.

MANNY: Arright. Who wants to go home first?

RED: I'm not goin' home.

MANNY: Where you goin'?

RED: Contigo.

MANNY: I don't got any more clothes for you.

RED: I don't need any.

ALONSO: Oh, shit.

[MANNY *starts the van.*]

RED: Hold up—let's wait for her.

[*Lights down on the trio in the car. Lights up on* NINA *in Santos' hospital room.* SANTOS *lies in bed;* NINA *is by his side. An IV is attached to his arm.*]

SANTOS: ¿Qué hora es?

NINA: 2:00.

SANTOS: It's so dark for the afternoon.

NINA: It's morning.

SANTOS: What are you doin' here so early?

NINA: I missed you. I'm sorry I couldn't come yesterday.

SANTOS: It's okay, mi'ja, you don't gotta come every day. What's today?

NINA: Wednesday.

SANTOS: They let you out of work already?

NINA: No. I'm off Tuesdays and Wednesdays.

SANTOS: Oh, that's good, give you time to do things during the week. ¿Y Nessa?

NINA: She moved out.

SANTOS: For real?

NINA: She took Gato.

SANTOS: Gracias a Dios, that cat was crazy—I could always tell by those eyes. ¿Y Chicky?

NINA: We may be gettin' together soon. She wants to see you.

SANTOS: Tell her to wear that midnight-blue dress. Oh, shit, I forgot my camera. Can you bring my camera so I can get a picture of her in that dress? I never got a picture of her in that dress.

NINA: Sí.

SANTOS: What's today?

NINA: Wednesday. Hey, you should try to sleep. I'm sorry I woke you.

SANTOS: You didn't wake me—it's them damn nurses, comin' in here every five minutes for this and that, blood pressure, temperature. They got this new thermometer now, shoots you in the ear. Girlfriend, they put that thing in, I thought my whole head was gonna fall off. ¡Son brutas! I think it made me a little deaf. I been hearin' buzzin' ever since. The one you thought was a drag queen woke me up to give me a sleeping pill. Entonces, esa viejita down the hall had a fit just before you got here. She started screamin' an' shit, "Who took my Mylanta? Somebody stole my Mylanta." I said, "Miss Thing, please, get your tired ass to sleep—ain't nobody want your Mylanta." Imagínate—they got enough Mylanta here to feed an army, all she had to do was ask for more. Tú sabes, my doctor told me he was puttin' me in here so I could get some rest, but who can rest? This is the last place to rest. I'd be better off at home. Then they sent that priest in here. I told him you don't need to be prayin' for me, you better pray for yourself and all your priest friends, you all havin' more sex than me. Mi'ja, ¿qué hora es?

NINA: 2:00.

SANTOS: In the morning?

NINA: Sí.

SANTOS: How did you get in? Was you flirtin' again?

NINA: Un poquito.

SANTOS: You better stop that shit, them guards carry guns now. Did you see the one by the x-ray room? Tan macho—and fine. Just the way I like 'em. Como Jon Secada, pero ¡más macho! Tú sabes, them macho ones are only macho on the outside. They're like whipped butter underneath. Are you hungry?

NINA: Not really. Are you?

SANTOS: Yeah.

NINA: You want your hospital sandwich?

SANTOS: No, that's for you.

NINA: Pero, you're hungry.

SANTOS: Not for that.

NINA: I made some pernil, but it has to be heated.

SANTOS: Put it in the fridge, I'll tell the nurse to heat it up tomorrow. My mother's comin' tomorrow.

NINA: Oh, I thought she was comin' Saturday.

SANTOS: Yeah, that's tomorrow.

NINA: Today is Wednesday. Tomorrow is Thursday.

SANTOS: Oh.

NINA: [*Holding up a pack of M&M's.*] Mira, I brought you M&M's.

SANTOS: The fuchsia?

NINA: Yeah.

SANTOS: Dame, I'm starving.

[NINA *pours out some into his hands.*]

SANTOS: [*Searching his hand.*] Where's the fuchsia?

NINA: [*She selects a red M&M and hands it to him.*] Aquí.

SANTOS: [*Staring at the red M&M.*] Girlfriend. You goin' blind. That's not fuchsia. That's red.

NINA: You're right. I lied. I couldn't get the fuchsia. They're not in the stores yet. By Easter.

SANTOS: When is Easter?

NINA: April.

SANTOS: April. What month is it?

NINA: February.

SANTOS: Ay, mi'ja, they probably all taste the same anyway.

NINA: Hey, Santos. I love you.

SANTOS: I know. I love you too, mi'ja. [*Pause, then in a teasing tone.*] But I'll love you even more if you get the fuchsia.

[SANTOS *laughs softly,* NINA *smiles. She holds his hand and rests her head on his bed. Lights fade.*]

Performance Pieces

WHILE PERFORMANCE ART AMONG Latinas is not new—indeed, we can trace its roots to the "Latin" performances of the 1940s (vaudeville, clubs, Teatro Latino)—its exponential growth in the last few years, and especially since the end of the 1980s, merits special attention. This vital, efflorescent theater movement among Latinas has become an important medium to express and articulate Latina identities that had been silenced or stereotyped in mainstream theater as well as in Latino theater.

By staging their own life experiences, Latina performers have transformed Latino theater. In their irreverent and provocative way of doing theater, and by telling and staging their own autobiographies, Latinas have created a space for a self-defined Latina protagonist. Sometimes funny, sometimes poignant, sometimes political, but always subversive in their acts of contestation, persistence, resistance, and negotiation, these one-woman shows speak to and beyond a Latino audience in stories of the self that authenticate their voices and experiences both honestly and defiantly. While intent on seeing themselves and their families realistically represented on the stage, they simultaneously continue to tackle issues that are of vital importance to them and their communities.

Rescuing the feminist platform initiated by Latina playwrights such as Cherríe Moraga, Dolores Prida, and Josefina López, Latina solo performers have moved a step ahead as they have highlighted those particular issues in their own given families, schools, workplaces, communities, and sexual positionings. In this manner, Marga Gomez, Monica Palacios, Carmelita Tropicana, and Janis Astor del Valle have given voice to lesbian sexuality, their feminism and body politics. Taking their work to alternative spaces that major urban centers can provide and to university campuses, these four Latina performers have established a following among multicultural feminist and lesbian audiences. These alternative spaces truly have become a kind of launching pad where not only Latinas but the entire gay community can identify as the performers dismantle taboos both political and sexual by breaking the silence. That the means to achieve these goals has usually been through parody and irony, laughter and catharsis, has assisted audience members in their ability to see themselves and speak the unspoken.

At the same time that hilarity is often a useful tool, it is not the only kind of performance. Other Latinas, such as Denise Chávez, Amparo García, Wilma Bonet, Silviana Wood, Yareli Arizmendi, Laura Esparza, and Ruby Nelda Perez, use their performance art to communicate the entire spectrum of Latina life and experience in their respective communities. Their work centers on their relationships with men, with other women, and with their families, a revisioning of history, political consciousness, open sexuality, and a cross section of representation of Latina life in its myriad forms. In this sense, these performers stage the multiplicity of roles that they have been performing both on and offstage for the last three decades.

NOSTALGIA MALDITA:
1-900-MEXICO
A STAIRMASTER PIECE

Yareli Arizmendi

GLOSSARY

Nostalgia: Pain caused by the memory of something lost.

Maldita: Cursed by Divine Justice—damned.

1-900: An emergency measure meant to fill the human void that industrial, hyper-civilized societies have created.

Mexico: A mythic idea of a place in the minds of those who have left its reality.

Reality: A set of rules and perceptions created by a tribe to make sense of the chaos handed down by the cosmos.

[*Voice-over is heard in the waiting room, encouraging audience to enter the circus to view the "unbelievable talking head" punished by the gods. Some audience members are handed toothbrushes arbitrarily. Others should see that not all are getting them and be left to wonder.* ACTRESS *is covered by a "circus style" decorated drape. Only her head can be seen under a tight, dim, pinspot.*]

VOICE: Eh, familia, you are about to witness the incredible firsthand account of the unbelievable talking head. She is 500 years old going on 501, and she's still talking. A ver, niños—I hope there's a lot of you out there—listen carefully, children, and learn the lesson well. [*To the head.*] A ver, head, tell us how you came to be in this pathetic state.

ACTRESS: Por desobedecer a mis padres. I didn't listen to them. I thought I had a right to dream.

VOICE: Are you sorry now?

ACTRESS: Sí, but it is way much too late.

VOICE: Do you have any advice for our children today?

ACTRESS: I have a story.

[*Light changes. Head starts to sing "There Was a Boy, There Was a Girl" by Donny and Marie Osmond.*]

ACTRESS: There was a boy; there was a girl. If they had met they might have found the world a joy [*Starts to climb under the drape, simulates an earthquake effect.*] but he lived on the other side of the border, and she lived on the other side of the hill. [ACTRESS *pushes drape up and throws it out towards the audience to reveal StairMaster. She is climbing.*] And I've been climbing ever since. I had a plan. Donny Osmond was my man. His favorite color is purple. Did you know that? I read that in *Tiger Beat.* I was a cute little Mexican girl, a Maria wanting to be Marie. Here's the thing. I would walk across the hill, dress up as a maid—oh, because not all Mexicans look like maids. Believe it or not, some need a disguise. I had a map. I knew exactly where Utah was and, of course, I knew everything about the Mormons because in fifth grade I chose the Mormon religion as my report topic. Can you imagine? There I was, sitting in my little classroom in Mexico City, looking into my options as a Mormon wife because, of course, Donny would ask me to marry him, and I would have to convert. I hated the part about men having multiple wives, but I thought, "Donny has to be different." How could he sing "Puppy Love" and be thinking about five different girlfriends? So there I was, dressed up as a maid and ready to knock on the Osmond's door. Mama Osmond would answer my call.

I would ask for work, just one more Mexican Maria asking for work. And Mama Osmond would say, "Oh, Mexico? I just love the pyramids." I would smile and nod, and not let her know I had never been out of my upper-middle-class neighborhood and had only seen pictures of the pyramids in my elementary school textbooks. Of course, it never occurred to her that in Mexico we speak Spanish, not English with a Texan accent. Yes, my English teacher was from [*Texan accent.*] Dallas, and I had picked up a perfect Dallas accent. Come to think of it, you don't seem too surprised yourselves. Must be that I dropped the Texan for the [*Valley accent.*] Californian. Okay, so, now I had work and my plan was in place. I was sweeping.

[*Begins singing "Paper Roses" as she sweeps.* DONNY *"appears," cutting her off.*]

DONNY: Maria?

MARIA: Donny!

DONNY: Was that you singing?

MARIA: [*Bashful.*] I think so.

DONNY: You sound like an angel. We must sing together.

MARIA: What about Marie?

DONNY: I'm a grown man. She'll have to understand—I'm a grown man; I need a partner, a wife.

MARIA: [*Utter surprise.*] Donny!

DONNY: I am sorry, Maria, but I've been in love with you ever since I saw you, and now with your voice—

MARIA: We are the perfect couple.

DONNY: Well . . .

MARIA: Oh, I know, you couldn't possibly marry a maid, and a Mexican.

DONNY: Maria, you know I love Mexico. I mean, the pyramids, the mariachis, the margaritas and all, but—

MARIA: Stop! I have something to tell you. I'm not really a maid. And I only happen to live in Mexico, but I'm really Spanish—a beautiful, ancient Mayan princess from Madrid. Y ¡olé! [*Flamenco stance, abrupt light change to bright indicates change of place.*] Excuse me, Mr. Director, I know Mayan and Madrid both start with "M" and, well, to make things more complex they are both followed by an "A" like MAyan and MAdrid, so this can get confusing. You may—I don't mean you personally, this could happen to anyone—I mean, one could think they're from the same country, or at least the same continent, but really they are two entirely different—[*Alarmed.*] Oh, no, no, no. I respect your work, I mean, you are brilliant, my hero. No really, I never meant—Aha, aha, aha. [*Fireball.*] Oh, I get it, you are right, it makes for a complex character, a great identity crisis. She could become a psycho, kill Spaniards in search of her Indian blood mother. I get you. No, really, I do. I'm not just saying that. I love it. I think it's—ah, what's the word?—ah, it's intense. [*Holds the smile, ready to cry.*]
You got to do what you got to do. I became Maria, the beautiful, ancient, Mayan, Spanish Princess from East L.A. and they loved it. I killed my Spanish father, killed my Indian mother—it was more dramatic that way,

you know. Plus surveys show that we all want to kill both our parents, and that most of us actually do, and hey, in California with a good lawyer you can easily pull a Menendez.

Well, now, parentless, with no one to tell me what to do, what to eat, when to brush my teeth, no one to remind me where I came from, I could embrace my gringa self, embrace the dream, turn off the culturally correct alarm clock.

[*An alarm clock is heard three times. "American Bandstand" music is heard. Four seconds later, multi-colored, festive lights go up.* ACTRESS *has a "Miss Fat Gram" ribbon, crown, and staff to match, and an exercise stick at her side, which she'll later use as a pointer.*]

ACTRESS: [*Valleyish accent.*] Welcome to Fat Gram City, where we are all Equal. [*Displays box of Equal.*] Take out your counters and let's start playing. [*Takes out fat gram counter.*] Now, put your social body fat number at the top of your mind. Are we ready? Now, listen carefully to the rules of the game. I'm going to measure the collective body fat of this group, okay? Remember, you want to make the low-fat decisions! If you can answer like non-fat it's better, kind of like credit. Now, answer yes or no, but be honest. We'll add up your points at the end and . . . I'll tell you at the end. Good luck and trim, trim away.

[*She eats carrots and celery sticks. What follows is an improvised segment in which the* ACTRESS *throws out the questions below and comments on the answers. She seemingly is on the side of a dehumanized but efficient society. She has a "no fat" sign, which she uses whenever a fat-incorrect (i.e., emotional, human) answer is given.*]

ACTRESS: Do you think money is sexy? [*Y*]
Do you think needing to sleep or eat is a sign of weakness? [*Y*]
Do you engage in sex for exercise? [*Y*]
Do you engage in sex for love? [*N*]
Do you want to have children? [*N*]
Do you want to raise your children? [*N*]

[*She periodically checks her pulse.*]

ACTRESS: Do you want to get married? [*N*]
Do you want to stay married? [*N*]
[*Taking up her exercise stick*] Do you think you'll die of a heart attack? [*Y*]

Do you think you'll die of cancer? [Y]

Do you think you'll die? [N]

[Pointing at a member of the audience.] Oh, you don't think that's a valid question? How can you be so sure you'll die? None of us can say for sure— we haven't died yet, at least I haven't. [Starts into a paranoid delusion, uses towel to wipe off the sweat, wraps around neck.] So stop looking at me like you're judging me, like I deserve to die or something, like you know what's right and what's wrong, and like I don't. [Gradual change of light to mystical atmosphere.] In the end, we'll see who's left standing, who exercised, who ate right, who stood in line, who wore blue contacts and dyed her hair, who got the promotion and the tract home with a pool, who owes more on credit cards, who has more cellular phones, who has more insurance, who's been on a talk show, who's been in a movie, who's—Forgive them, father, for they know not what they eat.

[Using the exercise stick, ACTRESS re-creates "Christ on the cross" as "Superstar" music comes on. Light change is complete.]

ACTRESS: [Image of "Suplicio."] I'm thirsty, I'm thirsty.

[Diet Coke descends to ACTRESS's hand. She drinks transfixed, swings the can as if to hypnotize audience and follows it herself for a beat. Gets rid of stick, prepares karaoke. Religious music plays in background. ACTRESS wears towel as the Virgin's veil.]

ACTRESS: [With manual karaoke device in hand.] Reality is divided into two great eras: BDC and ADC: Before Diet Coke and After Diet Coke. Diet Coke brings us closer to the true wealth we all aspire to: the spiritual. Thank you, Diet Coke [Coke can starts to be raised up and away.] Thank you, Diet Coke, thank you, Diet Coke. [Lift completed, ACTRESS abruptly turns off karaoke, launches into used-car-salesman pitch voice.] I know what you are thinking, that commonplace cliché, "Suffering is good for the spirit." No! Diet Coke goes way beyond that. [Turns on karaoke and returns to preacher's voice.] Limitations are good for the body, so that this body, with its never-ending material needs, starts getting used to not having—simply that, not having. And we will arrive at the only logical conclusion: that it is fantasy, the imagination, the spiritual dimension, what truly satisfies. [Turns off karaoke—sales pitch.] And this is precisely how Diet Coke helps us meet the challenge. Because we are imperfect beings— that is to say, materialists, consumerists. [Uses local restaurants and spe-

cialties.] A Fat Burger turkey-bacon cheeseburger, a Cha-Cha-Cha banana boat, a Pink's chili dog, all dangerous temptations that block the road toward a pure spirit, a pure essence.

[*Merolico/street vendor-like.*] In a country where homelessness, violence and despair are ever present, Diet Coke is our benefactor, our official sponsor, for it will help eliminate the human body. No diets. Take away hunger and suffering without adding a single pound, a single calorie, to the human body! [*Turns on karaoke—rapture.*] Can you feel it? Do you feel it? It's grandiose, glorious even, reduce, reduce, reduce without pills, without chemicals, except potassium benzoate, to finally arrive at the sublime evaporation of the body and the elevation of the spirit. Gracias, Diet Coke. [*The Spanish just "comes out."*] Gracias, Diet Coke. Gracias.

[*Abrupt light change cuts* ACTRESS *off at third "Gracias." Audio comes in.*]

VOICE: Are you Mexican?

ACTRESS: I used to be. No, wait! [*Surprised.*] I stand by the fifth. [*To audience.*] And I'm not talking about Cinco de Mayo.

VOICE: You look Mexican.

ACTRESS: Are you one of Pete's boys? [*Substitute any timely anti-immigrant stance.*]

VOICE: Are you Mexican?

ACTRESS: [*Screams.*] I used to be.

[*Audio Track: Thunderbolt.*
ACTRESS's *finger points at her accusingly. Battling against it. Hand tug-of-war. The right slaps the left. The hand takes off her sporty top to reveal her true colors: red, white and green—she is Mexican. Audio comes in.*]

VOICE: How long did you think you would last? How far did you think you could get? You are what you eat, you know. Of course you know. Did you think I wouldn't notice? Do you think they don't notice? [*Referring to audience.*] They're polite—that's why they let you go on pretending, but it shows you're a wannabe.

ACTRESS: I don't wanna be. I am. I'm not Mexican, I'm not American—

VOICE: You're nothing. And I condemn you to wander through the darkness, aimless, roadless, tortilla-less. And to think you did all for Donny.

[*Violent blackout. Three seconds. Video and sound track of "Return, Volver, Return" by Dr. Loco's rockin' Jalapeño Band, comes on. The video depicts nostalgic scenes from Mexico—lots of humorous moments. As she sings, the* ACTRESS *moves to the beat on the StairMaster. At the end of the song, she takes a sip of water as if it were a tequila bottle—she's tired. Audio comes in.*]

ACTRESS: [*Honest.*] Okay, I got your lesson, I agree, quiero volver . . . beam up.

VOICE: Ya te dije que you can't.

ACTRESS: Who says I can't go back?

VOICE: The StairMaster king.

[*The* ACTRESS *makes a "fuck you" gesture at the voice and tries to get off the StairMaster. She is stuck, glued to it. After third try, tape comes on.*]

VOICE: Remember when you turned off the culturally correct alarm clock?

ACTRESS: That was a long time ago, top of the show to be exact.

VOICE: Crazy glue. Just press down for 30 seconds and you're glued—for life.

ACTRESS: For life? Just for turning the alarm off? So I hit the snooze button, relax a little, big deal. I don't suppose you have traffic school? Is there no appeals process in this (mocking) stairwell land? So now what, sleeping's a crime?

VOICE: No, dreaming is.

ACTRESS: There must be a consumer protection agency, at least customer service—

VOICE: No return policy on this side of paradise.

ACTRESS: [*Negotiating a deal.*] Are you going to make a movie about this? That would definitely make this more bearable, you know, knowing that the eyes of god and the TV are watching.

VOICE: No "L.A. Law" to draw up the contract.

ACTRESS: Cute. Okay, I get it. You win. We'll do it your way. But you'll be so sorry, you know why? 'Cause ketchup is dead, and tortillas are the best thing since white bread. I'll be your worst nightmare. You'll think of me every time you pour salsa on your hamburger.

[*Lights to black. Immediately salsa video comes on, depicting images of the Latino presence in the United States.*]

ACTRESS: [*Scream.*] ¡Azúcar! Sweet and Low!

[ACTRESS *is dressing up for rumbera-aeróbica number. Lights will come up on her during the music-only interludes. She will be dancing a "weights-as-percussion" choreography. Salsa ends.* ACTRESS *receives the applause. Takes her pulse, wipes off sweat. Gets her cellular phone, puts on glasses.*]

ACTRESS: [*Infomercial host personality.*] Whew! Howdy! It's great to be here with you. You are all so beautiful, really. Give yourselves a hand, I mean it. [*Gets audience to clap.*] Are we ready to change our lives today? I sure hope so, because time is money, so we shouldn't waste any. Now, let me tell you a little about myself. [*As though reading a TelePrompTer.*] It's hard to believe that three years ago I was unemployed, recently divorced, short of cash, lonely, and in despair. I was looking around for something to do, something I'd enjoy, something that would make money—lots of money. When I got the idea to start, every single one of my friends said I was crazy. They sure don't think I'm crazy anymore.

[*"1–900–Mexico" video ad comes on. Late-night-ad look with images of national Mexican heroes intercutting.*]

AD: It's late, it's dark, but it doesn't have to be lonely. Nostalgia Maldita: 1–900–Mexico is waiting for your memories. Pick up the phone. I won't laugh at you. I'll cry with you. Your memories are safe with me. I won't tell. We welcome pesos. For a limited time only, receive an inflatable taco with your phone call.

[*Meanwhile,* ACTRESS, *in the dark, takes off hat. When the video ends, sexy lights up. Phone rings.*]

ACTRESS: Nostalgia Maldita: 1–900–Mexico, how may I help you? [*Changes tone to "sexy."*] So, what do you want to talk about? Well, you phoned in. Okay. I understand. It's been a long time, and you've forgotten how. Talking is like exercise: it hurts. Okay. Slowly now, let's stretch it out. Tell me, do you ever dream of enchiladas? I mean the real ones, with sour cream y todo? Oh, I know, just the cream alone is 95 percent fat, but that's okay. Your memory needs it. It's natural to feel guilt. You're not alone. [*Conversational.*] What else? Oh, I don't think you've forgotten, you just haven't used it in a while . . . it's one of the body's strongest muscles and you say yours is pretty big, right? It can be retrained. Let's see. [*Sexy again.*] Take it out, stick out, stroke it, wide, roll it, now try it, [*Orgasmic.*] "ferro-carril." [*Sticks out tongue.*] Good. "RR con RR cigarro, RR con RR barril, [*Speed up.*] Rápido ruedan los carros cargados de azúcar del feRRocaRRil." Whew! I'd love to meet someone who can do that! No! I won't laugh at your accent. Them—theirs is worse. Do you want to hear them? [*She gets the audience to roll r's; she comments on results. Then, sexy.*] Now I want to hear you. Tell me, what else? [*Conversational.*] Have you been eating in your car? Zipping down the freeway with a burrito in your mouth? The powder guacamole dropped all over your pants? Good. Aha, with Rosarita canned refried beans? Vegetarian? No lard? Oh, non-fat too. Hmm. Well, you may hate it, but that is where your memory is stored. Really, scien-tifically proven, fat is the only thing in your body that has time to remem-ber. Everything else is busy doing its job. Think about it, the heart is busy pumping, the brain is busy thinking, what's fat doing?

No, it doesn't mean you can eat everything in sight. You'll kill your arteries. Be selective. I'm talking good fat, productive fat, healthy fat. You know, the kind you eat with good friends, with your neighbors, with your parents, you know. Aha, aha, aha. Oh, I'm sorry, I didn't know that. [*Concerned, takes off glasses, really listens.*] Well, when you start eating alone, you know you have a problem. Loneliness is a disease, but there is something you can do about it. Do you cook? Hmm. No, the microwave doesn't count. [*Ponders slowly.*] I'll tell you what, let's start you out easy. Why don't you try eating with a fork and a knife. You'll most likely wind up at a table. Yes, you'll have to sit. Yes, it is possible that others will sit down with you. Yes, you'll have to talk to them.

Oh, I know, it's scary, but just think they are me. Just think how much money you're going to save when you learn to talk to your neighbors instead of calling me. [*Genuine laugh.*] What? Come on, say it. Come on. [*The following is very real for her.*] Of course I remember when we could go back, but now we can't. You know that. You are where you are, and you have to live with it, accept it, just deal. We can't go back, not now, not really, not ever. Where's your toothbrush? [*To audience.*] Your toothbrush, take it out. Take it out, I said, it's a trick of the trade. Now, brush, brush, brush. And remember, [*Reminding herself while putting phone down.*] home is where your toothbrush is.

[*Video and music: the Amexican anthem—a fusion of the American and Mexican anthems—with the waving Amexican flag. In the dark,* ACTRESS *picks up the "Amexican flag"—the American flag with green instead of blue background for the stars is mounted on a giant toothbrush—and starts to wave it. Light reveals her. End of video. The frozen image of the* ACTRESS *and flag is clearly lit. She lets the StairMaster carry her down holding the flag. Lights out.*]

GOOD GRIEF, LOLITA

Wilma Bonet

CHARACTERS

(all characters to be played by one person)

WILMA. Lolita's mom and narrator.

LOLITA. Age 4–7, Wilma's daughter; a pesky, precocious child afflicted with cystic fibrosis.

TÍA MARÍA. Wilma's aunt, born in Puerto Rico, lives in New York, loves to tell a good story.

FUNERAL DIRECTOR. Runs Sunset Mortuary, knows his business.

SONIA. Wilma's sister.

DR. AOKI. A nurse.

GEORGINA. Lolita's grandmother.

PINK PRINCESS

PINK QUEEN

SETTING

The East Bay–San Francisco Area, California–December, 1980

> There is a land of pure delight,
> Where saints immortal reign;
> Infinite day excludes the night,
> And pleasures banish pain.
> There everlasting spring abides,
> And never-withering flowers;
> Death, like a narrow sea, divides
> this heavenly land from ours.
> *—Isaac Watts (1674–1784)*

I do not grieve as I might have done. For I have good hope that there is yet something remaining for the dead, as has been said of old, some far better thing for the good than for the evil. *—Plato*

[WILMA *enters.*]

WILMA: Lolita, I wrote you a story. It's called "The Pink Princess." Would you like to hear it? You can keep your eyes closed. Once upon a time, in a different and much prettier place than our world, there was a Pink Princess who lived in a pink cloud castle. [LOLITA *snores.*] Lolita? Lolita? Great, she fell asleep again. [*The doorbell rings.* WILMA *opens imaginary door in apartment.*] Hi. Sure, come on in. She's sleeping. Yep, she's a real trouper. There's food in the kitchen. Help yourself. You're leaving, Father Golinski? Sure, I'll call you if anything happens. [*Walks him to door. Sees the audience.*] My daughter is dying. I wish this was all over. I want to go away— escape. [*Drums are heard playing.*] Whenever I'm not feeling so good, I dance. I rise above everything and look down from a different height, about 5 feet 8 inches. I see myself lying on a beach, listening to the waves calmly rolling at my feet with every beat . . . mmmmmm. I hear—barely—drumming in the distance, calling me. I must go and see who is playing. I hesitate . . . for a moment. I hear my name being whispered in every downbeat. Wil-ma, Wil-ma. As I walk faster, my feet decide to dance me across the beach. A beautiful red tree is dancing in the distance, its arms inviting me for a spin. I accept. I'm dancing through the tree's arms, swirling and dipping as if I were dancing with a good salsa dance partner at Caesar's Latin Dance Palace. This tree is good. It feels my moves. I move with the slightest impulse under and around the red blossoms. The tree stops and invites me inside of it to visit and have a shot of coquito—coconut milk with rum, so sweet I want more. The tree pulls out a hypodermic needle full of coquito, introducing my veins to its extended form and my new dance partner, Ivy—IV Bottle. I rock and roll with my new dance partner through the rainforest—yes, this tree has a rainforest inside of it. The drum is getting louder. As I get closer, I see the player of this drum—an old dark man wearing a white panama hat, all dressed in white. The drum sounds more like coquí sounds—coquí, coquí, coquí, coquí—singing frog sounds? From the drum? The old man looks at me and smiles. [*Music.*] His dark, wrinkled hands playing the tight skin of the drum, cupping his hands, he changes the sound. I hear coughing sounds coming from the drum. The old man smiles again and plays. He stops, lifts the drum, places it across his lap, and out leaps a tiny little brown tree frog from the drum's mouth onto my hand. Coquí, coquí. [*Cough, cough.*] Coquí, coquí. [*Cough, cough.*] What a strange little frog. It smiles at me. I can feel its heartbeat in my hand. Just as I'm about to touch it with my finger, it leaps out of my hand singing coquí, coquí, and transforms into a little girl dressed in pink. She laughs loudly, running into the forest—coquí, coquíhahahahacoquí, coquí. Hahahaha.

[*Cough, cough—repeat sounds segue into hospital sounds, and* LOLITA *coughing, spitting up mucus while watching cartoons. Another child is wheeled into the ward.*]

LOLITA: Hi. Is this your first time in the hospital? I've been here lots of times. What's your name? Jenny. I like that name. My name? Oh, my name is Lolita. It's Puerto Rican. I don't know where that is. I think it's in New York City. My teacher told me my name is not a real name, that it's a nickname. That my real name is Dolores—that means pain in Spanish. But my mom says that I was named after a Puerto Rican revolu-sirnary. Her name is Lolita and she's famous. I think she lived in New York City. Have you heard of her? My mom did a play about her. She was in prison for a long time—I think it's because she pulled out a flag and shot into the congress and wrote a poem about freeing Puerto Ricans. I don't know why they want to be free. Maybe they wanted to be able to dance salsa in New York City. What do you have? Sixty-five roses? You mean cystic fibrosis. You said it funny. I have the same thing. Do you cough a lot? Me too. I hate the physical therapy—all that cupping exercise, holding you upside down. Making you cough up the junk. Aghh! Oooh, I hate the medicine too. I hate that powder stuff they put on the food. It makes the food taste like throw up. Sometimes I throw it away—when the nurse is not looking. With the new nurse I can get away with it, but the old nurse stands there and makes sure I swallow. It's boring here, isn't it? But you get lots of presents. And you don't have to go to school—well, they give you homework, but it's so easy. And you don't have to do it if you're not feeling good or if you're tired. I'm always tired when it's time to do homework. Do you know who John Matuzak is? Brian, the big CF boy down the hall, told me that he plays football with the Oakland Raiders. He was here yesterday and gave me this poster. Do you want it? I don't like football either. The volunteer told me that Mickey Mouse and Goofy are gonna visit today. I want to see them. Wanna play? Let's go to the playroom. They have lots of toys there. I'll race you to the playroom. Silly, you can too race with your IV bottle. Just hold on to the pole, put one foot on the stand, and push.

WILMA: I've known Lolita was going to die since she was two years old. The doctors diagnosed her with the terminal illness—cystic fibrosis. Have you heard of it? I hadn't. At the time, I never imagined a disease that would automatically limit a child's life span. The average mortality rate is from three to five years. Lolita is seven years and two and a half months old. Most moms talk that way about newborns. I count every day. When Lolita was born, she looked like a frog. I swear. Ugly little thing. When the doctor placed her on my chest, all I saw was eyes. She was all wet, didn't have much of a nose, a squatty face, and the biggest brown eyes I have ever seen on a baby. But she looked like a little brown tree frog. A coquí, that's what I called her. Coquí. That's the national animal of Puerto Rico. More like the national amphibian. A tiny little brown frog with big eyes and powerful lungs. The coquí sings at night. Thousands of coquís come out to sing beautifully at night. Loud little guys, too. Scientists have tried to study the coquí, but they can't be relocated, because they die if they're taken out of the island. They are native only to Puerto Rico. Big brown eyes . . . when she stared at me that first time, I had the feeling that she was . . . talking to me, like she was sizing me up. "So, you're the one, the one who's gonna take care of me. You look a little frightened, but you'll do." Little did I know that it was gonna be a big job. There is no test for cystic fibrosis. They couldn't tell just by looking. She was pronounced "a cute, healthy baby girl." She was fine for most of her first year, except for her huge appetite. She was eating as much as her father and was having frequent bowel movements that were very loose. Diarrhea. I feel like I'm talking to a doctor. She got a cold when she was nine months old and the doctor prescribed antibiotics and the steam and said that she would be better in two weeks, but the cold wouldn't go away. For months. The doctors insinuated that I was not taking care of her properly, that I was being a bad mother. This went on for almost six months until this one doctor, who had just attended a CF seminar, noticed a layer of salt on her arm. He gave her a sweat test. This was the test. It was positive. At the hospital, it was twenty-question time. A team of doctors, nurses, and social workers entered the examination room—more like the interrogation room. The room was small. [*She sits.*] They were towering over me, staring with those sympathetic faces and apologizing eyes. "Hello. I am Dr. Aoki. Lolita has cystic fibrosis. Do you know what that is?" "No." "It is a hereditary disease Blah, blah, blah, characterized by excess fibrous tissue in glandular organs like the lungs and pancreas, and by excess, blah, blah, mucus secretion, which causes the blockage of the respiratory passages." "What does this mean, is Lolita going to be all right? Will I be able to do theater?" "It's a terminal genetic disease, one gene is inherited from both parents, blah,

blah, resulting in a 25 percent chance that the offspring blah, blah, blah, would be a full cys." "Excuse me, did I hear terminal? Is that like in bus terminal or like in kick the bucket, decease, and eventually die, terminal?" "Yes, but there are many preventive care measures we can take to keep her healthy. Was there anyone in your family that died from this disease?" "I have no idea. And don't ask me about her father. I don't know anything about his family. He'll probably say the same thing. And you'll have to ask him 'cause I'm not speaking to him. I just got divorced from him last week." That was a tough month, March. Everything marched right into my life—this disease, single motherhood, and a new second career. Nursing. [*Sits as nurse and does the cupping exercise, which resembles drumming.*] "There are eighteen positions to hold the child and administer the cupping exercises. One minute each position. After each position, you must induce the child to cough up the mucus in her lungs, but since your child is very young to cough on her own, you must use the suction machine. You place the child on your lap facing down. Are you right handed or left? Right. Then, with your left arm, you hold the child's legs, as there will be lots of kicking—the child does not enjoy this at all. Then you take the rubber hose apparatus and stick it through her nose and maneuver it to her esophagus, which will cause her to cough, which then will stimulate the mucus to move, which will be suctioned by the hose, and will show up in this neat little jar. Got it? It will get easier with repetition." Nope, it didn't get easier. The nurse forgot to mention that the apparatus will also cause her to vomit, and not only that, but I would be a sympathetic vomiter. The family that throws up together, stays together. I couldn't stand to do that suction thing. I was torturing her. She would kick hard. She didn't understand what or why I was doing this thing to her. She would flash a look at me after the whole mess: "I hate you." It broke my heart. [*Doorbell rings.*] My apartment feels like Grand Central Station. [*Opening door.*] Hi, come on in. She's hanging in there. [*To audience.*] It's been buzzing with people all week—friends dropping by to help, family flying in to lend support. My mom and dad flew in from New York with my Tía María; my cousin Lucy flew in from Florida with her Jehovah Witness husband, George; and José, Lolita's father, flew in from Puerto Rico with his mother, Georgina. They are born-agains. And there's a group of nurses who have volunteered to watch Lolita throughout the day and night. I don't even know their names. They've been staying in her room, sleeping on the floor next to her bed. Lolita's white canopy bed. There's an image of a prairie girl looking down on her from the pink canopy. She smiles calmly through the cloth, waiting to turn Lolita's cage into a sailing ship. But Lolita is anchored to a big green tank full of oxygen. I haven't been at her side all day. Father Golinski—he's the one that left earlier—he's Lolita's friend, a Jesuit priest. He's been by her side throughout the week. I'm not a practicing Catholic, but he asked to give Lolita her last rites and I said okay. Covering all bases, I guess. We got the Jehovahs and Catholics and the born-agains, and the socially politically correct. So why not? I'm tired—too many people coming through the door. Trying to get last-minute things together because it could happen any minute now. Grandmother Georgina is in Lolita's bedroom sitting on the rocking chair, praying. I've been in the kitchen, talking with José. You won't believe what he just said to me. My Tía María is stroking Lolita's hair. [*As* TÍA MARÍA.] "Wilma, mi'ja, ven acá un ratito. You haven't been by Lolita all day. Lie down here next to her and rest." I'm so tired, it feels good to rest next to Lolita. Life is so strange. José just asked me to marry him again. I can't believe it. He said he wanted us to have another child together. We've been divorced and separated for five years. I told him, "No way! I'm not going to bring another child like this into the world to suffer. Uh-uh." Besides, I don't want to be with him anyway. Lolita is breathing quietly. I hear crying. It's Grandmother Georgina. "La nena no se ve bien, la nena no se ve bien. She doesn't look too good." I'm thinking to myself, of course she doesn't look too good. She's dying. "Georgina, let her go. Let her go. She's suffered enough." "Ay, Dios mío!" Georgina and José, who found God in the Lincoln Tunnel, have a congregation of born-agains praying, in Puerto Rico. They claim that God is not going to let her die because they are all praying and God grants requests. [*Gasp.*] Lolita is dying. [*Calling all in the apartment.*] "Lolita is dying. Lolita is dying." We lay our hands on her little body. I can feel the warmth of her life leaving us. There are no tears being shed. A feeling of calm, unity, and love flows throughout the room. We're singing a Diana Ross song—Lolita's favorite song. We just started singing. [*Hum first; sing second; speak third.*] "Reach out and touch somebody's hand make it a better world if you can." I think it's her message. Her body is growing cold. She's gone. Is this it? I don't feel a thing. Is this really it? [*Drum with coquí sounds.*] She's gone. Come back, little coquí girl. I'm running through the rainforest trying to catch up to the pink dress, and she disappears. "Where are you, coquí girl?" I hear laughter behind me. I turn and the laughing seems to be coming from a rose growing in the forest. "Coquí, coquí, I'm here." "Where?" "Coquí, coquí, in the flower, silly." The rose opened its petals and a coquí scrambles out from the center. He-he-he. "You're a little brown frog again." The coquí smiles and leaps onto my shoulder. "Come with me." [*Music stops.*] I feel my sister move me into the kitchen. "Wilma, you are staying here with me." "But I want to go back to her bedroom." "No, you are not going into the bedroom. You are staying here with me. It's the funeral people. They'll take care of her now." "Sonia, I'm fine, I'm not going to fall apart. You expected the 'madre sufrida' bit. I get it. Come on, Sonia, I'm okay, really. Okay? I just want to see her one—What's going on? They're here already. I never heard the doorbell ring. Can't they wait a few minutes? There's the gurney. Oh, they're taking her away. Come on, Sonia, I'm fine, really. I'm not going to break down. She's fine now." I want to tell my sister that I don't feel this pain that is associated with the death of a child. That what I'm feeling is glad that it's over. But that doesn't sound right. Father Golinski is here. He was driving home when he felt her leave. He felt her leave. Other friends are at the door. I can see it in their eyes. They felt her leave too. I'm too tired. It's been a long day, a long week. It's over. My sister takes me to her house. She gives me a Valium. I guess the doctors thought I might need it. Well, what the heck, I deserve a good high. [*The pill is affecting her.*] Whoa-a! Lolita, I know you are feeling better. I know you're in a better, prettier place—that pink world in your pink castle. Lots of people around me. I feel sleepy. Lolita will come to me in my sleep. Lolita. [*Sung.*] Duerme, duerme negrita, que tu mamá está en el campo. Duerme, duerme negrita, que tu mamá está en el campo. Te va a traer muchos dulces para ti. Te va a traer carne de cerdo para ti. Te va a traer muchas cosas para ti y si la nena no se duerme, viene el diablo blanco y zas, le come la patita, chaca puma, chaca puma, chaca puma.

LOLITA: [*She's been playing with a friend, Solina. Walks into* WILMA's *bedroom.*] Shhhh. Mommy, are you awake yet? Mommy, wake up. Come on, wake up. Open your eyes. [*Fakes cough to get attention.*] I want you to read me this book. But first—what are they doing? It's Solina's book. She says that it's about sex. What is sex? Why are they naked? Tell me. I want to know. Okay, I'll wait until you get back from the bathroom. But hurry up, okay? [*Whispering.*] Solina, I think you are right, she does know something. Grown-ups try to hide things sometimes, huh? Not Mrs. Baker, my teacher. She tells us lotsa stuff. The other day, my teacher brought these two baby dolls to school, but when we took off the clothes, the girl doll had a vagina and the boy doll had a penis. None of the girls wanted to play with those dolls, especially when the boys started to laugh and make fun. Boys are so stupid, huh? My teacher asked the class how many girls had vaginas and all the girls raised their hands. Then she ask how many boys have penises and this boy Johnny didn't raise his hand. He thought he didn't have one. That's funny, huh? He said he has a lee-lee—that's what his mother calls it. He thought he didn't have a penis. Ha ha ha. Does your little brother know what he has? I know he's only three years old, but let's ask him. Look at him, standing by the bathroom door. He really is in love with my mom. Josue, come here, we want to ask you something. What do you call your thing down there, you know? A . . . pee-pee. You call it a pee-pee. [*To Solina.*] See what I mean? No, Josue, pee-pee is what you do when you go to the bathroom. That is a penis. No, not a peanut. God, Solina, your brother is so stupid. Here she comes. [*Mom is back.*] Time to read the book, Mommy. Yes, I had breakfast already. No, I'm not hungry. Yes, I took my medicine. Solina's mom gave it to me. Read. Me gusta tu perfume. What does that mean? I like the way you smell. What does that mean. Oh! Oh! Oh!

WILMA: Mmmmm, I smell pancakes, and chorizo con huevos. Better go see how Lolita is do—. That's right. She's gone. Right. Don't have to do the morning routine any more. Usually, I'd get up early, five or six in the morning. Then I would do the cupping exercise—that's at least an hour. I'd rub her stomach, while she coughed up the junk that accumulated in her lungs during the night. Phew, that stuff stunk. Then I would clean out the kidney shape dish—the hospital always let us take them home. We have a collection. Here are my dinner dishes, here are the kidney dishes. Then I would bathe her and change the sheets—accidents in the middle of the night. Then I would dress her. This would take a while. She takes so long to decide what she's gonna wear that day, and whether it was dress day or pants day, and the color, and the right color socks. She's just like her mother. Then I'd prepare the breakfast. The breakfast had to be rich in potassium. That particular nutrient kept her heart running, so we had to come up with a list of foods that are high in potassium. She liked raisins sometimes, bananas sometimes, and avocados a lot. Give her guacamole any time. I'd try not to give her mucus-forming foods, but she's a kid. She loves—loved—pizza, ice cream, and milk shakes. Then it was time for the medicine. I would prepare the pancreatic enzyme—her pancreas didn't produce the necessary enzyme to digest food, so I'd prepare this stuff in applesauce, and the vitamins and the oil to keep her lubricated. Does it sound like I was maintaining a car? We would joke about it. We would say every time she'd go to the hospital, she was going in for a lube job. Wait a minute. She didn't come to me in my dream. Why? I've heard stories of loved ones coming into your dreams to say good-bye or about how people actually have encounters with the spirits just before they go on, you know, to another world or realm. Tía María told me that her father's spirit had come to her in the middle of the night. He was wearing a panama hat and stood at the foot of her bed, glowing in the dark. The light seemed to radiate from his hat. He smiled and she felt him say to her that he loved her. When she got the call from Puerto Rico the next morning, she already knew that he had died. Lolita didn't come to me. I wanted to tell everyone, "Hey, she came to me and she's fine." But that's not going to happen. Maybe I'm not open to that kind of thing. Gotta move on. Gotta move on. We need to get the funeral arrangements done. The funeral arrangements. The funeral director . . .

FUNERAL DIRECTOR: Welcome to Sunset Mortuary. As I told your sister Sonia, we will be donating everything, so you don't have to worry. Let's go shopping. Funeral parlor humor—ha ha. Let's begin—the coffin. We have two models in the child size—walnut finish or a white brocade. I think the white one would be lovely for a little girl, don't you think? Well, that was easy. The plaques. We don't use headstones anymore because it makes the grounds look crowded. The plaques allows the meadows to blend in with nature. Lots of deer here, you know. It allows family members to come and picnic with their departed loved ones. I'm not joking. On holidays, this place is jumping. We have quite a few designs, both in marble and metal—both wear nicely. You can have the rose design—that's very nice for a little girl—or it can be simple, no rose, with just a border around her name. Or—you could have both. Yes, these do look very grown up. Let's look in the back of the catalog. I do believe there's one design—where is it?—oh, there it is. This may be lovely for her. The hand stretching out from the heavens, a little girl walking down a path. They're holding hands. Yes, I knew you would like that one. And what would you like on the plaque besides her name, birthday, and—aha. And "Our Pink Princess." Sure, I can add that. Now, tomorrow, I will post the announcement for the newspaper—the obituary. I want to make sure that the spelling is correct. You want to have a Back-key-nay. What is that exactly? A party. Really? A Puerto Rican tradition. I've never heard of it. Is it like an Irish wake? There's lots of drinking there too—and fighting. And the Afro-Americans sometimes have beautiful processions with lots of music and dancing. This sounds wonderful. In that case, I'll give you our biggest room. I think it is so much better to say good-bye like that. I'm in the death business and sometimes it can get morbid. We can use some cheering up. Of course, bring the children. Death is part of living. Let's go to the grounds now and choose her plot. So, tell me, what happens at a Baquiné?

[*The audience hears "people on the bus" sounds.* LOLITA *is going home from school.*]

LOLITA: The University Avenue bus takes us home, huh Mommy? That man is black. You are white. I am brown. But Chinese people are not really yellow. Why do people call Chinese yellow? Their skin looks white to me. Do you know whose birthday it is tomorrow, Mommy? It's Martin Luther King Jr. We learned about him in class today. He was an important person, huh Mommy? He marched and demonstrated so that black people can ride in front of the bus. We learned about how there are so many different color skins. I never noticed that before. When I play with Tanisha and Rainbow, it doesn't feel different. What makes us different? What is pre-ju-dice? Is that when people notice that you are different? Sometimes, the kids at school make fun of me when I cough a lot. That's like being prejudice, huh? The kids in my class don't because they know, but the ones not in my class are stupid. Ignorant? Okay. Like that man who told me to shut up when we went to the movies. Grown-ups are ignorant too. I jumped rope today. I jumped four times in a row, then I started coughing. That's a long time, huh? I wish I could jump for a long time without having to cough. I love jumping rope, and I love making bubbles, and I love dancing like a balle-rina. Mommy, that black man is sitting in the back of the bus. Excuse me, mister, you don't have to sit back there anymore. You can sit in the front now. What did I say?

TÍA MARÍA: Oye, Wilma, mi'ja, ven pa'ca. Te quiero decir algo. In Puerto Rico, when a child dies, they are considered little angels so you don't mourn, you party. Your grandfather, te acuerdas de él, maybe you were too little to remember him. He used to make people laugh en los Baquinés. He was un jíbaro and worked in the plantations cutting sugar cane with his machete grande. We lived en el pueblito de Yabucoa on the side of the montaña overlooking the sugar cane fields. Everything is so green over there, not like Central Park in New York—that is not green. From our casita, you could see la playa with the waves gently kissing the beach and the palm trees bai-lando with the breeze, tú sabe', suavecito. Everyone knew my papa, your grandfather. I think it's because he was a tough man. When you are good with a machine, you know how men are—they like to test each other to see who is más hombre—and he, me dicen, would win every fight. But a long time ago—'chacha, I must have been five years old—Papi took me to this Baquiné at this neighbor's casita down the road. The Martins. As we walked on this red dirt road, you could see the flamboyán trees in bloom with red flowers, and the pana trees heavy with breadfruit. All the casitas were very simple—some made of wood with cardboard roofs, and some were bohíos made of sticks tied together. Those would disappear during a bad hurricane. As we got closer, mi'ja, I could smell a pig roasting. I ask Papi if it was Christmas, because that was the only time that people would make lechón asa'o. He said que no, that we were going to a Baquiné. Bueno, right in front of the yellow casita was this huge pig on a spit being turned by el Señor Martín's brother, Papo. Señor Martín was all dressed up in his white guayabera that his wife made for him. He and the men were drinking pitorro, homemade rum—this was before Bacardi, sabe'—and the women were with la Señora Martín. She looked sad. She was staring at this white box that was on a wooden table underneath a flamboyán tree. The flamboyán tree looked like it was rocking the white box, its red arms swaying gently. In the box was a little girl dressed in white, with a wreath of white carnations on her head. I asked my father really loud, "¿Por qué la nena está durmiendo en la caja? ¿No tiene cama? Why was she sleeping in a box? Doesn't she have a bed?" ¡Qué tonta! ¿No? Papi laughed, "She's not sleeping, mi'ja. She's not with us any more, she's an angel now." "A real angel? Can we wake her up so we can see her fly?" "No, mi'ja. She doesn't need a body to fly. Her spirit is flying right now but you can't see her. This Baquiné is for her." I still didn't know she was dead. I went to play with the other children. We kept playing around the angel, hoping she would wake up and play with us. You really think differently when you're a child. Bueno, a group of men gathered together to play music. One was playing the cuatro, another a guiro, otro maracas, someone else was keeping time, playing los palillos. It was just like Christmas with aguinaldos, plenas, and bombas playing. The oldest of the men started improvising this song, making up the words from his head about el Señor Martín and something about how the little girl danced.

[Sung.]Lo le lo lai, lo le lo lai. Lo le lo lai, lo le lo lai.

Con su padre a'lao, bailaba la negrita.

Con su papi a'lao, bailaba la negrita.

Ahora baila en los cielos con todas las estrellitas.

Ahora baila en los cielos con todas las estrellitas.

He stopped—someone was crying. It was la Señora. She was holding a doll and saying something about her daughter. I know that it was sad, pues porque, you can feel those things. Tú sabes. All of a sudden, the drum started to play a bomba. A circle was formed. I ran to the circle and there was Papi, dancing and shaking his butt. Another man, with a lighted candle in his hand, was chasing Papi around the circle. He was trying to light a piece of paper that was sticking out behind Papi's back pocket. The flame touched the paper and Papi started dancing really fast, shaking his butt as hard as he could, trying to put the fire out in his pants. Everyone was laughing. Then I noticed la Señora was laughing too. She stopped crying. Your grandfather made her forget her grief. That's what he would do at the Baquiné. He was a payaso. How you say it? A grief clown.

WILMA: I told everyone to pass the word: it's going to be a celebration. No black. Wear Lolita's favorite color—pink. What am I going to wear? Pink, of course. But I don't have anything to wear that's pink. Wait a minute, I have this long pink scarf. I could wear that with my black crepe jumpsuit. Uh-oh—pants. I can hear Georgina now. "Pero, mi'ja, ¿por qué pantalones? What will people say? Wear a black dress. That is the correct thing to do." She is so dramática. Let's do the black thing. Let's show the world how much you've suffered, the cross you've had to bear. But the black jumpsuit does look good on me. Maybe I'll accessorize it with the pink scarf and I'll buy some pink earrings. But I don't want to wear black. It's too respectful. It sets a tone, a mood—I can't make up my mind. I wonder what Lolita will look like. I think everyone should get to know their local mortuary so that you look like the person you were after you kick the bucket. They do weird things to your face. My friend Cathy called. She was the first one to view her. She sensed my fear. "Wilma, Lolita looks like a doll. She doesn't look made up. They did a good job. She looks beautiful in her pink dress." [*Relief.*] Father Golinski called. He wanted to check in with me. He's the chaplain at Children's Hospital and Lolita's friend. He said that he knows that Lolita was named after Lolita Lebrón, the Puerto Rican nationalist political prisoner, and that he knows that I did a lot of political organizational work to help free her, and would I mind if he tied in all this with Lolita's life for the service? This is gonna be an interesting sermon.

LOLITA: [*In the hospital, sitting, doing acupressure under her foot and taking deep breaths.*] Go away. Go away. Go away. Hi, Father Golinski. Oh, this? This is a pressure point for my stomach. When I press it with my finger, it makes my stomach feel better. That's what my physical therapist told me.

[*Takes deep breaths.*] Father Golinski, why do they call you Father? How many kids do you have? You have lots of kids, huh? I don't call my daddy Father. I call him Daddy. I went to New York in an airplane to visit my daddy. No, I wasn't scared. I looked out the window and saw all the clouds. It looked really quiet. Can you stand on a cloud? My daddy told me that God is in the clouds but I didn't see him. Well, why can't you see him? He's everywhere. Hmmm, how does he do that? He's inside of you? And me. Well, if he is, then why am I sick a lot instead of being well like other kids, and why did he let Jenny go to the death room—that room across the hall? She never came back. And why are my parents not living together like other kids' parents? Well, I know why. Father Golinski, I think my daddy has the devil in him, but he doesn't know it because he lied to me. He told me that my Auntie Sonia and Uncle Steve broke my parents up. I believed him. But my mommy said that it wasn't true, that the reason they didn't live together anymore was because he—. He—hurt my mommy. She told me she never wanted me to know that he would hit her, because she knows how much I love him. He lied to me. Why? He didn't have to do that. My daddy has the devil in him. My daddy has the devil in him. [*Pause.*] I should forgive him. Why? If he hadn't told me, I would still love him anyway. I still do. He needs to pray a lot, huh? Okay, I'll pray for him. Do I have to say it out loud? [*Prays quietly and quickly.*] The end.

[*At Sunset Mortuary. Day of the Baquiné.*]

WILMA: Everyone whispers in a funeral parlor. Who are they gonna disturb? The funeral director greets me quietly. "Lolita is our celebrity. We're very happy to have her here." The smell of the place is definitely funeral parlor— the flowers. The silence. Someone opens the door. I walk toward the white casket. My heart is beating as if I'm about to meet a lover. She was the love of my life. [*Sees her.*] She looks like a doll in her long pink organza dress. A storybook princess—a Pink Princess. Her hair on her shoulders, drawn back with pink barrettes. On her feet pink crocheted slippers with pom-poms that Sonia had made for her. Her hands crossed on her small chest. You can see her little fat fingertips—the by-product from lack of oxygen. On her head, a crown of white carnations. She looks like she's asleep. She looks beautiful. They did a good job. [*Turns and see friends.*] My God, there's lots of people here. There must be at least a hundred and fifty people, all quietly seated, whispering, waiting, and all with something pink on. No black. Pink shirts, pink ties, both. What a fashion statement. I smell Arróz con Gandules—orange rice, Lolita called it orange—. There it is, in the back of the room, two long tables, set up with food—red beans, Pollo Guisao, and pork roast. Who made the lechón a'sao? Great. Red and white wine and Bacardi rum. ¡Qué chévere! There they are—school friends, hospital friends, theater friends, some with their guitar cases nearby. Flutes, conga drums, a fender ronde—wow!—pink and white flowers surround Lolita's white casket. Her drawings are on the walls around the room. Who put her drawings up? My sister, I bet. This party is paralyzed. I feel like doing a stand-up routine. Hey, everybody! It's so quiet here. Who died? Just kidding. You see these pictures on the walls? These are Lolita's self-portraits: Lolita with her IV bottle. This is my friend, Ivy. Wherever I go, she goes. [*Laugh.*] Today, please, no whispering allowed. Let's talk loud. Let's drink. And let's dance. Javier, play us a salsa tune, por favor.

[*Piano salsa music plays.*
Christmas at the hospital.]

LOLITA: Mommy, I did something stupid today. I broke my kissing Barbie doll's neck. I got mad at her because she wasn't kissing very good. She's supposed to kiss when I squeeze her arms, but she wouldn't. She's so stupid. Why can't she work right? And why are you so late? I hate it when you don't come when you're supposed to. This is the worst Christmas. Here comes another Santa Claus. I thought there was only one Santa. Why are there so many Santas? They must be actors, huh? I hate being here. I'm sorry, Mommy, for being so angry. I wanted to be home for Christmas, not in no hospital. There's nobody to play with. Is that for me? Are those the presents the real Santa brought me? Oh, my go—a Ken doll and a bed for Barbie. Just what I wanted. Barbie meet Ken. You see how stupid she looks. Her head keeps turning around like the exorcist girl. See? That looks funny, huh? [*Pause.*] Take me home, Mommy.

[*Salsa music.*]

WILMA: Javier, that was great. By the way, where'd you get those polyester pink pants? It's great to see so much pink. Pink power. Lolita loves it. Believe me. I gotta share something with all of you. Lolita knew she was gonna die. Check this out. I had just gotten her from the hospital. We're at my sister's house. Lolita was lying down in a room upstairs. I go up to check up on her—she's blue. I mean really blue. I say, "Lolita, what's the matter?" She doesn't say anything. I check the portable oxygen tank. "Lolita, it's empty. Why didn't you say something?" She looks at me with her big eyes and shrugs her shoulders. I said, "Oh, no you don't, you're not

leaving us yet. Grandma and Grandpa just flew in from New York to see you. You can't do this. We are not ready. We are not ready." I couldn't believe I said that. I could just hear her say, "Okay, I'll grant one last request, but after this, I'm outta here." Lolita said good-bye to all her favorite things. She said good-bye to the swing in the park. Here she is—so skinny—attached to the portable oxygen tank. She pulls off the oxygen thingamagig, gets on the swing, and starts to swing higher than she ever had before. As if she was trying to reach the clouds. After she was done, she stopped the swing with her skinny little leg. Then she calmly walked away and never looked back. The next night, about fifteen to twenty of her friends dropped by. Her room was full of people. She was talking with them and making them sing her favorite songs. Then she asked me to read "The Pink Princess" to them, a story I wrote for her that I thought she hadn't heard because she kept falling asleep every time I tried to tell it to her. Well, I told the story that night, and I realized that she had heard the story after all. It was her way to say good-bye to her friends. She said good-bye to her foods. It must've been around five o'clock in the morning. Tía María and my brother Edwin were in the room. She was having a tough time. I was rocking her. "Lolita, I love you. You know you're the Pink Princess in the story," and she said, "Uh-huh." "And you're going to a better, beautiful place" (as if I knew where). "Uh-huh." That's when Tía María got up and said, "Ay, Dios mío, ella sabe—she knows." Then I hear Lolita whisper, "I want a milk sh—." "What, baby?" "I want a pineapple milk shake."
"Honey, it's 5:00 A.M. No one is—"
"I want a pineapple milk shake."
My brother says, "I'll get her a milk shake."
"Pineapple!"
"It better be thick and lumpy."
"Thick and lumpy. Where in the world am I gonna find a pineapple milk shake at five o'clock in the morning?"
"Frostee Freeze, University Avenue, open all night."

GEORGINA: Stop it! Ay, Dios mío! ¿Qué haces? What are you doing? You are sacrilegious. You make fun of God. He will punish you. This should be a rosary. She is wrong. She is not real Puerto Rican. I am Georgina Bonet and I am Puerto Rican. There is no such tradition. Baquiné. This is not the way a funeral should be.

WILMA: Wait a minute. She loved music. She loved theater. She loved dancing. She may have been sick but that never stopped her from living. I did all I could to give her a good life. It wasn't easy. I could have given her up. I almost did. She was so stubborn sometimes. She wouldn't take her medicine every day, and I couldn't force it down her throat. Once—I was so tired that day—I'd been working eight hours a day and using public transportation. She refused to take her medication. She wouldn't let me do the therapy, and we fought. I got so angry at her. I remember telling her that if she didn't take the medicine, she was gonna die. And she said, "I don't care, Mommy, I would rather die. I hate the medicine. I hate the therapy. I hate it. I hate it, and I hate you." I smacked her. I hit her legs so hard. I know it was hard because my hand was burning. I had lost it. The next day I called the CF unit at the hospital and told them I wanted them to find a good family for Lolita. I wanted to give her up because I no longer had control over the situation and . . . and I felt like I was killing her. An emergency meeting was set up with the social worker, head nurse, therapist, and whoever else—I don't remember. They asked me did I really want to do this, and I said no, but I was burnt out. I told them what happened and I said I never ever wanted to hit her again, ever. Then they ask, "What can we do to help you keep her?" While I was with them, Lolita was in physical therapy talking to the head therapist, telling her that she didn't want her mother doing the therapy because she never gets a chance to be read stories at the end of the day like other kids in her class. The hospital made a few phone calls that day and a therapist was assigned to go to her school to give her the extra therapy she needed. We finally ended up having real mother and daughter time at the end of the day. Somebody sing, please.

TÍA MARÍA: Mi'ja, ¿Cómo te sientes? Don't let her bother you. Here, have some coquito. I made it. I think Lolita is very happy. Ay, Dios, here comes the funeral guy. Por favor, Georgina, take it easy.

FUNERAL DIRECTOR: Ms. Bonet, is everything going fine? The place is yours. Use the lobby as well. Why, thank you. I'll have a drink—coconut milk and rum—de-li-cio-so.

TÍA MARÍA: That funeral guy is nice. I like him. [*Drumming is heard.*] Wilma, mira, who's that guy with the panama hat?

WILMA: Standing by the door is an old dark man playing a beautifully carved drum. The drum is strapped across one shoulder. As he plays, the people in the room start to move their bodies as if they're under some kind of spell. My Tía María dances herself to the center of the room. The dark old man follows her around the room as if he is playing just for her. All of sudden, the whole room is swaying. Everyone is lining up behind the drummer, dancing, holding on to each other's hips. It looks like a snake dance. The party spills out into the lobby, in and out through doorways, circling around the flowers and the casket. The pink snake is getting longer and longer. Then it coils, tighter and tighter, spinning faster and faster. Everyone is losing their balance. My god, they're falling to the floor laughing. [*Laughs.*] The old dark man rises and with him a little girl dressed in pink. Hand in hand, they walk to the door. They turn and smile at me. Lolita, you want me to tell the story of the Pink Princess? Stay where you are. I'm going to tell a story. Once upon a time, in a different and much prettier place than our world, there was a Pink Princess, who lived in a pink cloud castle. On this day, Her Pinkness was walking in her pink flower garden looking very bored. "Oh dear, I'm so bored. I can't find anything to do. I wish I could do something different. I better go speak to the Pink Queen." So she went to visit the Pink Queen.

"Hey, Pink Queen, I am so bored with all this pink cloudy stuff. Isn't there something else to do?"

"What about picking flowers?"

"I pick flowers all the time."

"Do you still enjoy the pink milk shakes?"

"Yes."

"Oh I see. What about your pink friends, do you still play with them?"

"Yes, but—."

"Well, this is serious. We must find a solution."

The Pink Queen went to her "Solutions to Boredom" file (which happens to be pink) and found one in the pink of time.

"Pink Princess, how would you like to visit a different place? But it will only be for a little while."

"How different is this place?"

"Well, it's not pink. And you will live in an apartment instead of a pink cloud castle."

"WOW! An apartment! What's that?"

"It's a home. And you'll be staying with a mom and dad."

"Mom and dad, what are those?"

"Those are people that will take care of you until it's time for you to return."

"When do I leave?"

"You can leave right away. But firs—here, take this bag of pink dust. You will need to dust your face every day in order to stay there. But once the pink dust is gone, it will be time for you to return."

At the next sunrise, when the horizon was beginning to glow a soft pink, the Pink Princess went off on her trip. She stepped onto a pink dream cloud in the shape of a panama hat, laid her head down, and drifted into a sweet sleep. The next time she woke up, it was to a blue day with blue sky, blue sea and blue birds. She really grew to love Mom and Dad. She spent a lot of time with Mom and learned to make cookies and make puppets. She loved the hand puppets because she could be two people at the same time. There were always new people to meet. The little Pink Princess would make friends right away. Her pink smile and her pink charm were irresistible.

Years went by and the Pink Princess saw that the pink dust bag was nearly empty, but she wanted to stay longer in the blue world. So she began using only a teenie-tiny bit for her pink smile. But her smile got smaller and smaller and smaller. She knew it was time to go. Mom noticed that the Pink Princess was not smiling.

"What is the matter?"

"I have to go back to where I came from, so I must say good-bye."

Mom told the princess that she was going to miss her. The Pink Princess gave her a teenie-weenie smile and went to sleep. The pink panama hat dream cloud carried her back to the Pink Kingdom. When she awoke, all her pink friends, flowers, rainbow, and the Pink Queen were around her. A big smile came to her face when she saw them. That day, the Pink Kingdom had a big party to welcome back the little princess. But she kept thinking about her blue world friends and Mom and Dad. How sad they must be with no pink around them. The Pink Queen announced that it was time for the little Pink Princess to open her special present. "A special present for me."

[*She unwraps present.*]

"It's a beautiful mirror."

"But it's not just a mirror—it's a magic pink mirror. Whenever you want to see your blue world friends, you will. Just look in the mirror."

"There's Mom. But she looks sad."

"Touch the mirror."

[*She does.*]

"She has a smile. A pink smile."

A ROOMFUL OF MEN

A RADIO FOR THE EYES PERFORMANCE PIECE

Amparo García Crow

SETTING

A dark room. A blood-red gauze rope hangs off the wall and trails off toward a miniature "foundation" of what represents a house made up of two cement blocks that later become a platform to stand on and crouch over. To one side a large conch shell leans against the "house." On the other side is a pink, plastic doll with a plum-colored face/head. Further Upstage is a small bench that eventually becomes the front seat of a 1961 Chevrolet Impala that has two industrial-size cans of tomatoes on each side. One of the cans is filled with pennies. The other is full of tiny, plastic "naked babies"—miniature dolls, an inch tall. On the opposite side of the "car" is a ladder. Next to it is a clothes rack with a long red satin cloth, dark clothes, and a glow-in-the-dark "death mask" that hangs beside the attire. Downstage Left is a solitary starfish and sand. Draw shapes in the sand with a finger or two. A small box has been turned over to become a "table," on which a tiny pink tea set sits. Downstage Center there is a 60-mm projector.

ACT ONE

[Lights come up. I am standing in the center in a classic black-and-white 1950s dress with a red petticoat underneath. My bosom is stuffed with purple grapes and a green snake, but because they are hidden, it looks like I am a full-figured "babe." I stare at the audience in silence.
Sound: The skipping of a record, a film strip, or the like is heard over the projector, which comes on. An empty reel spins, creating an empty

"white" frame against the black wall. I am framed within this bright light, as if inside the square or frame. My mouth is moving, but there is no sound. Finally I speak, in person.]

ME: I've been sitting here, watching the crowds pass me by unseen. I think I've died and gone, not exactly to heaven, but to some dark room someplace, some Saturday matinee somewhere. I watch these reels like a mute. The sound coming from someplace outside myself, my mouth moving, words being said but one step removed, like the not-so-graceful dub of a foreign movie. [*Gesture: I grab a fistful of pennies and hide them in my bag, as if facing someone who has appeared out of nowhere.*] A woman keeps showing up, regardless of where I am and what I'm doing. She terrifies me. I don't recognize her at first. She always says the same thing: "Ay, this begging, it's a bad thing, but what can I do?" [*Gesture: Establish the "needy" gesture that will symbolize "Mother" during the rest of the piece.*] "What can I do?" I scream at her. [*Gesture: I mirror the distraught woman's violent arm gestures, then stop abruptly.*] I know she just wants change. [*Gesture: I dump a handful of pennies on the floor, my arm frozen in an upside-down "grip."*] I give her whatever loose change I have in my pocket in hopes that she will leave as quickly as she came, but not today. She just stands there, staring. "What are you looking at?" I ask. Finally, she hands me this compact. [*Gesture: The grip, turned over, becomes a distorted "compact." I look into my own palm, as if looking at a cosmetic mirror.*] "There's nothing in it," I scream, "but this piece of broken mirror." As I watch her disappear, I realize, oh my god—although she looks totally different, like somebody else—that's my mother.

[*Gesture: I hide the compact between my legs as if securing it in my own vagina. This is not literal, as much as it is a distinct movement that repeats at significant moments of "sublimation" throughout the piece. Song: "Ghost Town." Gesture: On all fours, I crawl to the "house," climb onto it as if a four-legged animal of some kind, and crouch over it as if I'm peeing.*
Song: "Ghost Town." Sound: Rhythmic rusty box springs—"the beat." I move accordingly, as if I have to pee, but am, at the same time, forced into involuntary convulsive motion. The sound should build into a climax.]

ME: I keep coming back to this house where I lived with my parents after they got married . . . the second time. It's a two-story, haunted, cement box built in 1878; that's why the rent is so cheap. Some of the windows are boarded up to keep the heat inside; it has running water and rats bigger than my cat Betsy. There's a stove connection, but I don't remember a restroom. "Is she asleep?" I hear them ask each other almost every night, before the rusty mattress coils turn my slumber into a trampoline, their sounds hungry and animal right next to me. I can feel strange, big sensations between my little legs, something radiating on and off, a round and round yearning I would eventually recognize as desire.

[*Gesture: I climb off the house, shake off as if something might be dripping between my legs. I bend down to take off the first pair of underwear. They get as far as my ankles.*]

GIGI'S VOICE: [*Recorded.*] Once you walked inside there, no other house or place existed anywhere near or around it. It was like you walked into another dimension.

[*Gesture: Surprised, I stare at the conch shell, as if Gigi's voice is coming from there.*]

ME: My cousin Gigi?

[*Gesture: I pick up the conch shell and hold it to my ear and listen. I do a "dance" with the underwear at my ankles.*]

GIGI'S VOICE: [*Recorded.*] I would have never stayed in there alone for nothing. It was dark. The stairs were dangerous—rotted through. There was always a "charco" in the front of the house, a leak from some broken pipe—like water had died there a long time ago, that dead pond smell. I don't remember a restroom. We pottied outside, next to where you had a box of play dishes, remember? It was a house of spirits, like the "Twilight Zone" for sure, and your dad—.

[*Gesture: I quickly kick the underwear off, pushing them away, as if wanting to hide them somewhere around the cement blocks.*]

GIGI'S VOICE: [*Recorded.*]—whenever he was around, I knew we were in for an adventure. He was bien "splendor," bien handsome. When he had money, he would spend it on everyone. I knew I would come home with something too. It was your mother I was always afraid of.

[*Gesture: I take the shell off my ear and take it over to the area where the starfish and sand are. I lay the shell down as the lights go off in that area. Sound: Abstracted electronic gadgets. Gesture: I climb a ladder and deliver this next section like a bad "industrial" actress delivering lines.*]

ME: Someone designed an experiment to study what I am, calling it "Seeing with Your Eyes Closed." [*Gesture: Rotating hands that eventually synchronize as the story describes "empathy."*] They took two people and they put them into separate rooms. Person A is put into a deprivation room. Person B is put into a separate room and given random electric shocks. Both are wired for brain waves, skin resistance, pulse, and breathing changes. Person A is asked to guess when Person B is given electric shocks. Well, at first A's guessing has nothing to do with B's shocks, but A's polygraph shows significant physiological changes over the time B is given an electric shock. Now, we may conclude A was not conscious of the shocks, but the polygraph shows that A was conscious on a more biological, fundamental level in his body. His body knew of the happenings, even if his mindbrain did not. [*Gesture: I take out "the compact" I stashed earlier and look at myself.*] Till this day, if you ask my mother about me she will say, "Amparo . . . she was never any trouble to me." [*Gesture: I climb down the ladder, turn my back to the audience, and re-insert the "compact" in my vagina.*] That was our compact, an agreement we sealed in the womb. [*Music: "Womb Theme." Gesture: One of my feet ends up on top of where the blood-red rope/cord ends, which represents the umbilical cord. I wrap myself around it and dance with it as I speak the following.*] The womb is a dark room where your skin is not your own. Your eyes can only see inward. It's like floating in an isolation tank surrounded by waves of sound. I have no sight. I am pure sensation inside of darkness itself. In the womb, I am a polygraph wired to my mother's brain waves, skin resistance, pulse, and breathing changes. [*Gesture: Turbulent movement that eventually forces me to the floor on my back. Music: Turbulent "Womb Theme."*] Whatever is going on out there today has got my mother's heart pounding adrenaline into my tiny veins. I suddenly feel hostile. "Don't fuck with brain—stop!" That's the message I send—"stop!" Via the bloodstream like a telegram— "stop! I won't be any trouble to you. Please stop!" [*Pause.*] That's too early in the game to promise anybody that. [*Gesture: Unravel myself out of the umbilical cord.*] My mother had figured out how to do abortions on herself at nursing school. She would insert a long red tube into her cervix and disturb her womb enough to expel whatever was in there at the time. When she heard my father was going to prison, she thought it merciful to expel the already perfectly formed girl fetus that was conceived before me and flush her down my grandmother's toilet. [*Gesture: I lay the cord down, empty. My hands take on the shape of a triangle as if looking into the womb of my mother's truth.*] When my mother visited recently, I asked, "Did you try to abort me?" "No, Amparo, not you, I threw hot water at your father." My mother has a way of answering questions indirectly. Consequently, she tells the truth accidentally. She answered me so quickly, so directly, it was obvious that we are remembering the same incident. The womb is not about facts; it's about sensation. In utero, my skin feels like those inexpensive walls they build cheap apartments out of these days. I can feel and hear everything that the neighbors do and say, and I only know I can hardly wait to get out of the neighborhood. [*Song: "Rest Of My Life." Gesture: I return to the "safe" area where the shell and starfish are. For these sections, I speak simply and conversationally with the audience, without the more elaborate gestures that represent "the unconscious" throughout. I have tea with an audience member and improvise "More tea? Sugar? etc." throughout the following monologue. Gesture: I establish the drinking of tea that will symbolize Vera falling out of the window later in the piece.*] Have you ever seen "The Secret Life of Plants"—the movie when they wire plants up to polygraphs as somebody chops lettuce violently right in front of them, causing the needles to go haywire like the plants are having sympathetic heart attacks? Same reaction when they throw live shrimp into boiling water; the plants empathetically feel the shock and distress of the shrimp, causing the polygraph to register it dramatically. [*Gesture: Establish arm gesture that will represent my father and his burned arms throughout.*] My mother threw hot, boiling water at my father the week I was getting ready to be born, and born I was in a little transient motel on North Beach in Corpus Christi, Texas, on April 4, 1958, where my father washes dishes at a seafood restaurant down the street. My mother follows him there, leaving the tiny, unemployed ranch community behind, hoping they'll both find work, but in reality their problems intensify. [*Gesture: A tumble backward, legs in the air, curl back in. My dress creates a tent-like effect out of which I am born.*] The night I am born, my father asks my brother if he would like to see a little angel; my brother assumes I am an honest-to-God angel for the first year of my life. By the time he finally figures out that I am a mortal after all, my parents have also figured out that their marriage is too. They divorce before my first birthday. [*Gesture: I tie the blood-red cord onto itself and hang it out of the way on the wall, then move Downstage Left and do the "Camel"—a yoga gesture*] *that has me on my knees, my back in a back bend, arms resting on my heels. Moving into and out of this posture, oddly, looks "erotic" in an abstracted way because of the neck and arched back extensions. Video: Still-life patterns of light rippling created by light. Music: "Ecstasy Theme."*] With my father gone, the house is unusually peaceful tonight. There is no hollering or dark, jungle moans in the middle of the night. I am alone in their bedroom in the center of their bed so that I can't roll off. I am very aware of my tiny infant size, limited to the use of only my head, like a primitive monocle or some camera that's been launched to the moon. I'm very attracted to the light on my right, the porch light, how it fragments through the blinds, creating a curious splatter of lines on the bed. For this moment, I feel as whole as a plant drawn instinctively to the light. I remember thinking this has to be the most beautiful sight I have ever seen. I can feel the ocean breeze pushing the blinds against the window. I can feel the cotton sheets on every inch of my electric infant skin, recording forever this sensation as my first sensual memory.

[*Gesture: I move to the seemingly "safe" place again and sing. Song: "Sanddollar." Gesture: I pick up the shell and listen.*]

MY MOTHER'S VOICE: [*Recorded.*] Pos a ver, Ampie. I don't remember—you get old y te patina el coco. I've been taking lysine—it's brain food. They have it there at the HEB. You should try. Pero a ver, that house . . . pos a ver, I think we had a restroom. Did we have a table?

[*Gesture: It becomes obvious that I am impatient with my mother's slow, distracted rambling.*]

MY MOTHER'S VOICE: [*Recorded.*] I remember Beto getting married—you remember Beto, my old boyfriend when I was divorced from your daddy? I remember watching Beto from that window where the bed was, getting married in the church across the street. Maybe the restroom was downstairs where the gatitos negros lived.

[*Gesture: The moment they are mentioned, I put the shell down, face up, as if its mouth remains open. I walk away from it, almost in a daze. I return to the side of the house and remove a second pair of underwear with which I repeat the earlier "dance." This time, the underwear stays around my ankles as I walk to the area where I repeat the "Camel" motion from the earlier section, suggesting the similarity between the "light" (flight) in both memories.*]

MY MOTHER'S VOICE: [*Recorded.*] I felt so sorry for them, somebody killed their daddy, remember, ah, sí, como tu papá, qué curioso.

MY VOICE: [*Recorded.*] My mother is talking about a family who lived downstairs. A single white mom and her two sons called Los Gatitos Negros, nicknamed after their dark-skinned father, known around town as the black cat who was killed in a brawl in some bar. All I remember about them is the strange smell of urine mixed with fresh tortillas toasting on the grill whenever I visited. One afternoon—no adult anywhere—I find myself downstairs in their house on the center of a full bed. I do not remember how I got there exactly, except that I am surrounded by a pack of adolescent wolves. Right as I feel the sensation of my underwear hitting my ankles, I feel limited again to only the movement of my head. I remember looking to the right as if looking frantically, as if looking for my first memory of the light, and then, suddenly, I'm gone. It's my first memory of flight.

MY MOTHER'S VOICE: [*Recorded.*] Your brother used to play with the boys, remember, sí, mira no más. Oyes lo que crees. I ran into Alfredo—did I tell you?—at the post office. A tear ran down his face when I went up and I took his hand. I said, "I forgive you, Alfredo, now it's between you and your god." Pos he's been out for a year. It's the anniversary of your father's death next week, you know, it's not like Alfredo doesn't know that. Beware the eyes of marsh, Alfredo, se lo dije, sí, se lo dije . . . ay . . . esta vida. Pos, that house, Ampie. Yes, I think there was a bathroom right by the porch, no? I think I had left your daddy. Sí, we got remarried y todo pero, I had left him again 'cause you know your daddy, bien smart—he had the highest IQ when they tested him in the Air Force, pero era mañoso. ¡Ay, Dios mío! Pos, he was with that Rosalinda, ¿como se llamaba?—Rosalinda Betancourt, era de la calle. Pos, se la mataron. Fíjate—

ME: [*Interrupting.*] Somebody killed her?

MY MOTHER'S VOICE: [*Recorded.*] Pos, they picked your daddy up. He was in jail for a while. They killed her in her sleep. Your daddy always said it was his crazy cousin René who did it—the one with the split personality. He had two, two personalities, that René. He comes from some real cuckoos, you know that?

[*Gesture: I walk up to the shell and turn it over as if hanging it up or closing its mouth, obviously agitated.*]

ME: All I asked was where the restroom was! [*Gesture: I stand on the "house" and look out. My tone is that of playful, curious "little girl."*] I can see the people next door from up here. The little brother with the magnifying glasses for eyes that make his long dark lashes look like guppies swimming in a fish bowl. He likes to watch me from behind that bush, like a hunchbacked Romeo watching his Juliet up on the balcony. He lives in that tiny, pink, shingled shack with his insane older brother, Wyoming, a misplaced Chicano cowboy in a Lone Ranger outfit, who roams the streets, talking to the invisible about Wyoming, and how he hitched a ride all the way there and back one day. They live with their three sisters, Las Búfalas, the town prostitutes. They are huge, identical in size and shape. They wear tiny skintight miniskirts with their peroxide hair teased tall and wide, giving them the unmistakable look but, of course, not the dignity of buffaloes, in the feminine form. [*Gesture: I play "sexy" with the audience, walking through the aisles, sitting on laps, etc., as if imitating the archetypal "whore" or streetwalker. Song: "Cowboy Dreams." Gesture: I deliver this like an edgy sermon, with an initial "chola"-like attitude that softens into the innocent, curious little girl.*] There usually wasn't any food in our house. I had to be hospitalized for a near-deadly kidney infection caused by dehydration and malnutrition, which is why I perfected the art of conversation early on to charm the landlady across the street. She would always have a plate out for me, like I just happened to get there in time for dinner, even if it was hours before or after. On my way to her house this time, I see the neighbor hiding behind the anaqua tree, off the road, toward the creek. He likes to sit there with his hand in his pants. Today he offers me a silver dollar if I'll play with him. [*Gesture: The innocent little girl fascinated with the money, I kneel obediently, distracted, until I look up and freeze in quiet terror—mostly stillness.*] What big eyes you have, I say, what big teeth, what big—. I thought he was a little boy. Now I see that he's a man. And, although I am only four years old, I already have more sense than he. "My god, little girl." His voice is now a thousand miles away. "You're such an angel. You want to see my bird?" [*Gesture: The dance of compromise, which ends with my palm in an upside down "flipping the bird" position in front of my vagina. During the second verse of this, the ghost projector comes on again. I stand in the square, pointed light, my back to the audience, interacting with my shadow on the wall. Song: "Dante's Dare." Music: Grooving, suburban theme with a funky fifties-style Hawaiian twang takes on a playful persona inviting me to play again.*]

I nod "no" initially, still inside the glare of the light. Finally, like a child who forgives and forgets, I put a scarf around my head and cat-frame glasses, looking like the glamorous "picture" of a 1950s Hollywood mama riding in an imaginary car.] I'm riding in a brand new '61 Chevrolet Impala. Already a tall, lanky thing for three, I'm standing on the car seat pushing against the roof with my head, leaning against my mother's driving arm. We'll cry next week when they repossess the car. The first of many etchings into my brain that nothing pleasurable is permanent. My mother could never resist free introductory offers of any kind. [*Gesture: I take the can of plastic babies and throw them grandly out into the audience, walking across the stage like a beauty queen throwing kisses.*] She would order away for merchandise, fully intending to keep it without the slightest means of paying for it. Consequently, we had the first three volumes of everything—*The Illustrated History of the Civil War, The ABCs of Medical Encyclopedias.* At least the encyclopedias proved useful when I used them to force my cousin Gigi into sitting there and watching my makeshift cabaret shows underneath the kitchen door proscenium—" 'Cause if you don't, I'm gonna read to you about cirrhosis of the liver or cancer of the colon." Gigi was terrified of the graphic photos of glands gone crazy—[*Gesture: I dig into the can and squish out plastic babies through my hands.*]—making people pus up or bulge up, photo after photo of war-torn leprosy skin or grodey cancerous organs devastated by alcoholic excess and greasy food. That was usually enough to get her to sit there quietly and watch me turn into Doris Day. [*Song: First three lines of "Qué Será, Será."*] I am loving this ride, just my mother and me. I feel snug and in motion, like a peaceful day in the womb. [*Song: Chorus of "Qué Será, Será."*] The car stops abruptly in front of a little shack with a mangy, barking guard dog. My mother honks and a strange man approaches. [*Gesture: The "compact"/gripping gesture appears, acting like a hand puppet of my mother, with which I interact.*] "I want you meet Ramón, your daddy," she says to me, like I'm supposed to know what that means. There hasn't been a daddy in the house since I was born. There's been a roomful of men parading through my mother's arms. I recall several boy-friends, particularly the Vitalis hair of one who rode in this very car just last week. [*Music: "Ecstasy Theme" is heard again.*] He sat right there as I watched him like an exotic animal at the zoo. Mesmerized, I reach for the back of his head to feel his barber buzz. [*Gesture: The "compact" viciously slaps my own hand as I reach for the imaginary head of this man.*] "No seas insimosa," my mother screams at me as if I had just touched his penis instead. [*Gesture: I push the "compact" away as if getting somebody out of my face.*] Insimosa is a term used to imply that a woman is fresh or all over a man—I'm three years old. It'll be years before I'm insimosa and with a vengeance, too. [*Gesture: My free hand struggles with my other hand, which now represents the "compact." I win, forcing the "compact" to face the audience as if guilty.*] She's talking about her own behavior as I have witnessed many times recently. Apparently, she's gonna marry Ramón—my father—again. She was fourteen when she married him the last time. An uncle had told her that if he saw her with my father or his kind, he would beat her, so when the uncle happens to catch her talking to my daddy at the drugstore one day, she doesn't ever go home again. They elope to the Duck's Quack, a seedy motel in the center of town. [*Gesture: Back in the car, I act out the following.*] All I can see of my father from where I'm standing is a huge tattoo on his left arm of a ship with a large sail. I can't read yet, but it's explained to me that my mother's name is ingrained on the sail of his brown skin. When he pokes his head into the car to take a look at me, I look away, staring at the plastic figure of the Virgin Mary on the dashboard instead. I get a very bad feeling about it all. [*Music: "Ecstasy Theme" reprises for a long moment.*] I liked the Vitalis man so much better. One afternoon, that same uncle calls my mother the black sheep of the family. [*Gesture: I tear off the scarf, hold my two arms up like fists arguing with each other. Music: Turbulent "Womb Theme."*] "You're the 'joto,'" she screams, "doing it with men on the side and then marrying a woman to cover it up." He tried to slap her, but instead, she violently pulled on my great-grandmother's tablecloth, sending plates and food all over the place, upsetting everybody's Thanksgiving that year. She dragged me back to this house with her, where she took a heavy cast-iron skillet and hit herself hard on the head, making herself pass out on the floor. I thought she was dead. [*Gesture: Holding the scarf, glasses still, then dropping them painfully into the heap, where the house is.*] I keep going back to that spot—the house where I lived when I was four years old. [*Gesture: I pick up the can of pennies and start dropping one at a time on the floor, as if popcorn or breadcrumbs to find my way back if I have to. This leads me back to the shell. I re-enact the "tea" gesture, the tumble gesture ending in a kneeling position, my "compact" arm slowing, coming to a painful rest, as if weighted down by the grief of it all. Every time a penny lands, there is a haunting musical theme that captures the "fun" yet melancholy existence of a child's imagination.*]

MY OLDER SISTER: [*Recorded.*] Vera and I were playing with pennies one day, Ampie, throwing them down the rain shoot, just to hear them clang and roll all the way down, when Ramón came home and found us throwing money away. Ramón would sell his blood for spending money. So in a way, it was his blood we were throwing out the window, right? So he unlatches the window and crawls onto the roof to get his pennies back. The thing is, he forgot to latch the screen back up. So a few days later, Vera and I are playing dishes. I'm sitting on a little chair, I'm four. She's three. So I pour her some tea. She takes it and swings it back real big, Ampie, causing her to fall headfirst out the window. She might have lived, because there's a man mowing the grass downstairs and she fell right on him. He broke her fall, but when she rolled off him, she cracked her head open on this big old rusty nail sticking out of some board on the ground, and that's what killed her really, besides her broken neck. If only Ramón hadn't left the window open. I don't know. For no reason, right after Vera died, her doll's head turned black, Ampie—plum-color black. The rest of her body stayed pink and plastic. Remember those dolls that had the marble eyes that rolled back behind their head? Well, her head turned completely black—black with blond hair and blue eyes. It was weird. But even weirder was that every night, for a long time afterward, she would come and talk to me in my sleep. Mama Elvira would see me sitting up, talking to her with my eyes closed, saying, "No, I don't want to go with you." She wanted me to play with her so bad. [*Gesture: I take the shell, gather the doll and the two pair of underwear, and put them inside the can of pennies, as if trying to put it all away somehow. I crouch over the house again like before. Music: "Sanddollar Theme" reprised.*] If you're supposed to get hanged, you're not gonna get shot or drown—that's what my grandmother would say. Fate is fate. For a long time, she kept the newspaper article with the picture of the window, showing Vera's fall with arrows. She kept all Vera's little dresses till the Hurricane Beulah flood came and forced eight feet of dirty creek water into the house. For a whole week, boats paddled around the roof like it was some giant rock jutting out of a lake somewhere. Finally, the water went back down, leaving a thick inch of dirt on everything inside and out. I was the first one to open the screen door when a water snake came slithering out the front door like it'd been shacking up in our living room the whole time we stayed downtown in the courthouse shelter. I jumped back, terrified as it slid past me, noticing a ring of all things, embedded in the dirt where my feet had been—an engagement ring the flood carried out of some neighbor's jewelry box. [*Gesture: I put on an imaginary ring.*] Me and the snake—engaged somehow. [*Gesture: I take the can of stuff and "sit on it"—hide it underneath the full skirt of my dress.*] So we had to throw away everything that didn't launder well, even that spooky doll of Vera's. My grandmother took my older sister and brother to live with her after Vera's death. "I'm too old to take three," she said apologetically, which meant I had to stay in this house with my parents, alone a lot of the time, since my mother had to be at the hospital at dawn. My father would stay home when he could drum up a sign or two. Like today, he paints "five hamburgers for a dollar" for the greasy, one-room diner down the street. This gives him time to rebuild his blood so he can sell it again for spending change. Mostly, he waits for the beer joints to open. He spends so much time there, I was always so sure he worked there. He stole four tires that year to buy Christmas presents, but he got caught when he forged the car dealer's signature on a check. He had to do six months in the pen for that. "He's just a little rat," my mother pleaded with the judge, "when there's such big rats all around." But they wouldn't listen.

[*Music: Dark "Snake Song Theme" begins. Gesture: I unzip my dress, remove it, revealing a short black slip, with a bra made of voluptuous purple grapes, a snake coming out of the fruit and coiled around my arm. I do movement evoking a tight-wire rope dance in "fuck me" pumps.*]

MY VOICE: [*Recorded.*]: I had a dream the other night of this house. My body's on the table in the kitchen as if it's some kind of examining table, my legs apart, forced into stirrups, like the ones my gynecologist has, while another part of me scopes out the room like a free-floating camera or something in midair that can fly. That's how I see that my father is asleep naked in the other room with an erection, while in the kitchen with me is a nerd of a man with coke-bottled glasses, holding a knife and a potato masher. "What are you gonna do with that?" I ask. I remember thinking a red ant bit me— that's why I'm swollen and it burns down there—but I was too embarrassed to tell or show anyone, so I kept the stinging pain to myself. My father knew of split personalities because, in essence, he was one. He could be in two places at one time and not even remember one of them. Always on the verge of passing out, a level of alcohol so high as if he was trying to disinfect a gaping, festering wound. The more dead I am at his side, the more affection he's showing me. My heart is beating and, although I've died right there next to him, my mind is flying far away into darkness. My body is alive and dancing like a snake. [*Song: "The Snake That Swayed."*

Music: Deconstructed theme of "The Snake That Swayed" that sounds like wails, trains in motion, and other themes evoked by the language. Gesture: I put on a skull/mask/scarf headpiece that gives me two faces— my own on one side, death on the other. I put on a long, black, lace skirt and a shawl over my head and begin to slowly climb the ladder, where I begin to rip a long red fabric of silk into many long shreds. Every tear is a slow-motioned movement.] I'm watching my father sleep, or so it seems. I swear I see his chest rise up and down like a wave every now and then. There's a long line waiting to see him. Every time somebody comes up to my mother to offer her condolences, the wails start all over again. When she starts her hollers and cries, we all do like a miniature Greek chorus. For some reason, I keep flashing to the cafeteria ladies at my school. I keep seeing them in my mind's eye, whispering to each other so that I don't hear, as I wait in line, embarrassed, for my serving of corn. So today, I cry for myself. I realize—like any twelve-year-old who starts to feel embarrassed about her parents—I am embarrassed, because it's my father who is the sensational murder of the year. This town has 4,000 people—about 3,875 are Chicanos and twenty-five total are white, with a hundred or so being a mixture of the two. There are no blacks in this ranching community that, for only a brief moment at the turn of century, was a booming train stop town. Nothing much happens here anymore, but when it does, it's gruesome. We have a white king of sorts, the last of the white patrones—bosses who run the town. Because around these parts Mexicans are still considered game: when they don't kill each other, they're easily disregarded. The boss offers protection in return for votes. The infamous Box 13, which got LBJ his senate election, came out of my town's cemetery. All my dead relatives voted as it turned out. The boss was nowhere to be found three nights ago when three brothers showed up at a drive-in burger place where my father, mother, and baby sister were out celebrating his fortieth birthday. I had been invited but stayed behind to watch the Beatles premiere their "Let It Be" video on *The Ed Sullivan Show*. Alfredo and his two older brothers showed up out of nowhere, it turns out, drugged out of their minds. My father had given the oldest brother a ride to work this week but was running late and wasn't able to deliver him to the doorstep. So tonight, because there's nothing else to do, they act like a vengeful pack of wolves, harassing my father for making the older brother walk a few blocks. Knives are flashed. My father, who is easily frightened—I have many memories of my mother chasing him across the house—says to them, "Have respect. My family is here." And before anyone can see, a knife slices an ear off and is plunged into his chest. My little sister screams at the top of her lungs like a siren, piercing the spell of this violent reality, sending the men running. For three days, the doctors at the hospital try to keep large amounts of blood in his body. On March 3rd, he died, after my mother asked him how he felt. "I never felt better in my life. They're coming for me. Let's go." The day he was buried, I had the undeniable feeling that his death was somehow for my own good, like we had agreed to this twist in the plot. From this day forward, I entered another "dark" room, a chrysalis-state, like some larger part of me went into a long, necessary sleep—with my eyes open, and my mouth moving, words being said but one step removed—like the not so graceful dub of a foreign movie.

[*Sound: The skipping of a record or film strip or the like that started the show over the projector spinning its empty reel. Gesture: I have slowly made my way back down the ladder, the red satin shreds behind me, some still hanging on the ladder itself. With the death mask on, I sing the funeral song a capella. Song: "Adiós." Gesture: The "ghost" projector comes back on, the bright light squared off Upstage, as Los Panchos' version of "Nuestro Amor" comes on. I do the funeral walk across the stage, the red satin trailing behind me. The look of me is like the classic, Spanish mourning woman with the dark mantilla and all, death glowing from underneath the veil behind me. Occasionally, I stagger, as if suddenly hit by the impact of it all. Finally, I make it back to the "frame" of light. This time the light is almost too bright; I shy away from its glare. Finally, I turn to look at my shadow again and, with my back to the audience, I kneel and repeat one more time the gesture that has symbolized flight/ecstasy. Because the death mask now glares out into the audience from underneath the veil, it appears for one moment like a skeleton taking its bow, except that my face, in that "Camel" arch, appears momentarily in my back bend, as the lights fade to black. Sound: During intermission, the sounds of my "transition" during the birth of my son are heard.*]

ACT TWO

[*Music: Rafael Ramirez's "Nuestro Amor" as sung by Los Panchos comes on in the darkness. Slowly, their voices fade as mine continues to sing the song alone. I am dressed in a skirt with a Mexican peasant shirt. I wear bullets like a Mexican revolutionary, with costume jewelry over them.*]

ME: My cousin Gigi's father owned "The Rialto," the movie theater in town that showed steamy Mexican movies. Gigi and I had never seen anybody kiss or touch like that so, of course, we reenacted what we could, kissing underwater in the swimming pool, pretending we were each other's boyfriends. [*Gesture: I slowly take another pair of underwear off, keeping the rest of my clothes on.*] We would hang onto the towel rack over my grandmother's tub, spreading our naked legs and behinds wide open in front of the face of the other, so we could see what we were each made of from the bottom up. "What do you see?" I'd ask. "Purple folds, like a rose," she'd say. "What do you see?" she'd ask. "An extra tongue and you're sticking it out at me." [*Song: "Inscription on Her Underwear."*]

I found Jesus Christ one night when I knelt in front of the television and accepted him as my personal lord and savior during a Billy Graham crusade. The way Billy explained suffering and violence away made me suspicious of priests who hadn't made a big enough deal about Jesus, for heaven's sake. Maybe if they had, those brothers wouldn't have murdered my father. And maybe my mother wouldn't have knocked herself out with a frying pan. So I send away for my "you are saved" card in the mail. I worried about my great-grandmother. She was old, the one I loved the most, and the only one in the whole family who refused to go to church. "Para qué, mi'jita, cada cabeza es otro mundo—every head is a different world," she'd say, as if tolerance and respect were the only true religion. "Those who go to church eat saints and shit devils, mi'jita." So she wanted no part of that hypocrisy. But she sat there patiently nonetheless, rolling her Bugler tobacco cigarettes, as I got her to repeat after me, "For God so loved the world—amá, ándale, repeat after me—that he gave his only son." And, even though she couldn't speak English, she ended up accepting Jesus, phonetically, as a favor to me.

I was awarded a four-year Achievement Scholarship to the University of Texas, where I temporarily became a Baptist and a drama major my first semester and met my first true love the second day I arrived on campus. We were assigned our final freshman acting scene together that fall, when, in rehearsal, he insisted that his character needed to kiss my character. "But he wouldn't do that," I argued, feeling like the blocking was all wrong and that I understood his character so much better than he. "Maybe he wouldn't, but I would." I was determined to be a virgin when I got married, as if to compensate, so we abstained from s-e-x those first few months, till he finally panted a proposal to me out of sheer sexual frustration, after we had rubbed bare every crotch of pajama or blue jeans we had tried to keep on in the process. [*Gesture: I breathe hard and heavily, in motion—the frenzy dance.*] The day the wedding invitations were mailed, he led me to a new church inside my body overnight. "Are you sure you've never done this before?" I asked. He seemed to know his way around, waking all of the sleeping parts of my body up at once. "I read books, that's all." "Take this body, eat this bread, and we'll sing a song of love, allelu, allelu, allelu, alleluia." Sex was my first true holy communion. It finally all made sense. We were young and in love and nothing could be sexier than doing God here, there, and everywhere, morning, noon, and night. For the next seven years, I stopped worrying about who was saved and who was not and devoted myself to loving till "death do us part." Of course, that proved to be challenging when we were both so very young and so very much alive. [*Music: East Indian mixed with Catholic, electronic tones— "Metallic Theme." Gesture: I stand in front of the projector this time, a thousand distorted images of what could be my face.*] Any one moment, when you hold it up to the light, looks like a thousand frames, a thousand mirror movements that make up any one gesture. Before there was language, we dreamed with our eyes open, like babies do. One night, I'm dreaming I am on deck of a huge ocean liner right as a Gilligan's Island storm is about to hit. It feels like I'm alone when I suddenly realize— [*Gesture: I pull on my own ponytail to indicate "husband."*]—ouch! My young husband. And together we are waiting for the storm to hit. He is there with some mysterious woman, who might as well have a blue dot where her face should be. Her identity is concealed. And I am there with him, right as the storm turns into a catastrophic one. "But I want to go swimming," my young husband says to me, implying he wishes to do so with this woman. I become aware that there are two of me—the one that is asleep having the dream, and the one who is actually in the dream. We think and feel very differently. The one sleeping tries to argue logically: "In a tidal wave? You'll drown. It hurts my feelings. I can't believe you'd rather drown with her." But what comes out of my mouth instead is: "You're a swimmer, dear." The part of me sleeping can't believe I just said that, but I said it so calmly, so truthfully, like I was a thousand years old.

Next, I'm standing at the end of a long maze-like hallway—same dream, second scene—my young husband is still standing there with me. When I open a door, we are both overwhelmed to see that instead of pillows, couches, and rugs—oh my!—this room is furnished with men. [*Gesture: I grab my own ponytail, caveman like.*] Who invited them? I have no idea. I only recognized a couple of them. The men were diverse in age and appearance, as if waiting for some kind of reunion to take place, like I had made appointments with them all. How could I have invited men I don't even know? Right then a wave of sound pierces my inner ear as if ringing an undeniable truth in my ear. "You invited them, my dear." The part of me still sleeping could have passed a polygraph, no problem. I've been faithful, devoted, the model of wifedom, but the one awake in the dream is more interested in when and how it happened. As if the important thing is to become aware of what it is I do that invites them, even if I'm convinced that I don't. [*Video: A pair of strong masculine arms climbing up a rope, as if in some kind of competition. Song: "In the Other Room."*

Gesture: Red overtakes the white light. New movement to indicate "the sword of truth." Finally, I find myself in yet another room—scene three, same dream. This room is empty except for this shield in the center of the room, like a shield of armor. It is red, thick, and plastic and it has a sword pushed through it. As I contemplate this curious shield, a loud voice trumpets in my ear: <u>*"This is the mother that needs to be destroyed in order to continue as necessary."*</u> *Before I can ask any questions, "that" which is always with me walks to the back of the room and pulls aside this heavy, black curtain. Gesture: Blinded by the most extraordinary light, supported by "lights" that actually saturate the stage, but focused and pointed, like a spear or laser at me, the original white light returns.*] Youch! The most incredible blinding light is shining through this window I didn't even know was there. It shines through me and this shield like a beam. The sensation is that of being pushed into an icy pool of water. I am awake beyond my control, my heart beating, breath accelerated, as if I had just run a marathon of some kind. I am coming out of my skin, sitting up trembling in the middle of the night, terrified.

[*Gesture: I pull on my ponytail once more, carefully and painfully taking the rubber band off, while pulling at the end of my hair to imply I am freeing myself from my husband's control. As I do, I watch him sleep, regretfully.*]

VOICE-OVER: [*Recorded.*] I sit here watching my husband sleep. By day, we banter like birds arguing property and personality. Staking out appropriate modes of responses, we volley like well-matched champions at the completion of their long, drawn-out season. I whisper to myself, "See how alone we are? Even if I could be with you every instant of my day and night." If wishing were all, if thinking were not, what a relief to know what supposedly I don't remember. Remember? To tremble at this knowledge I slowly rediscover, so easily distressed and lost—that is what is left to shiver about. Through me, not me, a spear through my soul on the way to its target.

Fire on the water—see.
Fire on the water—touch.
I'm fire on the water—free.

[*Song: "Waiting on the Will of Heaven."*]

VOICE-OVER: [*Recorded.*] Right around that time, I'm cast in the part of Adelita, the mythic Mexican female revolutionary in a play called *Pancho Villa's Wedding Day.* "I am being told that this play is your birthday party," the designer of the show tells me one day while she takes my measurements. I didn't dare ask her who was telling her all this. It was the dead of winter. My actual birthday was in the spring but, since it was rumored that she could see ghosts and hear the voices of the long departed, I listened. [*Gesture: Put on my "smile" mask.*] "You strike me as someone who has always had to smile," she told me as if reading my mind. "You come from a very—" she stopped, like she'd best be tactful, "—'earthy' people . . ." I must have laughed and shaken my head, earthy being the last thing I would call them. "Or are they very of the earth people?" she corrected. "Let me put it another way. Is there violence in your home?" I shrugged and nodded reluctantly. She and I had never spoken about any of this before. So I say, "Yeah, my father was murdered but big deal. It doesn't have anything to do with me really. He was in the wrong place at the wrong time—la-de-da-de-da." "You have developed to a fine art your ability to become invisible," she tells me. "You become invisible to withdraw from the situation emotionally and to remain free while chaos and confusion reign all about you. This was a technique of extreme value and importance for one as sensitive as you are, to retain your sanity. You believed you could not enter into the fray which you found around you and that, I am hearing, is the truth. You could not. You had to find a way to go away. And you did." She looks at me like, "do you remember?" I nod, petrified. "You mean the way I would melt into the light, into the blankness, and fly around like a bat in hell?" Of course I didn't say that but it was making me uncomfortable to deny it. "They are showing me a whole group of men. There seems to be a feeling of this group of men being somewhat ominous and threatening and they don't have to do anything—just their presence, because they feel angry—and I'm wondering if you experience masculine energy as anger? You must put your mother aside as the image of what it means to be female in any way. You carry, I'm hearing, a terrible sense of rage and resentment that you believe you should never have perceived." I was stunned. This perfect stranger was, in essence, reiterating my dream, my life—but in everyday language. No obscure symbols here. My mind went to a black woman who had recently appeared in my dreams to give me a new name, implying I was daughter of Hermes. In the process, she took my who-can-turn-the-world-on-with-her-smile off my face—and showed me that the true smile of peace and stillness is here. [*Gesture: A half-moon under my breasts, implying "inside."*] Not here. [*Gesture: Repeat the before and after smile mask.*] "You have a lot of pain to communicate," the designer went on. "That's what the old woman is telling me that works with you from the other side. She sees you as the bird." The designer looked at me like I should know what that means, for she most certainly did not. She was just relating the message. [*Gesture: I take out the "compact" from my bosom and contemplate it.*] So it's opening night. There's a party afterward when a reticent, shy man appears who has never spoken a word to me ever, although he's been a college classmate for four years. He comes up to me and says, simply, "I have always loved you. I just wanted you to know that." Oh, no, I remember thinking, you poor thing. I felt so sorry for him. Here I was married and happy, and I could tell how much it took for him to say that to me. I felt bad for him somehow. Still I thanked him, walked away, not giving it another thought, I thought. But that night, I dream I'm at a picnic with this man and he's telling me, like yet another messenger, that my husband is unfaithful. So why not enjoy where we're at? The food's all laid out and I seem to be hungry—starving in fact. [*Gesture: I put the "compact" back in my bosom and do the frenzy dance.*] A week later, I become obsessed beyond rational explanation. I cannot stop thinking about this man. For a year, I write it all out in my journal—how much I love my husband, how much I wanted to stay married, but how much I want to know other people, like for example this man, if I was having to pick a man, if I was going to. But of course, I'm not. I'm committed for life, even if I am just twenty-five. I just want to know what they—he—might be like. That same day, a co-worker tells me at work, "I had a dream about you last night. I saw you standing with a big sheet of glass, like a spear pushed through your torso, as if you'd been stabbed." I happen to go home early from work that day and surprise my husband, who is reading my journal.

His eyes are full of mad tears, and he won't talk to me. All I had written in my journal were tender impressions and endless pages of wanting to know what it might be like to let other people into our life. But he won't hear a word I have to say. Instead I hear a loud crash and some hammering in the living room. My young husband has broken our wedding picture against the sofa armrest and taken a large, rusty nail and nailed the picture on the wall, with the nail hammered through his heart. There's a piece of glass that barely remains hanging inside the gold frame, and it has managed to pierce my waist in the photograph. He tells me that he too has had temptations, but he's only thought about them, but never acted on them. "Neither have I," I cry, which was true, but I couldn't help noticing how much I sounded like the dream when he asked, "Who invited them?" And I honestly say, "I don't know." Neither of us bothered to take the picture down after that. I wrote "pain of glass" on a piece of paper and put it under the wedding picture, like the title to a piece of art in some museum. Most of our friends never noticed it hanging up there in that condition, except one, who looked at me quietly horrified and said, "I'm sorry." "Don't be." I explained, "It's the most honest wedding picture I've ever seen." Soon after, I dream of a woman with dark, wavy hair. We sit on a bamboo couch somewhere. She tells me that she really likes my husband. "I don't feel this way a lot about other people. It's something special." "I understand," I say. "He's extremely sensitive. He's extremely this and that. In other words, I like him too." "No," she clarifies, very serious, as if to say, please hear me out. "I really like him." Telepathy in dreams is more effective than any language in that it's not the words. It's the intention, which in this case was: I wish to be with him, as in a mistress, or some kind of intimate way. Again, there are two of me in the dream—the sleeping Mary Tyler Moore beauty who smiles when she shouldn't, and that calm, accepting, wiser me who seems to be talking more and more in the dreams these days. She is the one who looks at this woman straight in the eye and says, "That's between you and him. It has nothing to do with me." Needless to say, I woke myself up in a fit. "Do you know a woman by the name of . . . mmmmmm . . . Margie?" I ask my husband. (He shakes his head.) "Do you know a . . . mmmmmm . . . Maggie?" (Again, he says no, and shrugs.) "Well, whoever she is, she really likes you." Turns out, this woman moved into town a couple of months later to perform in a play that my husband was also cast in. Within the year, they would be living together. She had a bamboo couch just like the one we sat on in the dream and her name was— Molly. By then, I had finally announced to my husband that I had decided it was all right to finally go be with my messenger for what turned out to be one night, while my husband had to sit at home waiting while I drove there and back. He told me later that he followed me and sat in the car outside the apartment complex, watching his whole life get fucked right in front of his eyes. It snowed that Christmas, a rare thing in Texas. So we got snowed in for several days, during which he told me all of the truth. "I was never a virgin and, by the way, there was Nancy, there was Sally, and some other woman whose name I never even knew." And now, of course, there was Molly but she—at least—she was the necessary, fated Judas. After the last supper is said and done, it is Jesus who says to Judas, "Do what you have to do." Every transformative experience seems to require a willing Judas because betrayal and trust seem like necessary bedfellows and yes, we will have our moments in the garden of Gethsemane—later, when we wish that the cup of our destiny could pass us by, the very cup that we just toasted from in happier times. From that day forward, I swore to heed Merlin's advice when he says to King Arthur, "Honor who comes to your feast, daggers and all."

[*Song: "Forever To Be Told."*]

ME: So Mother is a red, thick, plastic shield, cursing her very own name. Mother is a red, thick, plastic shield, thinking she is Sodom's shame. Mother is a red, thick, plastic shield, grieving hard molten tears, begging to hide all of her fears. Mother is a red, thick, plastic shield, punishing her appetite, running scared with all her might. Come, then, sword of truth. Come, then, sword of man. Melt your way into this mold. Come into this empty room, then, and contemplate. When a person doesn't lament, they cause grief for others. That is the mother that needs to be destroyed. To continue as necessary is to not turn plastic, but trust that flame liquifies all that is red to flow as it will, all to flow as it might. What you have taught me, then, Mother dear, is moonshine. There's really not much to be done except to tongue the mouths of mutes, taste the intoxication off all exotic fruits. Every fear is a secret wish. To continue to fear the roomful of men is to fuel their presence, with a vengeance. So I send a dance card to the roomful of men and, full, it returns to me. For the next several years, I am dancing. [*Song: "Deep in Purple."*] My inner flame has merely gone astray.

[*Video: Many sperm attempting to break through into one solitary egg.*]

ME: Two men often arrive in my life simultaneously. One will introduce himself as a close-up, and he insists, [*Gesture: I grab my own face tight, with a death grip.*] "You must remember this face." So, of course, I am always impressed by how sure he is that we have met before and that we have promised to always find the other over and over again, even if it's in a different body, a different state, and always a parallel universe. Often, he looks like the mightiest of Indian braves, and somehow I know to trust how ancient he is, how familiar, how we have died in each other's arms, if not killed the other before. And always, he is too hard to resist. Even I soon regret the deep connection when after our first dance it is obvious that his intent is to always be "in my face." [*Gesture: I grab my own face and won't let easily go, without a struggle.*] The other usually arrives with the presence of a dove. I am initially impressed, because this dove has perspective. He flies high. He flies low. And he understands he's in the presence of a little girl who wants to play crazy eights with two decks and she wants him to teach her how. He realizes it could be difficult but decides it's not impossible. Love is not like money—the more you spend, the less you have. You cannot ask someone to be faithful. They have to want to do it on their own. Love is not possessive. And finally, where there is intent, there can be no blame. So he shuffles the deck, ready to begin, when the Indian brave always appears. The brave, who was there first, he insists, stares at the dove like the dove is his mortal enemy. He proceeds to attack the dove with a knife. The dove attempts to take the knife away, but in the process, the struggle intensifies, the dove proving to have more physical strength this time around. The Indian brave, however, refuses to admit defeat. He will have his way, no matter what. So he throws his body onto the knife, which the dove helplessly holds. It is the dove then that must carry the weight of the other man's self-destructiveness. Needless to say, the ensuing triangle always proves difficult and necessarily painful, proving yet once again that when a person doesn't lament, they cause grief for others. Monogamy has eluded me since the end of my young marriage. Even in committed relationships, it is understood that I prefer honesty to safety. If you want something, someone, you take it, for like Ovid's *Metamorphoses,* it is understood that there is nothing constant in the universe. All ebb and flow and every shape that's born bears in its womb the seeds of change. [*Video: My son's birth is seen, abstracted by the dark, natural light in the room, which makes it all appear in silhouette. Music: "Ecstasy Theme" reprised.*]

Three years after my son's birth, he's playing one day when he suddenly stops and starts to cry very sadly and quietly. "What's wrong?" I ask. "I dreamed I died," he tells me. "You want to tell me about that?" "I was swimming in the big river. My hand got bigger. My head got bigger. I'm swimming in the big ocean when I see the white house, and then I died." "You're remembering being born," I say, without even a breath between us. The womb is not about facts; it's about sensation, and I too remember this moment. While everyone present at his birth celebrated and welcomed him with cheers and claps, I myself felt that I was unexpectedly at a funeral. The most incredible sadness came over me the instant his little body left mine as if somewhere else others were saying goodbye to him right as we were saying hello. Was I feeling my son's sensation of birth, which he perceived as "a death"? Or was he feeling my loss—that for nine months, we had been one in our thinking and feeling and now that part of our togetherness was done? Turns out, he was born at home in a white house, just like he remembered in his waking dream. The moment his head surfaced, his hand appeared right alongside it like a platter for his head. What he calls his head getting bigger, his hand getting bigger, is not abstract at all—[*Gesture: I hold my own head in the platter of my palm.*]—for there it remained till the final contraction, which pushed him out of my womb like a wave. The womb is not about facts. It's about sensations. It is a powerful place this room, this womb—this empty room that is mother.

[*Song: "Post Parting Blues."*]

ME: The man who can hold my ear and play my wheel like a lute knows that I live in two houses on top of a cemetery. Unlike other people who plant flowers in their gardens, there are bones and headstones in my yard with an occasional perennial that grows of its own volition. When we make love like gods and then get into our separate cars and drive ourselves to our separate homes, he wonders and often asks if it is the fate of every man who enters my space to become part of that faceless mob in that room. "I see you as the many in the one, and you see me as the one in the many," he tells me, as if he would go ahead and pop the question if I only knew the answer to his question without a doubt. And, for that reason alone, we don't do what the neighbors do when they decide, beyond a doubt, that they have found their truest love within the other. While we know we share an eternity when we look into each other's eyes, we know that the day to day is a river which flows onward always, penetrating crevices, wearing down resistance, stopping to fill deep places and then flowing on— me and the snake engaged somehow. [*Gesture: I end up where I started— in front of the light.*] Any one moment, when you hold it up to the light, looks like a thousand frames—a thousand micro movements that make up the simplest of gestures. Before there was language, we dreamed with our eyes open, awake all of the time . . . [*Gesture: Seeing with my eyes closed—the original polygraph gestures, repeated.*] I finally know where my mother ends and I begin, but still I ask: who is this woman, then, who reserves a roomful of men to reflect upon? Sometimes I swear that every man in that room is the same man. Physicists say there are ten to the hundredth power plus, slightly imperfect copies of all of us running around constantly splitting into other copies that become unrecognizable, even when we run right smack into ourselves in some dark room—somewhere—without a light. For a long time, I carried my mother's rage and resentment as if they were my own. Of course, I couldn't recognize her—[*Gesture: Look at the compact one last time.*]—in myself, when she would come and beg me for some change. [*Gesture: The "compact" turns into a "cup," which I pantomime taking from the "ocean." Sound: The waves. "Sand-dollar" reprise.*] I can walk up to the ocean and cup my hands like this, and hold the ocean inside both of my hands. As if it is my true beloved, I can even say, "I have you, ocean, in my hands." It's not a lie to say that so long as I know that, directly in front of me, is also the ocean, which remains immeasurable beyond my attempts to grasp and to hold it. [*Gesture: I wash my face in the ocean. I take the shredded red silk fabric used earlier and dry my face with it.*] Who am I, then, and what is "that" which remains with me, even when I seemingly stand here all alone?

[*Gesture: Turn to the right to take in the now familiar light, look up at the light. Gesture: I sing as I repeat the gestural "language" I've utilized throughout the piece. Among the gestures: mother, womb, compact, polygraph, the "flipping of the bird," angel, half-moon smile on the "inside," etc. Song: "Angels Will Cry."*]

DESCRIBE
YOUR WORK

Monica Palacios

First of all, let me describe myself.
I am a cross between Lola Beltrán,
Frank Sinatra, Doris Day, Bobby Darin,
and Charo—
with the 1950s in my soul.
I'm as sexy as Sophia Loren's cleavage.
I've been called Lenny Bruce—who hasn't?—
but I feel like Woody Allen
without the
neurosis.
I'm Film Noir Meets The Lesbian Nerd.
I'm a Vegas lounge singer,
a storyteller,
a soothsayer.
I've got Cantinflas on my back,
I never thought the Frito Bandito was funny,
I eat Tofu Chorizo,
and I like wearing my black bra
when she . . .
. . . Mariachi mistress.

I perform words because this is how I speak.
Listen up cuz I'm the
Latin Lezbo Comic
and I'm bringing you
Greetings From A Queer Señorita
cuz I got
Confessions . . . A Sexplosion of Tantalizing Tales.
These one-mujer shows
come deep from the center of my Chicana Lesbian

corazón—
blood,
sweat, and
Tacos.

But people have tried to shut me up
because I like chicks
because my brown eyes ain't blue
because I'm just too bold.
I'm bold with boobs
y ¿qué?

Wasn't always this forthright.
Was a shy chavalita.
At the dinner table
I was sending notes:
"Hi, this is Monica, pass the butter?"
During these quiet times I was inhaling life,
listening to language,
learning what makes people tick.

The most entertaining tick-tock was
my father, Guadalupe,
the pseudo-mariachi guy—
had the guitar but not the outfit—
brought out the performer in me.
"And now damas y caballeros
¡Los Palacios Fabulosos!"
Dad on guitar, little brother on drums,
and me jamming on the ukulele.
Sometimes Mom would sing,
giving us a Partridge Family flair.
Mom and Dad crooning duets,
ah yes,
we felt sooooo middle class.

Mysteriously, life began in the sixth grade.
It was the year I read:
Everything You Wanted To Know About Sex But Were Afraid To Ask.
It was the year my mother told me to wear a bra—
all the time—even in the shower.

It was the year I became Funny.
I worked the room for lunch money.

High school was all girls and Catholic
because older sisters went there and
public schools were shit.
I was the school clown.
Adoring laughs and applause
from those gregarious giggly girls—
ha-ha, titter, titter—
Stand-up comedy routines came
in the form of an English class.
Addicted and thrilled.
But too young to go clubbing,
continued to glide my pen across those pages.
Jumped into college as a creative writer who
was dealing with
HOMO-
SEX-u-al-i-teee.
Was she or wasn't she?
Only her hairdresser knew for sure.

Who came first—the comic or the lesbian?
They busted down that closet door at the same time.
I was sizzling in San Francisco.
Performing in front of a queer audience
empowered my soul,
allowed me to believe in myself.

But mainstream clubs were tough—
did I say tough?—I meant
homophobic, racist, sexist.

They didn't want me.
They wanted to fuck with me.
So I said adios to those sleaze pits
and did my lezbo comic thing
until it was time for me to leave my cable car town.
I needed a change—a new haircut—new shoes.

Moved to L.A. because like many of you,
I was gonna get discovered by some young white male

who was gonna give me my own cheesy multicultural
TV show featuring David Hasselhoff.
"Do as I tell you and you won't get hurt."
"You're good but get rid of the queer stuff."
"Get rid of the Latino stuff."
"Don't talk about your period."

Excuse me, but I'm not talking—
I'm telling.
I'm telling you about my life because
I have every right to do so.
I'm letting you know that my queer Latina vida
is not stereotypical like you have ignorantly believed.

And stop telling me I need to be more mainstream
because the people in Middle America won't get it.
Well get this, apple pie:
I'm sick and tired of you
looking right through me—
I'm talking to you too, Raza.
Stop being all uptight and homophobic.
We all eat tacos—don't we?
We're coming from the same place, gente.
Let's organize,
act civilized,
go forth and kick butt.

I'm an AMERICAN with a tortilla aura.
Can you see it?
It's next to my salsa psyche.
Can you feel it?

Hey!
¡Oye!
Look for me in print.
Look for me on stage.
Look at me.
Look into me.
LOOK!

Testimonios

IF EPHEMERALITY IS THE essence of the performing arts, the only records remaining of productions in the theater are the scripts of the plays themselves. How can we reconstruct a history of theater when the only remaining "texts" are "sub"-literary and archival: playbills, reviews, box office receipts, communications among the members of the ensemble, and advertising? Behind these stand other objects such as costumes, lighting, set constructions, and subsequently recycled props. Nor do these objects tell the story of a production or the people in it. Besides these objects, what evidence is there of an actual production recaptured in its totality? What untold story does each production hold of the individual journey of its actors? Who will recount the actual events that led the company to its current position? Who will remember the pivotal, consciousness-raising moments that occurred while a production was in progress? In the increasing institutionalization of the arts, where does alternative theater, particularly theater written, developed, and acted by people of color, fit? With these and other questions in mind, we embark upon an archeological quest to recover the legacy of Latina acting, directing, performing, and, of course, playwriting since the late sixties.

In our effort to reconstruct Latinas' roles in theater, we found testimonios to be the most appropriate tool, literally, to bear witness to Latinas' legacy in the theater. Therefore, we asked Latina playwrights to contribute to this volume by writing short autobiographical statements that explained how they came to be Latina playwrights, directors, or actors. Many took a circuitous path that unfolded as a result of a variety of factors, as these testimonios evidence. While each testimony differs radically, the one common trait among them is that the authors have moved from their peripheral roles backstage to center stage as the protagonists of their own stories. Through the writers' testaments to this process, we are able to witness that remarkable transformation, as well as to perceive the long history of acting, activism, and the very presence of Latinas in teatro. Nearly every Latina playwright we have encountered has performed a multiplicity of tasks in the theater. Thus, in this section, we want to acknowledge those women who not only write for the theater, but also direct, produce, teach, act as dramaturgs and mentors, found new theaters, and nurture the theater in thousands of small but crucial ways.

Finally, this section acknowledges the countless women, perhaps not represented here, whose life work has been to keep theater and theaters alive, even against the greatest obstacles—political, personal, and economic. We salute these women for their inspirational work, persistence, and endurance, all of which have paved the way for younger generations of Latina playwrights and critics. We specifically wish to recognize the contributions of Maria Irene Fornes, Dolores Prida, Miriam Colón (Puerto Rican Traveling Theater), Rosalba Rolón (Teatro Pregones), Silvia Brito (Thalia Spanish Theater), Silviana Wood, Carmen Zapata, and Margarita Galbán (Bilingual Foundation of the Arts), Cherríe Moraga (Teatro Brava), Teresa Jones (Borderlands Theater), Elisa González (Teatro Vision), Ana María Mendez and Virginia McFerran (Teatro Latino de Minnesota), Nita Luna (Teatro Aguacero), Elena Parres (Zona de Teatro), Irene Oliver-Lewis (La Compañía de Teatro de Albuquerque), Cora Cardona (Teatro Hispano de Dallas), Diana Abrego (Teatro Cultural del Pueblo), Elsa Zambosco (Multicultural Theater Corporation), Sister María Carolina Flores (Tercer Acto), and Silvia Contreras (Teatro Carmen). Muchas gracias a todas y a cada una.

BATTLE·WORN

Laura Esparza

February 5, 1958. [*Clap.*] I was born in a hospital across the street from Milam Plaza, San Antonio, Texas, where my grandfather, Gregorio Esparza, was buried after he fell in the battle of the Alamo. It is a snowy day—the first in seven years. [*Clap.*]

February 5, 1995. I am in a restaurant celebrating my birthday with director Ping Chong, his cast from *Undesirable Elements/Seattle,* and my co-workers at The Group Theatre. Now I am a professional theater director and writer. This is the ritual that begins his play—now it is the ritual that begins my story. [*Clap.*]

My place in this world of 1958 is a tiny two-bedroom house on the Latino west side of San Antonio with five other siblings. My family has lived in this approximate location for more than three hundred years, long enough to feel the earth in my blood. My father had his own room because he worked the night shift at the post office for thirty-seven years. I slept on a couch until I was about fourteen or fifteen years old.

They lived inside the belly of the beast,
in the central chapel of the Alamo,
for thirteen days and thirteen nights.
Oh, holy war.
My grandfather shot a cannon on a high scaffold stuck in a window
with a patch of sky that turned blue and then black,
blue, black, blue, black.
Oh, holy night.

Down below Ana waited, the stench of death and the sound of dying
all around her.
Three frightened children and a baby stuck at her breast.
She waited.

She waited for that last day when Gregorio shot his cannon
and a cannon shot right back.
He caught a cannonball with his sternum
and fell from the sky into Ana's wailing arms.*

On my couch I read Ernest Hemingway, F. Scott Fitzgerald, J. D. Salinger, and Willa Cather. I'm sure I couldn't name a Latino writer then, but any book was an escape from these cramped circumstances. I often longed for something greater in life: I drew, I wrote poetry, I loved Margot Fonteyn and old movies, but I was not really expecting much more than my peers, who had husbands and babies by seventeen. I thought I would be very lucky to "get out" like my sister, who dodged the draft with her husband and became a Canadian.

Generalísimo Santa Ana won the battle
and ordered all survivors,
women and children,
out of the Alamo.
On a gray morning
my great, great, great grandmother
began her own battle;
Ana taking on Santa Ana
(no relation),
face to face.
No relation, except both were warriors;
no relation, except they both spoke the same language;
no relation, except they both had this land in their blood.*

I wrote poetry, was devoted to poetry, from the age of eight. I hid it because once my brother gave his girlfriend one of my poems so she would have something to turn in for a class assignment. Her teacher got it published in a magazine—under the girlfriend's name.

I knew it would be hard to break free when the time actually came. Leaving home is a big deal in many Latino homes. At the age of eight, I was the only girl at home; by the time I was ten, I was cooking and washing for my brothers. I felt isolated much of the time.

*From *I Dismember the Alamo,* by Laura Esparza.

My sister, my favorite person in the entire world, dodged the draft for the Vietnam war with her husband in 1971. When she moved to Ontario, she was the first to ever leave Texas for good. I think Ana might have done the same if she had had a choice. I think she too might have said no to any kind of senseless killing. She might have liked Canada, with its cool crafted landscapes, might have forgotten for a moment the burden of identity, the multiple colonizations of her land.*

Every morning my father drilled our English vocabulary from the fat Webster's Dictionary on the same squeaky black table where my mother rolled out tortilla dough. There was a dictionary in <u>every</u> room of the house. My parents' first language was Spanish, because my family had lived in Texas since before the American Revolution. Segregation never required a change in language until World War II took my father into the Pacific. My father is like the young man in the play *Soldier Boy.* In those days, returning from the war to work at the post office was an improvement over the jobs Latinos could hold before the war. Their vision for me extended only as far as nursing or home economics.

My grandfather had a brother named Francisco,
who lived in San Antonio too, but
who served in Santa Ana's army.
Brother against brother.
After the fall
he stepped forward,
begging Santa Ana for custody of Ana and her children.
They returned to the Alamo
   to the stench of body rot
   to the maggot-ridden graveyard,
   to the birthplace of our assimilation
   and countless colonizations.
Lit by the pyre that burned men's bodies
They dragged my grandfather's to bury in hallowed ground
   like a couple of Antigones in the night.
Oh, holy light.*

The double standard between what they expected for my brothers and what they expected for me had created hard feelings for me. I worked two or three jobs every summer to put myself through college and two jobs throughout the year. I went to an affluent university, the kind they call an Ivy League of the South, and I was one of only three Latinas in my dormitory. The realization hit me like a cannonball: there was a gulf between my working-class upbringing and the class of just about everybody else in school; I had to work much harder to put myself through school compared to what my brothers or my college roommates were afforded; and not only was there little financial support, there was even less emotional support for going to college. It forged a fierce independence, and anger really, that created the fortitude to go into a field that was so foreign to my experience: theater.

> For 13 days and 13 nights, she was death's midwife. She waited through the endless night until her husband fell from the sky like Icarus, a cannonball stuck in his sternum. Four babies and a bloody corpse. Four babies and a bloody corpse. Hero is too big a word to waste on the dead.*

The only theater that existed in my town was the San Antonio Little Theatre (which felt like one of those places that was off-limits) and the theater produced at local colleges. But in my early life, theater was the annual Easter ritual of the washing of the feet: on a huge flatbed truck parked in the school yard, the parish pastor washed the naked feet of the lay church leaders in the community. Theater was seeing a pachuco down the street stab his wife, then stack her on a kitchen chair in his front yard, until the ambulance came to get her and a police car came for him. Theater was the annual Posada, carrying candles and singing to the rude people who would not let Jesus in. Theater was watching the outdoor Cantinflas movies projected on a sheet draping the back wall of the parish hall. My mother was aghast when Cantinflas became too bawdy and she hustled us home as the bosomy women blasphemed the rock that Peter laid. Theater was seeing *Spoon River Anthology* at the age of ten after my father read it to me late at night after he came home from the post office. To see poetry get up and walk around—it is an image of theater that has followed me from childhood.

> Her cells are my cells.
> Her grito is mine.
> She lived past the glory,
> the hype of history,
> And I am here simply
> because she survived.*

Vancouver, B.C., and Tom Stoppard: While I was attending my first university, I dated a man from South Korea who was from a well-to-do diplomatic family.

The resonance of our two cultures was astonishing. We ate Kim Chee and enchiladas; we sang each other's songs in pidgin languages; the apartment we shared had a serape on one wall and a folding painted screen on the other.

During our courtship, he received a midnight call from his father. A marriage had been arranged for him to a sixteen-year-old girl from an affluent family in Korea. Our hearts were broken, but as the oldest son he was compelled to go through with the marriage. My parents, who were suffering a feigned ignorance of the whole affair, offered me a two-week vacation to visit my sister, now living in British Columbia. I took the plane ticket as a sign: the release papers for the rest of my life. After one week, I cashed in the return ticket and my sister called my mother to tell her I wasn't coming home—ever.

In Vancouver, B.C., I finally embraced the theater. I found I could see the shows at the "Queen E." if I worked as a bartender in their concessions stand. I saw a play I had studied in school, and I remembered my professor saying, "This is a play that is understood only in production." It was Tom Stoppard's *Rosencrantz and Guildenstern Are Dead.* Poetry got up and danced around the stage, and my heart was lifted higher than it had ever gone. I was twenty years old, on my own in a foreign country, writing lots of poetry, and practically living at the beach. In my heart of hearts, I felt the impossible had already happened—my life had been re-routed by an arranged marriage, and I had the rest of my life to call my own. An escapee of a predictable life, I decided that theater would not bore me. Theater would offer endless challenges and adventures. Theater would offer me the chance to integrate my life and my work. I wasn't wrong about any of that.

I went back to school at an alternative college in upstate Washington—the kind of college where you make up your own degree, and there are no grades; instead, you write and write and write and write and write. After playing trouser-roles (a part for a man played by a woman) three times in a row, I switched my studies to lighting design, even pursued a wiring course at a trade school. Lighting design was good for three years; it was fun to use tools, climb to the top of tall ladders, and carry heavy instruments with a kind of butch swagger. But, three years into my apprenticeship, I was bored with the kind of plays I was asked to light. And, despite having the best grades in the lighting class, I was never asked to work on the more prestigious mainstage productions. I was also the only woman in the class. The only way to shape my destiny in theater, I thought, was to direct projects of my choosing. And the only way theater or any other media was going to reflect women's reality was if women took charge. I wanted to influence what people saw on stage. I devoted my last year of college study to directing and found I had a knack for it (or as my mother puts it, I love telling people what to do; this was about the time she called to suggest beauty school).

One of the first productions I directed was a pair of one-acts devoted to the life and poetry of Sylvia Plath. I cast three wonderfully different women to play the single role of Sylvia Plath. For love of poetry that has always been my spiritual voice, we crafted a simple and moving act of remembrance for this wonderful woman. I'll never forget the day we closed. The actresses and I were sitting in my living room, drinking wine and watching a gorgeous Northwest sunset. We hated to leave each other's company and savored our last significant moment. The door blew open; a wind filled the room, and we looked at each other at the same moment with the same thought. We felt Sylvia had walked into the room, and I was grateful for the opportunity to love her in death.

Soon after this, I joined with a colleague, Stephanie Lourie, in forming a feminist theater company called SisterStage. SisterStage was devoted to the production of works by women and the training of women in all aspects of theater. The Women's Center was our sponsor; my college provided the physical theater. We produced six productions and a conference on pornography over a two-year period of time. I directed, lit, and designed the sets with the assistance of more than one hundred women. Our productions were low-budget financial successes. These early years taught me theater's necessary discipline, and the company of women provided me with a love that still drives me.

> Theater is like my woman lover because it is through women I grew to love theater and through theater I came to understand the love of women.

I moved to Seattle, tired and grieving the death of my sister. Patricia Van Kirk, Artistic Director of Front Room Theatre, a lesbian theater, offered me a chance to direct the world premiere of *Giving Up the Ghost,* Cherríe Moraga's first play. I was working at The Group Theatre in Seattle as a literary/directing intern, and enjoying the cultural mix at that theater. I longed for the expression of my culture while creating theater by women. I had difficulty finding a cast since there were so few Latinas who acted in Seattle anyway, and because some of those I contacted would not play a lesbian.

> Homophobia. I was not a lesbian then, but I was seriously questioning my sexuality. Ambiguity was shaking my core through this production because I was in love with a woman, because I was married, because I was working with a lesbian theater company when associates of the

company openly challenged my right to be there. Life and production wound like a double helix. Ah . . . the lover-theater bites.

I continued to direct in Seattle, discovering the plays of Maria Irene Fornes, taking her writing workshop, and creating a piece called *ChicanaTalk* with my comadres Josephine Ramirez and Peruvian actress Rose Cano. The short process was driven by creative improvisations, my new tape recorder, lots of Coronas and laughter well into the night. We entered a director's festival at the New City Theatre, and, to our utter shock, we won. Unfortunately, Rose had to return to Peru, so I jumped into her place overnight. It was here that I saw the wonder of memory becoming action, action becoming written word, the word like an unfamiliar dress, until memory overtakes the actress and becomes action once again. It was like watching a baby being born. *ChicanaTalk* was filled with painful memories of growing up without my parents' tongue. Two little girls growing up side by side, separated by a gulf in class and language—the cruelty of fate as each longs for the other's destiny when they meet by accident years later in a Planned Parenthood clinic.

I remember the champagne we broke open at 10:00 A.M. when we learned of our small victory—little parcels of love from my lover-theater.

By this time, I was working part-time at the library and "part-time" at The Group Theatre as the Administrative Coordinator of the Multicultural Playwrights' Festival. The Festival gave me the opportunity to meet many, many playwrights of color—for a while we truly created a "scene" that was very exhilarating. My first professional job in theater convinced me that I needed to know more, do more, and have only one lover: the theater. I applied for graduate school.

San Diego, January 1992: I am in graduate school at the University of California, San Diego, pursuing a directing MFA that also includes being a part of Dr. Huerta's Teatro army: a group of eight actors and two directors chosen for a pilot program in Latino Teatro sponsored by the Ford Foundation. Under the leadership of guest director José Luis Valenzuela, the Teatro students have undertaken the task to develop a play collectively about the "pepenadores" of Tijuana, the scores of Mexicanos who live on the trash heaps above Tijuana city. We are joined in this task by writer Luis Alberto Urrea, author of *Across the Wire* (Doubleday Books). Luis travels to Tijuana weekly with a church group, distributing food and clean water to the community high in the artificial hills—a community that makes its living gleaning recyclable materials, food, or usable clothing from the refuse of Tijuana. Luis invites us to join him on his weekly excursion, to meet the people of our play.

Our day begins with loading vans with fruit, cookies, clothes, and jugs of clean American water. The freeway to Tijuana is familiar to San Diegans—Interstate 5, the artery that ties Canada to Mexico, Seattle to Mexico, the hearts and minds of thousands of campesinos to Mexico. As I-5 approaches the border, large yellow highway signs with silhouettes of a fleeing family of four warn drivers to watch for pedestrians on the freeway, running for their lives from the migra, the coyotes (migrant-runners), or the pistol-happy skinheads that hunt illegal immigrants for sport. Passing through Tijuana, layers of shacks cut into the hills, we pass dead dogs rotting in a sun darkened by flies. When we reach the community, a line has already assembled to receive our gifts, and a line of children is assembled to receive their weekly baths from the church volunteers.

Afterward, we travel farther to twin peaks of garbage, the sound of millions of seagulls above us maneuvering among the pickers bent knee-deep in their task. I watch a woman recycle dirty Pampers for her baby. A man rips apart an old office chair for recyclable materials—with a rock. A large, dark woman in bright rags sells coffee and tacos from a large pot on an open fire, a counter constructed of bits of plywood, linoleum and Formica, in an improvised, open-air diner for workers.

Up on the second hill, a trash heap thinly layered by dust and ash, lies the small settlement of pepenadores. The assemblage of materials that makes their homes would bring any artist pride. A house made of doors, with a fence of mattress springs; the ghosts of familiar brand names on bits of wood and tin, strangely mutated into one-room shelters where people seek refuge from the strange, surreal air, sickly yellow with dust. The golden towers of downtown San Diego glisten in the distance.

Children follow our path; students make friends and are invited into homes for a meager taco of grease and unknown matter. I feel at home here, familiar poverty, language, and faces. We visit the cemetery a hundred yards away, where the bodies of children are buried in shallow graves of garbage—cribs, toys, and bits of wood painted in happy pastels to celebrate the dead. When we leave, everyone is sad. A bright little girl named Elena wants to come with me; she could be my sister.

Through a process of collective writing, common among Chicano theater companies, we create our play, *A Handful Of Dust/Un Puño De Tierra,* performed in five sites around San Diego County. When the local media's right-wing bias means only some news is disseminated news, theater becomes a necessary means of telling a story that rarely leaves the hills, a stone's throw from the border.

Border Boda, August 1993: A group of powerful women artists and scholars are meeting to read and discuss Gloria Anzaldúa's book *La Frontera,* among others, and to discuss the covert war at the San Diego/Tijuana border. They are angry with a local museum that paid for celebrity photographers from the Northeast to document life on the border in San Diego; the photographs are mounted in a gallery exhibition called "Los Vecinos" (The Neighbors). The powerful women artists who call themselves Las Comadres have been documenting life on the border for more than a decade. They decide to mount a rebuttal exhibition called "La Vecindad" (The Neighborhood). We are part of the Border Art movement that has centered itself at the Centro de la Raza, the vital throb at the heart of the Latino community.

Las Comadres has decided to stage a performance piece in the exhibition, and they ask me to direct it, even though I am new to the group. The only contingency is that the entire collective must dramaturg—determine the structure of—the play. This happens fairly quickly for a collective process, and I am handed the basic structure of a grandmother preparing a granddaughter for a wedding in the context of border politics.

The August night in San Diego is full of secrets. Sweet, soft air, disguising the smell of immigrant terror, running from la migra, the skinheads, and the crazy right-wingers in cars that "light up the border." In a canyon behind Rocío's house, I have gathered the women of Las Comadres to a fire-circle, to tell their stories of their immigrant past and the people they have met while documenting life on the border. In the light of my fire-circle, I see a group of courageous women whose lives have been utterly compromised by their commitment to their art and this issue. Their faces are shades of Russian Jew and Mexican Indian. We tell stories late into the night for four nights and, from these tapes, I create the rest of *Border Boda.*

My actors are not actors but the women themselves, some of whom have created acts of "performance art." Because the actors are also the visual artists who are creating the gallery exhibition, the art work is produced to frame the performance. Our set is the gallery exhibition, but the gallery exhibition has been created to resemble a kitchen in one room, and a TV studio in an adjacent room. Between the two rooms is a marvelous piece, created in collaboration for the performance, with an eight-foot painted cutout of the aura of Our Lady of Guadalupe behind a chain-link fence. The face of Our Lady of Guadalupe is a mirror; her heart is the blade of a circular saw.

The rehearsal process begins each day with a ritual around an altar that the collective has constructed. We begin by talking about the stories that we want to explore that day—the poems, stories, or newscasts that make our days what they are. Our vocal and physical warm-ups are incorporated into a ritual of wailing and yoga. After the warm-ups, we go directly into a "run-through" of improvisations based on the story board I have created from the day's yield. Every rehearsal is a run-through, and each day, we cull the pieces that worked the previous day and we re-work them, adding additional layers. At night, I script the pieces and the result is a full-length play with three performance spaces: a kitchen, a TV newsroom, and a mystical space behind the fence of Our Lady of Guadalupe with the sawblade.

The day of our performance, we begin our daily ritual behind a thirty-foot veil drawn across the kitchen. Audience members hush when they see our moving shadows, our murmurs and wails, and the flicker of candlelight. Television screens have been placed in the lobby of the gallery to accommodate the overflow crowd. The percussionists begin; Rocío's mysterious voice intrigues us with Mexican corridos as the aunt who cannot speak, but only sing. The grandmother gives advice to her granddaughter on the day of her wedding to an anglo man from Chi-"cago." But the grandmother has a mystical power and a secret from the girl's past. The domestic scenes alternate with the harder edge of the black-and-white world of television news and documentary. Video footage of the border collected by Las Comadres is the centerpiece. There is an interview with a woman who sells tacos at the border to men crossing at the fence, who claims to have been beaten by the U.S. Border Patrol. In the mystical realm behind the fence, the bride drifts into a dream world, where she glimpses the rumblings of her sub-conscious, hears voices and songs, and awakens to find that her wedding dress is concealing bleeding nails taken from the image in Frida Kahlo's painting.

> Four of our ex-husbands are there that night. There's been plenty of interpersonal drama. We've received a threatening letter from white supremacists that we reproduce onto a ten-by-eight-foot canvas rug in the gallery foyer. Someone accuses me of being homophobic, even though I am involved with a woman. A lot of people come; we make a lot of noise, but then night comes again, sweet, delicate, and screaming.

December 1993: I am rehearsing a play with a small Latino theater company in San Jose, California. There isn't much money, and nobody seems to know how we are going to pay for the musicians required for a carpa, our theatrical form of choice. Someone has a friend, who tells a cousin, who works with a man who plays accordion with a *conjunto,* and, on this bright Saturday morning a three-piece mariachi band—accordion, stand-up bass, and guitar— shows up at the door, unannounced, of this one-room Latino community center.

"Heard you need a band."

"Well, yes," I stammer. Knowing how word travels in small Latino communities, I am still thoroughly surprised. I decide, however, to be non-committal until I can hear them play.

"Do you have anything worked up?"

They laugh. "Pues, we've been playing together for years. 'Jaula de Oro,' " he calls to the band. And they start to play. There's no stopping them, and they're good, really good. This is not how I'd planned to spend my rehearsal. People from the community begin to gather, the cast starts to dance, and a few others join in. The stage manager has the common sense to start passing out flyers for the play and the band—well, they had their first rehearsal, for tips.

Sometimes making theater in small Latino communities is like making stone *caldo;* husband and wife may both act in the play, while the kids are backstage crew, handing out programs, or hanging on the edge of the stage through a performance, watching mommy and daddy act. Everyone feels good after the show—as Jorge Huerta puts it, the audience response is one of "grateful acceptance." But it's more. TV and movies have not satisfied our thirst for seeing our images defined and validated for America; many find the thrill of seeing their own images on stage through *teatro.*

This is the difference between community theater, a hobby in pursuit of itself, and a Theater of Community. Latino *teatro* is in the business of providing a source of emotional support for the battle-weary, a place where a community with common woes can feel a part of a greater whole and openly, freely love what we deeply love: our culture.

Mission Cultural Center, San Francisco: Even before finishing graduate school, I have taken a job developing the theater program and a theater space at the Mission Cultural Center in San Francisco. In fact, for three months, I commute weekly from graduate school in San Diego to my full-time job in San Francisco. (I have been cursed by a compulsive need to make my life very complicated.)

What I desperately want to do is establish a space where Latino theater can flourish. Space is a valuable commodity in San Francisco, where there are five Latino theaters and 150 Latino theater artists and no space that they can call their own. But even before I begin this task, trouble has begun.

Spring 1992. The renovation is done and *Heroes and Saints* is a big success. Then the Rodney King riots begin, right outside the glass lobby walls. The producer decides not to cancel the night's sold-out performance after checking with the police and the mayor's office. They can't afford to refund 180 tickets. The police agree to let our audience through the police barricades that have blocked the street, north and south of the theater. I watch the police beat up a kid five feet away on the other side of my glass cage. Three hundred people are arrested and on their knees fifty yards away. Fifty brave people are watching the show as an act of civil disobedience. The cast has fortunately shown up, but no one else has. I'm running the box office and watching the glass lobby walls very carefully. My partner is a man, who is at home and very worried about me, so he orders a pizza and walks to the theater and up to the police barricade. "Pizza delivery," he says, with an air of authority, and they let him through.

August 1993: My last day on the job at the Mission Cultural Center. We are concluding the last event of a wonderful festival of new Latino plays. On stage a panel is convening: the Artistic Director of The Magic Theatre, a guest playwright from New York, the Artistic Director of Teatro de la Esperanza. Suddenly a young boy runs into the theater and points a gun at the stage. Pow, pow, pow. We all hold one terrified breath and wait for blood to flow. Whose blood? No blood. A cap pistol. A prankster. I run outside just in time to see him take one look at me and duck away between buildings. This was only a rehearsal, but the Festival Director is crying. He was at a rehearsal in his hometown in Argentina when police burst in firing and took two or three of his friends away. This event has sent him back there.

> Saying good-bye to this theater that I have poured heart and soul into is irrelevant now. I did what I set out to do. On this day, all five of San Francisco's Latino theaters and many of its actors can call this home. But then, someone runs in, randomly, takes a potshot, and the theater is assassinated.

September 1994. Judy from Northwest Immigrant Rights Project called me when I moved back to the Northwest after a six-year absence. Now I am the

Associate Artistic Director of The Group Theatre and, in that capacity, I manage the Education Department. Judy used to work for the ACLU; now she is the NWIRP's Outreach Coordinator for the Northwest. She knows her audience well. Remembering the work of Luis Valdez in the mid-sixties, she asks me to write a short acto (agit-prop skit) in Spanish to teach documented workers about their rights when it comes to job discrimination. Our small troupe of three travels to theatrical meccas like Aberdeen, Idaho (church basement), Ontario, Oregon (parking lot of a labor camp), and Sunnyside, Washington (Día de los Muertos Fiesta, upstaged by the lowriders).

I am reminded of Jorge Huerta's words, "necessary theater," and how little the need for the acto form has changed. The lives of Latino people have not changed much either in the last thirty years; we're still struggling with issues of identity, language, and family, and figuring out a way to survive pesticides, poor wages, and pessimistic sub-standard schools. Teatro is still our language of choice.

DANCING WITH THE VOICE OF TRUTH

María Mar

The Writing on the Wall:

I pick up the brush my friend offers me and carefully write on the wall: "Searching for Maria." Then, with the same strong intent, I sign: "Maria." I am twenty and going to college, a promising young actress and a political activist. Having just met the man I will later marry, I feel happy. Yet tonight at this classmate's party, while other friends leave graffiti markings of their presence on the kitchen wall, I leave a marking of my absence.

Many years have passed since that writing on the wall. In more than two decades as a writer, performer, and group facilitator, I have worked with thousands of people: battered women, abused children, youth, dysfunctional families, and couples. I have worked both with human services professionals and with their clients. In most instances, I could feel a void in my clients that was kindred to mine. It stared at me through so many eyes that it grew, becoming a question demanding to be answered, or at least begging for a name that would give us permission to tend to it without being called mad.

The Black Hole in the Soul:

I'm in a shelter for homeless women and their families. The women have problems coming up with heartfelt images. I guide them through breath meditation to get them into their bodies and off their mental noise and confusion. I ask them to touch—both with the breath and their hands—their heart energy center. This is an area between our breasts, the place we touch with the index finger when we want to indicate "me." It is the seat of the soul. An African-American woman opens her eyes wide and says under her breath, "I can't. When I touch that center, there's nothing." The others, a multicultural group of Latina, African-American, and white Anglo-Saxon women, all nod in recognition. They, too, feel only emptiness. They describe this vacuum as a "black hole, like the one in space, that swallows everything."

The image of the black hole has appeared time after time when I ask workshop participants to touch their heart centers. Until recently, I also felt that emptiness whenever I dared to go deep within me. But five years ago, everything changed. I found a path that helped me walk through that void. Beyond the black hole, I found a window to the vastness of the universe, a state of Oneness with the sacredness of that universe. In contrast with my old way of seeking communion, which was neglecting myself to focus on others, this state of Oneness returned me to myself. As I came home to myself, I found a "me" whom I barely knew, but who had at her reach unlimited possibilities. This is what I call the total or True Self, or just Self, with a capital. At the center of this Self is a being, a Core-Self, whom I have named the Essensual Self, for this part of ourselves is our Essence or Spirit as it inhabits the sensual realm of the body. Other names I also use for this self are Soul Self and Tantric Self. This Soul Self nests in the heart chakra—or energy center—within us, and when it has been wounded to the extent that it has hidden from our consciousness, then all we feel when we go within is absence. The story of how I healed that absence is the story of the emergence of a new way of doing theater that is, in reality, the reawakening of an ancient way. It is called Theatre of Transformation.

When we were growing up, most of us were taught to repress our feelings and perceptions. We were told what our reality should be. To survive as children, we had to conform to our elders' views of reality, of themselves, and even of us. We kept our own truths a secret, and eventually we not only forgot them, but came to distrust our own perceptions of reality. Adulthood, then, marked the entrance into a world of illusion, which we accepted as the only possible reality. Things are the way they are, we still often say to ourselves. But our essence cannot be destroyed. Buried under the amnesia, illusion, and numbness in the way we live, it howls for our attention. Each time we muzzle its cry, we feel hunger instead. After years of stifling its call, we are left with an endless craving, a void that we desperately try to fill with outside things, from people to drugs to objects that we buy for illusions of power and control. This, in my experience, is addiction—the ineffective attempt to fill the hole in our soul with things outside ourselves. But nothing external can fill this emptiness, because in order to ful-fill ourselves we must feel our *Essensual Self.*

For years I had silenced the cry of my Essensual Self. Yet here I was, facilitating workshops to help other people, unaware that I myself was sick, that a little part of me was dying every day. I was addicted to cigarettes, food, romance, and relationships. I worked and took care of others compulsively in order not to feel my own truth. The theater which I did reflected not only my compulsion, but that of the world around me. Part of me believed this was indeed my mission as a playwright and performer: to help people reflect on the world they were creating, so that they could begin the process of changing it. But part of me felt there was something missing in my theater. Something important. Something that had to do with <u>touching</u> people's body/soul, and with <u>healing</u>.

While this was going on, I was also developing my faculties as an "Espiritista," the name Puerto Ricans give to their spirit-speakers. Unable yet to integrate body, soul, and emotions, I split myself in three: the theater person, the spirit-speaker, and the facilitator.

Journey to the Self:
I have just finished the production of *Those Who Most Love You Will Make You Cry,* a play about domestic violence. As usual, I interviewed the victims as well as the experts in the field. The characters and situations were constructed from a composite of many real stories, for as a playwright, I wanted to lend my voice to those whose voices have been drowned in the inequalities of society. All of a sudden I lose my voice. My throat burns as if a beast were gnawing at it. In a whisper I ask my body: "What are you trying to tell me? What do you want?" Then it hits me, loud and clear: I have given a voice to everyone but myself! In a flash, I understand that it is time to tell my own story with my own voice. For months now, my Ancestors have been asking me to set time aside to gather my experience into a coherent system. They have also told me that I need to heal myself. My body has been asking for rest, my soul for replenishment. But I have not listened. The Ancestors had to paralyze me with this silent scream in order for me to hear. I have never given myself vacations, but this time I do. I use half my time to rest and have fun, and the other half to start the task at hand. By the time three weeks are over, my new creative path has a name and I have drafted the eleven steps and the structure for the Theatre of Transformation Active Laboratory (TOTAL). I invite a small group of people to join me in this journey of exploration.

It was during the first year in the Laboratory that All Our Ancestors requested that I become a Shaman.

"You know how I am," I said. "I don't take well to following a closed doctrine or religion."

"Shamanism is not a religion in the way human culture sees it now. It is a path of spiritual evolution through your Earthwalk," my Ancestors explained. "You are becoming a Wounded Healer."

Now this was something I could totally relate to! Although the idea of being a healer terrified me then, I definitely knew I was wounded. I said yes because I knew in my soul that this was what I should be doing, even though at the time I could have never imagined what becoming a Performance Shaman would entail. Little did I know the courage needed to walk the path of the Shaman, and maybe it was best I didn't. During the first five years of training and initiation, I have been trained as Wounded Healer, Spiritual Hunter, Spiritual Warrior, and Performance Shaman, and my training is hardly over!

Like the Old Ones did in the ancient Initiation Ceremonies, the Ancestral Spirits "dismembered" me, "killing" me to my old self. The dismemberment happened when I met all my fragmented, dissociated Inner Selves. The Ancestors helped me to see these parts of me while at the same time detaching from them (something like the "V Effect"—or Distanciamiento—used by Brecht). Meeting the Shadows and Wounded Children who were "driving the car" of my life was not flattering. But the experience helped me realize that my wholeness had been shattered. As an actress, I grew because I had awareness of and access to my Shadows, so I could embody them, allowing them to infiltrate my creation consciously rather than subconsciously. I also found out that I was not alone with my Shadows. I have presented them during workshops in different countries and to people from a diversity of cultures. Most people recognize these Inner Selves immediately. Therefore, in exploring and enacting my Shadows, I now have access to Universal Shadows that help heal and transform others.

At the end of the first three years, which was my initiation, I had acquired my first Medicines, or personal powers. I understood that each of them was a lesson that I must pass on as part of the path of Theatre of Transformation. Some of these are: the Breath that Knows, Impeccable Truthfulness, and Shadow Hunting.

Each year since the initiation, I have been given a "Task of Power" that has led me to acquire new knowledge and power. The first one was to "remember" my Self after having been dismembered. This task led me to remember many of my past lives, and it took me to Mexico, where I met other Spiritspeakers and gained some students. I learned to see myself as an Infinite Self, existing simultaneously in the past, the present, and the future. Now when I perform or dance, I go to that place. There I find the place where my consciousness meets that of the audience. This makes it possible to engage audience members at a genuine level. The awareness that is the Infinite Self allows the Performance Shaman to bring out the healing as well as the divinatory powers of art.

My latest "Task of Power" is to achieve Inner Balance—between my Female and Male Shields—and Inner Congruence. To learn these lessons, the Ancestors have taken me to South Africa, where I am writing the final version of this article. Here I am conducting Shamanic Celebrations in which people dance, chant, drum, and channel poetry from a place of Oneness with the universe. What I am learning is that we need to marry our Essensual Self—the soulful, sensual, "feminine" aspects of the Self—to the aggressive, mental, or "masculine" aspects of the Self, in order for both art and healing to take place. I see that many people disown their creativity because they either cannot touch their Essence or cannot express it.

Through TOTAL—the long-term laboratory—and through these pathwalkers or clients who came to me for individual sessions, the Ancestors taught me the true nature of art. I healed the split that weakened my Medicine. I was now a teatrista, facilitator, and spirit-speaker, all in one. I was becoming a Shaman.

What I learned is that art, at its most fundamental, is a healing ritual. Poetry happens when the soul touches its truth. Painting and drawing are the footprints of the spirit. Dancing is connecting space within with space without, manifesting Oneness. Singing is sharing the language of life: vibration. Storytelling connects us with our Ancestors. Theater—through enactment—penetrates the mask that binds the soul, cracking it open.

The healings I now facilitated through art were quick, effective, and deep. If a dancer came to me, the whole session became a ritual of dancing through her obstacles in search of herself. If the pathwalker was a visual artist, she created a painting that came from within and then walked into the painting as a way of changing her reality from the inside out. People, through the language of their souls, found answers to questions they had been asking all their lives. They were able to put together those pieces of their existence that had been disowned, and to overcome the tyranny of abuse, rape, and enmeshment. This was what I had been looking for in my creative work! I saw now that not until I began my own healing could I have understood, much less have been a vehicle for, this type of art.

Not one of all my acting, directing, and playwriting teachers had ever taught me that I could do this with my craft. Why was the healing nature of art unknown in our society? I saw miracles happen in every individual, as well as in group sessions, yet no one I knew of was doing this kind of theater in this country. I soon realized what had happened.

When the first "civilized" men encountered the ancient ritualistic paintings, dances, dramas, and incantations, they labeled these as superstitions. They studied them with curiosity, to see how humans used to live before they "really" understood the universe. The limited scientific view of their days led them to believe that humans were the only conscious beings on Earth and that everything else either had no conscious life or no life at all. The men of the modern age rejected anything that threatened their view of the universe as a mass of matter following certain laws of cause and effect. The scientific man saw himself as separate, and his art lost its power to connect him to the universal field.

Since the Law of Relativity led to quantum discoveries, western man is realizing what the ancestral Shamans in Australia, Africa, India, and America have known for thousands of years. There is a universal field of energy that travels in a space-time continuum without being localized either in time or space. Energy everywhere follows the movement of consciousness and is one with it. And this universal law is what has enabled art for centuries to become a doorway to the infinite possibilities of the universe. The Ancient Ones were not ignorant savages, as modern man characterized them. The Ancient Ones simply possessed advanced knowledge that found no place within the culture western civilization had built.

My shamanic training and my experiences in the development of Theatre of Transformation led me to understand that we are lost to ourselves through separateness. It is the source of disease, alienation, and the overwhelming, chronic depression so many people feel throughout their days. When we see ourselves as separate from others and from the rest of creation, we are like a bird that has lost its wings. Oneness is the wind that allows us to fly consciously in the Universal Energy Field (UEF).

Those cave paintings can help us understand much more than the "working of the primitive mind." They can teach us the power of art as a means to connect human beings to nature, to each other, and to the Unknown through the UEF.

Another effect of separateness in our lives has been polarization, or dualistic thinking. We have learned to see the world in terms of opposites that preclude and fight each other: good and evil, black and white, male and female, love and power, the Shadows and the Light.

Through the creative process as a Shaman's Medicine, I was led to the Place of Paradox. I learned to dance my Inner Shadows into the Light, to sing my pain until it became a doorway to Power. I was taught to look at the material beauty of a person, tree, or landscape, and through it enter the world of Spirit. It was at this time that I received my first Medicine Name. I became *She Who Lights the Shadows with her Presence.*

When in training, I was led to *Hands of Light,* a book on the healing techniques of Barbara Brennan. There I found this passage.

In the 1920s, physics moved into the strange and unexpected reality of the subatomic world. Every time physicists asked nature a question in an experiment, nature responded with a paradox. The more they tried to clarify the situation, the stronger the paradox became. Finally, physicists realized that paradox is part of the intrinsic nature of the subatomic world upon which all of our reality exists.

Dancing with the Voices of Truth:
Two weeks to opening night. I am rehearsing the first play of Theatre of Transformation, *The Temple of Desire.* It is an AIDS-prevention play celebrating the body and sexuality from a female perspective. I struggle with a sequence that deals with the history of my sexuality. It talks about times in my early youth when I unleashed my sexual powers only to be shamed by the man I was with. I am trying to thrust my pelvis forward, but it won't budge. Suddenly my pelvis is thrown backward with such force that I fall some three feet back and crash-land on the floor.

I enter Dreamtime. The First People place a great value on Dreamtime. One's body suddenly enters another reality. It has sensations, visions, of its own. If one follows one's Dreambody, it will walk one through the time-space continuum in the universal field. The Dreambody will take a person into those experiences the body/soul needs to unravel the mystery of her present situation. The Dreaming may happen while one is sitting quietly or it may be a Dreamdance, in which case the dance takes place simultaneously in the space through which one is moving physically, within one's inner being, and in the UEF. A Dreamdance effects powerful changes within the dancer—at a cellular and auric level—as well as in her life and environment. Those observers who harmonize with the dancer will also benefit from her spiritual journey.

In my Dreamtime, I face an ancient temple in the center of a jungle. I know this temple to be my body. There is a magnificent lion sitting at the entrance, which I know to be my pelvis. This beast is beautiful, wild, and fierce, but it is made of stone. It is immovable and blocks the entrance to my pelvis and sexual organs. Its name is Leo. I touch its cold stone, and tears flood my face. The stone takes me back in time to a rainy day in which the jungle was thundering with chaos. A young, sensual woman is entering this temple. She wears a long, flowing skirt and a flower adorns her hair. I recognize her as my youthful self. She goes into the temple, her head lowered in shame. Scared of her own desires, of her hunger, and of men, she hides deep in the temple's chambers. Leo closes the entrance, becoming a stone so as not to allow any desires to perturb the young woman's retreat. I travel forward into the present, still in the jungle. I now know that the imprisonment of the sexual part of myself has caused the fibroid which has had me bleeding copiously for a year. I break into a deep sob that comes from my belly. Breathing into my pelvis, I reclaim my genitals, my sexuality, my passion. Leo begins to melt, to become a beast of flesh and blood. The entrance to the temple is uncovered. An amazon-like woman appears, her black hair dancing wildly in the wind. Her legs are as strong as a lion's hinds. "I am Majestad Salvaje (Wild Majesty). You were protecting the girl who entered here, not entrapping her," she says to Leo. "But that girl has grown into full power. I have been born. You guard me not because I am a prisoner or weak, but because I am a Queen."

I awaken from Dreamtime. My body is more open, my pelvis loose. I now understand what was going on in my being some minutes ago, when my pelvis refused to move forward. I understand it in ways that could never come just through analysis. This movement, which resulted from an apparent "failure" to follow directions, has given me a deeper level of insight about my life, my wounds, and my disease. I have also found the source that guides my intentions and movements in the sequence.

Before a shamanic play goes on, the process of rehearsals must also be a shamanic journey in which the artists take real risks. Anthropologist Arnold Mindell, who is himself a Shaman and therapist, describes several categories or stages in Shamanism. There is the Wounded Healer. There is also the Hunter, who tracks down the opponents, the Shadows, or the key element in a situation, depending on the context. Psychologist-Shamans, for example, tend to be Hunters.

Then there is the Warrior. The Shaman-Warrior is she who not only tracks down but seizes the prey. If the prey is, let's say, an Inner Shadow, the Spiritual Warrior becomes the Shadow and harnesses her energy into the Light of awareness, creativity, and love within herself and within the person she is helping. In this sense, the Performance Shaman is a Shaman-Warrior. As such, she walks through her fear into her power, through her wounds into her truth. This walk begins with the co-creation or development of the play or performance, and continues during its presentation.

The development of a play or performance is then a personal and collective voyage into the very heart of the issues addressed. In *The Temple of Desire,* for example, when the performers explored the reasons why we had had unprotected sex in our lives, the exploration led us to a labyrinth of Inner Shadows and wounded aspects of the Self. Among these were: co-dependence, our inability to love ourselves, a sense of invisibility and not valuing ourselves, ignorance about sex and safe sex, the mythification of the sexual encounter, and the belief that we would be seen as "bad girls" if we spoke about sex beforehand with a date. We also found ourselves in the midst of layers upon layers of fear. As we would peel an onion, we peeled these layers. The first layer was fear of being ridiculed. Then we found fear of abandonment. Beneath that was fear of saying the truth and losing our partners or male attention. Then we found fear of discovering the truth about the relationship. We found fear of trusting a man, but also fear of confronting a man—fear of standing on our truth and honoring our beings. And, finally, a fear of death that forbade accepting ourselves as mortals. All these Shadows, wounds, and fears garbled our thought processes, disconnecting us from our conscious intent. The result was that—even when we knew how to have safe sex or that we should have safe sex—we acted in ways that were dissociated from this knowledge.

The shamanic play deals with social reality, but must go farther. Truth lies, for the Shaman-Warrior, as well as for the Performance Shaman, in the Place of Paradox—in the center, where opposites converge to form a metaphor for existence. For this reason, the performers must explore their own polarized beliefs. This act is so powerful that it can transform the auric structure of a person, the template that holds her body together. A performer facing her duality can find herself in the middle of a subatomic restructuring of her being. Suddenly, she will start trembling from within and light particles will explode within her as her atoms are releasing the imprints of these old beliefs. The very substance of this process will be felt by the audience during the presentation, lending truthfulness, a sense of "realness," to the journey.

The Performer as Shaman must undergo the Shaman's training and initiation. This process, which I have briefly sketched, is best done as part of a group. It requires the guidance and power of a teacher. Sometimes she will be a Spirit-teacher, like in my case. But usually it is an Earth-teacher, someone who is still on the earth plane. This training entails a personal, psychological, physical, and spiritual death and rebirth. After all, the Performance Shaman is a Wounded Healer too. As such, she must have traveled the length and breadth of her wounds and must have emerged from this pain into her power. This is what gives her the empathy, compassion, knowledge, and energy to heal in the act of enacting the wound. No matter how good an actress she is, a performer cannot fake presence. Either she tells the story standing in the center of her Circle of Power, or she doesn't. If she does, the enactment of the wound becomes a path to power for those in the audience who choose to follow. If she doesn't, the dramatic action will not carry enough power to bring the audience into healing.

Whether the play has been written beforehand, is developed with the performers, or is improvised with the audience, it unfolds as a direct consequence of the performers' journey through the reality being explored. The director is responsible for facilitating this journey. Flexibility is her tool, for the solidity of the final weave—the performance—will depend on her ability to help the performers explore the fluidity of the threads and colors they are blending. Dance, poetry, installations, unspoken sequences, new dialogue, sound explorations, key metaphors, and participatory structures may evolve from the actors' journey.

If the performers are Shamans, the director is the Shaman of the Shamans. She is a teacher in the Shaman's Way. The performer must hunt her Shadow while maintaining her center. She must go to the very depth of her soul while keeping detached. She exists in two worlds at the same time. This Place of Paradox is difficult and can be dangerous. The beginning actor needs someone who holds the performer to her center, who helps bring her back if she starts to get lost. The veteran benefits tremendously from someone who lends her additional energy, witnesses her Act of Power, and gives her feedback. These are some of the roles the director of a shamanic play has. She is the Master Hunter, helping the performers seize their fears and resistance and use them as allies in the act of bringing forth an enactment that will transform the consciousness of the audience.

Theatre of Transformation is my way of rescuing the shamanic nature of art in a contemporary, non-traditional context. Many traditional rituals have a strict format in which not one verse or movement can be omitted or changed. The reason for this is that these rituals' function is to preserve the balance of creation. In contrast, a play or performance within Theatre of Transformation is a blueprint for journeying into the collective unconscious, bringing forth archetypal movements, forms, sounds, and energies that can help the participants move past their habits and obstacles into deeper insight and new possibilities. It is a tool for expansion and transformation.

Secular Play, Sacred Space:

April 1996. This is the first time that *Temple of Desire* as a full play will be presented totally as a shamanic experience. We have created a central installation. It is an altar to Ochún, the Yoruba goddess of female sexuality. I have represented her through a full-sized female "doll." I created this representation with black skin, African braids, voluptuous breasts, and the small but abundant frame of many Latinas and Caribbean women. This reflects the fact that the play is emphasizing the experience of Latinas, who are a "high-risk" population getting very few resources in New York.

The audience are staff, clients, and the families of clients of a nonprofit organization that helps people with AIDS and offers an AIDS prevention program at a city-wide level. We expect about fifty people, and as we open the doors to receive them, a thousand questions cross my mind. Can fifty people create the trust and intimacy necessary to travel into Dreamtime? How will those people from different cultures respond to our Caribbean iconography?

The audience enters a large room where the seats are arranged in a horseshoe formation. Around the audience area, there are several interactive installations. Each of them presents the audience members with an opportunity for healing in a variety of ways. Honoring the Ancestors, releasing grief, naming, touching, and opening the heart to joy are but a few Medicines contained in these installations. They embody the metaphors encountered by the performers in their Dreaming during rehearsals.

"The Tree of Life and Death" is the first installation audience members see as they come in. A dead tree with bare branches on which hang purple ribbons, it allows the spectators to send messages to their loved ones who have died of AIDS or related diseases. The performers start by hanging their own paper plate, dedicated to Ilka Tanya Payán, a friend and actress who died of AIDS and who was courageous enough to face public scrutiny as she shared her tragedy in order to educate others. The members of the audience write their own messages and hang them on purple ribbons. People's energy shifts from curiosity to reverence. They came in with a question on their faces: "Are you going to make me cry, or lecture me?" Now the answer comes from within: "There is a place where the spirits of my dead ones can flourish. The tree holds them and sends them my love." Actors and audience have found a common ground. It is no longer "them" and "us," but "we." The healing has begun.

As we move into the "Altar of the Sacred Spiral," we take our personal deaths and pain and place them in the arms of all our Ancestors. We are surrendering our guilt, mistakes, anger, and confusion to them. We ask for a true voice, a clear eye, and empowerment to change the course of human existence for us and for future generations. With low, deep, warm tones that come from the bones and find their way through fear and pain, the audience members begin to name that which needs healing. Naming is a sacred, powerful act.

   * I was into drugs. I didn't love myself, so how could I love anyone else?

   * I was young and immortal. Nothing could touch me.

   * I am asking help to heal my co-dependence. It is just so difficult! I can't be this hungry. I'm too vulnerable to danger.

Next we move to the Ochún altar, where, one by one, we embrace joy and open our hearts to the life force. We sing and gaze into each other's eyes, discovering Oneness and welcoming love. Twenty minutes into the opening, the lights let people know that the shamanic journey is beginning. The Performance Shamans now enact the script. Through the silence, we feel the closeness of people's hearts. Their breathing becomes one with ours, as if we were one large, living, moving organism. Every move we make happens simultaneously in space, in our innermost recesses, within the participants, and in the universal field.

I have come full circle in the journey for the search of my Self which I initiated as a young girl. On this journey, I have gone through studies in psychology, political activism, more than twenty years of professional popular theater, and more or less the same number of years as a facilitator of women and family groups.

What have I found? A path to Self. A Rite of Passage from our wounds into our gifts. A Sacred Space in which healing, understanding, and transformation are initiated. A way of doing art that brings body, mind, emotions, and soul together. A creative movement that restores us to Oneness with each other, with nature, with the universe, and with the Sacred World. A place where performers and audience join in the Act of Power that creative expression truly is. It is not the only path, but it is the one I have been given to travel and to share. I call it Theatre of Transformation.

SEARCHING FOR SANCTUARIES

CRUISING THROUGH TOWN IN A
RED CONVERTIBLE

Diane Rodríguez

Joining the Teatro Campesino was like running away to a spellbinding and forbidden tent show. Part circus, part evangelist revival, part political rally. It was grand. Difficult. Important. I learned how to act and commit to the act. I learned how to believe, create, do. Creer, crear, hacer. It was my haven. We belonged and believed in the magic of unity and social change. May we all continue to find such sanctuaries.

Most of us who joined the Teatro Campesino in the seventies were in our late teens or early twenties. I came to the Teatro as an eighteen-year-old girl-woman, attracted to an irresistible energy I couldn't explain but that I felt deep in my soul.

The Esparzas, my mother's familia, settled in San Jose, California, when the Santa Clara Valley was a fertile field for apricots and prunes, not megabytes and rams. It was a lush agricultural valley, surrounded by the Santa Cruz Mountains and the San Francisco Bay. They had followed the migrant path from the grapefruit orchards of the Coachella Valley to the garlic fields of Gilroy. My mother, Helen, was a smart, dark brown, desert kid who ran to school near the Morongo Reservation. My grandfather died at thirty-seven, leaving my grandma to raise nine children with the help of the Protestant missionaries, Mr. and Mrs. Smith, and Tío, my grandpa's brother.

Even though my dad's father, Alejandro, was a poor dirt farmer in dusty southern Texas, my father, Jacob, did as little field work as possible. My dad had aspirations. He was going to be an entertainer. So, he made his way to California in the late 1930s and never looked back. Texas had been his family's home for generations. The Rodriguezes had been there when Texas was Mexico. But as far as my dad was concerned, Texas was a dead-end street. Jake wanted action. He wanted out. Dad landed in Oxnard, California, that action-packed town of the Golden West. Worked his way to Hollywood, made a go of it as a singer at the Beverly Hills Hotel, looked deep into the eyes of many a movie star, and saw loneliness. Decided this wasn't the life for him. Packed his bags and moved to San Jose to marry my mother.

Jacob and Helen weren't going to be poor. Many Depression-era kids made the vow not to go back to the poverty of their family's past. Jake and Helen gave my sister, Martha, and me ruffles and a canopy bed, French provincial bedroom sets, Sunday dresses of crinoline and lace, roses and manicured front lawns, summer tans and Doughboy swimming pools, potato salad and summer picnics, fish sticks on Fridays, Yosemite and Bridal Falls, snazzy cars and the University of California. They also gave us la segunda, the thrift store habit, Grandma and Tío and las novelas, figs and loquats on a hot summer day, strawberry fields at Aunt Jessie's, Spam, Ma's flour tortillas, La Primera Iglesia Bautista Hispana Americana, which included Spanish sermons, conjuntos, y la Biblia.

My sister and I went to my parents' high school graduation when I was in junior high. My mother was working at Tri-Valley cannery. My dad was an orderly at San Jose Hospital. With more schooling, my mother became head of the EKG department at a local Catholic hospital and my father became a steam and maintenance engineer. They had come a long way from the dirt lands of Texas and the sunbaked streets of Indio, California. Where they came from was who my parents were, they never denied it, and that never changed.

The center of our life was the church. There were picnics, retreats, potlucks, fund-raisers, plays, rehearsals, choirs, quartets, Saturday cleanup, meetings, revivals, and home visits. The Rodriguezes and the Esparzas attended the Baptist church on 9th street in San Jose. They had built the church with their own hands during the sixties. They dug out the dirt to lay the foundation, built the walls, wired, painted, and bought the pews.

In the early years, my mother played the piano, while my father directed the choir. Not to be upstaged, I'd run up behind my dad as he was directing the coro and mimic him. Those were my first recorded theatrical improvisations. I was three. I began to find theater in the weekly rituals of church activity. As I grew older, I sang solos, read the Sunday morning scriptures, and acted in church plays. My most inspired and memorable role was that of the Archangel. My wings were fabulously huge and I was a big hit. Those white feather wings launched my career.

My entire extended family practically organized every church event and enterprise. They had all met when the church was a small mission at the end of a dusty, unpaved road called Sal Si Puedes, which had been home to César Chávez and Luis Valdez, too. It was a natural progression that, as my cousins and Martha and I grew older during the sixties and seventies, we became activists just as our parents had been active at La Primera Iglesia Bautista Hispana Americana.

Being in the Teatro Campesino was an extension of church for me. I was inspired, energized, and motivated. We did everything. We acted, answered phones, built costumes and sets, made props, signed contracts, booked tours, taught workshops, made adobe bricks, mended fences, did publicity, picketed, studied Mao, learned Nahuatl, made movies, performed on flatbed trucks and on German opera stages, married, had kids, divorced, and laughed. We laughed a lot. We were loud, wild, focused, funny, raw, and committed. Our agenda was to inspire, educate, and define what it was to be a Chicana/o. We had our differences. But for all the years I lived and breathed El Teatro Campesino, these differences were small compared to the vision of seeing my community unified under a banner of consciousness and self-empowerment.

If the sixties was a time of political awakening for the country at large, for me, entering consciousness occurred in the seventies when I joined the Teatro Campesino. Of course, I joined the Teatro Campesino thinking I would only learn how to act better. My voice was thin, sweet. It tried to please. I had no relationship with the center of my body. Over the next decade, I would peel away the shell I had created around myself, find my voice, my power, my center, and my community.

What changed for me was realizing that good acting, social consciousness, and activism were all intrinsically connected. I could only be a good actor if I made strong choices and committed to them. In that same vein, the Teatro considered acting to be activism, meaning that activism, too, was to act upon a choice in order to fulfill an objective. The Teatro Campesino used theater to inspire and challenge a community hungry for leadership and identity. This explosive marriage of art and activism caused a powerful connection between actor and community. It happened in Italy in 1976 when our set and costumes were detained at the French border. Five thousand people waited in an outdoor amphitheater. We were scared out of our minds. But we walked on stage and simply sang. The audience went wild. And then, five thousand Italians began to sing to thirteen Chicanos the Communist Internazionale. Their spirit entered me and I became connected to an international struggle. The world became smaller and I became larger. It was a great act. A pivotal moment in my life. I became a world citizen. Being in the presence of such unity is a spiritual experience. I was in church again.

My induction into the world of great acts and social movement happened during the summer of 1973 when Peter Brook, the undeniable master of directing, brought his company, The Centre for International Theatre Research, to San Juan Bautista, California, the home of the Teatro Campesino. Every day we'd sit in a circle in the Teatro's hot tin warehouse. Peter's company was made up of actors from Japan, England, Mali, America, Germany. They came in every color and size, dressed in African fabrics, turbans, long vintage skirts, scarves, long hair, rings, and tattoos. They were a fabulous sight dropped into the middle of San Juan Bautista, where the claim to fame was the California Mission, an Indian cemetery, and the San Andreas Fault.

The women in Peter Brook's company were incredible. For twenty years, their free spirits have stayed within me. Miriam, Natasha Perry, Michele George, Liz Swados, and Helen Mirren. Luckily for me, Helen and I would share a small room together with one big window, where I'd gaze out into the night sky and wonder what lay ahead. Helen took me under her wing that summer. Immediately, we drove to San Jose and my father helped her buy a cherry-red convertible, and she sped through San Juan Bautista, population 1200, in search of action and me in search of myself.

As we sat in the circle, Peter would outline the improvisational exercise for the morning session. Helen would literally dive in with wild abandon and take what came her way. She lost herself inside the circle. She died. She leapt into the unknown and landed with a womanliness that grounded her. She was fearless. It was a liberating sight and I wanted to join her dance, be invited to her party, sit at her table.

While I'd sit and admire the women of Peter's group, Luis's younger sister, Socorro Valdez, caught my eye. La Socorro commanded attention. She had a light inside that came from a belief in herself. She was hysterically funny and tragic at the same time. She took risks. She could play men better than men, somersault and back flip, and then make you cry. She never thought. She did. So I decided Socorro would be my measuring stick and Helen Mirren, for that fleeting summer, would be my tutor.

Never had two mujeres moved me so profoundly. Socorro was a comic, short, dark, Indian featured, and from San Jose, my hometown. Helen was sultry, blond, voluptuous, and English. Socorro had a male energy that drove her. She was the fire of the Teatro. Helen was wise, intelligent, and in touch with her femaleness. Both were razor sharp, willful, strong. They possessed an intensity and freshness that was riveting because they made strong, wild choices that set them apart from most. In a male-dominated field, their strong presence was a political act. They were deep and intense women who were not afraid to show it. They illuminated my way by their success and courage.

For me, the Peter Brook experience was baptism by fire. For the Teatro, it was a transitional moment. We had spent a summer finding a universal language of symbols and movement. We began to transition into a vision of the Chicano in the world scene. We envisioned ourselves as the creators of a universal theater, deeply embedded in Chicano/Indio culture. This new direction actively began that fall of 1973 as we delved into Luis's concept of Pensamiento Serpentino. I resisted. It was hard for me to sit still and meditate, listen to my heartbeat. I couldn't figure out what the feathered serpent had to do with being a good actor. Luis was ardent as he took us through the paces of finding our infinite potential through breathing, balance, tumbling, and free exercise. It took me years to connect with my body, to find its center, "to work from where you are, not from where you would like to be, or think you are." The simplest exercises became life's biggest challenges. These exercises laid the foundation for a life of consciousness on and off the stage.

From 1974 through 1980, I was on a fast train with few stops. In those six years, we went on three European tours, three national tours, filmed a couple of PBS specials, did runs in New York City, and performed a yearly Christmas show. And if acting wasn't enough, I'd design costumes, too. I can only remember years now in terms of tours, cities, and performances. They were countless. We had a fine group of actors, trained and untrained, who made you believe in what they were saying because they were believers.

It is true, the Teatro repertoire of women's roles, the wives, the girlfriends, the loose women, the Virgins, was tiresome and limiting. I was never very good at playing any of them. Looking back, I realize it was my way of resisting those roles. I was most comfortable playing androgynous characters: La Muerte in *La Carpa de los Rasquachis* or Satanás in *La Pastorela*, a shepherd's play. These roles offered more versatility and power. We women complained but, in the end, we accepted the roles. All of us could have walked away, but we didn't. I take full responsibility for what the group was delivering. I was a willing participant.

¿Y por qué no? We were moving a community to self-empowerment through art. The audiences were hungry and we fed them with unabashed social and political commentary. Through historical and mythical archetypes, we created cultural signposts. *La Virgen de Guadalupe, Tonantzín,* and resistance. El *Pelado, El Rasquachi,* and *Everyman. La Muerte, El Diablo,* and the collective voice. *Quetzalcoatl, Tezcatlipoca,* our deux ex machinas. *La Luna, El Sol,* and the earth. History and the past gave us power to expand and deal with our future.

By 1984, you could feel the climate change. Reaganmania was in full swing, touring became extremely costly, Luis became more focused on outside projects, plays, and movies. The Teatro struggled to support us all full time. Eventually, there seemed to be no choice but make the inevitable decision to disband the ensemble, the group, and consequently, the life, the energy, the force. I knew it was coming: most of us did. It was incredibly difficult to experience our public but sheltered life change. We talked endlessly about how it could have been prevented. But it happened and we had to deal with it. Soon there was an onslaught of new energy: actors from Los Angeles and other parts of California. Most didn't share our history. Some were interested, others not. Some were Chicanos with a certain social awareness, but their commitment to the group was dependent on the project they were hired for and little else. Working with the Teatro became an acting job in the mainstream tradition. I began to feel like a relic from the past, a Chicana Ranasaurus Rex. It was time for a difficult change.

So, J.D. and I followed our hearts and left the Teatro of our youth. J.D. lived the life for fifteen years. I followed with thirteen. Most of those years we had been married. An era had finally ended. We joyfully gave our lives in order to create a legacy: a passionate, physical, energetic, and vital theater that no one could deny and few could repeat.

Los Angeles called us like a siren and we answered. We left Sunday visits to Ma's and Dad's, and old friends who shared our secretos. Out of the Teatro's womb, we were re-born in the fast lane of Los Angeles's vida loca. Angels watched over us.

Our passage was nothing new. We repeated what my father had done, and his father before him. We left home and regret behind to find our tierra—packed up our cosas, and traveled south to a brightly lit land, with promise in our reach, in search of new sanctuaries. But unlike my father, I did look back. As we drove out of town, I gazed over my shoulder one more time, and did not turn my head until the twinkling lights of the circus dimmed and were no more. It was magic.

HOME, DESIRE, MEMORY

THERE ARE NO BORDERS HERE (A LATINA PLAYWRIGHT COMES OF AGE IN AMERICA)

Caridad Svich

Home, desire, memory: there are no borders here. The only borders that exist are the ones in your mind. What is it to be a Latina, a writer, a playwright in this country? I can say this: the road is long, hard, but it is rewarding. Or, as Edward Albee once said, "It is rough, unfair, and (very) ugly."

I suspect I have always been a nomad. Born in Philadelphia, Pennsylvania, five months shy of JFK's assassination, I awoke, albeit prematurely, to a world optimistic and unknowingly poised for tragedy and disillusion, a world where the pure rock strains of an English band called the Beatles filled the air in sweet naive splendor.

I started playwriting a long time ago, it seems. At least I started to think of myself as a writer at an early age—at that time when girls begin to doubt their minds because they are growing up too fast for their bodies.

I never saw the limits that could impose themselves on a writer who is a woman, Latina, in this country.

When I started playwriting, the pleasure of creating a world through language was all. This intense connection to the word and the page was inextricably linked to my first experience with theater, which was not as a spectator, but as a reader imagining the stage.

I remember opening a book sometime in the fourth grade and discovering a wealth of words that had nothing—and yet everything—to do with me. Words that tumbled, danced, played; sentences mysterious, confusing, foreign. These words belonged in a book, and it turned out that the book I picked up quite at random was Shakespeare's *A Midsummer Night's Dream*.

I didn't know what I was reading. I only knew that I loved the language, that it made a kind of perfect sense to this girl of a Cuban mother and an Argentine father with roots going back to Spain and Croatia.

These words said to me, "There are no borders here."

Where? Nowhere. Somewhere. Sense of place is central to my aesthetic. My characters are those who stay, but dream of going. Or those who are always going and yearn to stay. I see America as a land of travelers, wanderers, pilgrims. As a daughter of immigrants, my vision of America as a land marked by centuries of wandering and forced and unforced pilgrimages has been colored by tales and dreams of that other place that lives vividly in my parents' minds. Patria—the repository of memory. Although I acknowledge that my patria is this country where I was born and raised, there are phantom patrias that exist for me (Cuba, Argentina, Croatia, Spain). These phantom images of countries that are in my blood-memory have created in me an añoramiento, a longing, for places I hardly even know, and have made me feel as though I am also an exile. Out of this paradoxical state, I write, re-imagining the United States from within.

(This añoramiento, this longing, is, I think, made distinctly more aching because of the United States' border relationship to Latin America.)

My earliest true recollections begin at the age of four, this time in the semi-urban, Polish-Italian-German-Irish neighborhood of Paterson, New Jersey. Spanish was spoken and heard only at home then, or when we drove what seemed like many miles away to Union City or strange areas in New York called Spanish Harlem and Queens.

Didn't everyone have the same old records at home—records where the singer would say "Ponte Mameluco" or "Óyeme Cachita" in free and lively ways, records that made me laugh and dance, and made my mother shake her hips and my tango-souled father blush? If not, could I take a very secret pleasure in having what, for all intents and purposes, was a double life: one, northeastern and American, the other, Caribbean and Latin?

Another four years, and from New Jersey to Miami, Florida (not as an army brat, simply a passenger on my parents' quest for the "American Dream"). Here was a true Latin city. To say I experienced culture shock would be to put it mildly. I felt exposed. My private, familial language and rhythms were everywhere, commonplace. Everyone spoke Spanish, or so it seemed. Everyone heard the same music. Everyone wore azabaches and gold bracelets. I believe it was in Miami that I became a true American—a fusion of sensibilities incorporated body and spirit.

It was in the ninth grade, at that stage of doubt when girls are becoming women and are questioning their identity in a world of men, that I decided I would write a play.

"This is what you want to do? Then this is what you must do." My English teacher sent me to a shelf at the local library, and instructed me to read the form so that I could learn how to put it down on the page. Now I know that you put it down the way you see it, not the way others do. But I didn't know that then. How could I? So, I read. I read everything on that shelf, not noticing that all the plays were written by men.

In fact, from what I could see, the only plays on that library shelf that were written by a woman were ones by someone called Lillian Hellman. (Much later, I would come to discover Lorraine Hansberry, Ntzoke Shange, Adrienne Kennedy, Caryl Churchill, and so many others.) As I began to read Ms. Hellman's plays (unaware of her more formidable prose) I was embarrassed by how dusty, how overwrought, they seemed. They were certainly not as exciting as the plays by Aeschylus, Shakespeare, Brecht, Tennessee Williams, O'Neill, Lorca, Molière—plays that clearly belonged on a shelf in a library.

What was it about these plays by men that earned them the right to belong on a government shelf? At the time, the one word that seemed to answer that question for me was "adventure." The ambition, breadth, scope, and danger that these plays courted was adventurous almost to a fault. The writers took life in their hands fully, often heroically. This is exactly what I wanted from playwriting.

So, I turned my back on my sex.

Therefore, when I actually began the process of writing a play, feeling pretty serious about it as only a fourteen-year-old can, I decided if I was to write a true play, then the characters who inhabited its world must be men. Not that I couldn't conceive of women taking center stage, but surely those who moved the world were men. And if I was to prove myself in this world, then I had to write like one.

Voice. Sound and poetry. What I hear on the street, on the interstate, in the hum of voices that make up a day, I elevate, because that is what theater needs to do. To go back to voice and space. For me, the playwriting impulse is in first locating a place (an emotional, physical, intellectual terrain) and then discovering its inhabitants—characters whose voices resonate in the geography. These are the voices that will tell me the play, and so I listen to them without prejudice. Listen, and allow them to take shape, for theater is (uniquely so) a form where language is made three-dimensional, where sound and sense rub against each other to produce a strange, beautiful, dangerous noise.

At some point in college, I decided I was sick and tired of writing about men, of denying myself, of trying to see the world a certain way, when I truly saw it differently.

I do not mean to divide all writing along gender lines. However, I do think that if you are a woman who writes, especially for the theater, you cannot think that your body and your position in the world have nothing to do with your work.

It haunts me still what Virginia Woolf once confessed in her writing: "Telling the truth about my own experiences as a body, I do not think I solved it. I doubt that any woman has solved it yet."

I am a first-generation American woman who lives and writes in these United States. In my work, I strive to place a female, primarily (though not exclusively) Latina point of view at the forefront of the theatrical experience. At the same time, I wish to present a landscape that extends beyond immediate reality toward one of dreams. The result is a hybrid form—a theatrical voice poised somewhere between performance and art, poetry and narrative, where there are no borders.

Writing without denying my sex liberated my imagination. Coming to terms with my identity as a Latina playwright freed my work even more.

When I consciously decided to incorporate my heritages, my blood-memory, into my work's expression (doing so for the first time with my play *Brazo Gitano*) I discovered an authentic voice that was free to manifest itself unencumbered by traditional expectations of form and style. It was a freedom that held within it the imprint of "origin." I have since felt that it is this reminder of one's origin that allows a text to breathe its own particular rhythm and thus create its own linguistic destiny.

For a long time, I did not think of myself as a Latina playwright. I was simply a "writer," with no qualifiers. And I must admit that I still see myself as a writer first: no borders, no party lines, just my imagination and what it can produce.

However, I have to admit that my work, my way of seeing, is naturally influenced by who I am, who my parents are, my background and my upbringing; I do feel a natural kinship, a link to a tradition of art and playwriting that includes Borges, Lorca, Velázquez, Lam, el son, la rumba, el tango, y el balompié.

My journey as a playwright has taken me many places, but none perhaps more important at the developmental level than my four years as resident writer and member of INTAR's Hispanic Playwrights Lab in New York under the direction of Maria Irene Fornes. Ms. Fornes is certainly a seminal influence on the work of a whole generation of Latina(o) writers (both as a consummate artist in her own right and as a teacher). It was at INTAR that I found a community of writers with whom I could identify.

Here was a group of playwrights, mostly in their mid twenties to early thirties, who were exploring their identities as Latino(a)s in this culture, and doing so in a manner that was forthright, sexually frank, structurally complex, and ultimately very American. The fluidity of time and space, the spiritual to the material, and the playfulness of a language not quite Spanish, not fully English, were elements that had just begun to occupy my playwriting. I had just written *Brazo Gitano* and I was fresh out of graduate school in California—two turning points at once. To encounter not only a group of writers who were exploring similar issues but who were also of my generation was confirmation that the path I had chosen was one that would undoubtedly lead to further exploration and a deepening of my work.

I see a new playwriting coming into being: playwriting that places Latinas as part of the mainstream, that is, characters who are Latina with no questions asked, as simply part of the fabric of the work. In other words, a writing that is carving away the myth of marginalization. As the Latina arts movement continues to grow and re-define its various missions, what is increasingly clear is that what could be termed "first-generation" playwriting has been relegated to a secondary place in the vast spectrum of possibilities. Taking its cue from the established, fertile ground of Latina fiction, theater is beginning to break the kind of ground that poetry and the novel have already broken. Stories of assimilation and coming-of-age are no longer the only subjects available, although they are still the expected province of hybrid Americans. Complex and radical stories, both in form and content, are heard more and more. These necessary voices point toward a further re-definition of what is "Latina." The main obstacle I have encountered as a Latina playwright is that most theaters have an idea of what a "Latina" playwright should write. Now that regional theaters have received grants for New Voices, Other Voices, and Multi-Cultural Voices programs, an unmistakable brand of tokenism has crept into our mainstream stages. Slowly, and often presented in a manner both obsequious and patronizing, expectations are leveled at writers who must fit a pre-determined slot. Thus, one finds theaters overcome with dreaded "good intentions" who feel that a "Latina" writer must only write specifically "La-tina" material. We have become the "other, ethnic" slot, alongside the now-standard African-American slot in a mainstream theater's season. Thus, for every genuine, original voice, there are a hundred more palatable "ethnic" voices that do little more than confirm a mainstream society's idea of what a "Latina" is.

This brand of tokenism is made more egregious as the paucity of diversity in theater seasons (and this includes Latino theaters) throughout the country increases. Where there used to be two or three new-play slots in a standard season, now there is perhaps one. And that precious slot almost always is taken by a pre-tested New York hit or other regional theater hit from the previous season. True representation has been replaced by a phantom view of an imaginary cultural spectrum.

With practically a whole generation of artists lost to AIDS, the refusal of theaters to produce work that is representative and reflective of our time (i.e., true voices engaging in original dialogue with the philosophical and political concerns of our day) has made an accurate documentation of the art of our time a needlessly difficult task. In fifty or a hundred years from now, what record will there be of the work that was relegated to the margins, the work that was shoved aside in favor of subscriber-friendly drama of often too-little artistic consequence?

Tokenism and prejudice go hand in hand. This is why we must carve away at myths. As a matter of responsibility to the craft we practice and to the keeping of a record of the age in which we live, playwrights must take on what society refuses. It is not enough to say "how long will we be ignored?" when how long is too long.

As a playwright, my battle with the theatrical "marketplace," to use a vulgar term, has not been resolved. I suspect it will be constant. My thirst for experimentation in the craft of drama is an insatiable one. With each text I seek a new form, a new language, a new music to explore. Not for "newness's" sake, but rather because I think rigorous investigation can yield something unforeseen. It is this unknown that lies at the heart of my quest as a playwright, as theater's secret is its eternal mystery.

As for the future and what it has in store, I can only say I will continue to write plays and live in quest—a nomad, finding and leaving assorted places called "home"—examining issues of ethnicity, identity, and gender as my gaze as an artist turns toward the increasingly complex socio-cultural fabric. And no doubt a part of me will also be searching to recapture the gleam of magic I first fell in love with on the page, and the moonless night on one of many highways when Pérez Prado's "Cherry Pink Apple Blossom White" was on the radio and all I could think was, "Yes, I'm going home."

TALES OF A
SOUTH·OF·THE·BORDER/
NORTH·OF·THE·STEREOTYPE
THEATER DIRECTOR

Susana Tubert

Theater has always been for me the barometer of society at large. It mirrors, reveals, accuses, escapes, makes fun of, and even mourns the greater truths that evade us day to day. Theater is the bridge that allows us to travel in a few hours to new and foreign territories where the rules of reality may drastically change. Great theater makes the specific universal, and in doing so, demands that we reconsider our preconceptions and stereotypes. As I was preparing this testimonial, I decided to take you on my own personal journey through show business. I hope that through the retelling of my own personal and artistic journey, your stories and questions will connect to mine.

In 1991, I was awarded a National Endowment for the Arts Director Fellowship through an organization called Theatre Communications Group in New York. The grant enabled me to design the perfect "dream year" where I could draw a line across American theater and learn about it from the inside out. I assisted Harold Prince on the Broadway bound musical *Kiss of the Spiderwoman,* Peter Sellars on a seven-hour modern opera, *Saint Francois,* and Marshall Mason on Lanford Wilson's new play, *The Redwood Curtain,* at one of the major regional theaters in the country. It was an extraordinary culminating event after ten years of continuous effort developing myself as a theater artist. It was a landmark year that allowed me to look back and appreciate how far I had come.

I first settled in New York City in 1980 to pursue an acting career. Back then, "multi-culturalism" was not a concept. Nor did the term "artist of color" exist. Instead, most of us who didn't have the blond, blue-eyed, Anglo-Saxon look belonged in the "ethnic" file. An exception, of course, took place when a casting director felt that someone like myself was "too white to be Hispanic" and "too Mediterranean looking" for the so-called "American" parts. Those of us in this typecasting limbo were usually placed in the "exotic" file. This may have been a blessing in disguise, since most "Hispanic" actors were, and still are, only hired to perform as drug dealers, prostitutes, pimps, maids, and, if they are lucky (as I once was in *The Guiding Light*) as a Venezuelan peasant in the background.

Yes, it was a memorable experience that every once in a while (as I open a residual check for $1.07 from a rerun in some foreign country) returns to haunt me. I can still see my reflection in the mirror: Chiquita Banana gets pregnant and goes to Haiti. I was asked to wear a puffy-sleeved blouse, layered skirts, yellow plastic earrings, and the traditional bandanna tied up high with a bow on my head. "Muy típico!" And as if that wasn't humiliating enough, my colleagues and friends were dressed in Mexican peasant shirts, sandals, string pants that were too short, and straw hats. Our significant contribution to the storyline was to be the townspeople in the background, along with the two goats, while the American lead actor married a Venezuelan temptress (who was naturally played by an Anglo actress who needed help from us with the phonetic pronunciation of the Spanish dialogue). "Muy muy muy típico!" I have something to confess: when they asked the extras to ad-lib at the wedding party, I started cursing in Spanish—and not very softly either! I guess I was starting to find my political voice.

Needless to say, it was a very confusing time. I had moved to the United States with my family two and a half years before, leaving behind the economic and political fascism of Argentina. Because I had gone to the American school in Buenos Aires, I spoke English without a Spanish accent. According to certain members of the Screen Actors' Guild support group, this was to my advantage: "Susana," they'd all say to me, "you most certainly could pass as a non-Hispanic! All you have to do is lie to agents about your family history. Don't tell them where you come from." But growing up, it was within the nucleus of my extended family that I felt I truly belonged. And denying my cultural identity (because in some subliminal way I was being told that it was not as valid as everyone else's) was a betrayal of my roots.

Two years later, my life took a turn when my mother died of cancer, and coincidentally, I was invited to join the Don Quijote Experimental Children's Theatre Company. I say coincidentally because, strangely enough, the death of my mom helped me focus on my career in a different way. I was filled with a sense of urgency and a new understanding of the fragility of life. I had just turned twenty-three.

Don Quijote's shows toured to schools, museums, and libraries in the five boroughs of New York. This was a very exciting time as I began to experience control over my own creativity. In the first production, a musical on the subject of ecology called *Let's Take Back Our Planet,* I was not just a performer, but also the co-writer of the script (with director Gloria Zelaya from Nicaragua) and music composer. The second production, which I wrote and composed, initiated me as a director. It was called *A Day in the Life of a Robot* and dealt with the difficulties humans have communicating.

It was a very successful production, and yet, at the time, I remember feeling strangely divided between the aspirations I shared with my fellow actors to "make it" (in commercial theater, of course), and the incredible gratification I was getting from reaching hundreds of kids in the community with a play that spoke so much from my heart. One Saturday, after a wonderful matinee at Lincoln Center, as I walked to the subway under the snow, I told myself, "What are you doing <u>trying</u> to make it? You are already making it!"

It was during those years that I got to know and identify with the multiplicity of Latino cultures that inhabit the barrios of New York. A parallel career emerged for me in the field of arts in education. And it was then that I realized that although I had been an Argentinian all my life, it was through teaching and performing in the barrios that I had become a Latin American. It is ironic that I began to feel more Latin American in New York than I ever had in Argentina.

Coming to terms with this issue of identity was a big part of my decision to turn to directing. The other part had to do with accepting the fact that I would never be happy in the role of a "postcard actress," sitting by the phone waiting to be discovered. I had taken control of my life and of my art. As a director, though, the struggle against the Hispanic stereotype continues. Although I now happily own my cross-cultural identity, I continually find it necessary to assert to the producers that I would be just as comfortable directing a play by Chekhov (whom my grandmother used to read to me as a child) as I am staging a streetwise musical that reminds me of the Latin American populist theater I saw in the streets and parks when I was growing up.

The concept of transcending a label continues to threaten many people who easily become confused or frightened of what they do not know. Fortunately, I am now in my thirties and have no trouble educating people to the fact that being contacted by non-Latino theaters on the basis of my culture is something I can be proud of. I am finally able to contribute to the American theater from my real self.

It no longer interests me to measure anyone's ability to succeed by his or her ability to pass as "the other." I'm not suggesting that there is one right way and one wrong way to deal with these issues. I fully understand the liberation that comes from getting hired as the artist who happens to be the best person for a particular job. Not as a "Hispanic" artist. Not as a "female" artist. At South Coast Repertory Theatre in Costa Mesa, California, I was asked to direct the Irish play *Someone Who'll Watch Over Me,* by Frank McGuinness, which is about three male hostages in Lebanon. I often think about the non-naturalistic edge of this production and how it deviated greatly from the Broadway version. I suspect that where I grew up, we looked for the poetic in the everyday as an escape, or a form of survival. In Latin America, we know that magical realism is actually a way of life.

In the last nine years, since directing has become my profession, I have been working steadily and at a very intense pace. Many of the plays I've staged have been by writers who are Puerto Rican, Cuban, Mexican, Argentinian, Colombian, Venezuelan, Hispanic American, and Chicano. I've also worked with African Americans and Caucasian Americans as well as with European authors. I passionately believe that it's possible to get at the universal marrow of a culture by understanding and working with the specifics of it. At the same time, because my aesthetics are rarely naturalistic, I try to reach for the essence of each culture and avoid the anecdotal, the folkloric representation of itself. As a director, my interest has also been to translate to the American stage the distinctive South American affinity I feel for the absurd and the fantastic. By eliminating the imaginary walls that keep characters apart, the audience can witness whimsical coincidences and make ironic connections that do not necessarily respond to a logical sense of time and space. I never know how far this question will take me, but I am always fascinated by the opportunities provided by theater to blur the line that separates reality and illusion. A strong unifying theme in all my work is the transcendence of the emotional over mere physical reality. When two people have a strong spiritual connection, it seems to me that whether the other person is physically there doesn't matter; her/his presence will continue to bring great pain or joy. Hints of this spiritual question often recur in productions of mine as a way, perhaps, of trying to give a home to the inexplicable. Or perhaps as a way of accepting the losses of those dear to me throughout my life.

As the conduit of this mysterious journey called theater, I observe the phenomenon of cultures meeting with enormous fascination. It gives me great pleasure when I succeed in abstracting a world from the culturally specific that reaches out to all audiences.

Life and art are interconnected, and in my own daily living they cannot always be told apart. But when an elderly lady in a mall sees me pick up a plastic card by the cash register that explains in Spanish the various forms of payment, and she turns around and indignantly hollers, "What country are we living in?!"—when I'm quick to assert back, "We are in Brooklyn, New York, USA, and do you have a problem with this being in Spanish?!"—I know then that, at a much deeper level, her problem is not really with my language. And that's when I take a deep breath and say to myself, "Susana, this is 2000. You are a woman, a Latin American, and you've chosen to be a theater director. Your whole <u>life</u> is one big political act!"

CATCHING THE NEXT PLAY

THE JOYS AND PERILS OF PLAYWRITING

Edit Villarreal

All my life, I've had an enormous love for writing. I think a love of writing comes naturally from a love of reading. I remember distinctly the day I learned to read. I was in first grade, had mastered the alphabet, and was really bored with it. My teacher made us repeat it over and over again. Why are we doing this? What is this stupid alphabet for? I remember asking myself. Then one day my teacher wrote the word "the" on the board and pronounced it. In a flash, I learned what the alphabet was for. If I live to be one hundred, I'll never forget that moment. I ran home and read every "the" on the front page of the newspaper. It was such a special moment for me, I wrote a scene about it in my play, *My Visits with MGM (My Grandmother Marta)*.

The summer before I turned twelve, I read *Little Women* and *All Quiet on the Western Front* on my own. In my junior year of high school, we read *Moby Dick, The Brothers Karamazov,* and *On the Road* in English class. Each one of these books was a threshold for me. The next best thing to reading books, I thought, must be to write them. From that point on, I was hooked on the idea of writing. For a long time, though, I didn't do much of it—just a little poetry and short stories.

In college, I changed majors constantly. I wanted to study everything. But the desire to write kept gnawing at me. Eventually, I became an English major. What could be better than spending the rest of my life reading all the great books? Then I discovered a small hitch. In order to be a good English major, I had to develop a "scholarly prose." My English professors told me my writing was "circular," perhaps creative, but definitely not scholarly. My extreme lack of desire to develop a scholarly prose eventually drove me out of the English Department. It probably also turned me off to graduate school for years.

Nevertheless, I was determined to get an undergraduate degree in something. My last recourse was to major in drama, where I finally found a niche that I could tolerate. I read plays, slapped out enthusiastic papers for my

professors, and helped build sets. It was a perfect arrangement: I read literature that wasn't "snobby," and I spent hours around stage sets doing physical
work in which I took pride.

My exposure to theater, however, turned me in a direction I never antici-
pated. Every writer has a public in mind, even if that public is only one person,
the single reader reading your work. Plays can be read as literature, but ideally,
they're flat on the page and alive only in performance. Plays beg to be performed. In the same way, all theater people, even those working backstage,
are closet performers. As soon as I began to write my first plays, *Going Home,*
about a young Guatemalan woman who decides to return to Guatemala
against the wishes of her expatriate family, and *Pictures,* begun in Irene
Fornes's Playwrights Laboratory at INTAR Theatre in New York City, about a
tattoo lady in a carny, I discovered a commitment to my characters that I had
never felt before. I became very attached to them. I wanted them to shine.
Like a mother, I had created them and now I owed them a life. A life in the
theater.

But a life in the theater is neither easy nor simple. Theater requires an
immense collaborative effort on the part of a huge number of people. Theater,
especially professional theater, is also expensive. In spite of my uneven history
of writing, I decided graduate study in playwriting would be a good, and
probably necessary, thing if I was going to succeed at all. I applied to and was
accepted by the Yale School of Drama. I wanted to learn to write plays and
become a playwright.

Now that I've written a number of plays, I find myself increasingly ab-
sorbed by and committed to the spare kind of writing that playwriting demands. A good play must maintain a high level of energy while creating
personal moments between the actors on stage and the audience watching the
actors. At the same time, the only tool the playwright has to achieve these
high-energy moments is ordinary colloquial language. I think playwriting,
more than any other kind of writing, reflects best the world we are living in
right now, at the end of the twentieth century. Plays allow me to have
ambivalent and contradictory points of view. Plays are also about marginal
people, that is, people on the edges of society, either entering it, or being
exiled from it. I too have always felt marginal. As a Latina growing up in the
United States, as a woman playwright in professional theater, as a woman
professor working in academia, it is impossible to feel otherwise.

All of my plays up to now have been about marginal people, either because
of their ethnicity, their age, their sex, or their way of making a living. To date,
most of my characters have also been from the lower or middle class. I think,

however, that it's important to begin to address the emotional life of upwardly mobile Latinos, for example, Latinos in the professions. The emotional challenges and choices that such Latinos will perforce have to make in the near future are complex and very important to the future growth of Latino culture in the United States. I think the very human dilemmas encountered by upwardly mobile Latinos will, in the future, be presented as drama, comedy, or tragedy. In both of my new plays, I've begun to portray upwardly mobile Latinos. One play, *Minus Four,* is an unadulterated comedy about a Chicana surgeon and a Chicano marine biologist trying to get married. The other play, *Tracks,* is a spiritual evocation of the unique experiences felt by an upper-class Mexicano who arrives in the slums of Chicago in 1890. Both portrayals of "upper-class" Latinos are, I think, accurate. Increasingly, I feel more and more compelled to write characters who are nonconformists, because the nonconformists amongst us are precisely the people we stand to lose in Latino culture, and they are precisely the people we need to retain. However, they may change in the future; I feel very strongly that all Latinos, at all levels of society, should feel comfortable and proud of who they are.

My work as a Latina professor in academia is not very different from my work as a Latina playwright in theater. Both fields are male dominated. Neither field readily allows input from women at the highest levels. Both fields have an uneven representation of Latinos and Latinas. As I work in both worlds, I feel an obligation, because I've been trained professionally in theater and have had productions in regional theaters and teatros around the country, to share my experience, my talent, and my education with other Latinos. In both worlds, I am also seen, predictably, as a role model. But though I understand the desire to cast me as a role model, on a personal level, I find it disconcertingly final and complete, as if my work has been done and all goals achieved.

Currently, I'm Acting Head of Playwriting at the UCLA School of Theatre, Film and Television, where I teach graduate playwriting. What I want most to share with my students is my love for the ongoing everyday business of my craft, constantly looking for subject matter, marking and remembering conversations, jotting notes on interesting people, interesting dilemmas. I want my students to discover their own joy in their own writing. But I also want them to assume the responsibility that goes along with the craft and the joy—the commitment to create the best characters, to give them their best voice (i.e., rewriting). I also try to impress upon my students the necessity to take a stand, assume a point of view, and, if necessary, go down with your ship.

Besides trying to impart a philosophical approach to playwriting as I teach, I also have a practical reason for enjoying what I do. Teaching playwriting helps me retain my own writing muscles. As a student in graduate school, I realized early on that I could learn more from the mistakes my fellow students made in their plays than from their successes. As a teacher, I've discovered that I learn from my students as I teach them. Every student project presents another hurdle that I as a writer may have already faced, but will undoubtedly have to face again. Playwrights can never know everything they need to know, because each subject, each idea, each theme, requires its own form. The often-asked question, how do you begin a play?, has no answer. Every play requires its own world, its own rhythm, its own structure, its own vocabulary. The more I write, however, the more I realize that my best writing is not regurgitation of things with which I'm comfortably familiar. My best writing is a new and first-time exploration of people and dilemmas that I want desperately to understand. Before I can catch a play, the play idea has to catch me and then, caught, I commit myself to the excitement and hard work of rewrites and more rewrites.

Every year, I wish I had more Latino playwriting students at UCLA. Hopefully, in the future, I will. In the meantime, I passionately believe we Latinos need to be everywhere all the time. Because it is an institution of higher learning, I never forget my ethnicity at UCLA. Or my gender. There is still a lot of work to be done.

Full-Length Plays, Collaborative Works

FOR THE READER WHO IS jarred to see not only non-Latina names in this section, but a male one to boot, a word about our decision to include these plays in our book is perhaps necessary. In these two works, both co-authored by major voices in Latina theater, we witness their collaboration with a South African and an Israeli. It is clear to us that our book needed to include these two voices, in collaboration or not. Thus, for us, the issue is not that "this is not a Latina play" because one of the authors is not a Latina, but rather, this is a Latina play because one of the authors is Latina. That these two playwrights have chosen to work with other individuals registers for us a movement toward a future where a true multiculturalism is more visible and accessible. We are witnessing here a politics of affinity that reaches across racial, sexual, and ethnic barriers. To claim that these plays are not "authentic" is to undermine the transactions and negotiations of Latinas/Latinos in the theater, workplace, educational center, community, and other such places. In our choice to print these plays we celebrate the kinds of coalitions that these playwrights forge. To labor together (colaborar) does not diminish the value of the finished product, but rather attests to a dialogue that accommodates differences and is receptive to inclusiveness. When different ways of seeing meld, the end result yields a polyvalent, hybrid, enriched, and intertextual theatrical work. Indeed, this book has been an effort through which we, as editors of different ethnicities, have experienced the collaborative process firsthand.

F R I D A

THE STORY OF FRIDA KAHLO

Migdalia Cruz and Hilary Blecher

CHARACTERS

FRIDA KAHLO. Mezzosoprano

DIEGO RIVERA. Baritone

An ensemble of four players:

WOMAN 1—SOPRANO. CRISTINA KAHLO ("Cristi," Frida's younger sister), the voice of MRS. FORD

WOMAN 2—MEZZOSOPRANO. The voice of the MOTHER, LUPE MARIN** (Diego's wife when he met Frida), the voice of MRS. ROCKEFELLER, NATALIA TROTSKY**

MAN 1—TENOR. ALEJANDRO (Frida's teenage boyfriend), the voice of MR. FORD, LEON TROTSKY**

MAN 2—BASS. The voice of the PETATE VENDOR, a CACHUCHA, GUILLERMO KAHLO** (Frida's father), the voice of MR. ROCKEFELLER, the voice of EDWARD G. ROBINSON

The six puppeteers play:

**THREE CALAVERAS (Death figures inspired by the Day of the Dead and Posada)

*MOTHER, a peasant

*DIMAS, the peasant woman's dead son

*TOWNSPEOPLE, including a PETATE VENDOR and a PIÑOLE VENDOR

*PEASANTS

*SCHOOLGIRLS, Frida's teenage enemies

*CACHUCHAS, Frida's teenage schoolchums

*BUS PASSENGERS

*WEDDING GUESTS

*MR. AND MRS. JOHN ROCKEFELLER, SR.

*MR. AND MRS. HENRY FORD

*DIEGO'S LOVERS, a parade of women

*EDWARD G. ROBINSON

NURSE

FRIDA'S LOVER

ACT ONE

Scene One

Frida at the National Preparatory School—La Preparatoria—on the Day Frida Learns what Death Looks Like and the Revolution Comes to an End.

[*Overture: Festive music as a dark, empty stage is transformed into a busy street in Mexico City, 1925. A* FIGURE* *enters playing an accordion. He looks up and we see that he is a* CALAVERA*, *a Mexican death figure. The sun slowly rises to reveal a moving wall of puppets and scenery that forms the landscape of Mexico.*

The bright blue wall of the Preparatoria School now extends across the stage. In the center of the wall are green gates above which appears the inscription "Preparatoria" and the motto "Love, Order, and Progress." Brightly colored Mexican birds fill the air. The school gates open and a perfect line of pious Teenage Girls, *identically dressed in school uniforms, file out.*]

SCHOOLGIRLS*:
   Somos hijas de la Preparatoria.
   ¡Hijas buenas y llenas de gloria!
   Schoolgirls, sweet and clever—
   And, oh, so pretty and slim.

*Indicates a puppet
**Indicates a masked actor
Note: All words in bold italics are sung.

We don't speak to the Cachuchas,
Nor to that girl who acts just like them.
Somos hijas de la querida Preparatoria.
Tenemos para siempre decentes memorias.

[*Loud noise/disturbance Offstage. Suddenly, a wild group of bicyclists—*FRIDA, ALEJANDRO, *and their gang, the* CACHUCHAS*, enter and ride through the* SCHOOLGIRLS*, *shouting their school war cry and totally upsetting the girls' demeanor.* FRIDA *is dressed like the boys. She wears a striped skull cap, and her hair is cropped. The air current from the bicycles makes the* SCHOOLGIRLS' * *skirts fly up and they spin around in disorder.*]

SCHOOLGIRLS: [*As they see the* CACHUCHAS *approaching.*] Oh, no! Los malotes Cachuchas! La banda de Frida!

CACHUCHAS*: [*Shouting.*] Shi . . . ts . . . pum
Jooya, jooya
Ca-chun, ca-chun, ra, ra,
Joooya, joooya,
¡Preparatoria!

FRIDA:
Stupid escuinclas! Little dogs without hair!
Come run with Frida. Use your brains—if you dare.
Niñitas de la Preparatoria—
Don't just sing Hosanna y gloria.

SCHOOLGIRLS*: What a monster! What disgusting behavior for a girl!

FRIDA: [*Imitating the girls.*] "Oh, what a monster! Oh, how disgusting!"

CRISTINA: Frida! You shouldn't!

FRIDA: [*Laughs.*] I can't believe a sister of mine could be such a girl!
Where they should have brains—all they have are curls.

ALEJANDRO: [*To* FRIDA, *who reacts with disdain.*]
I love you.

FRIDA: [*Shooting* ALEJANDRO *a look of amusement.*]
And nothing is more boring than you, stupid, stupid girls.

ALEJANDRO:
I mean your mind.

[*During the following,* CRISTINA *tries to restrain* FRIDA, *who boldly encourages* CRISTINA *to join in the proceedings.*]

FRIDA and ALEJANDRO:

> **When you look at your reflections,**
> **Aren't you shocked at what you see?**
> **Ugly girls with empty eyes and the brain stem of a tree.**

CACHUCHAS*:

> **Not like us. We're Cachuchas—the greatest minds of Mexico.**
> **We devour Aristotle, Copernicus, and Marx.**

FRIDA:

> **We'll climb the Himalayas, walk the Moon**
> **And swim with sharks.**

CRISTINA:

> **Frida?**
> **How will you ever do that?**

FRIDA:

> **You'll see.**

[FRIDA *pulls* CRISTINA *toward her.* CRISTINA *reluctantly joins in.*]

CACHUCHAS*:

> **We're Cachuchas—the greatest minds of Mexico.**
> **We have a mission to rise above ignorance—**
> **To learn to make our country great.**

[*The music quickens as* FRIDA *lights a firecracker; the other* CACHUCHAS* *follow suit.*]

CRISTINA: Frida, no.

[FRIDA *and the* CACHUCHAS* *throw firecrackers at the feet of the girls*, who are startled and jump high in the air with fright.*]

GIRLS*: [*Throwing their hands into the air and running away.*] Anarchists! Subversives! Monsters!

[FRIDA *and the* CACHUCHAS* *laugh as they continue to throw firecrackers at the fleeing girls.* FRIDA *is stunned into silence when a mother*, holding her dead child (cf. Kahlo: "The Deceased Dimas," 1937) enters.*]

MOTHER*: [*In anguish.*]
> *Nothing . . . Nothing . . .*
> *Lifeless eyes . . . Empty faces . . .*
> *I walk circles through the city*
> *Looking for God. Looking . . .*
> *To ask, to pray for mercy . . .*
> *What else?*
> *What else . . .*

[*With great urgency, she turns towards the rolls/stacks of petates and begins rummaging frantically through them.*]

PETATE VENDOR*: ¡Oye! What the hell—. Those aren't free.

MOTHER*: My son. Please, a place to rest his—

PETATE VENDOR*: You want a petate, lady, then híjole—you pay for it. [MOTHER* *suddenly becomes aware that her child is dead.*]

MOTHER*:
> *My sweet Dimas.*
> *My sweet Dimas is dead. My sweet son.*
> *All light has died with him.*

CHORUS:
> *Darkness is Mexico.*

MOTHER*: [*In great anguish.*] Bread could have saved him.

PETATE VENDOR*: You let him starve?

MOTHER*	CHORUS:
You must pay for bread	*Darkness is*
and I have nothing.	*Mexico.*

FRIDA: That's where our fight begins—children must have bread.

MOTHER*: I would have cut my own flesh to feed him, but he's gone from me. Too late. Too late.

[*The* PETATE VENDOR* *takes the body of* DIMAS* *and places it on a petate.* FRIDA *places flowers, especially marigolds, around the body.*]

CHORUS:
> *Now he is dressed for Paradise. Now Dimas is dressed for God.*

FRIDA:

I'll never forget those staring brown eyes.
I'll see them in my sleep.

[*The* PETATE VENDOR* *crosses himself and begins to sing the Lord's prayer.*]

PETATE VENDOR:

Padre nuestro que estás en los cielos, santificado sea tu nombre.

ALL:

Mexico, you're stealing your own breath.

MOTHER*: It is enough.

CHORUS: [*With revolutionary fervor.*] It is enough! It is enough!

PETATE VENDOR*: Why do the rich live while the rest of us die?

FRIDA:

The only road to Heaven shouldn't be through Hell on Earth.
We must stop the children dying.

PETATE VENDOR*: In this world there is never enough—life is God's lie!

CHORUS:

El pan nuestro de cada día, dánoslo hoy . . .

FRIDA: [*Softly.*]

Mexico, you're stealing your own breath.

[*To* DIMAS *.*] I will remember you. Those honest eyes—

FRIDA: [*Cont'd, spoken.*]	CHORUS:
The eyes of death. Those eyes on	*Now he is dressed*
yellow-green straw mat. A ribbon of	*for paradise.*
pink to prove that you're a gift to the	*Now Dimas is dressed*
Earth. . . and surrounded	*for God.*
by yellow marigolds . . . yellow	
and green are death.	

[*The* MOTHER* *exits, followed by a grieving procession of all the other characters, including* FRIDA. *A moment of silence for the dead child is shattered by the sound of distant gunfire and bullets. Flat puppets appear above the blue wall and enact a scene depicting the execution* of Zapatista peasant revolutionaries by government soldiers. As the bodies of the dead peasant soldiers are shot down, a small figure of the revolutionary leader, Zapata, on a white horse, rises up in their place, leading his army of other ZAPATISTAS. These small figures are replaced by identical large ones as the blue wall opens to reveal a large, victorious throng consisting of Zapata on his horse, ZAPATISTAS*, the MOTHER*, the PETATE VENDOR, FRIDA, CRISTINA, ALEJANDRO, the CACHUCHAS*, who all sing a victorious anthem of liberation.]

ALL: [*With patriotic fervor.*] ¡Viva la revolución! ¡Viva Zapata!

[*Revolutionary Parade Song.*]

ZAPATISTAS*:

We want what we've earned with the sweat off our backs.
Land will set us free. Land is liberty.

ALL:

Glorious Mexico—the country where our fathers died—
Give us back our history, filled with strength and pride.
We will fight for our freedom, we will fight for our land.
Land!—to those unafraid of hard work and dirty fingernails.
Land!—away from the thieving rich who ride on foreign sails.

CACHUCHAS*:

We are the future, creating life from the death of our fathers.

CHORUS:

Viva, viva, viva Zapata.

CACHUCHAS*:

A new generation—raising our voices.

CHORUS:

Viva, vivan tierra y libertad.

CACHUCHAS*:

Proud of the Aztec dust beneath our feet.

CHORUS:

Viva, viva, viva Zapata.

CACHUCHAS*:

Mexicans for Mexico, standing together, our love is complete.

CHORUS:

Viva, vivan tierra y libertad.

ALL:

Viva, viva, viva Zapata. Viva, vivan tierra y libertad.
Viva, viva, viva Zapata. Viva, vivan tierra y libertad.

FRIDA: [*To the* CACHUCHAS.] I was born the same day as the revolution.

CRISTINA: No, Frida you were—

[FRIDA *puts her hand over* CRISTINA'S *mouth to prevent her true birth date from being revealed. The music swells in a jubilant march as* FRIDA *pulls* CRISTINA *into the parade of* ZAPATISTAS *, CACHUCHAS *, PEASANTS * with flags who move past celebrating Zapata's victory. (cf. Diego: "Parade in Moscow").*]

ALL: Viva Zapata! Vivan tierra y libertad! Land for the people! Down with the rich!

[*The parade exits. Lights cross and fade to Scene Two.*]

Scene Two

Frida Becomes a Woman.

[FRIDA *is having her first period. She stands, very clinically watching the blood run down her thighs as* CRISTINA *looks on, fascinated.*]

FRIDA: It's so amazing. A part of myself is running down my thighs. In this blood is an egg which, if I had been "lista" enough to catch one, a sperm could have penetrated and made into a baby. A little me and somebody. Alex is the only one handsome enough for me. It <u>has</u> to be his sperm. I thought it would never come. I must be the last girl in Coyoacán to become a woman.

CRISTINA: You shouldn't have worried so much about it, Frida. It's not such a big thing.

FRIDA: It was for me—eighteen and still like a boy.

CRISTINA: Frida! The things you say.

FRIDA: Today my bath water will be pink. I'll wash the blood from my legs into the water and the water will take it to new, foreign places. Into the ocean . . . into the mouths of a school of tuna . . . onto a beach in San Francisco. I'm going to run away to San Francisco. That's where life is for bohemians and artist-philosophers. And only intelligent people are allowed to live there. [*Pause.*] Oh, Cristi, do you think he'll still love me even though I'll have blood coming out of me all the time now?

CRISTINA: Of course he will.

FRIDA: My children will have my brains and their father's beauty. Or maybe my beauty and—my brains. Anyway, one thing is for sure—they have to be wild and unpredictable—

CRISTINA: [*Teasing.*] And nothing like you.

[*They laugh.* CRISTINA *exits.* ALEJANDRO *enters.* FRIDA *moves to him and they enter Scene Three.*]

Scene Three

The Bus Stop, September 25, 1920.

[PASSENGERS * *wait for a bus. (cf. Frida: "The Autobus") Soft sounds of conversation.*]

FRIDA: Look, I'm not some stupid little whore who'll drop her pants for anybody who asks me. [*She looks at* ALEJANDRO *intently, suddenly serious.*] It was the first time for me, Alex.

ALEJANDRO: Mine too.

[*They look at each other in silence for a moment.*]

FRIDA: [*Seriously.*] Promise you'll love me forever.

ALEJANDRO: Forever.

FRIDA: Kiss me.

[*He smiles, grabs her, and kisses her passionately. As they kiss, the bus arrives. The* PASSENGERS * *get on.*]

ALEJANDRO: [*Pulling himself, laughing, from her tight embrace.*] Frida, the bus.

FRIDA: [*Shouts.*] Hey wait! We're coming!

[*(cf. Frida: "Drawing of the Accident") The accident is enacted by puppets and models on a smaller scale than reality. The doors of the*

bus are about to close. Someone* holds them open. FRIDA* *and* ALE-
JANDRO* *jump on. The doors close. The bus moves off leaving the
Mexican landscape empty.*]

WOMEN'S CHORUS:

Aquí yo he venido,	*(Here I've come,*
porque ya he llegado	*because I've arrived*
y vengo muy descansada,	*and I'm very much rested,*
cantando canciones	*since by singing songs,*
me paso la vida	*I spend my life*
un poco más divertida	*a bit more amused.)*

CHORUS:

El autobús corría	*(The bus ran*
sobre la estrecha vía	*down the narrow street*
de pronto se fue a estrellar	*and suddenly it crashed*
contra un tranvía	*into a streetcar*
a todo dar por el medio	*going too fast down the middle*
de esa calle sin parar.	*of that street, without stopping.*
Fue en el año veinte—	*It was in the year of '20—*
septiembre, veinte y cinco,	*September, the 25th,*
cuando murieron varios—	*when some people died—*
pero no Frida de Coyoacán.	*but not Frida of Coyoacán.*
Llegó la Cruz Blanca,	*The White Cross arrived,*
llegó la Cruz Roja,	*the Red Cross arrived,*
a auxiliar a los heridos,	*to help the wounded,*
y allí encontraron	*and there they found*
que Frida no había muerto—	*that Frida hadn't died—*
pero su cuerpo estaba roto.	*but her body was broken.)*

[*The following happens in very slow motion. (cf. Frida: "Drawing of the
Accident") As bus and trolley collide, the bus breaks open, and the naked
broken body of puppet* FRIDA* *falls out. An Angel* flies in from above and
sprinkles gold dust over it. At the moment of impact, the actors* FRIDA *and*
ALEJANDRO *are thrown onstage and witness the accident. A* CALAVERA
moves to grab the puppet FRIDA* *away, but is stopped by the real* FRIDA,
who snatches back the broken doll representing her damaged body.]

CHILDREN'S VOICES: [*Offstage.*]

Dale, dale, dale.	*(Hit it, hit it, hit it.*
No pierdas el tino.	*Don't lose your touch.*

Mide la distancia   *Measure the distance*
que hay en el camino.   *of your path.)*

ALEJANDRO: A house painter had been carrying a packet of powdered gold. The packet broke and the gold fell over her like rain.

PASSENGERS*: [*In awe of her naked, golden body.*] ¡La bailarina! ¡La bailarina!

ALEJANDRO: With the gold on her body, they thought she was a dancer.

[*The* CALAVERAS *exit slowly.* ALEJANDRO *moves Downstage as he repeats his speech as a litany, almost inaudibly, as if by speaking it quietly, he could avoid reliving the horror of the moment.*]

ALEJANDRO: Frida had a piece of iron in her body. Her spinal column was broken in three places. Her collarbone was broken, and her third and fourth ribs. Her right leg had eleven fractures and her right foot was dislocated and crushed. Her left shoulder was out of joint, her pelvis broken in three places. The steel handrail had literally skewered her body at the level of the abdomen. Entering on the left side, it had come out through the vagina. Frida said she had lost her virginity on the bus.

[*The lighting becomes very white.* CALAVERA *moves* FRIDA'S *bed on stage.* FRIDA *hangs the broken* FRIDA* *puppet on the bed.*]

FRIDA:

I was once full of life
Dancing in a world of hidden colors,
Now my steps are slow and painful
Over shards of crimson glass.

ALEJANDRO: I was certain she was going to die.

FRIDA:

Death dances around my bed at night—
Gold-speckled redness on naked flesh.
My friends will be women slowly . . .
I'm old in an instant.

ALEJANDRO: The doctors were certain she was going to die.

FRIDA:

My faithful companion, the darkness—
Its shadow caresses my hair

Remember? We were to climb the Himalayas.
Don't touch the sun without me, mi vida!
Remember me as I was—not shattered like this.
Tell me something new, mi amor.
Dime que me quieres para siempre . . . para siempre.

ALEJANDRO: We were all certain she was going to die.

[*He exits.* FRIDA *turns longingly toward him as he exits.*]

FRIDA:
Today still goes on.
I feel the wind of my playful "Pelona."
What is ahead of me? Will my life once again be complete?
When I look in a mirror, one Frida looks out, one Frida looks in.
I'll wear a mask to cover my pain. I'll live my life upside down.
Death dances around my bed at night, but I refuse to cry.
Death dances around my bed at night, but I refuse to die.

[*During the following speech, a* CALAVERA *enters bringing* FRIDA *an easel and some paints.* FRIDA *begins to paint.*]

FRIDA: Dear Alejandro, I stole some oil paints from my father. And my mother ordered a special easel for me so I can paint lying down in bed.
The Fridas I see in these faces roam the world
While I lie here dipping brushes into paint the color of my heart
To create the Frida I want to be.
What I hope, what I am, what I know.

So Alex, I am painting this for you—my breasts and nipples, a magic talisman. So that one day soon, very soon, you will come back to me.

[*Musical interlude as* FRIDA *gradually recovers. She slowly begins to walk—at first painfully, and then, as she becomes stronger, with great ease and exuberance.*]

Scene Four

Frida Meets and Marries Diego, 1927–29.

[DIEGO *is working on his mural in the Preparatoria.* LUPE MARÍN**, *his wife at that time, poses for him on the scaffold.* DIEGO *is very intent on his work.* FRIDA *enters, dragging a reluctant* CRISTINA *behind her.* FRIDA *walks with a slight limp on her right side. They hide behind a column.* LUPE** *becomes restless and tries to get* DIEGO's *attention by singing a seductive tango.*]

CRISTINA: Is that him?

FRIDA: Yes—the greatest painter in the world.

CRISTINA: [*Incredulously.*] That's Diego Rivera?

[FRIDA *shushes her as* LUPE** *begins to sing, moving seductively around* DIEGO*.*]

DIEGO: Lupe, can't you hold still?

LUPE:

Diego, can't you stop to look into my eyes?
If I dance for you? Will you look at Lupe then?

DIEGO: I look at you all the time, Lupe.

LUPE:

Will you let me paint my name on your lips with my tongue?
Will you let me taste your milk white baby skin?

[*Suddenly spotting another woman's face in the mural; outraged.*] Who is that woman you're so busy painting in your mural?
Who is that woman—she isn't me.
I've seen her before, sniffing around our back door like a cat in heat, hanging around you like a whore.

DIEGO:

For a painter new models are essential,
Fresh blood to mix in with his paints.
A painter lives for inspiration.
That doesn't mean I don't love you, Lupe.

LUPE:** It's hard to believe you could need more women than me for your satisfaction.

DIEGO: But you're too beautiful—you distract me. Go play cards, nena, and then we'll make love.

LUPE**:
¡Mírame! Señor pintor.

[*They kiss.*]

LUPE**: Mmmm . . . you always taste like fresh-cooked chicken.

DIEGO: My women never go hungry.

[*He lunges for* LUPE** *again.* FRIDA *and* CRISTINA *begin to giggle.* DIEGO *pulls away from* LUPE** *to find the source of laughter.* CRISTINA *and* FRIDA *burst into renewed laughter.*]

FRIDA: Isn't he adorable?

CRISTINA: He looks so dirty.

FRIDA: So what? I'll bathe him.

CRISTINA: And he's got such a big potbelly. Oooey!

FRIDA: Cristi, don't you understand? It doesn't matter what he looks like—he's a genius. Imagine life with a man like that. He could teach me everything— everything I need to know. I'm going to tell him, "Diego Rivera, look at me. You don't know who I am now, but one day I'll have your son."

CRISTINA: What about Alejandro?

FRIDA: We're just pals now. I need love "con un hombre."

CRISTINA: ¡Ay, qué atrevida! But he's so old. You wouldn't dare.

FRIDA: Wouldn't I? [*She approaches the scaffold.*] Diego Rivera! Diego Rivera!

CRISTINA: ¡Qué sinvergüenza! Come back! ¡Ay Dios mío! Be careful.

[*The four sing a quartet.*]

FRIDA:
Diego Rivera!

LUPE**:
I think we have an audience.

CRISTINA:
Frida, you're crazy.

LUPE**:
Let's give them a little show.

[LUPE** *lunges at* DIEGO, *who turns to* FRIDA *instead.* CRISTINA *runs to hide behind the pillar.*]

DIEGO:

Yes?

FRIDA:

Could you please come down to me?

CRISTINA:

Be careful.

DIEGO:

What do you want? I'm working.

LUPE**:

Go away!

FRIDA:

I have something important to show you.

CRISTINA:

You can't tell Frida what to do about anything.
I'm just her baby sister. What do I know about men?

LUPE**:

Yes. Hurry down. Maybe she's not wearing any panties.

DIEGO:

Lupe! Your suspicions. There is something in her voice.

FRIDA:

I have something I want you to see.

LUPE**:

So, what am I, Diego? Don't you dare to leave me up here. Diego!

FRIDA:

Just come down for a moment.

DIEGO: [*To* FRIDA.]

All right. One moment.

[*He begins to descend the scaffold slowly.*]

I'll be right down.

LUPE**: [*To* DIEGO.]

Come back here.

[*To* FRIDA.]
How dare you?

CRISTINA: [*With admiration.*]
I know one thing, my dear sister, my dear Frida—

FRIDA: [*To* LUPE.]
I'm not afraid of you.

CRISTINA:
—I wish I could be more like you—

LUPE**: [*Shouted.*] I could tear your little tits off with my teeth.

CRISTINA:
—Every now and then . . .

FRIDA:
Don't be my enemy—

LUPE**:
Good for you.

CRISTINA:
About convention, Frida couldn't care less—

FRIDA:
You're much too beautiful for that.

LUPE**:
You're not afraid of me—

CRISTINA:
To test the waters, she plunges in headfirst.
Cristi takes a little longer.

LUPE**:
She reminds me of myself.

CRISTINA:
I don't believe in chance or fate.

LUPE**: Watch out, little one. He's the enemy. He'll break your heart.

[LUPE** *exits.*]

CRISTINA:

I take my time so I can change my mind before it is too late.
Come on, Frida, let's go before—.

[DIEGO *appears from behind the scaffold and sees the girls. He seems surprised by how young they are.*]

DIEGO: Little girls? Shouldn't you be in school?

[CRISTINA *runs off, intimidated by* DIEGO'S *presence.*]

FRIDA: I'm not here to flirt with you or anything stupid like that. I brought some of my paintings, and I want you to tell me if they're any good.

[FRIDA *lays the paintings down.* DIEGO *looks at them carefully, in silence.*]

FRIDA: I'm serious. I have to be able to support myself. So I need to know—do I paint or do I do something else?

DIEGO: [*With admiration for both* FRIDA *and her paintings.*] You should paint.

FRIDA: [*With growing excitement.*] Really? D'you mean that?

DIEGO: [*Laughs, enjoying* FRIDA.] Yes, I do.

[FRIDA *looks hesitant.*]

DIEGO: Now what's the matter?

FRIDA: What if you're just trying to sweet-talk me?

DIEGO: Why would I?

FRIDA: To get me in bed. They say you'll sleep with any woman who's not an absolute dog.

DIEGO: [*Amused.*] Go and paint some more, niña. I'll try to come to your house next Sunday to see what you've done and tell you what I think.

FRIDA: [*Elated.*]: Okay. I live in Coyoacán, Avenida Londres, number 126. [*She starts to exit.*] My name is Frida. [*She begins to exit, but then turns back.*] Kahlo.

[*She exits. A door appears.* DIEGO *knocks. It opens.* GUILLERMO KAHLO **, *Frida's father, steps out.*]

GUILLERMO KAHLO**: So now it's every Sunday. You're not in love with my daughter, are you?

DIEGO: Why else would I come all this way?

GUILLERMO KAHLO**: [*Trying to warn* DIEGO *off* FRIDA.] You know that she'll need special care. She may be an invalid for most of her life.

[DIEGO *nods.*]

GUILLERMO KAHLO**: She's not pretty, but she is very intelligent.

[DIEGO *is amused.*]

GUILLERMO KAHLO**: Also, she's a devil.

DIEGO: [*His smile getting broader.*] I know. That's why I love her.

GUILLERMO KAHLO**: Well, I've warned you.

[DIEGO *enters.* GUILLERMO KAHLO** *closes door. They exit. Door moves up/out, revealing* FRIDA *and* DIEGO, *who stand some distance apart. The following song represents their growing intimacy: they move closer and closer until they are standing together as if at a wedding ceremony.*]

DIEGO:
Paloma de mi alma, niña de mi corazón . . .

FRIDA:
Contigo soy completa, mis penas desaparecen.
I feel your power like the wall of a temple on my back
Holding me up, straightening my legs.

DIEGO:
Frida—a bold beauty born of pain—
Join me in a love beyond convention,
Unafraid of life's darker tints,
You create your life in colors
No one else dares touch.

FRIDA:	DIEGO:
Diego with his warm eyes,	*Like a ripe fruit*
his gentle breath,	*of a singular tree*
he tasted me.	*I'll devour her.*

FRIDA:

Take me away and teach me the wonders of your world.

DIEGO:

Savor your life like a ripe peach.
Follow voices to unknown places.

FRIDA:

Your warm, sweaty hands, stained plaster white,
Will lead me where I could never go alone.

DIEGO:

Let me awaken to the sound of your laugh—
that sound makes an old man young again.

FRIDA:

Mi alma, you take my sickness away. Yo soy completa.

DIEGO:

¡Paloma de mi alma! ¡Niña de mi corazón!

FRIDA and DIEGO:

¡Mi corazón!

[FRIDA and DIEGO are in position for the wedding, 21 August 1929.
Birds fly on with a ribbon retablo announcing the wedding. (cf. Kahlo:
"Frida and Diego Rivera," 1931) The wedding party enters including
GUILLERMO KAHLO**, ALEJANDRO, CRISTINA, and a bizarre procession of
other guests** wearing masks based on Frida's paintings: "Magnolias,
The Flower of Life," and "Diego and I." The wedding guests enter and
sing a lusty, mariachi-style serenade.]

WEDDING GUESTS:

¡Felicidades! ¡Felicidades! Que Dios les cuide todos sus días (toda la
vida).
¡Felicidades! ¡Felicidades! Que Dios los guarde siempre feliz.
¡Felicidades! ¡Felicidades! Dios les bendiga en este día.
Vivan los novios y la alegría. Que Dios los guarde siempre feliz.

[As the ceremony begins, two CALAVERAS enter carrying a moon and a
sun. They enact a parody of the ceremony in which the moon and the
sun symbolize the union between Frida and Diego.]

FRIDA:

You are the sun to my moon

FRIDA and DIEGO:

Together the perfect universe

FRIDA:

Where love will shine from your face onto mine.
A man who's a boy I want for my own.

DIEGO:

Remember, my sweet Frida,
Together the sun and the moon may light up the sky,
But each must follow its own orbit—
Never the same size.

FRIDA and DIEGO:

Together our brushes will bring gods back to the temples.
Together we'll paint a golden ring around the world.

[*The following lines overlap.*]

CRISTINA:

I warned her . . . I knew she'd fall in love too fast.

ALEJANDRO:

I was her first love. Is Diego meant to be her last?

GUILLERMO KAHLO**:

She's a devil, but I love her.

CRISTINA:

I hope he'll treat her well.

FRIDA:

You are the sun to my moon.

GUILLERMO KAHLO**:

Remember, my sweet Frida,

FRIDA:

Together the perfect universe—

GUILLERMO KAHLO**:

I hope he'll treat her well.

FRIDA:

—where love will shine from your face onto mine.

DIEGO:

Remember, my sweet Frida,
Together the sun and moon may light up the sky.
But each travels its own orbit.

[LUPE** *makes a dramatic entrance.*]

LUPE**: [*To* FRIDA.]

Beware all that light—
It will blind your little soul.
You'll feel the painful nips
That love cuts from head to toe.

FRIDA:

A man who's a boy I'll have for my own.

ALEJANDRO:

He'll give her everything—I can tell.

GUILLERMO KAHLO**:

He is marrying a child who loves him like a mother.

LUPE**:

How can he marry that monster in braids?
Can't he see what she wants from his skin?
A minor painter attached to a giant—
It's fame and fortune she wants from him.

[*Spoken.*] ¡Miren! [LUPE** *moves to* FRIDA, *grabs her, lifts her skirt to reveal her withered leg, then lifts her own skirt. To* DIEGO.] You see what you're getting and you see what you had? You're a fool! Pinche hombre!

[*The orchestra plays the rhythm of a well-known Mexican curse as* LUPE** *exits in a huff. General laughter, uproar. The wedding guests applaud. After a pause, the gentle wedding music returns.*]

FRIDA and DIEGO:

I want you, sweet Colossus.
My little dove.

CRISTINA and WEDDING GUESTS: ¡Qué vivan los novios!

[*The* GUESTS *explode into an orgy of movement.* FRIDA *dances with Guillermo, then* ALEJANDRO, *then* DIEGO, *who picks her up and carries her off as the others continue to dance and the lights slowly fade.*]

WEDDING GUESTS:

¡Felicidades! ¡Felicidades! Que Dios les cuide todos sus días (toda la vida).
¡Felicidades! ¡Felicidades! Que Dios los guarde siempre feliz.
¡Felicidades! ¡Felicidades! Dios les bendiga en este día.
Vivan los novios y la alegría. Que Dios los guarde siempre feliz.

Scene Five

1930. Diego's Murals Are Criticized.

[*Lights up on* DIEGO *on his scaffold, painting Zapata mural. On the other side of the stage,* FRIDA *sketches in a small notebook.*]

DIEGO: [*Calling down to* FRIDA.] What do you think, niña fista?

FRIDA: [*Looking up, sizing up the problem quickly.*] No balance. Too much red. Add some green.

DIEGO: Claro.

FRIDA: [*Indicating a horse in the mural.*] And, Sapo-rana, the horse Zapata rode, was black.

DIEGO: But white is more heroic. The people need heroes. And a hero needs a heroic setting.

FRIDA: [*Laughs.*] But it's not the truth.

DIEGO: I'm a revolutionary artist. I paint what I want.

[*Grotesque March: The* CHORUS *enters—five men each, with a three-sided rotating mask that represents the* GOVERNMENT, *the* BUSINESSMEN, *the* COMMUNIST PARTY. *All these elements in society were highly critical of Diego and were out to destroy him.*]

MEN'S CHORUS:

Revolutionary! Revolutionary! Revolutionary! Revolutionary!

DIEGO:

I'm a revolutionary artist. I paint what I want.

COMMUNISTS:

> *I spit in your eye!*
> *You paint only for the rich—not for the poor.*
> *What the poor people need is bread—*
> *Not the hot air that floats around in your head.*

FRIDA: [*Jumping up on the scaffolding.*]

> *Idiots! Can't you see? This man sees through the eyes of the poor.*
> *He shows to us a better world—painting our Mexican people.*

COMMUNISTS:

> *If you're a man, defend yourself. Come down and fight.*

[DIEGO *laughs, proud and amused by* FRIDA's *defense.*]

DIEGO:

> *What a tigress! She's got balls—cojones de oro!*
> *I love you more than any woman is loved by man.*

FRIDA:

> *¡Maricones! Can't you see this man is a man without equal?*

COMMUNISTS:

> *This hypocrite must be stopped—his ideals are spent.*
> *He paints to kiss the ass of the new government.*

THE GOVERNMENT:

> *Shoot him dead. Stop him painting. This hot-head is a communist*
> *agent.*

COMMUNISTS:

> *¡Mentiroso! ¡Maricón! You're the one who betrayed your people.*

FRIDA:

> *You imbéciles with your false praise—you envy his fame.*
> *You're content to play the pawns in a new fascist game.*

THE GOVERNMENT:

> *No more walls. No commissions.*
> *This trash is inciting the peasants.*

FRIDA: Government pigs.

DIEGO: Don't waste your breath on them, Frida.

FRIDA:

>*I fight beside my man, maricones! Just try to fight us.*
>*All of you! Government, our own party, businessmen.*

BUSINESSMEN:

>*He defaces our architecture with his monstrous creation.*
>*It's not art. It's not cubism.*
>*It's communist symbolism.*
>*And since when does a worker wear*
>*A perfectly pressed shirt without a single tear?*

COMMUNISTS, GOVERNMENT AGENTS AND BUSINESSMEN:

>*And those ugly naked women.*
>*Imagine going to bed with one of them.*

DIEGO:

>*Barbarians!*

[*Spoken.*] You wouldn't fuck a pyramid, but that doesn't mean it's not art.

FRIDA: ¡Cabrones! ¡Pendejos!

DIEGO: Bourgeois pigs! What do you know about art?

>*Art is ham for the common man*
>*To breathe like air—*
>*For all to share.*
>*Not caviar for the rich*
>*To snack on when they've got the itch.*
>*Not behind private walls,*
>*Nor in exclusive halls.*
>*Art is for the common man*
>*To celebrate his deeds*
>*And the labor of his hands*
>*In the fields and factories.*
>*Art is ham for the common man*
>*For all to share.*

[DIEGO *takes his gun out of the holster around his waist. He shoots his gun into the air.*]

DIEGO: Now get the hell out of here. I'm working.

[ALL* *run out.* FRIDA *and* DIEGO *laugh. Then* DIEGO *gets serious.*]

DIEGO: That's it! That's enough. We're getting out of Mexico. I can't work with everyone against me.

FRIDA: I can't just go like that. Like nothing. What about my family? Our friends? Our work? The Party? Everything!

DIEGO: The Party has betrayed me. All my commissions have been canceled. Mexico's revolution is over. [*Pause.*] Rockefeller and Ford have invited me. That's where we'll carry on the fight—we'll go north.

FRIDA: North? To that bloodsucking United States?

DIEGO: Why not? After all, you must know your enemy before conquering him.

FRIDA: I am not going. You'll have to kill me first.

[*Voices of returning* BUSINESSMEN** *and* COMMUNISTS** *are heard. Explosion; bullet holes appear in the mural. They dive to safety. Blackout.*]

Scene Six

The Riveras Dress for Dinner with the Rockefellers and Fords, 1933. The Millionaire Banquet—Where Frida and Diego Dine with the Capitalists on Ticker Tape.

[*All images of the Mexican landscape move out and are replaced with those of the United States. (cf. Kahlo: "My Dress Hangs There;" also, "Standing on the Boundary between Mexico and the USA" and "Memory")* FRIDA *and* DIEGO *move in and around the images of the United States from the painting "My Dress Hangs There."* DIEGO *hands* FRIDA *her Tehuana-style dress as he steps behind the image of Mae West. She dresses herself in it to attend a dinner with the* ROCKEFELLERS *and* FORDS.]

FRIDA: Pastels are a poison. Once carnation pink is in your soul, you never know who you really are. I am Mexico. And that's how they must see me. I create the story of my life with every ribbon, every ring—I wear two on each finger. This way, I become my grandmother's mother and her mother before her, or anything else I choose to be. The Tehuana is perfect—the everyday dress of the forgotten people. It's something different for these Yanquis from "down Mexico way." It was Diego's idea—to cover the limp, but I really love these dresses.

[DIEGO *enters dressed in a tuxedo.*]

FRIDA: [*Angrily.*] Why the hell are you wearing that? Is this a costume party we're going to?

DIEGO: [*Enjoying himself.*] It's not every day I get to dress like a capitalist.

[*Honking of a car horn. A* CALAVERA**, *dressed as a chauffeur, drives a cut-out of a new Ford convertible on stage.* DIEGO *whistles.*]

DIEGO: ¡Hijo de la chingada puta! Look what Ford sent to get us. Incredible! What a machine!

FRIDA: A toy for the rich. I'm not riding in that!

DIEGO: C'mon, Frida.

[DIEGO *climbs in.* FRIDA *hesitates, then follows him into the car.*]

FRIDA: Damn you!

[*The chauffeur shuts the door and the car drives off. The New York city-scape moves off to reveal the Rockefeller banquet. (cf. Rivera: "The Night of the Rich") A table is set up, slightly off-center, by the* CALA-VERAS**. *Around it sit the Rich People* of the United States, including* MR. AND MRS. HENRY FORD **,* MR. AND MRS. NELSON ROCKEFELLER **, and* MR. JOHN D. ROCKEFELLER, SR. **. They dine on gold ticker tape.* THE RICH PEOPLE* *are much larger than life-size. The women wear long, pastel, floor-length evening gowns. Sound of ticker tape as a long roll of it is passed from hand to hand. A* CALAVERA** *dressed like a bandleader enters, holding a megaphone.*]

CALAVERA** and THE RICH*:
The people here are happy, as happy as can be.
I think it's something in the air—that smells like being free.

THE RICH*:
We're so happy to be us—money's nice to have around.
Love that jingle-jangle sound.

FORD*:
Free to choose the way you wish to make a buck.

ROCKEFELLER*:
Free to find a better life with just a little luck.

THE RICH:

In America, everyone can eat steaks.

THE RICH [*Women.*]*:

Money's nice to have around.

MR. FORD*:

All it takes is hard work and a few lucky breaks.

THE RICH*:

Love that jingle-jangle sound.

MRS. ROCKEFELLER*:

But we need more than prime beef to keep us alive.

MRS. FORD*:

*The key to our sustenance is to own a Picasso
—perhaps four or five.*

ROCKEFELLER*: [*Laughing.*]

*We have the brilliance, we have the millions
to commission new paintings to hang on our walls
and lend them to museums
so anyone can see them in their halls.*

THE RICH*:

*We're so creative with our money—
We buy our own milk and honey.
When we buy art, our place in history is revealed.
Our sophistication can't be concealed.*

[*They raise their glasses in a toast.*]

THE RICH*:

To art! To art! To art!

[*Music crescendo. Fanfare.*]

CALAVERA**/BANDLEADER: Here he is! The Great Diego Rivera . . . and wife.

[*The Riveras enter,* DIEGO *in a tuxedo and* FRIDA *in her Tehuana dress.*
THE RICH *raise their glasses in a toast.*]

MR. ROCKEFELLER*:

To our new friends from lands afar.

MR. FORD*:

> *To new ideas with Christian outlooks.*

DIEGO:

> *To Mr. Ford's amazing cars.*

FRIDA:

> *To new loves and lovers.*

> [ALL *stare at her.*]

FRIDA:

> *Of art.*

THE RICH*:

> *To art.*

> [*Goblets are clinked. They all sip except for* FRIDA, *who throws back her drink.* ALL *notice.* FRIDA *notices them watching her and laughs.*]

MRS. ROCKEFELLER*: [*To* DIEGO, *insincerely.*] Delightful, isn't she?

DIEGO: She's more than that.

FRIDA: [*Smiling sweetly.*] She's right here. She can hear you.

MRS. ROCKEFELLER*: Oh, sorry, I—I—why yes. What an interesting dress.

> [FRIDA *stares menacingly at her.*]

MRS. FORD*: It's very—it's . . . Mexican, isn't it?

FRIDA: Yes. Like me.

MRS. FORD*: How . . . intriguing.

FRIDA: [*Leans forward to* MR. FORD * *and whispers.*] Mr. Ford, is it really true? I heard you don't like Jews. [*Awkward coughs from* THE RICH.] I'm just asking for my father. He's Jewish, you know.

> [*Deathly silence.*]

MRS. FORD*: How really very interesting you are, Mrs. "Riv-i-era."

DIEGO: [*Laughs, comes to the rescue by breaking the tension.*] Frida, chiquita, you're priceless.

FRIDA: [*To* DIEGO.] I can't stand women who wear pink. Just how low will you let yourself stoop?

DIEGO: Don't you see we are in Rome? We must dine with the devil.

[THE RICH *all turn away from* FRIDA *to concentrate all their attention on* DIEGO.]

THE RICH*: [*Raising their goblets.*] To Diego! To Diego Rivera!

FRIDA: [*To* DIEGO.]
What the hell are we doing in this very North America?
It's made you crazy. You're turning into one of them.

MR. ROCKEFELLER*: Rivera, tell us more.

DIEGO:
Well, your game of football is splendid for a start—
A powerful living picture. It's a new form of art.

MR. FORD*: That's capital, Diego Rivera.

FRIDA:
Doesn't anyone notice there are people standing in bread lines?

[*Awkward silence while* THE RICH * *all stare at* FRIDA *and then turn away, ignoring her question.*]

DIEGO:
And your American skyscrapers. Extraordinary.
Like pre-Columbian artifacts.

MR. ROCKEFELLER*:
I like that. Pre-Columbian artifacts.

FRIDA: If anyone bothered to ask me—[*Getting louder.*]
If anyone bothered to ask me
I'd say your skyscrapers look like . . . tombstones.

[*Awkward pause.*]

DIEGO: [*Ignoring her.*] Well, Ford's the real genius.

[THE RICH * *turn towards him with a sigh of relief.*]

DIEGO: And his machines are the true subject of our day.

MR. FORD*: Yes. Efficient and cheap. That's how I like it.

[*He laughs.* ALL *follow his lead. They all sit and begin to consume gold-colored ticker tape.* FRIDA *suddenly pushes her plate away.*]

FRIDA: I won't sit here eating steak when there are people in the street who don't have a thing to eat. [*Under her breath, to* DIEGO.] Let's get the hell out of here before I—

[*She starts to pull him away but he gently stops her.*]

DIEGO: Frida. Frida.

ROCKEFELLER*: Not so soon, please, not so soon. We need to know how you intend to decorate the wall of my new building—Rockefeller Center. [*Amused with himself.*] Will your art tell the people what we want them to think?

DIEGO:
Into old bottles I'll pour new wine.
I'll paint the story of a new mankind.
Science, factories, assembly lines—
That's the story of our time.

ROCKEFELLER*: Sounds good enough to me. You've got a deal, fella.

THE RICH*: Hurrah! Hurrah!

FRIDA: ¡Ay, qué sinvergüenza! Now we're in for it.

DIEGO: And now to celebrate. Frida, let's teach them to dance a jarabe in this magnificent North America.

[ALL *join in a jarabe dance.* FRIDA *leads* MR. FORD *. DIEGO *dances with* MRS. ROCKEFELLER *.]

DIEGO: [*To* FRIDA.] You're flirting.

FRIDA: [*Annoyed.*] Just trying to keep it interesting.

[*Dance finishes. Blackout.*]

Scene Seven

Diego Loses His Wall and Frida Loses Her Baby.

[BARKER/CALAVERA *appears on the scaffold. A drumroll.*]

BARKER/CALAVERA: Tickets! Tickets! Get your tickets here to watch the great Mexican painter, the fabulous Diego Rivera, at work. Diego Rivera at Rockefeller Center. Get your tickets here!

[*Lights up on* DIEGO *painting the mural "Man at the Crossroads," including the figure of Lenin, on top of scaffolding at the RCA building, Rockefeller Center. People enter to watch* DIEGO *at work.* FRIDA *stands behind the crowd watching the proceedings. Lights emphasize* FRIDA, *who's being interviewed by a reporter.*]

FRIDA: Yes, I'm also an artist, but not like Diego. Little things—nothing serious. . . . No, I didn't study with him or anyone else. One day I just started to paint. . . . He paints the big outside, and I paint the secrets inside. It makes for a very pretty marriage. Oh, [*Leans forward, whispers mischievously.*] and there's only one thing Diego likes to do almost as much as paint. [*Laughs.*] Make love, especially to me. No, it doesn't hurt. But I understand the question—me, with my uterus pierced by a handrail—like a sword through a bull. I'm small, but I have tough skin—it's the German in me, I think. Or maybe the Jew. I know how to fight and what to fight for. Love, sex, cigarettes, and tequila . . . no, not painting—that's just a fact, like taking a breath on a cold day—you see it going out before it has a chance to go down, proving you're alive. . . . Self-portraits? Well, why not look out and see yourself as others see you? I prefer to suffer in a Catholic way—publicly. And I never complain—well, almost never. I simply paint . . . and I want this baby.

[DIEGO *plays to the crowd. Laughter and applause.* FRIDA *moves Downstage to her easel, isolating herself from the action around* DIEGO. FRIDA *sits at her easel and begins painting. Soon she throws her brushes down in frustration.*]

FRIDA:

I cannot distract Diego—
He has his work that must come first.
But this one . . . but maybe this one.
I want to hold this little Diego
Growing inside of me.
My body betrays me, Dieguito.

DIEGO: Why don't you paint something? It'll help you pass the time. [ROCKE-FELLER* *enters. He looks at the mural. There is a sense of unease amongst the crowd.*]

MR. ROCKEFELLER*: [*Suddenly suspicious.*] That head—on the wall—surely it couldn't be the head of a—a certain Russian. Could it?

DIEGO: Why not?

MR. ROCKEFELLER*: There must be some mistake here, fella.

FRIDA: [*Accompanied by a reprise of the earlier "Dead Dimas" music.*]
Dieguito, mi'jito—
Your father wants to be my only son.
He doesn't want to be a father.

DIEGO: [*To* FRIDA.] Maybe you should learn to drive a car. [*To* ROCKEFELLER.] You suggested the theme "Hope For the Future," didn't you?

ROCKEFELLER*: Well—yes.

DIEGO: Well then, who else did you expect me to paint? [*Indicates the head of Lenin.*] Who else provides us with hope for the future? Lenin—only Lenin.

ROCKEFELLER*: But . . . listen fella—.

FRIDA:

No, I cannot afford to lose Diego.
I must never lose his scent from my pillow.
But this one . . . But this one . . .
This baby I have felt. This one I've had time to love.

Diego, I'm—

DIEGO: Frida, don't make me ask you again. Have you seen the doctor?

FRIDA: Yes, yes, yes, I have. But what use is he? He says I must stay in bed. I would rather be dead.

ROCKEFELLER: You've gone and painted a communist. How can I rent the office space now? This is a capitalist place, Rivera. Red is not our color. Too bad you couldn't paint the stars and stripes. Here's your check. Hasta luego, Diego.

[*The mural breaks into pieces; newspaper headlines are shouted as the mural goes off: "Vandalism," "Rivera Knockout at the Hands of Rocke-feller Family," "New York Times, February 13, 1934: Lenin Painting Destroyed at Night," "Fresh Fuel Provided For Political Art Contro-versy," "Rivera Loses 100 Pounds."*]

DIEGO:

No one has the right to assassinate human creation . . .
in this or any other nation.

[*There is a musical note of pain indicating the beginning of* FRIDA'S *miscarriage.*]

FRIDA: [*Clutching her stomach.*] Get a doctor!

[*A piñata of a pregnant Frida is flown in. (cf. Kahlo: "Henry Ford Hospital," 1932) The* CALAVERAS** *enter, open the pregnant stomach, and take out a purple orchid and other objects from the painting.*]

CALAVERA 1*:

She looks so small.
Like a girl of twelve.
Her braids are wet with tears.

CALAVERA 2*:

Huge clots of blood and Frida.

CALAVERAS 1* AND 2*:

Screaming . . .

CALAVERAS 1*, 2* AND 3*: [*Giving* FRIDA *the orchid.*]
Here is an orchid from Diego,
A lavender flower in full bloom.

FRIDA:

It looks like my body gaping open, so easy to tear.
A lavender orchid from Diego.

DIEGO: [*Standing on the scaffold.*] A woman is superior to a man.

CALAVERAS**: [*Imitating* DIEGO.] A woman is superior to a man.

DIEGO: There's so much pain that she can stand.

CALAVERAS**: [*Continuing their ridicule.*] There's so much pain that she can stand.

FRIDA: Drowned spiders, alive in alcohol. Children are the days . . . and here is where I end.

DIEGO:

Frida, you'll create something incredible out of this.

FRIDA: Can I be complete without a child to call my own?

DIEGO:

Pouring your agony on canvas—
You'll heal yourself like this.

FRIDA: I have a cat's luck. Lucky me—I do not die so easily.

DIEGO:

I can't stand to see how you make yourself suffer,
But I don't need a child to prove I'm alive.
Can't you see I need you, Frida?
Now they've turned my work to dust.
Stand beside me in the struggle against all that is unjust.
Frida, I can't stand to see how you make yourself suffer.
Be my friend, my wife, my lover.

FRIDA:

No one sees the pain, the pain you have inside your heart,
unless you paint it as your soul is torn apart.

[*Spoken.*] I am hungry for home. I dream of a boat sailing back to Mexico.

DIEGO: But my work is here now. This is where I feel alive.

FRIDA:

Diego, please, let's go home.

[*A big sun—Diego—and a little moon—Frida—move above a boat that travels back to Mexico.*]

ACT TWO

[*Note: The structure of this act is meant to echo the surrealist element in Frida's painting. "Her fantasy was a product of her temperament, life, and place: it was a way of coming to terms with reality. . . . It is a magic of her longing for her images to have, like ex-votos, a certain efficacy," said Diego Rivera. "Frida tries to tap the spontaneous process of thought through free-flowing color and form. The adventure of the unconscious mind and its ever-changing encounters at the cross-*

roads of consciousness are, after all, a principal reality, just as real as daydreams." FRIDA said: "They thought I was a Surrealist, but I wasn't. I never painted dreams. I painted my own reality."]

Scene One

The Riveras Return to Mexico.

[*A white scrim now covers the scaffolding from Act One. This back-drop will be used for shadow-puppet sequences, which represent* FRIDA's *thoughts and emotional and psychological states as expressed through the images contained in her work. Schematic renderings of* FRIDA's *and* DIEGO's *dual houses—the blue and pink houses at San Ángel—stand on stage. They are sleek, modern shapes, surrounded by a wall of organ cacti and connected by a foot bridge. A moon floats above* FRIDA's *blue house and a sun above* DIEGO's *pink house.* FRIDA *throws open the door of her blue house. She watches the sunrise, full of joy at being back in Mexico.*]

FRIDA: Finally—home again.
The sun and the moon are home again, in Mexico,
Where I can breathe—where I belong, in Mexico.
Here in San Ángel, we'll both be free.
He in his pink house, the blue one's for me.
Home in Mexico, where I want to be.
We'll paint our lives here, Diego and I—
on canvas and plaster and pieces of tin.
Full of my sex, my grace, and my sin,
Here's where I'll rest my chingada spine—
Mexico . . . Mexico is mine.

[FRIDA *knocks on* DIEGO's *door.*]

FRIDA: Diego! Come look! Our first sunrise back home.

DIEGO: [*Entering from the pink house.*] Damn!
Damn the Mexican sun!
My life will dry up like the cactus here.

FRIDA:
My heart is rooted in this magenta dust.

DIEGO:

> *Dust raised by people moving backwards.*
> *Don't you see, my life is useless here?*
> *Mujer, I can't be at your side every time you think you need me.*
> *At least let me paint to forget the misery of Mexico.*

[*Spoken.*] Leave me alone!

[DIEGO *exits into his house, banging the door in anger.*]

FRIDA:

> *Only a great love survives two doors between.*

[*A* PARADE OF WOMEN* *moves toward* DIEGO's *pink house and through the front door. As they enter the house, the lights go up and then down.* FRIDA *watches the parade.*]

FRIDA: [*With a shrug.*] ¡Así es la vida!
> *I am the wise and forgiving woman.*
> *The world can go to hell as long as we are one—*
> *The private moon, the public sun.*
> *I'm the wise and forgiving woman.*
> *In spite of what you think and do,*
> *I know you always love me too.*
> *Tragedy is foolish. Life is much too short.*
> *I'm the wise and forgiving woman.*
> *I'll allow your little sport.*

[*The* PARADE OF WOMEN* *moving into* DIEGO's *house continues.* FRIDA *suddenly sees* CRISTINA, *with a scarf pulled down over her head, enter as part of the parade.*]

FRIDA: [*Calling out innocently.*] Cristi!

[CRISTINA *pulls her scarf further over her head and quickly enters* DIEGO's *house. The lights in* DIEGO's *house go off.* FRIDA *realizes the truth of Cristina's and Diego's betrayal. Silence.*]

FRIDA: Oh, Diego, not Cristi. Please, not Cristi.

[FRIDA *moves to a table. (cf. "The Wounded Table")* FRIDA *cuts prickly pears. (cf. "Fruits of the Earth")*]

FRIDA: All the surgeon's knives never made me bleed as I am bleeding now.

[*She slices one cleanly in half, reaches into it and with both hands, viciously pulls out the red pulp. (cf. "Cactus Fruit," 1937) She runs the fruit down every finger, grinding it into her skin. She takes a pitcher of water and passes it over her hands. She sits in stunned silence for a moment.*]

Scene Two

The Trotskys** Arrive in Mexico.

[*Russian music depicts* TROTSKY'S** *arrival in Mexico.* FRIDA *rises to greet* TROTSKY** *as he enters.*]

FRIDA: Querido Comrade Trotsky.
Your visit to Mexico has been delicious.

TROTSKY**:
Oh yes, it has—not as big as Russia, but certainly warmer.

FRIDA: [*Looks at him flirtatiously.*]
You've had a great influence on our lives.

TROTSKY**: [*Flirtatiously.*]
On you?

FRIDA: [*Evasively.*]
On Diego.
He has new energy for his work.
He's so busy these days, I hardly see him.

TROTSKY**:
A man should always make time for such a beautiful woman.
Don't you see it's you I want to influence?

[DIEGO *enters, having overheard the previous conversation.* TROTSKY** *moves Downstage to a table where his wife* NATALIA** *is seated. She is very depressed and sits tearing up* FRIDA'S *face from photographs.* DIEGO *strides up to* FRIDA, *who sits at the wounded table. The two unhappy couples, each in its own house, sing a quartet.*]

DIEGO:
Tell me, Leon, why did your fellow Russians throw you out?

TROTSKY**:
I chose to leave, Diego—to escape their cowardly doubts.

Frida 373

NATALIA**:

What are you doing with that woman and her mustache?

TROTSKY**:

Don't be ridiculous.

NATALIA**:

Do you play Russian songs on her little white bed?

DIEGO:

There's an ancient rat in my house—
He takes my hospitality
and my wife. My wife.
His wizened little tail leaves a trail of semen by her door.

FRIDA:

Listen to "El gran macho." El gran macho—
Afraid you can't compete with his intellectual charm?

TROTSKY**:

Natalia, she stimulates me with her mind—
We exchange ideas and books.

NATALIA**:

I've seen the looks you exchange.

DIEGO:

His intellect I too admired, until it moved
From his head, down his chest, to that withered third leg.

NATALIA**:

I've seen the love notes.

[*Lights up on* CRISTINA, *in a separate stage area, lighting candles as if at a mass.*]

CRISTINA:

His brush exposed my nakedness on canvas—
His touch exposed my heart like a lily under glass.
He painted his wife's sister and made love to her—
I pray for Frida's forgiveness in a private mass.

FRIDA:

Diego, you don't understand—his sex is in his brain,
Committed to relieve his country's pain.

DIEGO:

I admired him—the ancient rat,
So committed that every country but Mexico turned him away.

FRIDA:

This old man who befriends your wife sets off alarms.

DIEGO:

I offered him my home. I should have offered him a fist
Instead of giving him a hand.

[*Spoken.*] Which he bites.

FRIDA: He doesn't bite.

NATALIA**:

She's a demon, a demon disguised as a Mexican whore.

TROTSKY**:

Don't be ridiculous, Natalia.

FRIDA:

¡Para macho sí, pero hembra no!
For the man yes, woman no!

DIEGO:

I'll kill him.

CRISTINA:

Each time he entered me, I felt alive, and yet
How could he betray her? How could I?
My mother taught me to ask forgiveness—
I'll pray for Frida's mercy in a private mass.

NATALIA** and FRIDA:

Do you think I want to live in the shadow of your life—
You play and I stay home, the perfect wife?

DIEGO and TROTSKY**:

Other women are just diversions—you know that's the truth.

FRIDA and NATALIA**:

Why couldn't I be all you needed?

CRISTINA:

I pray, dear Frida, you'll forgive—

ALL:

> *Why do those you love the most*
> *know best how to torment you?*
> *Why do those you love the most*
> *know best how to torment you?*

[DIEGO *and* TROTSKY** *move away from their wives in exasperation and collide.*]

TROTSKY**: I heard you enjoy playing the great artist—dressed in tuxedo black.

DIEGO: I see why you surround yourself with such prison-like security. You make a man want to kill you.

TROTSKY**: How can you call yourself a communist and rub elbows with the rich? You betrayed the Party.

DIEGO: You betrayed my trust.

> *I warn you only once—stay away from my door.*

TROTSKY**: [*Phonetically.*] Zhopa! (Bastard!)

DIEGO: ¡Vete al carajo! (Go to hell!)

TROTSKY**: Yop tvayu mat! (Fuck off!)

DIEGO: ¡No me jodas, hijo de tu chingada madre! (Don't fuck with me, you son-of-a-bitch!)

[DIEGO *takes out his pistol and fires into the air.* TROTSKY** *and* NATALIA** *run off.*]

DIEGO: I forbid him to come here anymore, Frida.

FRIDA: Hypocrite! You can't compare Trotsky to one of your sluts. He's a man of substance. A world leader. Not some cheap gringa tourist begging you to show her the pyramids and your prick. Don't throw your own shit back at me! I know what you've done.

DIEGO: Nothing you didn't know from the beginning. I've never tried to deceive you.

FRIDA: But with Cristi, Diego? With my blood? How dare you?

DIEGO: Stop playing games, Frida.

FRIDA: Games?

DIEGO: Yes. Games. You set it up. You encouraged Cristi to model for me. What did you expect would happen with you sick in bed all the time? Leaving me alone to paint Cristi—who is, after all, an irresistibly beautiful woman? And since we're talking about sex, Frida—what about you?

FRIDA: For me, it's not only a matter of sex, Diego. I don't just have sex.
I have love—I make love.
I like the urgent feeling of a man's hand on my back—
The softness of a woman's cheek against my own,
No space between us—it's in the touch for me.
Fingers sweeping gently across my lips.
A tongue in the soft, wrinkled folds of my hand.
It's in the touch for me.
Not the penetration. Not the invasion.
I have love. I make love.
And I know what you have done.

DIEGO:
Inside your love
I see why I'm still here.
I will not leave you—you need too much from me.
I'm not a hero to save you.
Will what I have ever be enough?
You take so much from me.
A life without doctors and the constant smell of blood.
You deserve better and so do I.

[*Spoken.*] Stop draining me of my life.

[*As the lights on him fade, he exits.*]

FRIDA: I have a life too, Diego.

[FRIDA *moves to her own house and enters it, slamming the door behind her.*]

Scene Three

What the Water Gave Her: Frida in the Bath.

[*The two houses move apart to reveal* FRIDA *in a bath, facing the audience. The large white scrim is now illuminated to represent the painting "What the Water Gave Me." At first, the only elements present are* her feet—the right one cracked and bleeding, the upper edge of the bathtub, and grayish mass representing the water. All the following scenes are "filled into" (played against) this backdrop with shadow puppets—"The Dead Dimas," the child in the womb from "Moses," and FRIDA holding the baby Diego from "The Love Embrace of the Universe."]

FRIDA: I have visions in the water. They're often very dark. Not wanting a child but still mourning for the children I have lost—frightened gasps from a wounded deer, drowning in my bath.

[Silence to include a sense of suspension. FRIDA lights a cigarette. Insects* move across a tightrope suspended above the bath—also a CALAVERA*. A Spider* reaches down and touches her neck. Slowly, sounds are introduced. Sound of her breathing, water washing over her skin, tap dripping. Blood drips from her cracked foot.]

FRIDA: [Slowly and sensuously.]
Naked, I'm reminded of my passion,
Remembering the world I once held in my hand,
Remembering the touch of love on my skin.
Rough scars recall the pain that pleasures bring.

[Gentle laughter. Image of two women—FRIDA* and the DARKER WOMAN*. (cf. "La Tierra Misma/The Earth Itself") During the following sung sequence, the foliage behind the WOMEN* moves and intertwines. The MONKEY's* tail tightens slowly around the branch of a tree. The WOMEN's* arms embrace and legs entwine.]

FRIDA:
Love is all that bathes me clean,
Wipes away the broken flesh.
Love makes an island of my soul.

CHORUS: [Offstage, a duet for two women.]
Love is an island surrounded by time,
Waiting . . . waiting.
Will someone come and find me? Or see and pass me by—
love sinking into all that came before?

[FRIDA is helped out of the bath by a female NURSE/LOVER who sensually dries her off.]

FRIDA: [*Deliberately and slowly.*] Slow, slow. Flesh tight and smooth. A thin splinter of pain enters me, and its warmth closes my eyes.
Make love, have a bath, make love, have a bath.

FRIDA and LOVER:
Make love, have a bath, and then make love again.

[*They gently laugh.*]

FRIDA: [*To the* LOVER.] Diego has a woman's breasts. That's why I still love him.

[FRIDA *and* LOVER *exit as the bath moves off. The shadow puppets are replaced by depictions of Frida's self-portraits.* DIEGO *enters and stares at the screen.*]

Scene Four

Frida Sells Her First Paintings, Finds Independence, and Loses Diego.

[*Images of Frida include "Self-portrait with Monkey" (1938), "Fulang-Chang And I" (1937), and "Self-portrait—the Frame" (1938). These "shadow paintings" do not attempt to be full reproductions, but instead stress certain elements, such as her eyes, her eyebrows, her breasts in "The Broken Column" (1944).*]

DIEGO: [*Checking his watch.*] Movie stars are always late.

[EDWARD G. ROBINSON* *enters with brassy "show-biz" music.* DIEGO *shows him Frida's paintings.*]

DIEGO: See, Edward? Why waste your time buying my paintings when Frida's the genius?—No one paints a face as well as she does.

EDWARD*: Your pretty wife? Does she paint as good as you?

DIEGO: Not merely paints, but breathes life onto a canvas—hard as a diamond that can split your soul in two.

[EDWARD* *looks carefully at her paintings.*]

EDWARD*:
Those eyes are so strangely hypnotic—
That face makes me feel so erotic.

DIEGO:

Those eyes are a trap. They could tear your heart apart.

EDWARD*: Curious about her: Freda Carlo.

Curious about her: eyebrows that meet,
Eyes frankly staring, daring not sweet.

DIEGO:

You'll be the first one to own those eyes.
They'll always mesmerize the one who buys.

EDWARD*:

Her paintings pull no punches.
That face should be seen on a big silver screen.

DIEGO:

Thunder and lightning over the sea . . .
Will you take two or three?

EDWARD*: She's a sexy broad.

Those eyebrows—it's those eyebrows I adore.
I'll take four.

DIEGO and EDWARD:

The paintings of Frida create their own myths.
What a joy to possess.

EDWARD*:

No ands, buts, or ifs.

[*A cocky aside to audience, spoken.*] Yeah, and what d'you know, I'm the first American to buy her work.

DIEGO and EDWARD*:

Frida Kahlo, you'll be famous.

EDWARD*: All that blood and organs and things—I kind of like that.

DIEGO and EDWARD*:

Wait and see.

[EDWARD* *hands* DIEGO *the money.* DIEGO *takes it.* EDWARD* *exits with the paintings as the wall moves out to reveal* FRIDA *sitting in a wheelchair, painting at her easel.* DIEGO *moves into the scene, victoriously holding the money out to her.* FRIDA *whistles, astonished, as* DIEGO *approaches and hands her the money.*]

FRIDA: [*Triumphantly counting the bills.*] ¡Híjole! Eight hundred dollars! And all for me?

DIEGO: He loved your paintings.

FRIDA: He did? That crazy Yanqui actor, Edward Gee?

DIEGO: Robinson.

FRIDA: All right! Okay! I like this Edward G. Robinson. [*They laugh.*] Diego, I really wish you'd come with me to that rotten Paris.

DIEGO: It's you they've invited. Think of all those admirers waiting for you— André Breton, DuChamp and Picasso in Paris, and that handsome photographer, Nickolas Muray, in New York. You might have so much fun, you might not even want to come back.

FRIDA: You know I'll always come back . . . to Mexico.

DIEGO: Of course.

[*As* FRIDA *exits,* DIEGO *sings.*]
Frida Kahlo, you'll be famous. Wait and see.

[*Entr'acte. French accordion music, then New York–style jazz depicting Frida's journeys. Lights fade. Cameras flash. Lights come up on* FRIDA *seated in a New York hotel-style bedroom chair during a photographic session with her unseen lover, Nickolas Muray, the famous New York photographer. The way* FRIDA *moves and poses and the camera flashes denote his presence. She smokes a clipped joint as she speaks.*]

FRIDA: I'm so happy to be back in our New York, Nick. I hated Paris. I used to hate it here too, but it's beautiful now because everything makes me think of you. The "Half Moon" at Coney Island is your lips, and every tree in Central Park shades only us from the sun. [*Pause. She has lifted her blouse so her breasts show. A rectangle of light is on her torso.*] It seems I'm always offering these to my lovers. What do you think of my nipples, Nickolas. Too big? Unnatural? They feel unnatural sometimes, but that's why I like them. André liked them too. He liked everything about me. My paintings. My body. He liked how I stared at his wife. She has perfect breasts, like mine. Anyway, that's why he brought me to Paris. The Louvre bought a painting. Do you think that's good? [*With a laugh.*] I got some dough anyway. [*Pause. She inhales deeply.*] I'm killing myself with this, but it feels so good going down. I imagine the blue-black smoke filling out my legs, making me whole. This poison is like sex—breath that pounds my heart, parts my lips, so that pounding can get up between my thighs. [*She takes another drag.*] I get daydreams about all the lovers I've ever slept with. I keep a hand on my hip, covering the bruises from the needles. A woman pulls it away and rests her lips there. It's always a woman who knows where I need to be kissed. [*Pause.*] Hurry up, Nicholas, I'm getting tired. I'm always so tired lately. Will you show everyone these pictures? At least if I'm not remembered for my paintings, someone might remember my breasts. [*She smiles, takes a deep drag.*] I love you, darling Nick, almost as much as I love Diego.

[*Lights come up to reveal* DIEGO.]

DIEGO: I want a divorce.

FRIDA: What the hell are you talking about, Diego?

DIEGO:

You flaunt your lovers in my face—

DIEGO:	FRIDA:
Your lovers!	*As I learned from you, Diego.*
Freedom yes,	*I'll be as free as you.*
But not this mockery.	
You're beginning to discover	*What a hypocrite!*
your own life.	
	Damn you!
You don't need me.	*Can't you see, Diego—*
You don't need me anymore.	*don't you know you are my heart?*
It's over.	*I thought we had love.*

[*Shouts.*] Then go!

[DIEGO *exits as the houses move Offstage to denote the break in their marriage.*]

Scene Five

Frida Paints.

[*The three* CALAVERAS**, *dressed as doctors, enter, wheeling* FRIDA *in an apparatus suggesting both an operating table and a barbecue spit.* FRIDA* *is turned around in the spit like an animal in the furnace of hell.*

(cf. "The Broken Column") FRIDA *stands alongside the spit cutting off the puppet* FRIDA's *long hair.* CRISTINA *has entered with the doctors and stands outside the immediate action, observing the scene of* FRIDA's *torture with horror.*

CALAVERAS**:

Look, if he loved you, it was for your hair.
Now that you're pelona, he won't love you anymore.
Two Fridas—one Diego loves. One he loves no more.

FRIDA and CALAVERAS**:

Cut off the hair he loved—cut off my/her womanly disguise.
Whoever needs the love of men is helpless and unwise.

CALAVERAS**:

Mira que si te quise, fué por el pelo,
Ahora que estás pelona, ya no te quiero.

[FRIDA *finishes the haircutting and collapses into the wheelchair.*]

CALAVERA 1**: All the usual childhood diseases.

CALAVERA 2**: Plus polio at eleven.

[*Lights on* CRISTINA, *who stands crying over* FRIDA*.]

CRISTINA:

She never really walked, you know.
She flew and hopped like a bright young bird.

[CALAVERA 2** *laughs.*]

CALAVERA 1**: I loved that.

CALAVERA 2**: [*Stifling his laughter.*] After the accident . . .

CALAVERA 3**: Three months in the Red Cross Hospital.

CALAVERA 2**: Nine months in a plaster corset . . . and every now and then for the remainder of her life.

CALAVERA 1**: Normal sex life.

CALAVERA 2**: Really?

CALAVERA 3**: Congenital malformation of the spine

CALAVERA 2**: A little trophic ulcer in the right foot.

CALAVERA 1**: The cracked one—the one that always bleeds.

CALAVERA 2**: Scoliosis. And a fusion of the third and fourth lumbar.

CALAVERA 3**: And so many operations—thirty!

CALAVERA 1**: Twenty-three.

CALAVERAS**: [*With a barbershop-quartet sweetness.*]
She's almost ours.

[*The* CALAVERAS** *exit with the spit as the* NURSE *enters with Frida's wheelchair. She helps an exhausted and ill* FRIDA *into the chair. She comforts* FRIDA *and then wheels her to her easel Downstage. She exits.*]

FRIDA: My life is painted bread—a promise of food that leaves you hungry. I'm starving so I paint [*Mocking herself.*] and paint and paint and paint some more. [*Pause.*] My comforts—portraits of me. Empty space where my heart used to be. Messages for you, Diego.

[*A musical interlude follows, underscoring Frida's continuing transformation of her life events into art.* FRIDA *picks up her paintbrush and begins to paint. The following sequence, created through overhead projections and puppets, appears on and in front of the scrim behind* FRIDA. *(cf. "The Wounded Deer") The entire visual canvas is filled with images. This is the "Wounded Deer" sequence: a background of a stormy sea and sky is established. Against this, a branch of a tree falls as a forest is established, one tree at a time. The Wounded Deer*, a bunraku puppet with* FRIDA'S *face, appears from behind a tree. The deer moves amongst the trees. Suddenly, a* CALAVERA** *wearing a* DIEGO *mask appears from behind a tree and pierces the* FRIDA *Deer* with an arrow. A bleeding wound appears. Out of the wound falls an object such as Diego's face, "The Flower of Life," etc. This stabbing sequence is repeated nine times by different* CALAVERAS**. *Each time the Deer* recovers. In fact, she seems to become stronger and more audacious. From the last blow, however, she takes longer to recover. She confronts the audience without moving, as milk tears fall from the sky, filling the canvas. (cf. "My Nurse and I") Lights fade on the Deer* and come up on* FRIDA *at her easel.*]

FRIDA: [*Wistfully.*] Nine antlers. Nine arrows. [*Recognizing her own joke with a laugh.*] And nine lives for Frida.

[FRIDA *continues to paint as the* CALAVERAS**/MONKEYS *enter and crowd around her. They pose themselves around* FRIDA *to evoke "Self-portraits with Monkeys."*]

CALAVERAS**:
She paints so many monkeys. We wonder what it means.

CALAVERA 2**:
Is it because they're so cute and small?

CALAVERA 1**:
Or is it a sexual scene?

CALAVERA 2**:
The children that she never had?

CALAVERA 1**:
The love of sex that drove her mad?

CALAVERA 2**:
Something small to call her own,
Something to keep her from feeling alone.

ALL:
She paints so many monkeys. We wonder what it means.
Is it a sexual scene?

FRIDA:
Monkeys help to keep me sane.
Monkeys help me laugh at the pain.
When a tear rolls down my cheek,
They lift my skirts and take a peek.

CALAVERAS**: They don't leave you as long as you feed them.

[*The* CALAVERAS** *make the sound of approaching footsteps.* FRIDA *looks out expectantly.*]

FRIDA: Diego?

[*The* CALAVERAS** *laugh.*]

FRIDA: Puñeta!

[CALAVERA 3** *touches her hair.* FRIDA *enjoys his touch.*]

CALAVERA I**: He's not coming back.

[FRIDA *pulls away from* CALAVERA 3**.]

FRIDA: He's a bastard!

CALAVERA 2**: A pig!

CALAVERA 3**: ¡Un mierda!

CALAVERA I**: ¡Un maricón!

[CALAVERA I** *hands* FRIDA *a drink in a flask.*]

FRIDA:

Yes, that's easy. Cognac y marijuana . . .

[*Spoken.*] makes me feel . . . half human—for almost a day.
Until I look in a mirror. Then I know it's just a lie.

[CALAVERAS** *exit.*]

FRIDA: Don't forget me, damn it, I won't let you say good-bye.
Acuérdate de mí, compañero.
Cuando mires mis cuadros, cáete en mis ojos.
Look at my paintings and fall into my dark eyes.

[*Spoken.*] I will learn to live alone in this empty world.
[*With a sense of discovery.*] **That's how I'll keep from lying to myself.**
That's how I'll keep from dying.

[*With a sense of victory.*] That's how I'll keep from dying.

Scene Six

Frida's Death.

[*The* NURSE *enters and crosses to* FRIDA. *The* CALAVERAS** *wheel on a hospital bed and sit beneath it. The* NURSE *wheels* FRIDA *to the bed and, with difficulty, helps the physically weakened* FRIDA *onto the bed, tucks in her bedclothes, exposing the painted corset* FRIDA *now wears. Above* FRIDA, *on the screen behind her, we see an image of* FRIDA *as if in prison.* FRIDA *begins to writhe in bed, trying desperately to remove her corset, which restricts her movement and her breathing. She is having* *a nightmare. She raves disjointedly over the music as a flood of haunted images appears in her head/on the screen—a sense of confusion, chaos, and delirium.*

FRIDA: *Stop! I can't—breathe. Breath! Let me—catch—I must—get out! I have to—get out!*

[*An image of* TROTSKY's *head appears on the screen behind her. A* NURSE/CALAVERA** *enters and begins to interrogate* FRIDA.]

NURSE/CALAVERA**: Yellow?

[*An ice pick appears on the screen over* TROTSKY's *head.*]

FRIDA: Madness. Sickness. Part of the sun. Damn you, Diego, for running off and leaving me like this!

[*The ice pick stabs* TROTSKY's *head and the screen turns red depicting the murder.*]

FRIDA: Trotsky? Oh my God! Diego, they think you did it!

NURSE/CALAVERA**: [*Shouts.*] Black?

FRIDA: Black. Black is nothing. Don't you understand? Get out of here! Oh God, please leave me alone. [*In a small voice, with a laugh.*] Red . . . no black . . . nothing . . . really nothing. Stop! [*She screams.*] You're torturing me. Nurse! Some Demerol. Please. I can't take anymore. They arrested me and Cristi. Because of him—all these questions. Where the hell are you, Diego? ¡Ay, Virgen de Guadalupe! Please get me out of here.

[FRIDA *screams and sits bolt upright as if coming out of a nightmare as the image of* TROTSKY *fades. She sees* DIEGO, *who has entered the room playing a tambourine. He proceeds to dance around her like a bear in an effort to amuse and seduce her back into loving him as he sings a funny, Mexican-style love song. At first,* FRIDA *is too stunned to respond. Then she willfully does not respond, and then she can't help but start laughing.*]

DIEGO: [*Gentle and playfully suggestive.*]
¡Soy el oso negro de la montaña roja,
Y tengo mucho hambre por tu miel sabrosa!
["Miel" meaning honey with sexual connotations.]

¡Soy el oso negro de la montaña roja,
Quiero beber un trago de ti, hija!

FRIDA: Bastard! So finally, you've come back to the wife who made you sick with all her sickness.

[DIEGO *kisses* FRIDA.]

DIEGO: I need you, Frida.

FRIDA: But I don't need you anymore, Diego Rivera.

DIEGO:

Marry me, we need each other.
Let's take this last chance—
spend the rest of your life in my arms.
Make my life dangerous again, chiquita.

FRIDA: Marry you? Again? What for? You're crazy, Diego!

DIEGO: Maybe. But marry me anyway.
My little dove.

FRIDA: I can live without you now—but you're an old fool, and I still love you.

[DIEGO *lifts* FRIDA *gently. She pushes him away, standing on her own to sing.*]

FRIDA:

The Frida you see before you
on our second wedding day—
not Raphael's Madonna,
nor Da Vinci's flirting Mona Lisa—
I am a woman as seen by a woman—
Frida as seen by Frida herself.
Not as a man designs me,
Nor as a man desires me—
but as I conspire to be.

That's all I ever wanted. [*Pulling off her corset.*] ¡Viva la vida!

[*The sense of* FRIDA'S *victory as a woman, the triumph of her life, is picked up and explodes in a carnival of life and death. All the wedding* guests from the first wedding, even LUPE, enter. Each takes his/her turn dancing with FRIDA. They sing as they all dance.]

ALL:

Life's a gift, so tear it open.
Laugh at death y ¿por qué no?
La pelona loves a joke or two—
Taking souls not yet due.
Life's a gift so let's unwrap it.
Dance away this long black night.

FRIDA:

¡La vida es para romper!
I am not sick—I am broken.
So what if I am in pain—
I am happy to be alive to
paint and paint again.

CALAVERAS**:

La raza baile con alegría—
¡Mañana traerás más tequila!

[A musical interlude represents DIEGO's last dance with FRIDA and her realization of her approaching death.]

FRIDA:

I hear the silence dropping.
Night is falling in my life.
Yesterday I fought for freedom—
Now I'm fighting for my life.

[DEATH/CALAVERA** enters, waiting to dance with FRIDA.]

Death dances around my bed again tonight—
This time I won't turn her away.
This time I'll let the music play
Until I've fought my last fight.

[She moves to the CALAVERA.]

La Pelona, my oldest Cachucha—together at last.

[FRIDA kisses Death.]

Viva la vida, la alegría, and Diego.

[Death sweeps FRIDA up in his/her arms and dances with her Offstage as if with a precious trophy of victory. The stage floods with color. Frida's image appears on the scrim. A halo of flames illuminates and then destroys/consumes the image. All the players enter.]

QUARTET:

De petate a petate—from birth to death.
Mexico mourns Frida Kahlo—a daughter of the earth.
The one who gave birth to herself
Writing the most beautiful poem of her life.
De petate a petate—from birth to death.
Her colors go out into the world
To the world, forever.

MEMORIAS DE LA REVOLUCIÓN

*Alina Troyano
(a.k.a. Carmelita Tropicana)
and Uzi Parnes*

CHARACTERS

CARMELITA TROPICANA. Artist/revolutionary

PINGALITO BETANCOURT. Conductor of M15 bus/philosopher

MACHITO TROPICANA. Brother/poet/revolutionary

BRENDAH and BRENDAA. American tourists

ROSITA CHARO. Singer/friend

CAPITÁN MALDITO. Chief of Police

MARIMACHA. Singer/revolutionary

LOTA. German spy/granddaughter of Mata Hari

NOTA. Lota's adopted daughter

EL TUERTO. Killer/policeman

PROLOGUE

[*New York City, 1987.*
CARMELITA TROPICANA, *a modern-day Carmen Miranda, appears in front of a slide projection of a postcard of Cuba with a rose in her hand, singing "Memories."*]

CARMELITA: Memories, we all have them. [*To audience.*] You do. And I, Carmelita Tropicana, have them of my beloved country Cuba. [*She looks back to the slide projection.*] Who knew in 1955 what was to happen to us? Who knew then what destiny was to be? If maybe my baby brother

Machito had his mind more on the revolution and his date with destiny than on his date with the two americanas, who knows? Who knows?

[*She flings the rose at the audience and exits. Blackout.*]

ACT ONE

Scene One

[*Slide changes to the capitol building in Havana. American tourists* BRENDAA *and* BRENDAH, *dressed in similar polka dot dresses, enter and stand in front of the slide. They are waiting.*]

BRENDAA: Oh Brendah, I can't believe we are actually in Havana—love capital of the world. Everything is so romantic. [*Looking in a dictionary.*] Albóndigas.

BRENDAH: Albóndigas. [*Looking in the dictionary.*] Meatballs.

BRENDAA: Brendah, I never knew Latin men could be so—

BRENDAH: Sexy, virile, gay caballeros.

BRENDAA: Yes, but so sweet and gentle. Machito would never hurt a mosquito.

BRENDAH: Well, I saw him first. I'm more his type.

BRENDAA: Says who?

BRENDAH: I say.

BRENDAA: Well, we'll just have to see when he gets here.

BRENDAH: What time is it? He should be here by now.

BRENDAA: Brendah, in the tropics everything is slow. Maybe he overdid his siesta.

[*Blackout. Then lights up on* CARMELITA TROPICANA *waiting in front of a slide of a street scene in Havana with a flower cart. She is pacing anxiously. She is wearing dark sunglasses and is writing in a little notebook.*]

CARMELITA: Ay, Dios mío, Machito.

[MACHITO *enters disguised with a beard and dark glasses.*]

MACHITO: Maní . . . Manicero se va . . . Peanuts, señorita?

CARMELITA: Beat it. I'm busy.

MACHITO: Señorita, don't you want to buy some peanuts [*Removes beard.*] from that handsome brother you got?

CARMELITA: [*Hitting him.*] Machito, idiota. I kill you. I wait here an hour for you. This is dangerous. He's going to pass by any minute now.

MACHITO: I'm sorry, Carmelita. I didn't know.

CARMELITA: Never mind. The money.

MACHITO: Here. Minus $3 for the beard and the peanuts.

CARMELITA: Here are the papers. Now listen. I've been trailing him for a month. It's always the same, like clockwork. At 8:00 El Tuerto picks him up at the house and they drive here to that store to get his shoes shined and pick up a newspaper. At 9:00 he is at the police station. At 9:10 he goes to the bathroom, and by 9:20 he is ready to torture. He eats at 1:00, and at 2:00 El Tuerto brings him a woman from Casa Marina. He likes that brothel the best. It's where the U.S. Navy goes.

[MACHITO *gets really excited.*]

CARMELITA: Can you believe it, Machito? On the door it's got a sign with a little American flag saying "American Surgeon General Seal of Approval." On the door. What do they think, this is part of the Good Neighbor Policy?

MACHITO: [*Interest aroused.*] Every day a different woman?

CARMELITA: Yes. Disgusting. But quick, because at 2:30 he is snoring. By 3:30 he is back to torturing until he leaves at 6:00. It takes him an hour to get home because he stops to snack along the way: three orders of frog legs at the Pickin' Chicken, two dozen oysters at San Rafael, and flan at El Carmelo.

MACHITO: I think I'm sick.

CARMELITA: At 7:00 he is home. Between 7:00 and 7:30 he is in the bedroom—that's when you strike.

MACHITO: Between 7:00 and 7:30.

CARMELITA: Then meet me in the Malecón. Quick, Machito, I think that's his car coming this way. Go. That way.

[MACHITO *exits.* CARMELITA *waits, looks around and exits also. Slide changes back to the capitol building where* BRENDAA *and* BRENDAH *are still waiting. They are pacing.*]

BRENDAH: He must have been bitten by some tse-tse fly. He's more than an hour late.

BRENDAA: Oh, there he is.

[MACHITO *enters.*]

BRENDAA: Hola, you tamale.

BRENDAH: ¿Cómo estás, macho?

MACHITO: Hola, muchachas.

BRENDAH: ¿Cuando begins el tour grande?

MACHITO: I'm very busy today. I can't go on tour, but here are two tickets to Tropicana, the hot night club of Havana. You get in free. I meet you there tonight, okay?

BRENDAA: But I got all dressed up for the cigar factory.

BRENDAH: I got my bikini underneath. [*Seductively.*] Muchas polka dots.

BRENDAA: [*Touches him.*] You promised.

BRENDAH: [*Demandingly.*] We paid in advance.

MACHITO: Okay. We do the quick tour.

[*The slides in the background change to the tourist spots Machito names. He drags them as they are, in place, or from side to side.*]

MACHITO: This is the capitol building.

BRENDAH: I know. We've been standing here for an hour.

MACHITO: El Morro Castle.

BRENDAA: Can we go in?

MACHITO: No. No. This is the statue of Maceo.

BRENDAH: I can't run in these heels.

MACHITO: The arch of . . .

BRENDAA: Weren't we here before?

MACHITO: You americanas crack me up. This is the beach. Well, I gotta go. See you in Tropicana.

BRENDAH: That was some fast tour. I know this island is small, but this is ridiculous.

BRENDAA: I told you we should have gone to the Dominican Republic.

[*Blackout.*]

Scene Two

[*Later that night. The slide changes to the outside of Capitán Maldito's mansion. Slide changes once again to a window. In the darkness,* MACHITO *and his cohort,* MARIMACHA, *are dressed like musicians and carry music cases they will open to take out machine guns. They are about to assassinate Capitán Maldito.*]

MARIMACHA: [*Taking a kung-fu stance.*] I don't like it.

MACHITO: What do you mean?

MARIMACHA: It's too much like an American gangster movie—dressing up like musicians.

MACHITO: Shh. Listen.

[*They get closer to the house and peer through the window. They hear lovemaking noises.*]

WOMAN [*Offstage.*]: Dámelo, Papi. Papi, dámelo. Dámelo.

MACHITO: Pig. Let's go.

[*There are machine-gun shots; a woman screams. Dogs bark.*]

MACHITO: Oh, shit. That's not Maldito. Marimacha, run. Where's Pepe with the car?

[*They exit. Car sounds are heard.*]

Scene Three

[*An hour later that night. Inside a bus crowded with passengers, including* BRENDAH *and* BRENDAA. *The conductor of the bus is taking money when* MACHITO, *in disguise, jumps onto the bus and holds a gun to his head.*]

MACHITO: Do you believe in Cuba?

PINGALITO: The country or the singer?

MACHITO: Don't be a wise guy.

BRENDAH: ¿Cuánto dinero, señor?

BRENDAA: ¿Dónde está Malecón?

MACHITO: Tell them to—.
    Passenger 1: Hey, this is my stop!
    Passenger 2: Thief! ¡Ladrón!

MACHITO: Tell them to be quiet or else.

PINGALITO: Mi gente, relax. I'm okay. You're okay.

MACHITO: I have a little time and so do you. Have you ever been to Tropicana?

[*The passengers, who have been eavesdropping, repeat in a chorus, "Tropicana."*]

MACHITO: My sister, Carmelita, is the manager there. You let me be the conductor in this bus tonight, and I will spare your life and let you into Tropicana for free. If not, you'll die; but worse, Cuba will not be free. She will suffer. Go take this message to Carmelita: "The banana was not sliced." Do you understand?

PINGALITO: The banana was not sliced.

MACHITO: Gracias, hermano. Brother, we will win.

BRENDAA: Oh, they're brothers.

[*Blackout.*]

Scene Four

[*Later that night at the Tropicana nightclub. A red lamé curtain with green ruffles hides the performance area, and two tables in front of the platform area are set up to give the appearance of a cabaret. A cigarette girl comes out, taking pictures of the audience, and tries to sell them cigarettes.* ROSITA CHARO *comes out and signals the cigarette girl to beat it, the show is about to begin.*]

ROSITA: [*Standing in front of the curtain, pointing out that her dress is made from the same fabric as the curtain.*] Bienvenidos, damas y caballeros. Yo soy Rosita Charo. Bienvenidos a Tropicana. Welcome, ladies and gentlemen, to the most fabulous club in the world—Tropicana. Presentamos hoy. We present for you today the Tropicanette salute to our neighbors in El Norte, the United States.

[*The curtain opens, revealing a platform stage and two tables. On one is seated* PINGALITO. *There is a Rousseau-style drop in the background with lots of palm trees and flowers. The Tropicanettes are posed in front of it.* ROSITA *joins the Tropicanettes in a song and parody of "Yes, We Have No Bananas." The Tropicanettes have large fruits attached to their costumes on their rears.*]
[*At the end of the song,* PINGALITO *sings, "the banana was not sliced," and when the curtain closes, he stands in front of it speaking to the audience.*]

PINGALITO: [*Smoking a cigar.*] Life is strange. One day you go to your job, you punch tickets, and the next day the tide of history has swept you out to sea, and you have to sink or swim with the sharks. "The banana was not sliced." Code words for the attempted assassination of Capitán Maldito, Havana's Chief of Police and most feared man in all of Cuba. Bienvenidos, damas y caballeros [*Gestures with his hat.*] al show du jour, "Memorias de la Revolución," the personal memoirs of the daughter of the Cuban Revolution, star of stage and screen, Carmelita Tropicana. This revolution you witness here tonight happened in 1955 in Havana, but you do not find yet in the history books. This is why Carmelita calls me, Pingalito Betancourt, in Miami, to come here and present media extravaganza.
In 1955, I was the conductor for the M15 bus route that go from La Habana Vieja to El Vedado. Let me explain. [*He grabs his crotch while talking.*] In Cuba, there were two people on the bus—the bus driver, the muscle of the operation, and the conductor. [*Proudly.*] The brains, the financial advisor— in short, I, Pingalito, I am the Socrates of the M15 bus route. The first time Carmelita get on my bus and I smell the heavensent perfume, what can I do? I forget my job as financial advisor and let her in

for free. When I remember that day, ladies and gentlemen—los pelos se me paran de punta—my hairs stand on end. In that tight red dress, Carmelita was the symbol of Cuban womanhood. Like Carmelita, Havana in 1955 was very gay like the music: mambo, rumba, y cha-cha-cha. But underneath, the political climate was turbulent, churning, growling like the starving stomach of a 500-pound football player. In order for you to enjoy the show tonight, I will give you my own perspective of Cuba—from history, geography, culture. As a matter of fact, I have in my possession a document. [*He takes out a placemat with a map of Cuba and facts.*] Audiovisual aid number one, this placemat I pick up in Las Lilas restaurant of Miami. It say facts about Cuba. As you can see, the island of Cuba is shaped like a Hoover vacuum cleaner with Pinar del Río as the handle. How many of you know fact one? Cuba is known as the pearl of the Antilles because of its natural wealth and beauty. And the first thing we learn as little children in our history books is that when Cristóbal Colón, Christopher Columbus, landed in our island, kneeling down he said, "Esta es la tierra más hermosa que ojos humanos han visto." This is the most beautiful land that human eyes have seen—the beaches of Varadero, the majestic mountains of La Sierra Maestra. But, ladies and gentlemen, none can compare with the beauty of the human landscape. Óyeme, mano, estas coristas de Tropicana, those chorus girls of Tropicana with big legs, big breasts. In Cuba we call girls carros, and I mean your big American cars—your Cadillacs, Pontiacs, no Volkswagen. No. Like the dancer Tongolele. Que Dios te bendiga. [*Overcome with emotion.*] I swear to you people, or my name is not Pingalito Betancourt. You could put a tray of daiquiris on Tongolele's behind, and she would walk across the floor without spilling a single drop. [*Emphatically.*] That, ladies and gentlemen, is landscape. Give me gun for that landscape, I fight. Fact two: Cuba is 759 miles and is smaller than Pennsylvania. Wait a second. I got a cousin in Pennsylvania. I been there. [*Looking at map.*] Oh, I see, Springmaid. This is written by Americans. Mi gente, don't believe everything you read. Let's see if fact three is correct. Spanish is the official language of—. This is true. And it's a beautiful language. You talk with your hands; you talk with your mouth. There is an interesting expression in Cuba when you want to find out the color of someone. You say, óyeme, mano, y ¿dónde está tu abuela? Tell me, brother, where is your grandmother? Which brings us to fact four—three-fourths of all Cubans are white of Spanish descent, and a lot of these three-fourths have a very dark suntan all year round. It reminds me of a story my grandmother told me about a fancy restaurant, El Alcázar, run by a woman from Spain, Doña Pilar. It is a very expensive restaurant. One day, a black couple comes to the restaurant. They are very well dressed. It is the first time a black couple comes. Doña Pilar serves them very polite. But what do you think Doña Pilar do when they leave? Eh? In front of all the customers, she took every plate and smash them. When they ask me, Pingalito, "Pingalito y ¿dónde está tu abuela?" I say, "Mulata y a mucha honra." Dark and proud. Fact five: the name Cuba comes from the Indian word Cubanacán, meaning "center place." Because we Cubans know we are the center of the universe. In Cuba there is a saying: No quedó ningún indio para contar su historia. There was not one Indian left to tell their story because the Spanish conquistadores kill them all. But Cuba did not forget her Indians, no. She names her ice cream after the beautiful Indian maiden, Guarina—better than Haagen Daz. She names her national beverage after the Indian Hatuey—malta Hatuey, and the great Cuban composer, el maestro Lecuona, honors that Cuban Indian Siboney. Ladies and gentlemen, I think you now know all there is to know about Cuba, so let us relive those memorias with a tribute to that great Cuban Indian Siboney.

[PINGALITO *exits. Curtain opens to reveal* ROSITA *and* MARIMACHA *singing a parody duet of "Siboney" in the area designated as the stage of the Tropicana. The story of Siboney is re-enacted through dance. The dance is a reconstructed satire of a cabaret-style Indian dance in which there are two Indian maidens who love the Indian Siboney and a white hunter who kills him. At the end of the dance, Siboney is revived by the Indian maidens, and* MARIMACHA *kisses* ROSITA'S *hand.* ROSITA *exits.* MACHITO *comes in and sits at the table, and* MARIMACHA *joins him.*]

MACHITO: Juanita, dos Cuba libres.

MARIMACHA: The night is still young. We will try again. You scared?

MACHITO: Me, Machito, scared? Jamás. [*Gulps down drink.*] It's in my blood. This time, Marimacha, we do it right. We don't make the same mistake. We get Capitán Maldito or my name is not Machito. I'll never forget, when I was four years old, my papá calls me to his room. He say, "Machito, come over here and stop playing with the cucarachas." I was a kid, what did I know? To me they were my friends. I made them a little house. "Ven acá," Papá said. "You, Machito, you are hombrecito now—little man." He says he has to go away soon. He goes to the drawer and takes out a pistol and bullets and puts them in my little hand. "From now on, Machito, you will protect your mama and sisters: Carlota, Carmelita, Cachita, Conchita,

Cuquita, y Baba." That night, I hear whispers. I see Papá tearing up photographs. Mamá puts me to bed. In the middle of the night, I hear a knock on the door, heavy footsteps on the stairs. I hear my mamá cry. They take my papá away, that pig, Capitán Maldito, and his man El Tuerto, the one-eyed. I swear on that day revenge. Venceremos. Brother, we will win.

[*They toast. A flurry of shots is heard, and they duck under the table. After the shooting is over, they come up.*]

MARIMACHA: It's begun—stage one of "Operation Fry the Banana."

MACHITO: Maduros or tostones?

MARIMACHA: Maduro, of course. They taste better with beans.

MACHITO: Full steam ahead like a locomotive. There's no going back. Maldito will squeal like a pig. [*Squeals.*] Dead pig. You and me, Marimacha, we've been through a lot.

MARIMACHA: Remember our first time? Biba and Beba.

MACHITO: The twins with the cute little mustaches. And their father, the big-shot engineer. Thinks we're not good enough. Lowlife chusma. Asking us which beach club we belong to. [*Imitating father.*] "We go to the Havana Yacht Club." The high-class high life makes me sick.

MARIMACHA: Well, we fix him good.

MACHITO: Oh, I would have loved to have seen his face when we knocked off the power generator in his plant. Ha. The big cheese gotta go to the office, we little cheeses run off with the twins.

MARIMACHA: [*Toasting.*] ¡Viva Biba!

MACHITO: ¡Viva Beba! [*Sadly.*] "Oh, juventud, divino tesoro . . ."

MARIMACHA: You are right. Youth is a fine treasure. We are still young. [*Trying to coax him out of his mood.*] Machito, think of the future. History will remember us, our revolution, our art. Hey, [*Pointing to herself.*] who is the Cuban Bing Crosby? [*Pointing to* MACHITO.] Who is the Cuban Emily Dickinson?

MACHITO: You are right, but there is still one thing I hate about these dangerous missions.

MARIMACHA: What?

MACHITO: Sweating. I can't keep my shirt from sticking to me. Sometimes the smell is so strong it can kill.

MARIMACHA: Maybe we should change our plan. Just bust into Capitán Maldito's office and when he says, "Arriba las manos—stick 'em up!"

MACHITO: [*Raises his armpits.*] Die, you bastard. Ha. Sonomabitch. [*They drink.*] I went out with an American girl once. Jane Hayes. Blonde hair, blue eyes. American girls don't take showers every day like us.

MARIMACHA: I know.

MACHITO: She didn't wear a brassiere.

MARIMACHA: Yeah. American girls are loose. Not like our Cuban flores.

MACHITO: What time is it? Carmelita should be here by now.

[*Another flurry of shots is heard, and again they duck under the table as* BRENDAH *and* BRENDAA *enter.*]

BRENDAH: Are you sure this is the Tropicana? It doesn't look like much of a hot spot.

BRENDAA: The sign outside said "Troiana." The "p" and "c" were missing.

[*They go to sit down at the table where* MARIMACHA *and* MACHITO *are hiding.*]

MARIMACHA: Machito, looks like this table has more legs.

MACHITO: My little turistas americanas.

BRENDAA and BRENDAH: ¡Machito!

MACHITO: Brendaa and Brendah, I like you to meet my friend, Marimacha.

BRENDAA: Mucho gusto, señor. [*To* BRENDAH.] I'm beginning to speak like a native.

BRENDAH: Machito, can you order me something to wet my whistle?

MACHITO: Whistle?

[*He whistles.*]

BRENDAH: Drink—tomar.

MACHITO: Oh, sí, drink.

BRENDAH: Do you have any blender drinks?

MARIMACHA: We have Cuba libre. [*Yelling.*] It means free Cuba. Cuban rum and American Coca-Cola. Very good. You like it.

BRENDAH: Your name is Mary-macha?

MARIMACHA: Marimacha. I am a singer.

BRENDAH: I love a serenade. Brendaa, I see you're not doing so bad yourself.

BRENDAA: Oh, Brendah, [*Pointing to her wedding ring finger.*] maybe we'll leave Havana with a big rock.

BRENDAH: Machito, maybe you need a private secretary to take dictation.

[*Flurry of shots is heard, and* MACHITO *and* MARIMACHA *get under the table.*]

BRENDAA: Are those fireworks?

BRENDAH: What happened to our gay caballeros?

[MACHITO *and* MARIMACHA *raise the tablecloth as they talk.*]

MARIMACHA: "Operation Fry the Banana." Carmelita should be here by now.

MACHITO: Dios mío, Marimacha. I think I get confused. I had to meet Carmelita at Tropicana, but it was the americanas at Tropicana and Carmelita at the Malecón. Oh, she'll kill me this time—with her temper. Don't tell her about the americanas, okay? [*To* BRENDAA *and* BRENDAH.] Bye.

BRENDAA: That man of yours is always leaving. At least mine is still here. [*Looking at each other, they make a dash for* MARIMACHA *under the table. Under the table, there are cries of delight and then surprise.*]

BRENDAH and BRENDAA: Oh, Marimacha. Oh, Marimacha. Oh, Marimacha!

BRENDAA: The banana has been sliced.

BRENDAH: Oh my God. It's a she.

BRENDAA: I'll never be able to have children.

[*They come up and sit on their chairs. Enter* LOTA HARI, *a Mata Hari-type seductive spy in a black dress carrying a cigarette holder. She sits down at another table on the side and takes out a little notebook and pen and begins to write.* CAPITÁN MALDITO *enters with* EL TUERTO. MAL-*

DITO *wears a white tuxedo and carries a cigar.* EL TUERTO, *a policeman with a patch over his eye, in battle fatigues, holding a machine gun, goes menacingly to the table where* LOTA *is sitting.*]

EL TUERTO: Arriba las manos.

MALDITO: Relax, Tuerto. Let's see if we can catch a couple of bees with a little honey.

EL TUERTO: Sí, mi capitán.

MALDITO: Come check out this table.

[*They go to the table with* BRENDAH *and* BRENDAA.]

BRENDAA: This must be the bad element they warned us about.

BRENDAH: They can't do anything to us. We're American citizens.

MALDITO: Americanas, of course. Skinny, flat-chested. Passport.

BRENDAA: Somos americanas, señor.

EL TUERTO: Your name.

BRENDAA: Brendaa.

EL TUERTO: Your name.

BRENDAH: Brendah.

EL TUERTO: Twins, mi capitán.

MALDITO: Don't believe everything you see.

BRENDAH: I'll say.

MALDITO: Tuerto, the test.

EL TUERTO: [*Taking out a piece of paper.*] Who won the World Series in 1951?

BRENDAA: [*Getting excited.*] The Yankees.

EL TUERTO: Correct.

BRENDAH: Maybe we'll win something.

EL TUERTO: What do you put on your hot dog? Is a trick question.

[BRENDAH *and* BRENDAA *confer.*]

BRENDAA: Mustard.

EL TUERTO: Wrong. Sauerkraut. I told you it was trick. What is the name of your President Eisenhower's dog?

BRENDAH: [*Haughty.*] Muffy.

EL TUERTO: Correct.

MALDITO: Two out of three. Not bad. Tuerto, go check out the back. See if we have a couple of worms hiding.

EL TUERTO: A sus órdenes, mi capitán.

[*He exits.* MALDITO *goes to sit at the table with* BRENDAH *and* BRENDAA *and snaps a finger at* MARIMACHA.]

MALDITO: You want five to life or you want to pull up a chair for an illustrious gentleman like myself? [MARIMACHA *pulls out the chair.*] That's what I like—fast service. A man knows quality when he sees it. Quality likes quality. Recognizes itself. That's why I smoke Tabacos Partagas. [*Smelling the cigar.*] Cuba, cigar capital of the world. They take years to make. Lots of negroes in the field singing. Singing and rolling. Ay, mamá Inés, ay mamá Inés, todos los negros tomamos café. I'm like the sweet jerez of Spain. But I guess you American girls can tell that just by looking at me. I bet you are here—like all the americanas we get—to look for the real thing. Un macho who will make you feel like a real woman. A macho like me. I am El Macho de Machos. A macho among machos. I have two cocks. One's named Adolph for Hitler, the other Rudolf, for the reindeer. I've got them the best equipment—custom-made German stirrups. Ah, there's nothing like a cockfight. But don't go wearing white. Always wear red. You can say I always had an affinity for poultry. My grandfather used to take me to the marketplace. The chickens would be cackling. My grandpa taught me responsibility. He'd say, "Which one?" and I got to finger the chicken I wanted. The Chinaman in the market would grab the chicken I chose [*He demonstrates, grabbing* BRENDAA.] with his left hand, and with his right, the ax. We would lay the head on the block and whack. The head would roll. Minutes later, the body would be shaking in a cha-cha-cha. That's the macho way. I never liked my grandmother's way. With a sharp knife she would cut the jugular vein until it bled to death. The head would go in circles and finally die like Alicia Alonso in Swan Lake. I don't like ballet. Faggot stuff. I like real entertainment. I hear there's a singer I used to know here tonight. [*Yelling.*] Isn't that right, Rosita?

ROSITA: [*Disguising her voice.*] Rosita went home.

MALDITO: You don't fool me, Rosita.

ROSITA: I can't. I'm busy.

MALDITO: You want El Tuerto to come get you?

ROSITA: [*Entering.*] No, not that.

BRENDAH: Maybe it's time we banana split.

[*They try to sneak out, but* MALDITO *restrains them.*]

MALDITO: You americanas will stay to hear Rosita sing. Come on, Rosita. [MALDITO *grabs her forcefully.*] Show them some real singing.

ROSITA: No, Maldito.

MALDITO: What did you say?

ROSITA: Tropicanettes, the banana number.

MALDITO: No banana number. Our song.

ROSITA: No, Maldito. Not in front of—

MALDITO: Sing it to me while we dance.

ROSITA: Please, Maldito, not here.

MALDITO: Enough fooling around, Rosita. Now.

[*While* ROSITA *sings a parody of "Bésame Mucho," a romantic ballad,* MALDITO *dances brutally with her, throwing her around, twisting her arms, pulling her hair, bending her fingers, finally dropping her on the floor.* ROSITA *sobs.*]

MALDITO: That was touching, Rosita. I couldn't have sung it more beautiful myself.

[EL TUERTO *comes in with* MACHITO, *who is handcuffed.* EL TUERTO *throws* MACHITO *on his knees.*]

EL TUERTO: Look at the worm I found in the alleyway, mi capitán.

MALDITO: Good work, Tuerto. Machito Tropicana: bad poet, bad revolutionary. You look like your father, Camacho, only more stupid. You try twice to kill me, but first you kill my dog Buster. Then you kill my wife. I get big fat insurance. We are going to hear mucho from you tonight down at police headquarters. It is going to be pretty poetry. Ha. Not like this. [*He reads from a matchbook.*] The police found this in my house. Read it, Tuerto.

EL TUERTO: "Oh, beautiful Brendah y Brendaa." Ah, the twins, mi capitán.

MALDITO: Tuerto, read.

EL TUERTO: "Oh my beautiful Brendaa, my heart to you I will—. I will—."

[*He goes to the americanas to ask what the word is and as he does,* MARIMACHA, *who has been at the table, grabs a bottle and smashes it over his head.* EL TUERTO *is momentarily slumped over the table and dazed.* MALDITO *takes out his gun and shoots, but* MARIMACHA *and* MACHITO *run out. Both Tuerto and* MALDITO *exit.*]

MALDITO: [*Running out after them.*] Coño, Tuerto, you fool.

ROSITA: [*Screaming.*] Run, Machito, run.

[*While this has been going on, the two americanas have been oblivious to the action, instead fighting with one another over who will get the matchbook with the poem.*]

BRENDAH: "Oh, beautiful Brendah y Brendaa."

BRENDAA: "My heart to you I will surrendah."

BRENDAH: "Embrace Machito, great poet of Havana."

BRENDAA: "Oh, skinny and loose americanas." [*Happily.*] That's us.

BRENDAH: "Let's rumba tonight at Tropicana."

BRENDAA: "My heart to you I will surrendah." Oh, it's beautiful.

BRENDAH: Latin men are so sensitive.

[ROSITA *is prostrate on the floor, sobbing, as* CARMELITA *enters from the back.*]

BRENDAA: There she is. I saw her picture outside. That's Carmelita Tropicana.

ROSITA: [*Sobbing hysterically.*] Oh, Carmelita . . .

[ROSITA *continues to sob.*]

CARMELITA: What?

[ROSITA *continues sobbing, and finally,* CARMELITA *slaps her.*]

ROSITA: Thank you, Carmelita. It was awful. Maldito came.

CARMELITA: Machito doesn't get him again.

ROSITA: The pig makes me sing "Bésame Mucho" and El Tuerto comes and he finds Machito and it's bad, he's kneeling and the matchbook . . .

CARMELITA: What happened to Machito? Dios mío. Tell me, Rosita.

ROSITA: He's kneeling and they know him and they hit him on the head and then MARIMACHA gets a bottle and hits El Tuerto and Maldito takes out a pistol and bang bang.

CARMELITA: They shoot Machito and Marimacha?

ROSITA: No, they shoot and Machito and Marimacha run fast. It was awful.

CARMELITA: ¡Gracias a Dios! Marimacha is with Machito. She protect him. But this is bad, Rosita. Very bad. You have to go home now and tell the Tropicanettes to go home also. I have very important urgent business tonight.

[CARMELITA *hugs* ROSITA.]

ROSITA: Save us, Carmelita.

CARMELITA: I try.

[CARMELITA *goes over to the table where the americanas have been sitting.*]

CARMELITA: [*To* BRENDAH.] The banana is frying.

BRENDAH: I'm sorry, greasy food is not good for my complexion.

CARMELITA: [*To* BRENDAA.] The banana is frying.

BRENDAA: I ordered the plantains.

[CARMELITA *spots* LOTA HARI, *who is smoking a cigarette at the opposite table, and goes over to her.*]

CARMELITA: The banana is frying.

LOTA: The wasp sweats. The bee stings.

CARMELITA: The monkey with the bell rings.

LOTA: Ding a link.

[CARMELITA *goes over to the americanas' table.*]

CARMELITA: Time to go, americanas. Tropicana is closed. You make enough trouble for my brother Machito already.

BRENDAH: Somos americanas. You can't treat us this way.

CARMELITA: Out.

BRENDAA: What manners! Let's go, Brendah.

BRENDAH: We paid and we didn't even get to see the floor show.

[*They exit.*]

CARMELITA: [*Excited.*] Lota?

LOTA: Ja, Carmelita.

CARMELITA: Sí, ¡viva Cuba!

LOTA: [*Cool and detached.*] Viva.

CARMELITA: Finally you arrive. We have been waiting for you.

LOTA: [*Looking at her watch.*] Und I have been waiting for you.

CARMELITA: A little delay. My brother Machito is a great poet, but not so good revolutionary. He forgot he gotta meet me at the Malecón.

LOTA: He is a little geshtunka.

CARMELITA: I know geshtunka, but what can I do—he is family. Let's talk revolution.

LOTA: Let's talk business.

CARMELITA: Very well. You have the equipment and supplies?

LOTA: Ja.

CARMELITA: 200 machine guns, 100 submachine guns, 300 rifles, 2,000 grenades.

LOTA: Und von tank.

CARMELITA: Loaded?

LOTA: My guns are always loaded.

CARMELITA: $25,000.

LOTA: That is correct.

CARMELITA: And ammunition?

LOTA: That is not in the contract.

CARMELITA: Maybe we change the contract a little.

LOTA: $5,000 for ammunition.

CARMELITA: But, Lota, we are poor.

LOTA: It's business.

CARMELITA: It's revolution.

LOTA: That is not my problem. I am a spy, a professional.

CARMELITA: Lota, people are dying; children are hungry.

LOTA: It is business. $5,000 for ammunition.

CARMELITA: But, Lota, what good is guns without ammunition? It's like a flower without petals, a car without wheels.

LOTA: I'm sorry.

CARMELITA: Couldn't you give the revolution a little break?

LOTA: I feel for your position but—

CARMELITA: You feel?

LOTA: All right. This goes against all my principles. $4,000 for the ammunitions.

CARMELITA: $4,000?

LOTA: $4,000.

CARMELITA: The hungry children . . .

LOTA: $4,000.

CARMELITA: The starving artists . . .

LOTA: $3,500.99. This is the best I can do.

CARMELITA: Give me your hand, Lota. I see you are a stubborn Leo.

LOTA: Ja, Leo. Nein, stubborn. Sensible. How did you know this?

CARMELITA: I see many things, Lota. I am voyeur. I feel many things. This is why I am artist revolutionary. I sing; I fight. [*Looking at her palm.*] I see you have been a spy all your life.

LOTA: That is correct.

CARMELITA: I see two women in your life.

LOTA: Ja. Meine grandmother, the great Mata Hari, and her daughter, meine Mutti Wata Hari.

CARMELITA: They used to put you to bed singing.

CARMELITA and LOTA: [*Speaking the lyrics.*]
Men and women swoon
Whey they see my arms aflutter.

LOTA: They begin to stutter.

CARMELITA: They call me Mata—. Mata

LOTA: Mata Hari.

CARMELITA: My dance is like a wild safari.

LOTA: Better than a kama—

CARMELITA: sutra Indian in a—

LOTA: —sari. This is incredible. Carmelita, you are—.

CARMELITA: Your Grossmutter, the great Mata Hari, is a great spy, a dancer. She doesn't say business all the time like you. She has passion. She feels. She feels for everyone—for the French, the Spanish, the German, the Dutch. That's why they kill her. I see a little girl trying to come out to express herself. To feel, to be free. Like the Cuban people. Our struggle is your struggle. Freedom, Mata. Can you taste it? Like cold coconut water? Freedom from the tyranny of men like Maldito. Cowards. Little, big, fat men with prejudice, who torture, kill, and beat up women. I cannot pay you with gold, but as a woman, a revolutionary, I can make sacrifice. Myself, Carmelita, for ammunition. Good men kill for less.

LOTA: Carmelita, I feel—. I feel strange. Like it is the very first time . . .

[LOTA, *overcome with emotion, is about to kiss her. They are staring into each other's eyes in an embrace when* MARIMACHA *runs in very upset.*]

MARIMACHA: Carmelita, quick. We have to leave. Machito has been captured with Sergio and taken to police headquarters.

[CARMELITA *almost faints, but they catch her.*]

MARIMACHA: You must be strong. He wants you to be strong. Maldito gave orders to come burn Tropicana. He found guns in Sergio's car and knows about us. We have to leave at once. There is a boat waiting for us at the Malecón. Pronto. [*To* LOTA.] You look gorgeous.

CARMELITA: Vamos al Malecón.

[*Blackout.*]

ACT TWO

[*The action takes place in the middle of the ocean on a row boat as* CARMELITA *escapes with* MARIMACHA *and* LOTA. *It is night. There is a painted backdrop with clouds.*]

CARMELITA: How long have we been here, Marimacha?

MARIMACHA: Let's see. Night . . . mmm. I will say about twenty hours.

CARMELITA: We should see Key West already. We should go right, not left. Why did we listen to the German?

LOTA: I heard that. It's because Germans make the best precision instruments in the world. My instrument in the tropics is not so precise.

CARMELITA: Great, Lota.

LOTA: I am trying to find our course due north by northwest. It takes a little time. It takes something you hot-tempered Latins don't know—how to be quiet.

MARIMACHA: Well, when you find it, please let us know. I'm tired of rowing.

CARMELITA: I'm hungry.

MARIMACHA: I'm starving.

[*She remembers she has a candy bar she is hiding from them and sneakily takes a bite.*]

LOTA: I also.

CARMELITA: [*Seeing her chewing.*] Marimacha, what you got?

MARIMACHA: Nothing.

CARMELITA: Milky Way. Give us some.

[*They struggle for the candy bar.*]

MARIMACHA: I was about to offer you some.

[*The sound of a ship's horn is heard.*]

MARIMACHA: Carmelita, look—a boat.

LOTA: Das liebe boat. The Love Boat.

CARMELITA and MARIMACHA: We're here. Save us. Aquí estamos.

LOTA: Sit down, both of you. They can't see us.

CARMELITA: Lota, get up and scream. Maybe they hear us.

LOTA: They can't hear us. Stop rocking the boat. We will capsize.

CARMELITA: No tienes sangre en las venas. Tienes hielo, hielo, hielo.

MARIMACHA: You are frozen, like an iceberg. Frozen, frozen.

LOTA: I heard you the first time. Sit.

CARMELITA: You don't order us no more. You hear? Enough. We row for twenty hours and for nothing. Look at my hands. I'll never get to play the castanets again.

MARIMACHA: I didn't know you played the castanets.

CARMELITA: [*Punching* MARIMACHA.] Why don't you do something good—like fish. You told me you were a fisherwoman. Prove it. Catch us fish with your precision instrument.

LOTA: Very well. I will teach you both how it is done. First the hose. [*She removes her stocking.*] I need something to attract the fish. Earrings.

CARMELITA: No, it's the only pair I take out of Cuba. I can't.

MARIMACHA: Carmelita, we are starving and you're thinking of jewelry. Look over there.

[*She grabs the earring out of* CARMELITA's *ear.*]

CARMELITA: [*Smacking her.*] Marimacha, how can you? You know who you talk to. Look at me. You become an animal.

MARIMACHA: [*Crying.*] I'm sorry, Carmelita. I don't know what comes over me.

CARMELITA: [*Comforting her.*] What happen, baby?

MARIMACHA: Remember the Maine? I lost my mother, my father, my two older brothers in a boat at sea. Ever since then I have such memories. I can't go to the beach. If I see suntan lotion, I start to shake.

CARMELITA: Come over here, Marimacha. It's okay. You are fine, Marimacha. Let it all out.

MARIMACHA: Thank you, Carmelita. I needed that.

CARMELITA: [*Giving her the earring.*] Here, Lota, do what you have to do.

LOTA: [*Attaching earring to hose.*] Here, Marimacha. Like this. I am sorry, Carmelita, I call you hot-tempered Latin.

CARMELITA: Is okay, Lota. You teach us now to fish. We survive. You are masterful with the hose.

LOTA: I learned to fish in the Black Sea. Black—your eyes are black. Schön.

CARMELITA: Schön?

LOTA: Beautiful. Your hair is schön. Your mouth is schön.

CARMELITA: Your nose is schön.

[CARMELITA *and* LOTA *embrace and are about to kiss.* MARIMACHA *interrupts.*]

MARIMACHA: Help, hey, you guys. The fish. The fish. I lost the fish.

CARMELITA: I lost my earring.

MARIMACHA: You lost the oar.

LOTA: I lost my head.

[*There is the sound of a storm. The waves start to get rougher.*]

LOTA: Sit down. We will capsize.

MARIMACHA: I see a storm ahead.

CARMELITA: Lota, where are we?

LOTA: Mein Gott in himmel. I think we are approaching the Bermuda Triangle.

MARIMACHA: The Bermuda Triangle?

LOTA: Bad currents. The most powerful, but ships like the Love Boat have been swallowed.

CARMELITA: Marimacha, give me your oar.

MARIMACHA: I'm gonna die. Like my brother, my mother, my father. I wanted to die in the revolution. Not here.

[*She cries.*]

LOTA: Marimacha, hold on two more minutes and it will be over. Hold onto the side of the boat.

[*Sounds of storm, thunder are heard on tape until finally the storm ends. The waves subside, and both* MARIMACHA *and* LOTA *fall asleep. Two angels appear and open doors on the backdrop, which has painted clouds. It resembles an altar triptych with painted cherubs on either side. In the middle there is a screen for a film projection of an apparition of* La Virgen.]

VIRGEN: Carmelita. Carmelita.

CARMELITA: What is this? Am I, Carmelita Tropicana, hearing things? Marimacha, wake up. Lota.

VIRGEN: Shulum alechen vei gest du?

CARMELITA: ¿Habla español? What's going on here?

VIRGEN: Carmelita, don't worry so much. I have a tie line to you-know-who, and I promise you a happy ending.

CARMELITA: Who are you? Here I am in the middle of the ocean and—

VIRGEN: I'm Mary, the Virgin. Listen, Carmelita. You have been chosen by the Goddess herself to be the next hottest Latin superstar, but you gotta wait.

CARMELITA: I always knew my destiny.

VIRGEN: But listen, Carmelita. There's a little problem. There is a difficult road ahead.

CARMELITA: Difficult road?

VIRGEN: Cuba will no longer be your home. Her revolution will not be your revolution. Yours will be an international revolution.

CARMELITA: But what about my brother, Machito, and Maldito?

VIRGEN: Carmelita, please, hold your oars. Fate will have you meet your nemesis, Maldito, and when you do, you will know what to do. As for that geshtunkene brother of yours, you two will be reunited. Where was I? Oh, yes, the revolution. Let it be through your art. Your art is your weapon. To give dignity to Latin and third-world women—this is your new struggle. If you accept, you will be gifted with eternal youth. You will be as you are today, twenty-one.

CARMELITA: Nineteen, please.

VIRGEN: You will suffer much. Spend years penniless and unknown until 1967.

CARMELITA: That is a lot of years, but for nineteen is okay. I accept.

VIRGEN: But listen, Carmelita, there is more. You must never, ever, ever . . .

CARMELITA: What? You are killing me.

VIRGEN: Or all the years will return like to that nasty Dorian Gray.

CARMELITA: Never do what?

VIRGEN: Never let a man touch you. You must remain pure, like me.

CARMELITA: Oh yes. Never let a man touch me. Believe me, to Carmelita Tropicana Guzmán Jiménez Marquesa de Aguas Claras, that is never to be a problem.

[*The film projection of La Virgen ends, and lights change as* CARMELITA *sees land.*]

CARMELITA: Marimacha, Lota, wake up.

[*Both wake up.*]

CARMELITA: Look, it's Miami Beach.

[*Blackout.*]

ACT THREE

[*The action takes place at the Tropicana-A-Go-Go in New York City in 1967.* MALDITO *enters through the audience. He has a broom in hand. He has aged physically and lost weight. He is wearing a janitor's cap and uniform.*]

MALDITO: You disgusting, filthy kids. I'll put bullets in your stupid, pinko brains. [*He walks over and tears a large poster for the opening of a new nightclub, Tropicana-A-Go-Go.*] Who put this? Agh. [*He opens an envelope with a letter and reads.*] "Dear Mr. Maldito, We regret to inform you that you have failed the 1967 Paramilitary Operative Examination. However, do not be discouraged. Our office has created positions in the Civilian Counterinsurgency Specialist Patrol, for which you may apply. To apply for the CCSP all you need to supply us with is intelligence information leading to the arrest of subversive civilians engaging in or promoting direct or indirect" . . . hmm. I think I got my ticket.

[*He looks at the poster, starts to laugh, and the laugh turns into a coughing fit. He exits.*
Blackout.
The curtain opens to reveal the same set of the Tropicana nightclub in Havana with the exception of a cage in the back with a dance-machine-a-go-go dancer.
MACHITO *enters. He is in a 1960s outfit, including bell bottoms and little glasses. He carries a punch bowl.* ROSITA *is at the counter.*]

MACHITO: Here's the punch, Rosita, and the tablets.

ROSITA: Tablets?

MACHITO: Yes, to make the punch taste good. But wait till I tell you when to give them out, okay?

ROSITA: Okay.

[BRENDAH *and* BRENDAA *also enter in 1960s-style mod outfits.*]

BRENDAA: Peace, Brendaa.

ROSITA: [*Not recognizing them at first.*] Oh, Brendaa y Brendah. I am so happy to see you charming americanas at the opening of the fabuloso Tropicana-A-Go-Go in Nueva York.

BRENDAA: I wouldn't have missed it for the world.

BRENDAH: The day I got my invitation, I went shopping at the Luv-In Boutique. How do you like it?

ROSITA: It is charming, like you. Carmelita is going to be so happy you come to the opening.

BRENDAA: It's been so many years. But you know, Rosita, in the picture in the marquee, Carmelita looks just like she did in 1955—so young.

BRENDAH: A little retouching around the eyes, perhaps.

ROSITA: No, Brendah. It is true. Carmelita looks always the same. Is incredible.

BRENDAA: Oh, Brendah. Maybe she goes to a different guru than we do. Could be her diet, maybe rice and beans and plátanos maduros. And speaking of plátanos, will Marimacha be attending this soirée tonight?

ROSITA: Yes, but she change a lot. Maybe you don't recognize her when she come in.

BRENDAA: Well, so have we, Rosita. It's the sixties. Brendah and I are part of the sexual revolution.

ROSITA: I been living in the Sowezer—the Eighth Street section of Miami. I don't know this sexual revolution you talk about.

BRENDAH: Rosita, don't tell me you never attended a C.R. group?

ROSITA: C.R.? What is C.R.?

BRENDAA: Consciousness-raising. When you talk in a group of women and you discuss women's issues and you come to terms with your sexuality.

BRENDAH: Yeah, like *Our Bodies, Ourselves.* We demand an orgasm.

ROSITA: [*Embarrassed.*] Oh, you are still charming americanas.

BRENDAA: I've come to terms with my sexuality. That is why I'm hoping I'll meet Marimacha again.

ROSITA: Well, she be here soon.

BRENDAH: Rosita, is this the punch?

ROSITA: Yes. And tablets. Machito told me to give them out.

BRENDAH: We'll help you give them out. Okay? We'll take half.

ROSITA: That is very kind.

BRENDAH: [*To* BRENDAA.] I'm not taking any chances on getting stiffed again. You know how these Cubans are.

[BRENDAH *and* BRENDAA *walk further into the club and meet* MACHITO.]

BRENDAH and BRENDAA: Machito!

BRENDAA: My God. This looks just like the Tropicana. I can't believe my eyes. And I haven't even taken anything yet.

MACHITO: Brendaa and Brendah, welcome to the Tropicana-A-Go-Go. Is exact replica of Havana nightclub. Carmelita spared no expense. The curtains, the palm trees.

BRENDAH: Machito, what have you been up to all these years?

MACHITO: I now have the life of a Renaissance man. I write "happenings." One musician plays guitar with his toes, another sits on a tuba, two girls read newspapers and pour spaghetti on their heads.

BRENDAH: With sauce?

MACHITO: Of course. For texture. And there is also my poetry. But I am stuck. Is so hard to write in another tongue. This English words. [*Looking at pad.*] What rhymes with twirl?

BRENDAA: Curl.

BRENDAH: Hurl.

BRENDAA and BRENDAH: Berle. Milton Berle.

MACHITO: Rain of fire. Rain of fire. Swirl and twirl like Milton Berle. Groovy, let's dance.

[*They dance.* MARIMACHA *enters in turban hat and orange jumpsuit. She goes to* ROSITA.]

ROSITA: Marimacha, I love your—hat.

MARIMACHA: Na mash ren go go, na mash ren go go, na mash ren go go.

ROSITA: Marimacha, are you consciousness-raising?

MARIMACHA: No. My consciousness has already been raised. I'm on a different plane right now. When I chant my mantra, my chakra goes into a different tantra.

ROSITA: Chantra? Mantra? I live for years in Miami. Ah. This is the sexual revolution. Our bodies, ourselves. I want an organ.

MARIMACHA: No, no. I am beyond the sexual revolution. That was last year.

ROSITA: You mean . . . no more? You know—I can't say it.

MARIMACHA: Exactly. It's the new Marimacha.

ROSITA: Let me check your hat.

[MARIMACHA *joins* MACHITO *and* BRENDAH *and* BRENDAA.]

BRENDAA: Marimacha.

MARIMACHA: Brendah and Brendaa, this is a spiritually uplifting experience for me.

BRENDAA: Likewise, I'm sure.

BRENDAH: Oh, Marimacha. I've been looking forward to this day for years.

[PINGALITO *enters from the back of the club. He is wearing the same outfit as in Act One.*]

PINGALITO: 1967. It was a very good year. As you can see, the hot event of the year was the opening of the nightclub Tropicana-A-Go-Go. After Carmelita landed in Miami in 1955, she and Lota went off to Germany. But in 1958, she came back to the United States, to Columbus, Ohio, to be reunited with her brother, Machito, who had just come out of jail. He was in very bad shape and needed her. In 1965, Lota Hari gave up the business of spying to become a very big Hollywood producer. That same year, Carmelita was on a plane that crashed in Nepal. Everybody thought she was . . . But in 1967, Carmelita came back and Lota was so happy, she beg Carmelita to take money for a new nightclub. Tropicana-A-Go-Go. But to go back to 1955 when Carmelita and Lota were vacationing in the Black Forest of Germany. They saw a terrible car accident. The two people in the car were dead, but out came a little blonde girl with tears on her face, crying "mein Vater, meine Mutter," tut, tut. Lota and Carmelita adopted her and named her Carme Lota Nota Hari. Nota for short. Lota taught her spying, Carmelita singing. Let us welcome that little girl, who has blossomed into the folk singer of today, Nota Hari.

[PINGALITO *exits.* NOTA HARI *enters the stage with guitar in hand. She is wearing hot pants.* MACHITO, BRENDAA, BRENDAH, *and* MARIMACHA *all focus their attention on* NOTA.]

NOTA: Before I begin my song I'd like to read a telegram from my adopted mother, Lota Hari. "Dear Nota and Carmelita, My body is in Hollywood, but my heart is in Tropicana-A-Go-Go tonight. Much success. Signed: mother, lover, executive producer—Lota." This is for you, meine mutti.

[NOTA *sings a parody of "Both Sides Now." Everyone claps, and* NOTA *goes to join* MACHITO, BRENDAH *and* BRENDAA, *and* MARIMACHA. MALDITO *enters but is not recognized by* ROSITA, *who is at the counter.*]

ROSITA: Check your— [*Smelling his cigar.*] Partagas. Maldito.

MALDITO: After all these years, Rosita Charo, you still have it for me?

[*He tries to kiss her, and she fights him off.*]

ROSITA: You are repulsive.

MALDITO: Playing hard to get. Oh, Rosita. So many years. I need your titties on my face.

ROSITA: You disgust me, you skinny gross pig.

MALDITO: [*Grabbing her hand.*] It's still big.

[*He starts to cough.*]

ROSITA: I throw up. Your lungs will come out in black heaps.

MALDITO: I'm still young. I have plans.

ROSITA: What plans?

MALDITO: I need something on Carmelita.

ROSITA: You never get anything on her. She is a saint.

MALDITO: What is this?

ROSITA: This is punch and tablets. Not for pigs.

MALDITO: [*Examining the tablets.*] I knew it. This place is a front. Evidence.

ROSITA: [*Screaming.*] Carmelita, Machito, is the pig Maldito.

[CARMELITA *runs on stage.* MACHITO *lunges for* MALDITO *but trips on his way.*]

MACHITO: Coño.

CARMELITA: No, Machito. No, Marimacha.

MARIMACHA: [*Suffering a split from conflict.*] Na mash ren go go, na mash. Pig swine. Na mash . . . My hat, my beads. I want to kill the sonomabitch.

CARMELITA: No violence. It is the age of Aquarius.

NOTA: But, Mami, I heard about this greaseball. Let me give him one deadly karate chop.

CARMELITA: No, Nota.

MALDITO: [*To* NOTA.] You can't do anything to me. I am Maldito. Carmelita Tropicana, after all these years, we finally meet again. I have evidence against you, Carmelita. Look, tablets of drugs. I knew this place was a front for drugs and revolution. Once a revolutionary, always a revolutionary.

MARIMACHA: Once a pig, always a pig. Na mash ren go go.

MALDITO: This evidence will get me into the CCSP, the CIA. I will be on top again.

[*While* MALDITO *is speaking,* BRENDAH *shows* CARMELITA *the tablets she is holding in her hand;* CARMELITA *signals for* BRENDAH *to put them into the punch.*]

CARMELITA: Capitán Maldito. Yes, yes, yes. [*Signals to* BRENDAH *to put tablets in the drink.*] Finally, we meet again. You are a better man than I am. You have beat me. The better man won.

MALDITO: CIA, CCSP, here I come.

CARMELITA: A toast.

[BRENDAH *seductively hands* MALDITO *a glass with tablets.*]

BRENDAH: Maybe you need a secretary to help you take dictation.

MALDITO: Maybe I do. [*He drinks.*] Good punch. Now I give up my job as janitor of the junior high school. I am in command once . . . the c . . . the c is coming out of my mouth.

[MALDITO *is tripping. A film of op-art images is projected onto the stage.*]

BRENDAH: That's not all that's gonna come out of your mouth.

MALDITO: Oh, oh.

[*He goes over to the dance machine, which has been go-go dancing throughout the act.* MALDITO *kneels in front of her, but she doesn't pay attention.*]

MALDITO: Buster, Buster. Don't you recognize your master?

[MALDITO *staggers Center Stage and everyone surrounds him.*]

CARMELITA: I, Carmelita Tropicana, in the name of all here at Tropicana-A-Go-Go, j'accuse Maldito. Let the witnesses to your crimes step forward. Marimacha, step forward.

MARIMACHA: I saw you torture for no reason, kill good people. Na mas ren go go. But when I see your face, I want to get on a tank and roll over your decrepit body.

MALDITO: Ah, tank, my legs.

CARMELITA: Machito.

MACHITO: You kill my papá when I am four years old. I never learned to play béisbol with him. Two years in jail. [*He lifts his shirt to show scars.*] Look at my scars. Touch them.

[BRENDAH *grabs* MALDITO's *hand to put on* MACHITO's *back.*]

BRENDAH: Feel him, touch him, heal him.

MALDITO: I didn't mean to.

CARMELITA: You didn't mean to. Rosita.

ROSITA: You humiliate me. You beat me.

[ROSITA *steps on* MALDITO. *She is overcome with emotion;* CARMELITA *goes to her.*]

CARMELITA: Rosita, enough. Basta. It's my turn now.

[CARMELITA *goes into an incantation and during it, the chorus chants "bongo, bongo, bongo," and does a line dance while she recites a poem.*]

CARMELITA:

Maldito, if justice prevails
In hell you'll burn

But before that
Your earthly fate you can't escape.
Tonight in full you will be paid.
Oh, moon of Nepal,
Oh, moon of Cooch Behar,
Appearing, disappearing,
Playing peek-a-boo
Like Desi Arnaz,
We sing to you,
Babalú, Babalú, Ay.
Oh, Gods of Africa
Yemayá y Obatala
Grant favor to your humble servant
Who speaks Shakespearean verse
And transform this flesh and spirit
To another universe.
Let my incantation
Be full of syncopation
With the heartbeat of the jungle
The drumming of the bongo.
Bongo bongo bongo,
Bongo beats a beat.
Bongo beats a beat
For my dancing feet.
I can't stand still
'Cause I got no free will.
Obsessed, possessed
With the bongo beat
Everything in me shivers—
My hips, my lips, my liver.
My pelvis moves like Elvis
To the bongo beat.
Molecules are jumping,
Bullfrogs in the night are humping
In Peoria, Illinois
I hear the rooster sing to you cock-a-doodle-do.
In Santiago de Cuba el gallo sings to me ki-ki-ri-ki-ki.
Incarnation, incantation,
Alchemy divine

Ingredients like white sugar so refined
Magic potion
Containing
Extract of electric eel
Foreskin of baboon
Human hair with pigeon droppings
A dash of pepper
A twist of lime
Help to exorcise
The evil in this big, disgusting guy.

[*Toward the end of the incantation, the group, chanting "bongo, bongo, bongo" in chorus, surrounds* MALDITO, *hiding him from the audience. At the end,* CARMELITA *sprinkles glitter on him. When he gets up, he is wearing a chicken costume. He acts like a chicken.*]

MALDITO: Ki-ki-ri-ki-ki. Cock-a-doodle-do.

BRENDAA: Wow, Carmelita, that was great. But what was it?

CARMELITA: Brendaa, is a little trick I pick up in Nepal. Maldito always has affinity for poultry. Well, he be cackling for the rest of his life.

BRENDAH: What a happening. Mind blowing.

ROSITA: Very groovy.

CARMELITA: Oh, Rosita, seeing Maldito today brings such sad memories, but now that he is a chicken, the good memories come back of the place we come from and never can forget. Because where you are born, that place you carry in your heart. Let us always remember que la lucha continúa and art is our weapon.

[CARMELITA *recites first verse of "Guantanamera."*]
[*Lights fade.*]

JOSÉ GALVEZ

ELAINE ROMERO

RITA PRATTS

DOLORES PRIDA

JEAN WEISINGER

CHERRÍE MORAGA

MONICA PALACIOS

JANIS ASTOR DEL VALLE

YARELI ARIZMENDI

AMPARO GARCÍA CROW

SILVIANA WOOD

AL RENDON

DIANE RODRÍGUEZ

DOREEN STONE

J.P. HOUSE AKA A. SVICH

CARIDAD SVICH

EDIT VILLARREAL

SCHULTZ BROS. PHOTOGRAPHY

DIANA SOLIS

MIGDALIA CRUZ

Production of **BOTANICA**, by Dolores Prida.
(photograph © Gerry Goodstein)

LAS NUEVAS TAMALERAS, Jump Start Performance Company, Burras Finas Productions, San Antonio, Texas. December 1996. (photograph by Marilu Abirached-Reyna/Burras Finas Productions)

NOSTALGIA MALDITA: 1·900·MEXICO,
video clip. (photograph by Sergio Arau)

NOSTALGIA MALDITA, American flag with stars on
green background. (photograph by Sergio Arau)

Amparo García Crow in a scene from **A ROOMFUL OF MEN**. (photograph by Fabrizio DeRold)

"Frida and Diego Dine with the Capitalists on Ticker Tape," a scene from **FRIDA**, produced by the American Music Theater Festival. (photograph by Jack Vartoogian)

Carmelita Tropicana (center) and Uzi Parnes (right) in performance of **MEMORIAS DE LA REVOLUCIÓN.** (photograph by Dona Ann McAdams)

Contributors

YARELI ARIZMENDI was born in Mexico City and has resided in California since 1984. She received her B.A. in Political Science and her M.F.A. in Theater Arts from the University of California, San Diego. As a playwright, dramaturg, and performance artist, she develops work for the contemporary stages of both Mexico and the United States. As a trained dramaturg, she has translated various Latin American plays and novels into English and worked in that capacity with important regional theaters such as The Old Globe Theatre and La Jolla Playhouse. She translated the screenplay version of *Like Water for Chocolate* and the novel *Simple Prayers* (into Spanish). As an actress, she starred in the film version of *Like Water for Chocolate* and has continued to work successfully in both film and television since then. As an Assistant Professor, she participated in establishing the Interdisciplinary Arts Program at California State University, San Marcos. *Nostalgia Maldita: 1–900–MEXICO* has been produced in Mexico and the United States in various locations.

Arizmendi may be contacted through Alroy and Schwartz Management, 2934½ Beverly Glen Circle, Suite 107, Bel Air, California, 90077.

JANIS ASTOR DEL VALLE, Borinqueña (Bronx-born, second-generation Puerto Rican), lesbian, writer, actor, and producer, is a member of the Primary Stages Writers and Directors Project. At age seven, Janis Astor del Valle was uprooted from her beloved Bronx and transplanted amidst the cornstalks and whisker-wheat that was once New Milford, Connecticut. On weekends when she ventured back to the Bronx with her parents to visit their extended family, Janis often wrote and directed scenes in which she and her cousins performed at their grandparents' house. Her first play was written at age nine. During her college years, she was a radio announcer at various locations. In 1986, she returned to her native New York, where she received a B.A. in Theatre Arts from Marymount Manhattan College. Since then she has performed her plays and poetry in many New York City venues. Astor's full-length lesbian romantic comedy, *Where the Señoritas Are,* premiered at the Nuyorican in 1994 and won the Mixed Blood Theatre's National Playwriting Competition that year. An excerpt from her full-length play *I'll Be Home Para La Navidad* also ran at the Nuyorican and is published in *Amazon All Stars: Thirteen Lesbian Plays.* She is a founding member of She Saw Rep, and a co-founder of Sisters On Stage (SOS), a multicultural trio dedicated to fostering the development of aspiring lesbian playwrights. She was employed by New York University's Creative Arts Team as an actor and teacher and is currently pursuing her M.F.A. in film at Columbia University.

HILARY BLECHER emigrated to the United States from South Africa in 1981, where she was resident director at the Market Theatre and taught at the University of Witwatersrand. She made her New York City debut with the Obie, Drama Desk, and Laurence Olivier (London) award-winning production of *Poppie Nongena.* Other American productions include *Frida* (conception, book/director), produced by American Music Theater Festival and Houston Grand Opera, which opened Brooklyn Academy of Music's (BAM) Tenth Anniversary Next Wave Festival and was selected as the best realization of "opera/music theater" by the New York Times in 1991; *Sacrifice of Mmbato* (writer/director), commissioned and produced by BAM and the Market Theatre at BAM in 1994; *Trio,* a jazz opera by Noa Ain presented at Carnegie Hall; *Brightness Falling* (writer/director); *Black Novel* (adapter/director), with Argentine author Luisa Valenzuela; *Slain in the Spirit,* with composer Taj Mahal and writer Susan Yankowitz; and *Many Moons* (librettist/director), adapted from the James Thurber story with composer Rob Kapilow.

For more information on Hilary Blecher, please contact Peter Hagen, Writers and Artists Agency, 19 West 44th Street, Suite 1000, New York, New York 10036, (212) 391-1112.

WILMA BONET, an accomplished award-winning actress whose many hats include playwriting, directing, and teaching, premiered *Good Grief, Lolita!* at the BRAVA! Studio and performed the piece at the Solo Mio Festival. She just completed directing and performing in *Lady from Havana* at TheaterWorks. She is known in the San Francisco/Bay Area for her work with local major theater companies, including The American Conservatory Theatre, Berkeley Repertory Theatre, and El Teatro Campesino. Bonet was a member of the Tony Award-winning San Francisco Mime Troupe (SFMT). While with SFMT, she performed extensively in San Francisco and toured the United

States, Canada, Europe, and parts of Latin America. She received a Bay Area Critics Circle Award for ensemble acting and the L.A. Drama-Logue Award for outstanding performance. Since SFMT, she has performed at the Bilingual Foundation of the Arts and the Los Angeles Theatre Center, the Old Globe Theatre in San Diego, the Eureka Theatre, the Magic Theater, El Teatro De La Esperanza, the Marin Theatre Company, and the Dallas Theater Center. Ms. Bonet has appeared in numerous films and commercials. She is Rhonda Bird in the PBS children's series *You Can Choose.* She is co-founder (co-madre) of the Latina Theatre Lab. Last year, she was honored with the Marion Scott Actor's Achievement Award in recognition for her artistry and work in Bay Area theaters.

MIGDALIA CRUZ, a published playwright of twenty-seven plays, musicals, and operas widely produced in the United States and abroad, has worked in venues as diverse as Playwrights Horizons (New York), Théatre d'aujourd hui (Montréal), and Foro Sor Juana Inés de la Cruz (Mexico City). Her plays include *Miriam's Flowers, The Have-Little, Lucy Loves Me, Dreams of Home, Telling Tales,* and *Lolita de Lares.* She was nurtured by several institutions such as Irene Fornes' Playwrights' Laboratory at INTAR (New York), the Royal Court Theatre/New Dramatists Exchange '94 (London), and the Sundance Institute Theater and Film Conferences.

Among Ms. Cruz's numerous awards and fellowships are the NEA, the McKnight, a Connecticut Commission for the Arts award, the Susan Smith Blackburn Prize, and a 1996 Kennedy Center Fund for New American Plays award for *Another Part of the House,* a re-imagining of Lorca's *La Casa de Bernarda Alba,* produced by Classic Stage Company in New York, where she was a 1994 PEW/TCG National Artist in Residence. In 1996, she was a playwright-in-residence at Steppenwolf Theatre (Chicago), which is where her play *Salt* was born. She is under commission to write another Puerto Rican political history play for the Joseph Papp/Public Theater (New York). She has been writer-in-residence and Director of Theater Programming at Latino Chicago Theater Company since July of 1996. An alumni of New Dramatists, Cruz was born and raised in the Bronx.

For further information and performance rights, please contact Peregrine Whittlesey, 345 East 80th Street, New York, New York 10021, (212) 737-0153, fax: (212) 734-5176.

LAURA ESPARZA is a theater director, writer, administrator, and performance artist whose work reflects her passion for Latino and women's theater. She is one of only two directors to hold an M.F.A. in directing and Latino Theater from the University of California, San Diego. As founding director of Teatro Misión at the Mission Cultural Center in San Francisco, Esparza forged a Latino Theater Center with year-round mainstage and children's performances by Bay Area Latino Theaters. She toured the United States as one of four directors chosen nationwide to receive the prestigious Theater Communications Group/National Endowment for the Arts Directors fellowship. Following the fellowship she joined the Group Theater in Seattle, Washington, as Associate Artistic Director/Education Director. In 1997, she became Arts in Education Program Manager for the Mexican Heritage Corporation in San Jose, California, founding a theater, a gallery, and an arts education facility for a Latino cultural arts center.

Ms. Esparza's play *I Dismember the Alamo: A Long Poem for Performance* is forthcoming in *Latinas on Stage: Criticism and Practice* (Third Woman Press). Her extensive directing credits include *When El Cucui Walks, Miriam's Flowers, Harvest Moon,* and *Roosters.* Other unpublished plays include *Chicanatalk, Border Boda,* and *Paco, Flaco y Esperanza,* an informational acto for the Northwest Immigrant Rights Project. She is currently writing and performing two dramatic pieces about La China Poblana and sexual harassment among Chicanos.

Ms. Esparza was born and raised on the west side of San Antonio, Texas, with four brothers and a sister. She is a descendent of Gregorio Esparza, who fought in the Battle of the Alamo, and Ana Esparza, who survived it. She attended Rice University in Houston and Fairhaven College at Western Washington University, graduating with an original degree entitled "Community Arts Development."

AMPARO GARCÍA CROW is an award-winning, multi-disciplinary artist who acts, directs, sings, and writes plays. Her new play, *Under a Western Sky,* received its world premiere off-Broadway in a co-production by INTAR and The Women's Project after receiving development at South Coast Repertory Theater's Hispanic Play Festival. Her other full-length play, *Cocks Have Claws and Wings to Fly,* received its world premiere at Latino Chicago and was awarded the Larry L. King Playwriting award for Best Texas play.

Ms. Crow's work has been commissioned and produced at Plaza de la Raza in Los Angeles, as well as at the Texas Latino Theatre Festival and at the Planet Theater in Phoenix. She was a James Michener Fellow at the Texas Center for Writers at the University of Texas, where she received an M.F.A. in writing and is presently teaching playwriting and performance skills. She is an equity actress who has performed in television and film projects as well as at various regional theaters, including the Kennedy Center and various theaters in Austin, where she currently resides. She was named an NEA/TCG Director's Fellow in 1991 during which time she worked at the Mark Taper Forum, San Diego Repertory Theater, and Broadway's Roundabout Theater.

Ms. Crow has two independent releases of her original songs, "Inscription on Her Underwear" and "A Long Way From Alchemy," and has written songs for independent films. She and her husband conduct yoga/writing/acting workshops and retreats that incorporate movement, improvisation, and writing not only for creative development, but personal growth. She is the mother of two children.

For more information, please contact Bruce Ostler, c/o Bret Adams Limited Artists' Agency, 448 West 44th St., New York, New York 10036, (212) 765-5630.

MARÍA MAR's mission in the world has always been to be a transformation shamanness through the medium of the arts. She began her studies at the University of Puerto Rico in psychology but eventually made a commitment to the Drama Department. Movement back and forth between both worlds has informed much of her academic training since then. She arrived in New York in 1978 and continued her theater studies at Brooklyn College and Fordham University. During that time, she did poetry performances such as *Tiempo de beso, Mujericana,* and *Latina.* Simultaneously, she worked as an actress in the Puerto Rican Traveling Theatre and the Centro Cultural Cubano. More recently, her work has concentrated on what she calls Testimonial Theatre about family violence and violence against women, incorporating Augusto Boal's theories of Theatre of the Oppressed. This experience has helped to bring her to her current position in the Theatre of Transformation, which she has brought full circle in *Orisha Medicine,* a year-long Ritual Theatre celebrating one Afro-Caribbean Orisha per month.

After working in the Houston theater community for many years, ALICIA MENA moved to San Antonio in 1993 where she worked with the Guadalupe Cultural Arts Center as writer, director, and actor. *Las Nuevas Tamaleras* premiered in Houston, Texas, in 1990 and has been produced in Texas, New Mexico, California, and Colorado. In 1995, Ms. Mena founded Burras Finas Productions with the mission of staging an annual Christmas production of *Las Nuevas Tamaleras.* Since then, the play has continued to draw sellout audiences in San Antonio.

CHERRÍE MORAGA is a poet, playwright, essayist, and co-editor of *This Bridge Called My Back: Writings by Radical Women of Color.* She is the author of numerous plays, including *Shadow of a Man,* winner of the 1990 Fund for New American Plays Award, and *Heroes and Saints,* winner of the 1992 Pen West Award. Her most recent book is *The Last Generation,* a collection of poems and essays. A recipient of the National Endowment for the Arts Theatre Playwrights' Fellowship and an artist-in-residence at Brava Theatre Centre of San Francisco, Ms. Moraga premiered her newest play, *Watsonville: Some Place Not Here,* at Brava. *Watsonville* won the 1995 Fund for New American Plays Award.

MONICA PALACIOS is a Los Angeles–based writer/performer who continues to tour with her four highly acclaimed one-woman shows: *Latin Lezbo Comic, Confessions: A Sexplosion of Tantalizing Tales, Greetings from a Queer Señorita,* and *My Body and Other Parts.* She has been awarded a fellowship from the Los Angeles Mark Taper Forum's Latino Theatre Initiative to develop her play *Clock.* She has taught at numerous colleges such as UCLA, University of California–Berkeley, University of California–Santa Barbara, University of Massachusetts, and University of Texas–San Antonio. Palacios is anthologized in *Living Chicana Theory, Latina: Women's Voices from the Borderlands* (Simon and Schuster), *A Funny Time to be Gay* (Simon and Schuster), *Chicana Lesbians: The Girls Our Mothers Warned Us About*—winner of the Lambda Literary Award—and *Lesbian Bedtime Stories, Volume 2.* Her upcoming publications are included in *Latinas on Stage: Practice and Theory* (Third Women Press) and *Out of the Fringe: Latino/a Theatre and Performance.* Palacios also has a column in the monthly magazine *Lesbian News.* She produces the annual event Chicks and Salsa, an evening featuring outstanding Latina lesbian artists from all mediums in Los Angeles. As co-chair of VIVA, Lesbian and Gay Latino Artists, Palacios produces performance and art shows, leading the group in discovering, empowering, and promoting lesbian and gay Latino artists.

UZI PARNES is a native Israeli performer, writer, and director of alternative theater, film, and video working in New York City. He co-wrote (with Carmelita Tropicana), directed, and designed *Memorias de la revolución, Candela, Candela, Azúcar,* and *The Conquest of Mexico as Seen through the Eyes of Hernando Cortez's Horse.* Parnes holds a doctorate in Performance Studies from New York University.

DOLORES PRIDA, one of the foremost Latina playwrights in the United States, is the author of ten plays. Five of them have been published in the volume *Beautiful Señoritas and Other Plays* (Arte Público Press, 1991). Her work has been staged by numerous theater companies in New York City and throughout the United States and is included in several anthologies. She's a frequent lecturer at colleges and universities and teaches playwriting techniques. She was a Distinguished Visiting Professor at Dartmouth College for the spring and fall 1995 terms, and Visiting Professor at the University of Michigan, Ann Arbor, for the winter 1997 term. She's also a television scriptwriter, editor, and journalist. Prida was born in Caibarién, Cuba, and she has resided in the United States since 1961. She majored in Latin American Literature at Hunter College. In 1989 she was awarded an honorary doctoral degree of humane letters by Mount Holyoke College for her contributions to the American theater. Prida lives in East Harlem, New York City.

DIANE RODRÍGUEZ is a triple-threat director, writer, and actress who began her career as a thirteen-year member of the internationally renowned Chicano theater company El Teatro Campesino, directed by writer/director Luis Valdez. At nineteen, she was a founding member of the Chicano theater company Teatro de la Esperanza, and later of the comedy troupe Latins Anonymous, whose successful anthology, *Latins Anonymous: Two Plays,* has gone into its second printing.

She is a commissioned theater writer and her monologue, "Water," is included in the anthology of women's humor, *Crème de la Femme.* She has written for the *Los Angeles Times.*

She was the winner of a 1997 Professional Guest Director/Choreographer Award for her work with Cornerstone Theatre and is a 1998 winner of the National Endowment for the Arts/Theatre Communications Group Director's Career Development Award.

As an actress, Ms. Rodríguez has appeared in twenty-five film and television projects and more than forty plays. She is currently the co-director of the Latino Theatre Initiative at the Tony Award-winning Mark Taper Forum Theatre in Los Angeles.

Author of thirty plays, ELAINE ROMERO holds an M.F.A. in playwriting from the University of California–Davis. She is the recipient of the Theatre Communications Group/Pew Foundation National Theatre Artists Residency grant, and was awarded a residency through the 1997 National Endowment for the Arts/Theatre Communications Group Residency Program. For her TCG/Pew residency, she is serving as a playwright-in-residence at the Arizona Theatre Company in Tucson and Phoenix. As an NEA playwright, she is writing her latest drama, *Barrio Hollywood.*

Ms. Romero's other plays include *If Susan Smith Could Talk,* produced by the Actors Theatre of Louisville, the Planet Earth Multi-Cultural Theatre, and City Theatre in Florida. A finalist for the Humana Festival and the Heideman Award, the play was published by Samuel French in *Ten-Minute Plays from Actors Theatre of Louisville, Volume 4.* Ms. Romero developed her drama *¡Curanderas! Serpents of the Clouds* while in residence at the Guadalupe Cultural Arts Center in San Antonio, with composer Alize Gomez, choreographer Javier Romero, and director José Manuel Galván as part of the Gateways '96 program, sponsored by the Ford Foundation. The play was a finalist for the Humana Festival and the Jane Chambers Playwriting Award, and received second place in Stages Repertory Theatre's Women's Repertory Festival in Houston. *Walking Home,* originally commissioned by Borderlands Theater, premiered at the Planet Earth Multi-Cultural Theatre. It won first prize in the Chicano/Latino Literary Contest of the University of California at Irvine, and was published in Ollantay Teatre Magazine. *Undercurrents* won the Tennessee Williams/New Orleans Literary Festival One-Act Play Contest and the Invisible Theatre's One-Act Play Contest—the Arizona Story. It was developed at the Invisible Theatre, the University of New Orleans, the Miracle, Stagebrush Showcase Theatre, Old Pueblo Playwrights, and Theatre By The Blind in New York. *Living Dolls* was commissioned by and premiered at the Invisible Theatre. The multi-character play was produced as a one-woman show, starring Lisa Suarez, at Jumpstart Performance Company in San Antonio.

Ms. Romero's published work has also appeared in *More Monologues for Women by Women, The Alaska Quarterly Review, Rosebud Magazine, Tucson Guide Quarterly, The Storyteller 95,* and the *Tucson Weekly.*

Ms. Romero is a member of the Dramatists Guild. She lives in Tucson.

ALBERTO SANDOVAL-SÁNCHEZ is Professor of Spanish at Mt. Holyoke College. He is both cultural critic and creative writer, having published a bilingual volume of poetry, *New York Backstage* (*Nueva York tras bastidores*) (Chile 1993), and produced a theatrical piece based on his personal experience with AIDS, *Side Effects* (Mt. Holyoke College, 1993). He has published widely on U.S. Latino/a theater, Latin American colonial theater and identity, Spanish baroque theater, Puerto Rican migration, and issues of AIDS representation. His book,

José, Can You See: Latinos On and Off Broadway, is forthcoming from the University of Wisconsin Press. Sandoval-Sánchez and Nancy Saporta Sternbach have co-authored a second volume of Latina theater entitled *Stages of Life: Latinas in Teatro,* forthcoming from the University of Arizona Press.

NANCY SAPORTA STERNBACH is Associate Professor of Spanish and Women's Studies at Smith College, where she teaches courses on Latina and Latin American literature. She is co-editor of *Breaking Boundaries: Latina Writing and Critical Readings* and has published on Latina and Latin American women's literature and feminist movements. Currently she is completing a book about women and representation in Latin American modernismo titled *The Death of a Beautiful Woman.* She and Alberto Sandoval-Sánchez have co-authored a second volume on Latina theater, *Stages of Life: Latinas in Teatro,* forthcoming from the University of Arizona Press.

CARIDAD SVICH, a playwright/poet and translator of Cuban, Croatian, Argentine, and Spanish descent, was born in Philadelphia and now lives in Los Angeles. Credits include her play *Alchemy of Desire/Dead-Man's Blues* at Cincinnati Playhouse in the Park, the Royal Court Theatre in London, and Lincoln Center's Directors' Lab. Among her awards are an NEA/TCG residency at the Mark Taper Forum for 1998–99, a Mark Taper Forum Theatre Writing Fellowship, a California Arts Council Fellowship, and a TCG Hispanic Translation Commission. She has been a visiting lecturer at the Yale School of Drama and a playwright-in-residence at INTAR Hispanic Arts Center in New York.

CARMELITA TROPICANA is a Cuban/American writer who has collaborated with Ela Troyano and Uzi Parnes on numerous projects. She wrote with Ela Troyano *Carmelita Tropicana: Your Kunst Is Your Waffen,* winner of best short at the Berlin Film Festival '94. Her solo *Milk of Amnesia* was published in *The Drama Review* (1995), and her fiction has appeared in *The New Fuck You: Adventures in Lesbian Reading,* an anthology published in *Semiotexte* and winner of a Lambda Book Award. She received a CINTAS fellowship in 1995–96 for her literary work; she is currently working on a play based on Sor Juana Inés de la Cruz and on a screenplay with Ela Troyano.

SUSANA TUBERT's extensive directorial credits include regional productions and workshops at Denver Center Theatre, South Coast Repertory Theatre, Mac-

Carter Theatre, Alliance Theater, Actors' Theatre of Louisville, Hartford Stage, Sundance Institute, Victory Gardens, Seattle Repertory Theatre, Gala Hispanic Theatre, and Seattle's Multicultural Theatre.

In New York City, Ms. Tubert's work has been seen at The Public Theatre, Women's Project, Lincoln Center Institute, Playwright's Horizons Theatre School, Young Playwrights' Festival, Repertorio Español, Puerto Rican Traveling Theatre, and Circle Rep Lab, among others. Most recently, Ms. Tubert staged *Santa Concepción* at the Joseph Papp Public Theatre. She was a George Abbott Resident Director at New Dramatists, as well as a guest artist in Toni Morrison's Atelier at Princeton University, collaborating with Joyce Carol Oates on *The Identity Project.*

Ms. Tubert's upcoming projects include world premieres of *The Knee Desires the Earth* at the Women's Project; *El Mozote* with Pasqual Rioult Dance Theatre Company at the Guggenheim Museum; *Barrio Babies,* winner of the Richard Rodgers' Award for new musical; and *Squall,* recently workshopped by Ms. Tubert at Denver Center's US West TheatreFest.

Ms. Tubert is a member of New York Theatre Workshop, The Lab, and the Society of Stage Directors & Choreographers (ssDC). She has served on the New York State Council on the Arts for three years. As writer/composer, two of her musicals, *A Day in the Life of a Robot* and *Let's Take Back Our Planet* (co-written with Gloria Zelaya), were produced by the Don Quijote Experimental Children's Theatre.

Ms. Tubert was awarded the 1991–92 Theatre Communications Group/National Endowment for the Arts Director Fellowship, which enabled her to assist directors Harold Prince, Marshall Mason, and Peter Sellars. She was also a nominee for the 1996 Cal/Arts Alpert Award, the 1996 and 1995 Allan Schneider Award, and the 1994 Princess Grace Award.

Ms. Tubert has lectured at universities throughout the country and was profiled in Rebecca Daniel's new book, *Women Stage Directors Speak: Exploring the Influence of Gender on Their Work.* Ms. Tubert staged the Hispanic Heritage Awards at the Kennedy Center, which aired on NBC.

EDIT VILLARREAL is a playwright, screenwriter, dramaturg, and adapter. Her plays have received productions throughout the country. An early comedy, *My Visits with MGM (My Grandmother Marta),* was first produced at Borderlands in Tucson, Arizona. *MGM* subsequently received more than twenty productions, including equity productions at San Jose Repertory Theatre, Milwaukee Repertory Theatre, and The Bilingual Foundation of the Arts in Los Angeles. Another play, *The Language of Flowers,* a contemporary adaptation of Shakespeare's *Romeo and Juliet*, received its equity premier at A Contemporary Theatre. Her latest comedy, *Marriage Is Forever*, was commissioned by the Mark Taper Forum Latino Theatre Initiative. Another new play, *Chicago Milagro*, was commissioned by South Coast Repertory Theatre.

A member of the Writers Guild of America, West, her television credits include "La Carpa" (PBS, "American Playhouse," 1993), and "Foto-Novelas" (PBS, 1998). "Foto-Novelas" continues to garner awards, most recently a prestigious 1998 Peabody Award nomination for the series as a whole and a highly regarded 1998 HUMANITAS Award nomination for one of the four half-hours in the series, "The Fix," written by Ms. Villarreal and her husband, screenwriter Bennett Cohen.

A 1986 graduate of the Yale School of Drama, Ms. Villarreal teaches graduate playwriting at the UCLA School of Theatre, Film, and Television.

SILVIANA WOOD, a native of Tucson, Arizona, is well known for her bilingual comedies and dramas as well as for her famed television character, Doña Chona, on "Reflexiones," KUAT-TV. She received her M.F.A. in Creative Writing from the University of Arizona and has worked in Tucson's theater community since the 1970s. She is the author of many plays, including *Amor de hija* and *Anhelos por Oaxaca* and *A Drunkard's Tale of Melted Wings and Memories*. Her most recent play, *Yo, Casimor Flores*, was produced last year at the historic Guadalupe Theatre in San Antonio, Texas. Her next play, *Pagando mandas que no debo*, will be set in Magdalena, Sonora, Mexico, during the fiesta de San Francisco.

Credits

Botánica was commissioned and first produced by Teatro Repertorio Español in New York City—where it's still in repertory—with a grant from the Lila Wallace–Reader's Digest Foundation. Subsequently it was published in *Beautiful Señoritas.* The first performance took place on January 15, 1991. The play has toured extensively throughout the United States, produced by Repertorio. This is the first version to be published in English, translated by Dolores Prida.

Heart of the Earth: A Popol Vuh Story first opened on September 14, 1994, at The Public Theatre as part of the Jim Henson Foundation's International Festival of Puppet Theatre. The play was directed by Ralph Lee, who also created the puppets (from hand- to giant-sized), and written by Cherríe Moraga. The music was composed by Glen Velez. The opening included the following cast (in order of appearance):

Daykeeper/Ixmucane/Bat	Doris Difarnecio
Ixpiyacoc/Blood Sausage	William Ha'o
Cucumatz/Patriarchal Pus	Sam Wellington
Hunahpu (both generations)	Joe Herrera
Vucub/Ollas/Ixbalanque	David Noroña
Tecolote/Wooden-Man/Rat	Julie Pasqual
Ixquic/Conejo	Adriana Inchaustegui

Heart of the Earth had its world premiere at INTAR Theatre of New York on January 11, 1995. It opened with the following cast:

Daykeeper/Ixmucane/Bat	Doris Difarnecio
Ixpiyacoc/Blood Sausage	William Ha'o
Cucumatz/Patriarchal Pus	Curtis Cook
Hunahpu (both generations)	Joe Herrera
Vucub/Ollas/Ixbalanque	David Noroña

Tecolote/Wooden-Man/The Rat   Caroline Stephanie Clay
Ixquic/Conejo   Adriana Inchaustegui
Musicians were Iris Brooks and David Simons. Choreography by Sigfrido Aguilar. Set by Donald Eastman. Costumes by Caryn Neman. The Stage Manager was Jesse Wooden Jr. and the Assistant Director was Laura Esparza.

The Fat-Free Chicana and the Snow Cap Queen premiered at the Miracle Theatre/Teatro Milagro in Portland, Oregon, after being developed there and at Borderlands Theater in Tucson. It was recently produced at El Centro Su Teatro in Denver.

Fuchsia premiered in New York City at the Nuyorican Poets' Cafe on April 11, 1996. Directed by Dolores Prida, with the following cast:

Santos	David Zayas
Red	Eric "Trance" Smith
Nina	Janis Astor del Valle
Manny	Dennis Vargas
Alonso	Roylan Díaz
Chicky	Carmen Kelly

Nostalgia Maldita: 1–900–Mexico, A StairMaster Piece has been performed throughout the United States and Mexico.

1–900 video clip director	Isaac Artenstein
Recorded voice	Marcos Martínez
Video shows	Fidel Arizmendi
Production design	Sergio Arau and Yareli Arizmendi
Salsa costume and wardrobe consultant	Carlos Brown
Stage Manager	Chris Fox

Music:

"The Amexican Anthem," conceived by Sergio Arau and Yareli Arizmendi, music performed by Juan Colomer, sung by Yareli Arizmendi.

"Volver Volver," original by Fernando Z. Maldonado. "Return Volver" by Dr. Loco's Rockin' Jalapeño Band.

"Moliendo Café," original by J. Manzo, updated version by Azúcar Moreno.

"Stars and Stripes Forever," John Philip Sousa (1897).

"Washington Post March," John Philip Sousa (1889).

Special thanks to About Productions and Theresa Chavez for taking the risk; Isaac Artenstein and Jude Eberhard for originally believing; Avi Jamgochian and Lili Barreto; Enrique Martinez; Los Angeles Dental Society; Mexico and the United States.

A Roomful of Men: A Radio for the Eyes Performance Piece was performed at Fronterafest, Hyde Park Theatre, Austin, Texas, January 28–29, 1997. The production was directed by Daniel Alexander Jones; music scored, arranged, and co-written by Amparo García Crow and Vinnie Caggiano; visuals created and designed by Kevin West; costumes by Yvonne Miller.
Songs by:
"Ghost Town," Amparo García Crow and Michael Slattery
"Rest of Life" and "Cowboy Dreams," Amparo García Crow and William Dunlap
"Dante's Dare," Amparo García Crow and Arthur Shane
"Sanddollar," Amparo García Crow and Todd Kassens
"In the Other Room," "Waiting on the Will of Heaven," and "Deep In Purple," Amparo García Crow and Vinnie Caggiano
All other songs/music, Amparo García Crow.

An earlier version of "Home, Desire, Memory" was originally presented at the *Stage of Their Own/Un Escenario Propio* symposium/festival on Spanish, Latin American, and U.S. Latina women in theater sponsored by the University of Cincinnati, Cincinnati, Ohio, 1994.

"Tales of a South-of-the-Border/North-of-the-Stereotype Theater Director" was excerpted from a talk presented by the Hispanic Organization for Latin Actors (HOLA) at Hunter College, New York City, 1996.

Frida: The Story of Frida Kahlo, monologue and lyrics by Migdalia Cruz, book by Hilary Blecher, © H. Blecher and M. Cruz, 1991. Music © Robert X. Rodriguez, 1991. *Frida* was first published in *Plays from the Women's Project* (Applause Books).
 Production history for *Frida: The Story of Frida Kahlo:* (1) Plays and Players Theater (Philadelphia), April 1991, produced by American Music Theater Festival, Marjorie Samoff and Eric Salzman, producers, directed by Hilary Blecher; (2) American Repertory Theatre (Cambridge, Massachusetts), Robert Brustein, artistic director, produced by American Music Theater Festival, Marjorie Samoff and Eric Salzman, producers, September 1992, directed by Hilary Blecher; (3) Next Wave Festival at Brooklyn Academy of Music

(Brooklyn, New York), October 1992, produced by American Music Theater Festival (Pennsylvania), Samoff and Salzman, producers, and the Woman's Project (New York), Julia Miles, artistic director, directed by Hilary Blecher; (4) Houston Grand Opera, Houston, Texas, June 1993, produced by the HGO, David Gockley, artistic director, directed by Hilary Blecher; (5) City College of San Francisco, September 1993.

G. Schirmer, Inc. controls the rights to the work and anyone wanting to perform the opera must contact that organization at 257 Park Avenue South, 20th floor, New York, New York 10010, (212) 254-2100.